THE ANGRY BUZZ

This Week and Current Affairs Television

Patricia Holland

I.B. TAURIS

LONDON · NEW YORK

Published in 2006 by I.B.Tauris & Co. Ltd
6 Salem Road, London W2 4BU
175 Fifth Avenue, New York, NY 10010
www.ibtauris.com

In the United States of America and Canada distributed by Palgrave
Macmillan, a division of St Martin's Press, 175 Fifth Avenue, New York,
NY 10010

ISBN: 1 84511 051 X
EAN: 978 1 84511 051 2

A full CIP record for this book is available from the British Library
A full CIP record for this book is available from the Library of
Congress

Library of Congress catalog card: available

Typeset in Palatino Linotype by A. & D. Worthington, Newmarket
Printed and bound in Great Britain by T International Ltd, Padstow,
Cornwall

CONTENTS

'We need the angry buzz of current affairs'
Professor Sylvia Harvey

PREFACE

This Week was launched by Associated-Rediffusion Television in January 1956, three months after the beginning of independent television (ITV) in Britain. It was continued by Thames Television, which took over the commercial franchise for London weekdays in 1968. For eight years, from 1978 to 1986, Thames's main current affairs series became *TVEye*. The name *This Week* was reinstated in 1986 and the series finally closed when Thames lost its franchise in December 1992. For ease of reference, in this book I shall often be using 'This Week' as a shorthand for both series.

The book is part of a broader project on the history of the series, which began when Rediffusion had its licence removed in 1968. In 1971 Vicki Wegg-Prosser became documentary acquisitions officer for the National Film Archive (NFA) and found herself checking the Associated-Rediffusion materials which the new company, Thames, was clearing off its shelves. The collection included scripts and original film material – some complete programmes made on film, and some short sequences which were inserted into live studio broadcasts. The film was put into the Archive's store in Beaconsfield, where its cans rusted and it was largely forgotten.

In 1989 Vicki was invited to give the Ernest Lindgren Memorial Lecture, which each year focused on different aspects of the Archive, at London's National Film Theatre. She chose *This Week* as her topic and showed extracts retrieved from the early days, including such gems as the Happy Wanderers New Orleans style street band cheering up the drabness of 1950s London, and the scoop interview with Archbishop Makarios in exile from Cyprus. It was the beginning of a long project to rescue and preserve the *This Week* material. The task was far from straightforward, as film decays over time and formats change. In particular the technicians at the Archive had been warned not to handle the magnetic sound film, as it gives off poisonous vinegar fumes as it decays. Vicki had to rewind it cautiously or the rescued items would have had no sound to go along with them.

Next she persuaded Thames Television to restore some of their own filmed programmes. These were stacked away in Thames's vault, where, from time to time, they were dredged up by film researchers when producers wanted to re-use sequences, or when a repeat was needed to replace a programme which was delayed or not ready in time for transmission. Some programmes had become familiar through frequent re-use, some had had second lives through overseas marketing, but some cans had not been opened since the film had been neatly rolled up and packed away. As a result of Vicki's initiative, a number of key programmes were preserved on master tape, and Vicki's company, Flashback Productions, arranged with Thames to re-broadcast some of the more notable of them – ranging from the short sequences of the 1950s, to programmes that had become celebrated, such as 'The Unknown Famine' (1973), or notorious, such as 'Death on the Rock' (1988). The first transmission of 'Twenty-Five Years on the Front Line' was delayed by another front line. It was scheduled for 15 January 1991, the day American planes bombed Baghdad in the first Gulf War.

That same year Thames Television itself lost its licence to broadcast and, in January 1993, was replaced by Carlton as the franchise holder for the London weekday schedule. I had been helping research the retrospective series and was aware of the wealth of printed information that was held in Thames's written archive, guarded by librarian Bill Parker. I was lucky enough to get permission to spend a couple of months tucked away in that basement filling 20 A4 notebooks with densely written notes on the programme scripts and a wealth of other background material stored away in the files. Every programme has its own file, which contains the post-production script (the record of the programme that was actually transmitted), the PSB forms ('Programme As Broadcast' – the form filled in by the programme secretary which gives details of production personnel, the people who appeared in the programme, music used with its precise lengths, and other copyright details which are necessary for any future trans-mission), as well as an unpredictable lucky dip of other mate-rial. The files were particularly rich for the period of the 1970s, stuffed with internal memos, technical requirements lists and, perhaps most fascinating of all, letters from viewers. These were especially numerous – and especially abusive – following controversial programmes such as those on sex education and the Middle East conflict. Vicki and I supplemented our various notes – her card index on the 1950s and 1960s, my notebooks on the 1970s and 1980s – with interviews with the main protagonists. FremantleMedia, who eventually came to own Thames, allowed us to obtain rough VHS copies of many of the programmes for research purposes. All this educational material is now lodged in the Bournemouth Media School archive.

Through Bournemouth University and the British Universities Film and Video Council we have now been able to transmute our scribbled notes into a comprehensive database which records not only the topic of each *This Week* edition, but also the reporter, the producer and the names of most of those who appeared in the programme. It also indicates the style and technology used and adds extensive researchers' notes on many of the programmes. In this way, it has been possible to trace changes and developments over the 36 years of *This Week*'s existence, in topic and approach as well as personnel, and to make this documentation widely available to those who are researching political and social history, as well as the history of a television genre close to the centre of UK political culture.

In this book I shall focus on the issues and debates that challenged the series over its lifetime, rather than on personalities and anecdotes. So the book moves between the broad and abstract and the detailed and concrete, from the wider picture to the minutiae and the intimate close-up. I have decided to give some very detailed examples – in particular that of Northern Ireland – while keeping a wider impression of the series as a whole. I know I will have left out some remarkable programmes, and I regret that very much. And I apologize in advance to the many individuals who have made substantial contributions to the series, but whom I have not been able to mention by name – reporters and producers, as well as cameramen, sound recordists, picture editors, researchers and the ever supportive and hard-working production assistants and secretaries – the whole team that keeps a series going. They have all been deeply committed to the final product.

I would like this book to make sense to at least two audiences, but I am acutely aware that the interests of the two are not necessarily compatible. The first is an academic audience, for it is the writing of academic historians and theorists that has informed the ways in which I have formulated the problems I want to consider. But the book is not intended only, or even mainly, as an academic text, as I also want it to make sense to television practitioners – those who have been involved in the making of these and similar programmes and are all too aware of the accidents, the clashes of personality and the sheer contingency of the business of programme making. All too often the abstract analysis that theorists find so exciting seems like so much irrelevant self-indulgence when you have lived through the day-to-day muddle, arguments and pressures. As a practitioner it is virtually impossible to perceive a programme as a smooth and finished product, since every frame has a story behind it, and you are always aware of ways in which it might have been different. I want the book to reflect something of the texture of programme making – not just from the perspective of those with the influence to shape the direction of the series, but also of the whole programme staff.

ACKNOWLEDGEMENTS

So many people have helped with this long-running project that I am bound to have forgotten some in these acknowledgements, so I apologize to them in advance.

I am deeply indebted to Dr Vicki Wegg-Prosser whose brainchild this project is. It draws on her extensive research, including her work in making the materials available in the first place, the contacts she made amongst programme makers and others, the careful interviews she conducted, and also her unfailing support as I took the research forward and undertook to write it into a book. Her historical precision and understanding have tempered some of my wilder speculations.

Some of the material is developed from conference papers I have delivered in the decade since I first studied the archive, and articles I have published elsewhere. I would like to thank Thames Television, which became Pearson and is now Fremantle, for access to the archive and permission to quote from the programmes and background materials. The essential financial backing was given by the Harold Hyam Wingate Foundation which generously supported the first phase of my research, Bournemouth Media School which took it up, and the Arts and Humanities Research Council which gave two substantial grants for the construction of the database. Finally the Shiers Trust gave a grant towards the writing of this book. I am deeply grateful to all of them.

Many of the programme makers and other practitioners generously gave their time for interviews or informal conversations with Vicki and me – a list is appended. Special thanks go to Peter Taylor and Peter Denton for their comments on my Northern Ireland chapters, and Peter Denton for giving me access to his collection of photographs; to Phillip Whitehead for his comments; to Jeremy Isaacs and Peter Morley for letting me read their unpublished manuscripts; to Jim Pople for showing me his fascinating scrapbook, and to Nicholas Mellersh for lending me his copy of Bryan Magee's book. My thanks are also due to Len Whitcher now head of Fremantle Archive Sales, Bill Parker of the Thames written archive, Mike Maddison of the Thames film archive, Professor John Ellis for supporting the *This Week* project at Bournemouth University, Roger Laughton, at the time head of the Bournemouth Media School, and many other people at Bournemouth including librarian Matt Holland (no relation), Hugh Chignell and others who have engaged in helpful discussions, especially around the 2003 conference *Current Affairs, an Endangered Species*. Also to Professors Sylvia Harvey and John Corner for inspiration and helpful advice.

The following *This Week* people have been interviewed or consulted:

Roger Bolton, Joan Churchill, Brian Connell, Reg Courtney-Browne, Debi Davies, Peter Denton, Jonathan Dimbleby, David Elstein, Peter Gill, Margaret Gilmour, Sheila Gregg, Jeremy Isaacs, Robert Kee, Julian Manyon, Stacey Marking, Robin Marriott, Nicholas Mellersh, Claudia Milne (Twenty Twenty Television), Peter Morley, Stephen Peet, Jim Pople, Lewis Rudd, Jack Saltman, Peter Taylor, Peter Tiffin, Mike Townson, Denis Tuohy, Phillip Whitehead, Jenny Wilkes, Peter Williams, Paul Woolwich.

AUTHOR'S NOTE

The aim in presenting this book is to be as unfussy as possible, so there are minimal references and no notes. The list of References at the end contains the books, television programmes and talks I refer to in the text. When I quote from interviews done by myself or Vicki Wegg-Prosser, our initials will appear in brackets ('to PH' or 'to VWP'). Contemporary memos and other programme information are quoted from the programme files.

More information about *This Week* can be found on the Bournemouth University *This Week* database, available through the British Universities Film and Video Council (BUFVC), 77 Wells St, London W1T 3QJ. www.bufvc.ac.uk

Phillip Whitehead and some of the *This Week* team at a Friday meeting in 1969. Sitting, left to right: John Morgan, reporter; a blurred image; Phillip Whitehead, Producer; Anna Arki, Phillip Whitehead's secretary; Andrew McNeil, researcher; Gill Morphew, programme organizer; John Edwards, reporter, later to be series Producer; Mary Horwood, production assistant; Peter Williams, reporter; Llew Gardner, reporter. Standing, left to right: Peter Lee Thompson, film editor; Jolyon Wilmhurst, director; Tom Steel, researcher; Trevor Waite, film editor; Colin Martin, researcher; an assistant film editor; Arnold Bulka, director, later to be series Producer. Courtesy FremantleMedia.

DEMOCRACY AND PUBLIC SERVICE TELEVISION

Current affairs and democracy

We are nowhere if television loses its ability to tell us something and for us to respond: 'Bloody hell, I didn't know that' and follow up with the obvious supplementary: 'something must be done'. That is part of democracy and you endanger it at your peril (*Guardian* 1998).

Current affairs television in the UK, in more than half a century of programmes, has set out to tell us something we didn't know with all the urgency that political journalist Kemal Ahmed so graphically evokes, treating its audience as citizens with the right – and also the ability – to demand that 'something must be done'. Over their 36-year history, the current affairs series *This Week* and its replacement *TVEye* helped to mark out that democratic project.

'If the job of a news service was to tell us what was happening at any given moment, then the job of current affairs was to help us understand what was happening,' said Jeremy Isaacs, the producer and executive who was the single most important influence on the series (Paulu 1981:211). And the key is in that desire to *understand*. When *This Week* was launched in January 1956, current affairs was just beginning to create a powerful and flexible space for television journalism. It was evolving as an eclectic and hybrid genre, and developing an angry buzz of inquiry and dissent. I shall be tracing *This Week*'s place within this wider pattern. 'Current affairs' has not been rigidly committed to a single format or regular style, nor has *This Week*. The genre has embraced many different types of programme, including interviews, investigations, documentary reports and public debates.

Items may be based in a studio or a distant location; they may be live or pre-recorded; they may involve observational filming, dramatic reconstructions or elaborate graphics; they may feature a known and respected journalist or be led by an anonymous commentary; they may be filled with meticulous detail or strive for popular accessibility using narrative and personality. Above all they set out to illuminate the social and political scene and are prepared to ask awkward and difficult questions. Current affairs is political television in its widest sense, a project that is jealous of its status and political centrality, which constantly proclaims its aim to dig behind the headlines and to explain, explore and challenge as well as to tell.

Numerous short series and many individual programmes have made up the current affairs project on UK television, but for many years the genre was led by a few giants – series which were easily recognized, widely respected and long-running: *Panorama* (BBC 1953–); *This Week/TVEye* (Associated-Rediffusion 1956–68, Thames 1968–92); *World in Action* (Granada 1963–99) and *Dispatches* (Channel 4 1987–). The history of *This Week* interacts with these other series, and, despite their different characters, many personnel moved back and forth between them. Together they provided a high-profile outlet for television journalism in depth, a weekly monitoring of the social, political and global landscape with the occasional spectacular revelation – such as *This Week*'s 'Death on the Rock' (1988) on the shooting of IRA terrorists in Gibraltar – which reverberated throughout the political establishment and beyond. Of course there were bad patches and difficult moments, but the regularity and the very existence of such committed and prestigious series secured the place of current affairs as an essential component of 'quality' television. Their seriousness and sense of purpose underpinned television's, and particularly commercial television's, claim to nurture informed citizenship and the core values of democracy itself.

Public service television

When *This Week* was launched in January 1956 by the new commercial company Associated-Rediffusion, television was beginning – if tentatively – to create a national forum for social and political debate. It was developing a 'social eye' which reflected the lives of the nation at large; it was persuading politicians that it was more than a mere 'robot organization' (Winston Churchill's words) and worth taking seriously; and it was exploring new forms of visual journalism. At the same time, the advent of the group of companies that made up the Independent Television network (ITV) was hastening the expansion of the medium as the primary source of relaxation and entertainment for the population at large. The 'mirror in the corner' was gathering a huge audience from all sections of the population, with regular viewing figures of 16–18 million. Journalism that set out to take the whole of this new audience seriously and to approach *all* of its members as participating citizens rather than passive viewers, was bound to run into trouble, especially when, in its current affairs form, it moved beyond a factual news report to make full use of the visually exciting resources of the popular medium. Many of the challenges faced by *This Week* derived from its position as a 'serious' programme on a 'popular' channel.

The life of *This Week* spans the decades in which broadcasting in the UK gave priority to public service principles. ITV was launched in 1955 as a commercial channel funded by advertising, but it was also subject to stringent regulation and public obligations. From its early days there was cross fertilization with the licence-fee-funded BBC. ITV tempered the BBC's self-importance and solemnity and forced it to compete for popular appeal, while the BBC had prestige, a stated commitment to quality and the power to drive innovation free from commercial constraints. The two approaches were complementary: the 'popular' and the 'serious' posed a constant challenge to each other, and the glue of a public service commitment held together their sometimes contradictory imperatives. While competition for quality in programming was seen as essential, 'it remained the general view that competition for audiences and revenue would lead to a lowering of standards and was to be avoided' (Isaacs 1989:3). It was a classically social democratic project; current affairs, with its appeal to understanding, reason, explanation, participation and universality, was at its heart. The genre was the 'conscience of the programme companies' which might otherwise be 'entertainment-makers entirely given over to the show-biz mind' – at least that was the view of the first director general of the Independent Television Authority, the body set up to supervise the companies and moderate their cruder commercial impulses (Briggs 1995:69–70).

Yet, although few practitioners would accept such an absolute division between 'conscience' and 'entertainment', there remained a sense that *This Week* was constantly in danger, and many of the shifts in its mood and approach grew from the need to maintain a delicate balance between conflicting demands. Throughout its life the series inhabited a space where the public service project was at its most fragile, and, for that very reason, at its most important and most effective.

The series came to an end in 1992, as the public service consensus faced serious challenges – on the one hand from developments in technology which brought a multi-channel landscape with a global reach, and on the other from the shift in ideology signalled by the 1990 Broadcasting Act, and a move towards a more market-driven system.

ITV and its audience

Current affairs programmes have been described as part of a 'public sphere' in which the audience is considered to be made up of thoughtful, participating citizens who use the media to help them 'learn about the world, debate their responses to it and reach informed decisions about what courses of action to adopt' (Dahlgren and Sparks 1991:1). But, over its 36-year history, *This Week*'s aim to address viewers as such active citizens had to be set against the need for what its first producer, Caryl Doncaster, described as 'the commercial element' and 'audience strength'. The ITV companies were funded solely by advertising and, at the crudest level, their job was to deliver audiences to the advertisers – without such revenue the channel could not exist. Reflecting an increasing prosperity and an ever more comfortable lifestyle, this imagined audience was made up not of citizens but of consumers who must be attracted to the programmes and to the goods advertised in the commercial breaks. Consumers have a right to view according to their preference, and this too could be described as a 'public service' – especially by those whose judgements are based on commercial success. ('A public service should aim to give the majority of the public what the majority wants to see' was the attitude of *This Week*'s producing company in the 1950s (Black 1972:194).) From this point of view, if viewers do not watch a programme, arrogant broadcasters pursuing their own interests (and awkward and opinionated journalists fall all too easily into this category) have no right to take up space on the airwaves.

Trapped within such contradictions, current affairs journalism on ITV has been particularly vulnerable, but the desire to attract viewers is not necessarily in contradiction to the desire to produce important and relevant programmes. Indeed, the broader the audience, the more successful the programme was thought to be. *This Week* set out to maintain a productive interaction between commercial and non-commercial aims, and between attractive and accessible programme making and serious journalism, walking a tightrope between the temptation to 'sensationalize' and the danger of speaking only to a small and educated circle. At its most successful, the series was able to hold these conflicting pressures in balance and develop powerful journalism for a very broad audience. Significantly, it was when 'corporate cash and the creative drive [were caught] on the same upswing' (Fiddick 1984:11) that *This Week* achieved its 'golden age'. In the late 1960s to mid-1970s it was supported by a strong commitment from the management at Thames Television, which largely backed up the risks taken by the series, and created an atmosphere in which slow and painstaking investigations, not necessarily showing immediate results, were possible (see Chapters 3 and 4).

But the pendulum swung in both directions. By the end of the 1970s there was a sense that risky journalism must be restrained. The series was taken off the air in 1978 because, in the words of Mike Townson, the editor of its replacement *TVEye*, it was too journalist-centred and had become 'boring' (see p 168). Townson was credited with 'grafting tabloid style and values on to broadsheet journalism' but his argument was a powerful one, with which few would disagree. Current affairs, he wrote, 'should be driven by the desire to communicate to as many people as possible' (Bolton 1990:31; Townson in *The Listener* 4.1.90).

But by 1991, as the series neared the end of its life, Thames's market researcher was reminding *This Week* that even a current affairs programme must remember that 'the consumer is King' (see p 209).

Style and television journalism

A more important reason why *This Week* was taken off the air in the late 1970s was that it had offended the government of the day with its persistent coverage of Northern Ireland and its determination to reveal uncomfortable truths about the abuse of detainees in Castlereagh detention centre in Belfast. I shall be looking in detail at the coverage of Northern Ireland and its consequences in Chapters 5 and 6. But over the years *This Week* drew criticisms from many directions, and its approach to its audience, reflected in the form and style of its programmes, would be as controversial as their content.

The challenges faced by the series involved a number of balancing acts. Many of them grew out of its position as a 'serious' programme on a 'popular' channel, but others came from a wider suspicion of television itself as a medium for serious journalism. For many the very nature of television tends to the commercial and the vulgar, reflecting a debased popular taste. Indeed one of the most celebrated of television journalists, Robin Day, concluded that 'television ... was a medium of shock rather than explanation, it was a crude medium that strikes at the emotions rather than the intellect. And because of its insatiable appetite for visual action, and for violence very often, it tended to distort and trivialize' (Lindley 2002:124).

At *This Week*, a balance had to be maintained between verbal reporting and visual spectacle, between rational explanation and emotional appeal. At some points the series was slated for a collapse into 'infotainment' – and its early lightweight format was rejected as being insufficiently 'serious' – and at others it was criticized for moving too close to a highbrow aesthetic style. Again and again worries about inappropriate styles came back to a suspicion that the medium itself was an unsuitable vehicle for information and analysis. In 1975 John Birt, at the time head of current affairs at London Weekend Television, wrote of a 'bias against understanding' in current affairs programmes because 'film imperatives override journalistic concepts' (*The Times* 30.9.75). Flamboyant camera work or elaborate video graphics, the emotive use of music, slick dramatic reconstruction, a reliance on personality, the appeal to emotion to convey an argument; all have been suspect. But television genres are never hard and fast. As the serious and the popular continued to challenge

each other, television journalism had to be constantly re-invented
– and in my view strengthened – by harnessing and channelling
developments within the visual medium.

History and *This Week/TVEye*

It is rather daunting to realize that a history of a current affairs
series that ran for 36 years also reflects the history of those 36
years in both international and domestic affairs. And yet these
programmes have themselves contributed to the mapping of that
history. Although the series frequently declared its intention to
be 'current', a fleeting part of an ephemeral medium, the genre
also challenged that sense of immediacy by looking *behind* the
headlines and placing the news within a longer history. On a
long-running series, the angry buzz of current affairs was able
build up its own invaluable histories, using its archives and its
collective memory. At *This Week* news stories were revisited, the
political scene was reviewed and re-assessed, and journalists
themselves were able to question their own previous judgements
and put forward new ones.

Although it sought out topics of public importance, the scope
of the agenda was never taken for granted. *This Week* dealt with
crisis, disaster, wars and the daily workings of politics. It firmly
inhabited the public realm but it also explored areas of private
behaviour as an expansion rather than a negation of the political
sphere. Programme makers argued that it was equally important to include issues such as domestic violence, mental health,
sexuality and child care which have traditionally been seen as
private, but which, nevertheless, have a very public dimension.

In telling the history of the series I shall also be bearing in
mind the institutional history and historical development of the
current affairs genre itself. As well as considering the programmes
I shall be bearing in mind the pressures of a weekly output as
well as looking more closely at certain individual editions and
topics – their forgetability as well as their memorability. I shall
be exploring issues which include the scope of the current affairs
agenda, its obligations and its limits; the practice of responsible journalism in relation to audience appeal and attractive
programmes; the practicalities of time and technology; regulation and public service television; accusations of 'tabloidization'
and dumbing down; and issues of gender in relation to this very

'serious' genre which was dominated by men for a large part of its history. (As Vicki Wegg-Prosser, who began the research into the series, and I are both women looking at a genre which was for much of its history heavily dominated by men, the question inevitably arose, why was it that, in the period that many would claim as the 'golden age' of *This Week* – roughly the decade of the 1970s – women were so strikingly absent?)

I hope that by looking at the routine regularity of production as well as its remarkable highlights, I will be able to convey a sense of the daily experience of making such a series, as well as the broader social, political and economic factors that have influenced and shaped it.

This Week began in the mood of the frivolous fifties (Chapter 1), but dissatisfaction amongst its own journalists and complaints from the statutory Authority pulled it back to a new seriousness in the 1960s (Chapter 2). In that decade, it entered what many of the journalists who worked on it described as its 'golden age', when they were able to pursue their stories with a great deal of freedom (Chapters 3 and 4). In particular, *This Week* reported the conflict in Northern Ireland with a thoroughness and a persistence that was definitely unwelcome to the government and the authorities (Chapters 5 and 6). But other voices were being heard, complaining that a style of journalism that pursued its ends with too much dedication was ignoring the interests of the wider audience. *This Week* was taken off the air and replaced by *TVEye* (Chapter 7). Following *TVEye*'s eight-year run, *This Week* was reinstated, but Northern Ireland once more proved a breaking point. Prime Minister Margaret Thatcher was outraged by 'Death on the Rock' (1988) which brought her government's counter-terrorism measures under scrutiny. That programme is widely credited with strengthening her resolve to introduce legislation that not only brought *This Week* to an end, but also caused the demise of Thames Television as a broadcaster, and of the regulatory body, the Independent Broadcasting Authority (Chapter 8). Since the early 1990s, current affairs as a whole has faced an uncertain future (Postscript).

Through all its vicissitudes, *This Week* was at the heart of a social democratic project, which sought, in the words of the inspirational documentarist John Grierson, to address its viewers 'in all the complex drama of their citizenship' (Grierson 1938). Its prioritizing of an informed and politically active public remained at the heart of its project, and I will argue that its political and informational strength lies in the ability to mobilize different dimensions and draw strengths from a broader range of programme styles. When it closed down, critic Allison Pearson mourned the loss of a contribution to 'that broad and civilizing consensus about the common good' (*Independent on Sunday* 13.9.92).

The history of this single series shows something of the indispensable place of the genre within the overall ecology of UK broadcasting, on a commercial channel which was nevertheless an integral part of a public service system. A live history never merely remains in the past, but has a real purchase on the present and the future.

1

MORE FUN THAN *PANORAMA*: CURRENT AFFAIRS IN A FRIVOLOUS MEDIUM

More fun

This Week had an uncertain start. 'The "window on the world" which opened last night' was like looking 'through the alcoholic haze of a West End cocktail party. At times it seemed the window had opened at the wrong moment and the smog had got in', wrote the *News Chronicle's* television critic, James Thomas. That first edition was transmitted live from the Hungaria Restaurant in London's Lower Regent Street, but it seems that the smog (and those eye-watering pea-soupers were all too familiar to Londoners before the Clean Air Act of 1962) had as much to do with technical problems as with too much good living. However, the fact that the series was launched from a convivial public space did signal its intention to be, in the words of another critic, 'more fun than *Panorama*' (*Daily Sketch* 12.7.56). And the intention to look beyond the metropolis was also made clear. The programme was billed as 'a window on the world behind the headlines' and the title came up behind a revolving globe, triumphantly accompanied by a portentous fanfare selected from a gramophone library of musical effects.

This Week was produced by Associated-Rediffusion (A-R), one of the new companies licensed by the groundbreaking Television Act of 1954. This ended the BBC's monopoly of television broadcasting and created space on the air waves for a commercial channel. In the words of the *Daily Mail's* critic, Peter Black, British broadcasting was 'wrenched ... violently out of the orbit it had swung in for thirty years' (Black 1972:28). Independent Television (ITV) was set up with a regional structure and A-R had gained the plum job of broadcasting to the London region on weekdays. It was also one of the four major companies which controlled the national network. From the autumn of 1956, *This Week* was networked at 9.30 every Friday evening, and its reach expanded across the UK as the ITV regional network was built up.

A-R had been created out of a set of complex agreements which involved Rediffusion, a pioneer in cable communications, in partnership with the huge electronics firm British Electric Traction (BET). They were joined by Associated Newspapers, which owned the *Daily Mail*. The new company took over a substantial building on the corner of Kingsway in central London which had been the headquarters of the wartime Air Ministry. Adastral House was renamed Television House and reconstructed at high speed into studios and offices to meet the launch deadline. Independent Television News (ITN), which was to provide news for the whole ITV network, was based on the seventh floor where it remained until 1968. The building work was nowhere near finished when the station went on air, and there were stories of narrow escapes from falling concrete, and, according to one observer, 'the girls' were given a weekly hair dressing and dry-cleaning allowance 'to repair ravages to coiffures and clothing by the all-pervading dust' (Courtney-Browne 1975:2).

A frivolous medium

The political battle around the launch of commercial television had been long and hard-fought. When the BBC had resumed its television service immediately after the Second World War, its prestige had been enormous. Its wartime radio mix of popular entertainment and reliable news – from *ITMA* and *Workers' Playtime* to the *Brains Trust* and Richard Dimbleby's war reporting – meant that it had placed itself at the heart of British culture and a British sense of identity (Cardiff and Scannell 1987:157). The Corporation had experimented with public television transmissions in the late 1930s, but these had only been received by a few thousand homes in the London area. Once the war was over it felt that its moral and cultural prestige had given it the right to use what its founder and first director general, John Reith, called – a little tactlessly – the 'brute force' of its monopoly to develop the new medium in its own image, 'giving the public the best of what it knew, and continually enlarging the range of what it knew' (Black 1972:9). Yet BBC pundits considered television to be very much the junior partner. 'They thought it was a frivolous medium,' said Grace Wyndham Goldie, 'wholly unsuitable for serious communication.' Goldie was speaking in a *This Week* programme which reviewed the political jousting behind the launch of ITV on the channel's 20th anniversary (16.9.76). She had, herself, been a driving force behind political broadcasting on the expanded BBC television service, a hard-working advocate of television journalism and largely responsible for the weighty and respected *Panorama*. Her comment, then, was heavy with irony, but highly significant. Her memoirs recount innumerable ways in which the early television chiefs, who had learnt their craft in sound broadcasting, prioritized the spoken word and distrusted the visual as automatically trivializing (Goldie 1977:45, 54, 58). In the context of the 1950s, when television was only just finding its feet, such distrust seemed based in real anxieties, and a similar distrust would recur with great consistency over the history of television journalism and of current affairs in particular. Facing the visual with all its connotations has continued to be a major challenge and will be a regular theme in this exploration of the history of *This Week*. The visual has continued to be linked with frivolity, triviality and a lack of seriousness, as well as an excess of emotion and even with femininity, which, in the 1950s, itself had a distinctly frivolous air.

Undoubtedly, amongst the wider audience, frivolity was a highly desirable quality, and the campaign to open the BBC to commercial competition, where it was assumed frivolity would have plenty of scope, built up strength in the post-war years. In America commercial television was funded by sponsorship as well as spot advertising, but in the UK a government committee on broadcasting – chaired by William Beveridge, famous as the architect of the post-war welfare state – rejected the US model and agreed that the BBC's monopoly should continue. Yet pressures from commercial interests were very strong, especially those with entertainment and newspaper involvement, and they had some powerful backing from within the Conservative Party and from some broadcasters who were concerned that the BBC was not allowing television to develop its potential. Selwyn Lloyd,

Conservative member of the Beveridge Committee, produced a much publicized dissenting report, which argued in favour of commercial competition and spoke scornfully of the 'compulsory uplift' provided by the BBC. He wrote of the 'four scandals of monopoly: bureaucracy, complacency, favouritism, and inefficiency' and recommended regionalization and advertisements confined to a 'natural break' in the programmes, rather than sponsorship. These proposals were eventually adopted in the Television Act (Negrine 1998:18–19).

The debates were very much of their time, but they have a remarkably contemporary ring. Opponents of commercial broadcasting expressed fears of what would in the 2000s be described as 'dumbing down' – Americanization, cut-price programming and pandering to uneducated mass taste. MPs warned of 'an orgy of vulgarity', and of 'Caliban emerging from his slimy cavern' (Black 1972:57, 62). Those who favoured commercial television argued that the broadcast media needed to be much more popular in tone and that an appeal to a wider audience would be less patronizing and more democratic. In the post-war mood of growing prosperity and domestic consumerism, the BBC was portrayed as solemn, paternalist and snobbish, while commerce made no bones about its appeal to the mass as it pursued its primary purpose of making money.

The 1954 Act established a workable compromise between the two positions. It set up a public authority, the Independent Television Authority (ITA), which would own the new transmitters, issue licences to the new companies and monitor their output to ensure that their commercial instincts were tempered by public service principles. Parliament voted to label the new channel as 'independent' rather than 'commercial' and the service was described as 'additional' rather than 'competitive'. The scholarly Sir Kenneth Clark, director of the National Gallery and chair of the Arts Council ('probably the most cultivated person in Europe' (Black 1972:69)), was appointed to chair the Authority. The ITA decided on a network with a regional structure so that the companies did not compete with each other for advertising. 'The ITA might equally well have been the BBC governors,' wrote Peter Black. Even so, John – by then Lord – Reith, whose powerful advocacy of public service and citizenship had forged the BBC, denounced the new channel in the House of Lords, 'They have sunk a maggot into the body politic.' Competition, he declared, would be for 'cheapness not goodness', and MP Patrick Gordon-Walker added 'with commercial television we are, by definition, not dealing with gentlemen' (Corner 1991:5; Thumim 2002:209). But the BBC was not particularly gentleman-like either. The ITV launch night featured the classy Hallé Orchestra, and the BBC grabbed the opportunity to entice the audience away by staging the death of Grace Archer, popular heroine of the radio soap opera *The Archers*.

This Week was launched against this background: a political contest that had succeeded in drawing a compromise between free-market principles and a paternalist, educational approach, reflected in a cultural debate around quality of programming and the detail of content. The relationship between the commercial companies and an Authority whose brief was to ensure that commerce did not drive out quality was to be a crucial factor in the development of the series over the years.

When *This Week*'s first Producer, Caryl Doncaster, described her aims, she encapsulated the conflicting pressures in the following way,

> *This Week* will be a programme of stories behind the news worldwide. ... It won't be all political. There will be a bit of everything in it, including humour and glamour. It won't be highbrow because we want a wide audience ... with everything geared to the commercial element we cannot afford programmes that do not pull their weight in viewer strength (Courtney-Browne 1975:2, 7).

In linking 'the political', the 'highbrow' and 'what does not pull its weight in viewer strength' on the one hand, and opposing that to a cluster of ideas that included 'humour and glamour' and 'what appeals to a wide audience' on the other, she clearly laid out the antithesis that current affairs programme makers – and not only on the commercial channels – needed to negotiate in different ways over the following half a century.

Doncaster, Gillett and the commercial element

> Let's face it once and for all, the public likes girls, wrestling, bright musicals, quiz shows and real-life drama. We give them the Halle Orchestra, Foreign Press Club, floodlit football and visits to the local fire station. Well, we've learned. From now on what the public wants, it's going to get.

So wrote Roland Gillett, A-R's first Controller of Programmes (Sendall 1982:328). Gillett had American experience and was also television adviser to the Conservative Party (Cockerell 1988:29). Frivolity, humour and glamour were high on his wish list. Even so, when he recruited Caryl Doncaster to help launch a group of magazine programmes at A-R, he employed someone whose experience was in social documentary rather than entertainment. Doncaster had a degree in history, had done postgraduate work in social and political sciences and had ten years' experience in Paul Rotha's innovative Documentary Department at BBC Television. Rotha had tried to develop a specifically televisual style of documentary, heavily dependent on primary research, which was then scripted and re-enacted in the studio. Although purist documentarists later poured scorn on such reconstructions, it was a real attempt to create a form suited to the new medium, and a forerunner of the dramatized documentaries of the 1980s and 1990s (Bell 1986). Doncaster described it as 'one of the few art forms pioneered by television'. Her programmes included a five-part investigation into the problem of youth, a two-part report on the situation of women, and programmes on marriage and old age. (Laing 1986:160; Scannell 1979:101 lists Caryl Doncaster's work for the BBC Documentary Department.)

At A-R she was in charge of regional magazine series including *Big City* and *Look in on London* as well as *This Week*, which aimed for national political status and was broadcast across the ITV network. She was its first hands-on Producer, but after a few programmes Peter Hunt took over the day-to-day running, helped by director/producer John Rhodes. As Head of Features she continued to oversee the shape of the series, its finances and its public-relations profile.

In that first year of ITV it was doubly important for producers to be 'geared to the commercial element'. The start-up costs for the new companies had been substantial; not enough television sets which could take ITV had been sold and the take-up of spot advertising was slow. From the point of view of the advertisers the new viewers were not prosperous enough to buy costly durables, so commercials tended to be for cheap, mass-produced consumer goods, which needed to sell in very large numbers to make an expensive advertisement worthwhile. By March 1956 the losses projected for Associated-Rediffusion's first year of trading were around £4 million (Sendall 1982:167). 'No new commercial venture ... had ever so lost so much money so quickly,' wrote Peter Black (Black 1972:96). Like the other ITV companies A-R's solution was to build up audience numbers by scheduling light entertainment in peak times, especially variety shows and quiz shows with money prizes, including Hughie Green presenting *Double Your Money* (1955–68) and Michael Miles with *Take Your Pick* (1955–68). There was a move to cut back on news, but the ITA intervened to guarantee at least 20 minutes daily. In this climate, *This Week* provided a useful compromise since it set out to be news-based as well as entertaining. Even so it was a brave decision to continue backing the series, especially as, in August 1956, Associated Newspapers, joint owners of the company, pulled out, arguably breaking the link with journalistic expertise. BET and Rediffusion Ltd were left to pour in yet more money (Sendall 1982:185–7).

Fundamental seriousness and audience strength

But that first edition had been chaotic.

The plan was for programme controller Roland Gillett to introduce the new series live from the Hungaria Restaurant, which would have entailed huge outside-broadcast vans parked in Regent Street. A number of short items would follow, some live, some pre-filmed, all linked from the restaurant by the well-known journalist Réné Cutforth and co-ordinated by director John Rhodes. No fewer than nine different items were to be crammed into that hectic half-hour with commercials coming half-way through. In the event, Cutforth withdrew because he did not like the script and, on the very day of transmission, Gillett abruptly left the company. Fortunately the television stalwart Leslie Mitchell was now A-R's Head of Presentation and was co-opted for both roles. This meant that *This Week* was fronted by the man who had introduced the first public television programme in 1936 and the resumed BBC television broadcast in 1946. Everything was last minute. Jim Pople, *This Week*'s first film editor, was still assembling the filmed items for Part Two while Part One was on air. He swears that one item was transmitted still held together by a paper clip. (This business of last-minute rush editing continued throughout the programme's history, but the risk of a paper clip jamming up the works reduced as editing equipment grew more sophisticated.)

Half a century later, many of the items in that first programme still have resonance. There was some investigative reporting related to foreign affairs, as Neville (known as Nick) Barker introduced an item on the sale of army surplus tanks to the Middle East (in January 1956 relations with Egypt were becoming sensitive) and there was a filmed interview with the wife of an intelligence official who had defected from East Germany (the Cold War was at its height). Tucked between a discussion of the January sales and a glimpse of the growing child star Margaret O'Brien, other items reflected the focus on the Middle East: an interview with an Englishman born in Egypt who had no passport, and a discussion of polygamy between MP Dr Edith Summerskill and a person described by one reviewer as 'a Moslem'. In fact several muslims, men and women, were featured in the item. Reporter Michael Ingrams introduced Jalal Adin Hal of the Muslim Welfare League and plunged in with the crucial question, 'Mr Adin, how many wives do you have?' Mr Adin had only one wife but he described the privilege granted to men by the Koran and pointed out that many Islamic countries were modernizing. Dr Edith declared with equal forthrightness, 'I do not believe in the subjection of women and polygamy symbolizes that. ... Can Mrs Adin take three husbands?' Begum Ikrimullah, wife of the High Commissioner for Pakistan, pointedly linked Islamic and Western practices: '[we] object to the usurping of the first wife's home and happiness by the second wife – whether by divorce or polygamy.' Turning to the camera in a dramatic close-up, Michael Ingrams declared, 'It's a tricky problem. The East is divided on it; the West is divided on it. What do you think?' Ingrams had been thrown in at the deep end, and had to research, write, direct and conduct the filmed interviews himself (Courtney-Browne 1975:1). The item was uncomfortably stiff by today's standards, but it was at least a stab at posing controversial issues concerning race, religion and gender against a background of global politics, and, well before the age of interactivity, it challenged the audience to form their own opinion. But it was not well received. 'Viewers might be stung into an interest in polygamy, but not like this,' wrote Peter Black (*Daily Mail* 7.1.56). The programme also included a 'blurred impression' of some Rank starlets and a threat that the well-known quizmaster Plantagenet Somerset Fry may shave his beard next week.

Reviewers agreed that Caryl Doncaster had tried rather too

hard. 'What a hotchpotch – take it easy,' wrote Herbert Kretzmer (*Daily Sketch* 7.1.56). James Thomas agreed that she had overdone it, 'cramming her programme chock-a-block. ... The programme should take one or two big stories and make a real job of them' (*News Chronicle* 7.1.56). Peter Black concluded dryly, 'The programme will succeed, because programmes like this always do.' And, of course, it did, and retained its mixed magazine format – although less tightly packed – for nearly ten years. The 1,000th programme celebration was held in the same restaurant in December 1975 – at that time re-named The Hunting Lodge.

By the end of 1956, reviewer Bernard Levin was paying tribute to 'Miss Doncaster's admirable news magazine, a programme which straddles comfortably the yawning gap that separates being fundamentally serious and being delicate in style' (*Manchester Guardian* 22.12.56). But the history of *This Week* over its first decade turned out to be a move – albeit a rather slow one – towards Thomas's recommendation to make a real job of the big stories. The series shifted gradually away from the lighter, audience-grabbing format and towards greater 'seriousness'. Disputes over the balance between 'fundamental seriousness' and 'audience strength', and over the possible meanings and ramifications of those two concepts were to recur with great regularity during its 36-year history.

By the end of 1958, Peter Hunt had taken over as Head of Features and Doncaster had become a producer of special documentary programmes. Reg Courtney-Browne, who joined the programme in 1958 as a researcher and location organizer, later wrote an informal history of the series and claimed that Doncaster had been 'frozen out by Mac the Knife' – a reference to General Manager John McMillan, successor to Roland Gillett – who was allegedly jealous of her success.

News and magazines: the serious and the delicate

Television was rapidly becoming the main expression of popular culture, and ITV was oriented to domestic leisure rather than political participation. Most of its programmes were unashamedly populist – in the 'girls, wrestling, bright musicals and quiz shows' mode favoured by Roland Gillett – but others set out to find ways of making more demanding topics accessible to the expanding audience. *This Week*'s multi-item magazine format

suited the balancing act that was needed between the 'the fundamentally serious and the delicate in style', and there were plenty
of precedents in which trenchant journalism and a serious political project had been mixed with humour, showbiz and human
interest. For example, the news magazine *Picture Post* (1938–57)
had risen to the challenge of the Second World War and had
juxtaposed powerful photo-journalism with features on fashion
and entertainment; radio was broadcasting popular magazines
such as *In Town Tonight* (1933–60), which interleaved celebrity
interviews with songs and newsy items; and, of course, there was
the entertaining mix of down-to-earth reporting, gossip, sport
and celebrity news, together with plenty of pictures, which was
building the readership of newspapers such as the *Daily Mirror*
as the wartime restrictions on newsprint finally came to an end.
On BBC Television, there was *Panorama* – launched in 1953 as a
lightweight magazine – and the topical news magazine *Highlight*.
Significantly, the magazine format also seemed a suitable one to
attract a female audience (Leman 1987). Magazine programmes
were the first to risk unscripted interviews on television and
created an outlet for journalism which would go beyond the
dry, factual reporting that was the heavily protected province of
broadcast news (Bell 1986). 'Round-table debates of pedestrian
slowness cannot be expected to hold an audience', argued Caryl
Doncaster. Instead, she said, programmes should be 'presented
with on-the-spot emphasis, filmed illustration and lively, unfet-
tered comment' (Courtney-Browne 1975:7). Current affairs was
being established as a genre with its own identity, clearly separate from news.

Television news itself had been uncertain in finding its feet,
chiefly because of the BBC's deep suspicion of the visual, which
many feared would distort the sacred commitment to truth and
impartiality. Even showing newsreaders in vision was considered a dangerous step which would distort its bland neutrality.
'If a news reader were seen while giving the news,' wrote Grace
Wyndham Goldie, 'any change in his [sic] visual manner, a smile
or lift of an eyebrow, might, however little this was intended,
be interpreted as comment. The sacred line between fact and
comment could be blurred' (Goldie 1977:194–5).

It was because the Corporation's News Division continued to
prioritize radio that its energetic Television Talks Department set
out to pioneer new, televisual forms of political journalism. They

sought out the stories behind the headlines, and declared that if a visual medium could not avoid commenting, then a Talks programme would make a *virtue* of comment (Goldie 1977:41–6, 68; Scannell 1979:98–100). When they launched a 'news magazine' they refused to allow the News Division to insert a bulletin in its familiar neutral style, and, as a result, *Highlight* (1955–56) became 'the first series to look at the news with the cool and independent stare of good popular journalism' (Black 1972:132).

This institutional distinction between the news and the more eclectic series was maintained on ITV, despite the fact that ITN was adopting a more audience-friendly style. News on ITV was not averse to allowing its viewers to see facial expressions as well as hear lively language. 'Personality should not detract from the news, it should give it added meaning and vitality,' wrote Robin Day, who was prominent amongst the new American-style 'newscasters' (Black 1972:117). But news bulletins were still very short, and the companies were anxious to protect their right to create more exploratory series, including Granada's *Under Fire* and *Make Way for Tomorrow*, as well as A-R's *This Week*. They complained that ITN was going beyond its remit when it developed *Roving Report* as a 'news programme in depth'. Robert Fraser of the ITA declared that 'documentaries and news features are the consciences of the programme companies'. If they were taken away from them and given to ITN, the companies would be only 'entertainment-makers entirely given over to the show-biz mind' (Briggs 1995:70).

From the first, critics compared *This Week* to *Panorama*, whose tag line 'the window on the world' it had borrowed. As competition from ITV loomed, Grace Wyndham Goldie had revamped *Panorama* into a much more substantial vehicle, fronted by the formidable Richard Dimbleby and designed to be taken seriously by politicians as well as the thinking public (Goldie 1977:191). *This Week* saw itself as a challenger to *Panorama*, but it also shared the approach of *Highlight* and that programme's successor *Tonight* (1957–65). As a weekday early evening series, *Tonight* went for shorter items; it had a genial and engaging presenter in Cliff Michelmore and a distinctly flippant style. 'The notion then that television programmes should be either serious or entertaining struck us as false and rather insulting to the audience' said its editor, Donald Baverstock (Corner 1991:8). In a similar spirit, on *This Week* the serious and the entertaining sat side by side, and it was – at least at first – accepted that neither would detract from the other.

April 1956

The number of items in each edition gradually settled down at between four and six, within the half-hour slot. Longer items sometimes stretched to eight minutes, the shortest could be no more than two. At first the items nested comfortably around the commercial break, which by the end of 1956 was around 2 minutes 5 seconds with three to four advertisements per break (Wegg-Prosser 2002:205). These early commercials themselves give a glimpse of a 1950s living room; a television set polished with Gleam (60 seconds) is in pride of place, and the family settle down with their television dinners of Cheeseburgers (30 seconds) and Walls Ice Cream (30 seconds). Father wears his Mr Burton suit (15 seconds) even while relaxing.

I have picked 6 April 1956 more or less at random to give an idea of a *This Week* from that first difficult year. The four items were introduced by a sleek, moustachioed Michael Westmore, who had taken over from Leslie Mitchell as presenter. First came a fashion-conscious, celebrity-centred, pure entertainment item with a Royal touch – a six-minute film of Grace Kelly's wedding to Prince Rainier in Monaco. The film was from an agency, EMI, and a commentary by Nick Barker was added in the studio. Next was a plug for a book. In *The Long Walk*, a 'Mr Rawitz' described his escape from a Russian prisoner of war camp and his 4,000-mile walk to safety. He was interviewed by *This Week* reporter Jeremy Thorpe, at that time an ambitious journalist with an eye on politics. (His career was to move through leadership of the Liberal Party to an accusation of murder, a court case and disgrace.) The item played on those nagging preoccupations of the 1950s: the Cold War, the ideological confrontation with communism and the fear of Soviet power. Then, after Gleam, Cheeseburgers, Mr Burton and co, the programme went straight to the heart of Westminster politics with an interview with Prime Minister Sir Anthony Eden on a year of his premiership – a recognition of the standing *This Week* had gained.

By 1956 it was clear that the battle for politicians to appear on television had been won. The days when Winston Churchill scorned the new medium like a '17th-century aristocrat rejecting

the right of the mob to look at him' (Black 1972:44) were definitively over. However, political television was at the height of
what historian Michael Cockerell has described as 'Edenvision'.
Anthony Eden had become an accomplished performer who was
pushing his right, as Prime Minister, to broadcast to the nation
whenever he thought it necessary. In the *This Week* programme
his interviewer was Aiden Crawley, the first Editor-in-Chief of
ITN. This was the man who had introduced 'newscasters' instead
of the neutral 'newsreaders' used by the BBC, and was encouraging a more direct style of interviewing on the American model.
The coming of ITV was helping to shake up political television
which had, in its early days, 'veered between the deferential and
the sycophantic' and had approached politicians 'in a manner
that could only be called grovelling' (Cockerell 1988:37). Even so,
it seems that by today's standard this interview was fairly bland.
Eden was to be challenged much more strongly when the Suez
crisis came to a head later in the year.

Reporting politics on television in the early 1950s was an
uneasy business because of the '14-Day Rule'. This forbade
the broadcasting of talks, discussions or debates on any issue
currently before parliament or for two weeks before a parliamentary debate. The device had been conceived by the BBC with
the aim of ensuring that parliament remained the first forum of
debate, and that its power was not usurped by unselected broadcasters (Paulu 1981:208–10). But journalists were increasingly
irritated by what they saw as an unnecessary gag on democratic
comment. The forum for the expression of opinion was widening, and at issue was the legitimacy of television as a political
space. In the summer of 1955 the BBC had announced it would
abandon the rule, but Winston Churchill had responded that
'It would be a shocking thing to have the debates of parliament
forestalled on this new robot organization of television.' This was
when, in Michael Cockerell's words, 'Edenvision won' and the
14-Day Rule got the force of law. There had been some doubt as
to whether it would also apply to ITV, but the Postmaster General
(the minister with responsibility for broadcasting at the time)
decided that it should, with the caveat that he 'hopes to be "hands
off"' (Cockerell 1988:40).

In the last item of that 6 April edition, the potent issue of race
was floated through an entertainment item on American musicals featuring black performers, Eartha Kitt in *New Faces*, and

Dorothy Dandridge in *Carmen Jones*. Race, racism and racial prejudice would be themes which were to recur across the years. *This Week* was proud of its topicality, organized from week to week. For the first few months the wind up was always the same, 'and from *This Week*, that's it. For us, next week's edition begins 30 seconds from now!' The 'now' cued the (hand-cranked) roller caption showing the programme credits, and the (hand-spun) gramophone record which backed them up. This was now the stirring Intermezzo from Sibelius's Karelia Suite. Film editor Jim Pople helped choose Karelia which 'won by a nose over Beethoven's Leonora 3 Overture' (JP to VWP). The original recording was deleted by Decca but the theme became so popular that it was re-issued on a 45rpm disc. The same music ended the series 36 years later, when, for the first time, viewers watched an orchestra performing the piece.

The space of 1950s television

This Week aimed to provide a window looking outwards towards the world – whether the celebrity world of Hollywood or the dangerous world of the Cold War – but we should never forget its domestic location and the intimacy of that small screen, with its ghostly black-and-white low-definition image. However dramatic the events it portrayed, they were embedded in the 1950s home, where consumption was gaining importance, and 'affluence' was becoming a buzzword (O'Sullivan 1991:167). As well as looking out towards the world, television personalities and journalists also needed to look inwards, towards the notional viewers, the man in the Mr Burton suit and the housewife clutching her Gleam-soaked polishing cloth. The television studio was an intermediate arena where characters of all sorts and backgrounds met on more or less equal terms – and, like Michael Ingrams in the very first *This Week*, they could turn to those at home and ask them what *they* thought.

Television technology in the 1950s depended on live broadcasts, which might have come either from a studio or, as with *This Week*'s original foray into the smog-bound West End, from a more distant location through the use of cumbersome outside-broadcast equipment. 'Liveness' seemed the very essence of the medium and the cast of characters who appeared on the screen became like friends of the viewers at home. Unlike similar personalities on radio or actors in the cinema, these were real-life individuals, existing in the here and now, who defied the laws of space and looked the viewer directly in the eye. It was a new phenomenon. Here was a group of celebrities with whom the viewers could, apparently, exchange glances, and who built up a convincing sense of familiarity and continuity of acquaintance, able to combine, in John Corner's words, 'show-biz, glamour and cosiness' (Corner 1991:4). They included announcers, presenters, linkmen and women, reporters and interviewers, as well as jokesters, comedians, actors and performers of many sorts who spoke to those who were watching with unprecedented directness. In the *Television Times, This Week* producer Peter Hunt claimed credit for 'launching several personalities who are now friends of yours'. Many of them had had the experience of being stopped in the street (1.9.57).

Television's liveness gave rise to the convention of locating a magazine programme (and originally a whole channel) within a studio which had a 'current' temporal and spatial reality. The studio was 'here and now' and the presenter – or anchor – shared a co-temporality with the audience. It was a second home into which the presenter sometimes welcomed guests, performers and other participants, and sometimes invited viewers to travel away, as it were, to a real or a fantasy location for a filmed item at one remove from the shared time frame. The personality of the presenter was clearly all important, as it set the tone of a series. His (and on *This Week* it was almost always 'his') was the familiar face which would become the face of the programme, commenting, joking, sharing a comfortable relationship with the audience, but also able to meet the eminent guests on an equal footing. He needed to shift the mood between a suitable gravitas and a chatty good humour and had to be knowledgeable without being patronizing. Leslie Mitchell had stepped into the breach for the first month, but by the fourth programme introductions and links came from Michael Westmore. With horn-rimmed glasses, an airforce moustache and sleeked-back hair, Michael Westmore had originally come from the BBC to head A-R's children's programmes. His presentation was informal, jocular and liberally laced with folksy comments and asides.

The series itself needed to establish different registers for the different items. Interviewers faced politicians who were rapidly learning to lose their stiffness (and Prime Ministers Anthony

Eden, Harold Macmillan and Harold Wilson all appeared in the
early days); foreign dignitaries, 'experts' and pubic figures such
as the philosopher and anti-nuclear campaigner Bertrand Russell
(9.1.58); quirky characters such as the early specialist in body
piercing (18.12.58); as well as authors, performers and showbusi-
ness celebrities. Celebrity interviews on magazine programmes
like *This Week* prefigured those chat shows with their relaxed
and genial hosts that would later become a mainstay of popular
viewing. As television genres became more clearly demarcated,
this was one area which came to seem inappropriate for current
affairs and by the 1960s celebrity items had all but disappeared.

And then there were interviews with ordinary people – some
who were in the public eye for a particular reason, and others
who were just swept into the mix (an interview with an elderly
widower who could not afford electricity was described by the
Daily Sketch as 'one of the most heartrending interviews ever
televised' (Courtney-Browne 1975:16)). The late 1950s was a time
when the public spaces of London and other major urban centres
were changing from war-torn wastelands to busy commercial
centres. People could now be simply out and about, and the vox
pop (derived from the Latin *vox populi* – voice of the people) was
a telling television innovation. Passers-by were stopped in the
streets and asked for a quick opinion – whether on a political
issue such as the Suez adventure, or the latest fashion. A range of
everyday voices and faces – many accents, women and men, old
and young – were more or less randomly chosen and the snip-
pets edited together, giving a real impression of an exchange
and diversity of opinion as well as a fascinating glimpse into the
1950s crowd.

Finally there were the filmed sequences, which covered news-
worthy topics such as the racial demonstrations in Little Rock,
Arkansas (4.9.58), and slices of life, such as East Enders picking
hops in Kent (9.9.59). These mini-documentaries foreshadowed
the shape of future *This Week* programmes, and this was where
the reporters came into their own.

Reporters: measuring a story with their eyes

When *This Week* began, very few reporters were familiar with
television techniques, especially as 'crossing over from the BBC
to the commercial channel was akin to heresy – like forsaking the

established church for a new, unorthodox and not quite respectable sect' (Courtney-Browne 1975:1). 'We had to root around,' wrote producer Peter Hunt. 'One of the great difficulties is to find writers who have a news sense and also know what they are talking about when they ask for long shots or pans, who can measure the quality of a story with their eyes.' The role of the reporter was by no means clearly defined. Recruits were expected to write scripts and direct as well as conduct interviews and make reports. Michael Ingrams, who had been an actor, claims to have been told 'it doesn't matter that you don't know anything about television – hardly anyone else does' (Courtney-Browne 1975:1). The series was given weight by an experienced group of visiting journalists, whose authority was underpinned by their reputations. Tom Hopkinson, the former Editor of *Picture Post*, and William Hardcastle, Deputy Editor of the *Daily Mail*, were brought in as advisers on news gathering and as occasional interviewers; James Cameron of the *News Chronicle* and Kenneth Harris of the *Observer* were commissioned to present items on a one-off basis – in particular interviewing heavyweight politicians, economists and scientists. Relying on 'the knowledge and opinions of people outside the staff for the solid background material that goes into our items' was regretted by Peter Hunt, but, he went on, 'all that is changing. Our own people are rapidly developing the necessary knowledge that adds authority to conviction: a new generation of television feature journalists is on the way' (*Television Times* 1.9.57).

One of these was Dan Farson, described in one obituary as a 'legendary drunkard of the old Soho school of alcoholism'. His background was similar to that of many who joined television in the late 1950s. He had been a photographer on *Picture Post*, a journalist on the *Evening Standard* and *Daily Mail*, and was the son of Negley Farson, a celebrated writer, foreign correspondent and man of action – with whom he appeared in a *This Week* programme. Farson left the programme in 1959 with director Rollo Gamble to produce and present series with titles such as *People in Trouble*, *Out of Step* and *Living for Kicks*, dealing with the emerging problems of post-war Britain and putting a new focus on personal life, youth culture, 'coffee bar teenagers and the "sexpresso kids" '(*Guardian* 29.11.97). Many of his *This Week* items followed his interests in music, Soho and youth culture.

As time went on others of the audience's friends created by

This Week appeared across the ITV schedules. Nick Barker, with his suave good looks, hosted and edited a game show for youth clubs called *Answers Please*.

Women and glamour

This Week had promised glamour and the 1950s was possibly the last decade in which glamour could be celebrated simply for itself, without self-consciousness or irony. On BBC and ITV glamorous women fronted television programmes, made the links between them and appeared in game shows in their halter-necked evening dresses. And glamour was high on *This Week*'s agenda. 'The glamorous Miss Sheila Bradley', Britain's 'safety ambassadress', promoted an item on industrial accidents (9.8.57), and women's obsession with fashion and appearance was a regular topic. Michael Ingrams reported on the book *Dior by Dior*: 'Poverty is an astonishingly magic wand. A woman who can only afford to buy one dress, generally goes to such trouble to choose it that she makes a good buy' (8.2.57); an item on the revolutionary 'sack' dress concludes with Vernon Greeves's wind up 'Oh you women! How much easier it would be if you'd stuck to fig leaves' (27.9.57).

Many consumer programmes on the new ITV were addressed specifically to women (Leman 1987:85–7). There were afternoon programmes for women and a whole bunch of advertising magazines (known as admags) which wove promotion of domestic items into mini-narratives. They included *It's a Woman's World* with Daphne Padell and *Let's Go Shopping* with Ruth Dunning. Women were expected to be amongst the audience for a magazine programme such as *This Week*, too – but 'women's topics' gave rise to plenty of nudges and giggles from the male presenters – and wind ups such as 'One day I'll find a question women can't answer. Goodnight!' (6.2.58). A great deal of attention was given to film stars, including Marilyn Monroe and Grace Kelly ('that wedding'), but it was men like the actor Peter Ustinov and the grand old politician Sir Winston Churchill who were named 'Man of the Week', while an item on the publishing phenomenon of the decade, women's magazines, had not a woman in sight, just the old stalwarts and experts on the press, Percy Cudlipp and Francis Williams (20.2.58). There was a sprinkling of female guest reporters in the short items which made up each edition, but when Mary Hill, presenter of ITV's daytime programme for women, appeared on the series, her subject was predictably, 'Fashion for Next Year' (28.12.56). Women were present and visible, but the gender divide and the association with frivolity was clear and re-emphasized with every item. With the departure of Caryl Doncaster it was difficult to find a woman with authority in the production team, and only occasionally did they have the journalistic authority of a responsible reporter.

An exception was Elaine Grand. She had been 'the most famous woman on Canadian television' and 'the person Canadians most wanted to be interviewed by' on a Toronto-based programme, interestingly named *Tabloid*. Like *This Week* it was an eclectic half-hour of news, public affairs and interviews. She joined A-R in 1956 where she became one of the four female presenters on *Afternoon Plus* which was 'a switch from the daytime diet of light items aimed at housewives, to an interview programme tackling a wide range of people in an intelligent way' (*Independent* 23.5.01). From March 1957 she gained a regular slot on *This Week*, broadcast live from Manchester in an arrangement with Granada Television. As *This Week* was transmitted across the ITV network, these items, with their distinctive Northern flavour, carried a sense of locality largely abandoned in the days of high seriousness in current affairs. Sometimes they simply reflected local life, such as watching the Grand National from a crowded bar in Liverpool (29.3.57), sometimes they dealt with social problems. Grand reported on school children who were smoking (5.4.57), the condition of old people in Manchester (26.4.57), outbreaks of polio in Coventry and Lincoln (9.4.57), and the Asian flu epidemic – particularly as it hit the Sheffield Wednesday team (23.8.57). (In that same programme Dan Farson, as ever in search of the quirky and the eccentric, profiled British nannies in an item from Kensington Gardens.)

The women on the series felt that they were not treated with respect, and were often forgotten or pushed aside. Sheila Gregg was a rare female director who had been Caryl Doncaster's assistant at the BBC. She occasionally produced the programme and felt that her potential was not used (to VWP). As always, the secretaries and assistants provided the backbone of the fast-moving production schedule. When Bryan Magee enumerated the *This Week* location crews, he noted that the film director's assistant was – and he put it in brackets – '(always a girl – the only one in the group)' (Magee 1966:52). Many of the other women on the series were similarly bracketed.

But at the 1956 Radio Show, Associated-Rediffusion mounted a competition for an interviewer for *This Week*. 'Are you one?' asked Michael Westmore, 'Why not go along to Earls Court and see. And perhaps I might have the pleasure of meeting you next week.' Apparently nearly 300 visitors to the Radio Show competed, and the winner was announced as Mrs Kraftcheck. On 31 August 1956 she was interviewed by 'the man who first introduced a television service to the world, Leslie Mitchell'. She was paid £5.5.0d at the end of transmission and, as far as I can make out, was never heard of again.

The *This Week* agenda

What do you do if the script has been prepared in a hurry and is changing right up to the last minute – even after the programme has begun? If you are Peter Hunt, producer of *This Week*, or John Rhodes, the show's news editor and director, you keep calm and the programme goes on the air as smoothly as if it has been rehearsed for days.

wrote the *Television Times* in August 1957, and Peter Hunt continued,

We seldom work more than a week ahead. This makes for rush and inconvenience, but I firmly believe that news features produced under some pressure carry an immediacy that evaporates under conditions of leisure. ... Our aim is to present you the news behind the news in *This Week*. We wish we knew what is going to happen next week. But this is a young unit. We look forward to it (9.8.57).

The series ran for 52 weeks every year and Hunt was writing after 80 weeks without a break 'which represents some 500 little productions'. Five years into the series it had failed to appear only four times – three weeks during the election campaign of 1959 and on Good Friday 1956.

There were weekly programme meetings attended by all staff, when ideas were put forward and selected. At times the search for items to fill the slot (27 minutes or so, depending on the commercials) became close to frantic. Topics were chosen in a variety of ways, from a government report, a newspaper item, a film or publicity release, a request to a politician for an interview, and occasionally a news scoop. Some were more or less blatant PR exercises (Jim Pople flew over the North Pole to Japan, courtesy of Scandinavian Airlines, for the launch of a new route (1.3.57)). Nevertheless the future current affairs agenda was previewed to a remarkable extent in those early days. Within the first months there were hints at the range of stories that were to preoccupy the series over the next 36 years, from human interest to overseas reporting and high politics. Despite the brevity of the items, a current affairs map (Jonathan Dimbleby's term) was being laid down. The first 50 editions contained no fewer than 300 items, shifting focus rapidly between politics, social awareness and overseas reports, interleaved with humour and glamour. It was 'tabloid television' before the label became a pejorative one.

Social and cultural items

Like other current affairs programmes, *This Week* rapidly developed a 'social eye' – an awareness of the population in all its diversity linked to an exploration of social 'problems' (Scannell 1979). It reflected the social readjustments of the 1950s: domestic consumerism, welfare and education, the rise of the meritocracy together with a recognition of continuing poverty, disadvantage and unemployment, the new youth cultures, youth consumerism and youth rebellion – giving space to the inarticulate working-class Teddy Boys as well as the vocal young Angries of the new middle class.

Nineteen-fifty-six was the year of the Angry Young Men and their well-publicized disenchantment with respectable values. Colin Wilson's *The Outsider* and John Osborne's *Look Back in Anger* both came out in May 1956. Wilson was interviewed while eating fruit; Osborne was asked to comment on the upper-class debutante season. Presenter Michael Westmore concluded, '*What* an angry young man! I don't think I agree with him at all.' Unfortunately the angry text does not survive (31.5.57). The Teddy Boys were the first post-war group of working-class dandies who dressed 'to be seen' in public places, and asserted their presence through visibility and style. On television, viewers of all classes were invited to share this urban spectacle without venturing into the public space themselves. Society was becoming 'spectacularized', commented the critic Raymond Williams, but arguably the spectacle could also be seen as a real expansion in diversity and inclusiveness.

Domestic issues

Inevitably these included housing and poverty. The evening news described an item on poverty in Liverpool, as the 'shock of the night', revealing 'conditions of filth and damp unimaginable to any believer in the Welfare State. ... They've been on housing lists since 1932. ... If this is true then someone in charge of housing in Liverpool needs shooting – and at once' (17.3.56). Items covered unemployment, crime, health (Rollo Gamble's report from an accident hospital in Birmingham was the first of a long line of 'casualty' stories (2.11. 56)). Homelessness and separation from home became a regular Christmas theme, culminating with the gloomy programme on the lonely death of a homeless man which ended *This Week*'s 36-year run in 1992.

Individual injustice

The desire to right individual injustice – to aid the individual at the mercy of an uncaring system and to praise those stubborn characters who stand up for their rights – would also recur. Peter Whitehead 'has spent the last 12 years of his life in a home for mental defectives, [and] was released after a formal admission he'd been wrongfully detained' (14.12.56); farmer Dudley Glanfield threatens to blow up a pylon the Central Electricity Authority plan to put on his land (28.9.56). In a characteristic switch in mood, an item on the Happy Wanderers New Orleans style street band was followed by an emotional interview with William Bentley, father of 19-year-old Derek Bentley who had been hanged as an accomplice to a murder committed by his 16-year-old companion. 'We haven't changed anything in his room for four years. I promised my son I'd carry on the fight, especially because it's a stigma on his brother' (19.7.57). (It was to be a long-running campaign, and was taken up by *Storyline*, the programme that succeeded *This Week* in 1993. After a feature film and several refusals by Home Secretaries, Derek Bentley's name was cleared.)

Window on the world

Publicity stressed *This Week*'s internationalism, with 'exclusive news flashes, features and interviews from all over the world' (*Television Times* 30.8.57). Visiting politicians, writers, performers and musicians passed through the studio, and it was always tempting to suggest an overseas trip, especially as first-class travel was the norm. But 'yearnings for exotic places' ('Has anyone taken a look at the Dalai Lama recently?') were, according to Courtney-Browne 'wistful rather than practical ... bearing in mind the slim budget'. Cash was always short and a producer who went abroad needed to bring back several items. Inexperience did not help. Several crews set out without checking customs regulations and wasted valuable time negotiating over impounded equipment (Courtney-Browne 1975:4).

Michael Ingrams reported extensively from Latin America, including Argentina and Chile. (In early 1959 he was told there were not enough funds to move on from Venezuela to Cuba which was in turmoil. He went anyway, but was thrown out and missed getting a precious interview with Fidel Castro as the new regime took over.)

But the chief focus was on parts of the world linked by Commonwealth ties, particularly Australia and New Zealand. In Cyprus there was a full-scale civil war between Greek and Turkish Cypriots, and *This Week* gained a scoop interview with the exiled leader of the Greek faction, Archbishop Makarios (6.2.58). But Indonesia, Japan, China, the Indo/Pakistani dispute over Kashmir, all had at least passing recognition. 'We are too often drawn by the sound of gunfire,' said *This Week* producer Roger Bolton, 30 years later, and from the start overseas topics followed the focus of global conflict – particularly that which involved Western interests as the overarching framework of the Cold War slid into place.

Cold War fears continued to be echoed in items on spies, surveillance and civil liberties – not always serious in tone. 'Telephone tapping is legal!' declared Michael Westmore, and played back a conversation recently recorded (1.11.57). And fear of nuclear Armageddon was almost tangible. Appearances by protestors against the H-Bomb tests included 63-year-old Harold Steele and his wife who threatened to 'sail into the test area and offer themselves as human sacrifices in protest' (29.3.57).

Frivolous items

Social, political, international and cultural items were always juxtaposed with 'humour and glamour'. There was fashion (lots of it), an item on the debutante season and one on Dominic Elwes and Tessa Kennedy 'misbehaving' at upper-class balls (31.5.57; 13.12.57). There was the cinema, film stars and other celebrities (lots of them), and the Royal Family's 'keyhole reminiscences' (19.10.56). There was classic human interest (two children adrift in a boat for 32 hours survive (17.8.56)), and the topical, including the introduction of parking meters (3.8.56). And then there were the oddities: Dr Gerald Gardner admitted to being a witch. Tom Fallon asked, 'Could you put a curse on me?' 'I could, but I wouldn't' (3.5.57). But the man who taught a goldfish to speak turned out to be an April Fool's joke (1.5.59) (Courtney-Browne 1975:9).

Frivolity overflowed into the presentation of the more serious items: a stuffed wildcat introduced a rash of unofficial strikes; an item on inflation began, 'Twopenny ha'penny post is going to become a thruppenny one. ... If this sort of thing continues somebody will be getting a fourpenny one' (19.7.57). From July 1957 there was a regular report from cartoonist Al Capp on the American scene, and, more seriously, the historian A.J.P. Taylor could be relied on to plug a gap with a spontaneous, unscripted lecture on a huge variety of topics. Keeping its reputation for what the *Daily Mirror* described as its 'flair for the dramatic' (17.3.56), the series brought (an illegal) street bookmaker into the studio to plead for the legalization of betting shops, and disguised his identity by masking him. The live studio brought its unanticipated moments – the poet Dylan Thomas's wife Caitlin got 'overemotional' and was faded out; anti-nuclear protestors infiltrated the 1959 New Year edition. Links and wind ups became ever more ingenious with corny jokes and gimmicks, and a variety of animals and zany props enlivened the studio. Michael Westmore found himself in an apron to cook 'Drunks' soup from the Esquire cook book' (14.12.56), and apparently upside down for an item on Australia Day (27.1.56).

The series set out to reflect its times, and sometimes it did so inadvertently. But to a large extent its writers, directors and producers simply got on and did what seemed interesting to them. For example, the early *This Week* had its own aviation correspondent, ex-fighter pilot Colin Hodgkinson, 'who lost his legs training to fly Spitfires'. He provided the programme with snappy and inventive stories for several years and built a two-seater plane for £500 in a shed on the Isle of Wight. 'Turbi' items on *This Week* followed his progress, paralleled by features in the photo magazine *Illustrated* (from 5.4.57).

Life on *This Week*

After a live transmission the team would wind down at the local pub (there were some heavy drinkers) and at the Good Friends restaurant. There was a real sense of esprit de corps, working under pressure, especially as many of them had no previous television experience (Sheila Gregg to VWP).

Just as directors and journalists were new to television, so were the technical crews. There were no experienced news cameramen available to the series, and the film industry was accustomed to operating in a quite different way. Cameras were large 35mm Cameflex or Arriflex, made even more cumbersome by the blimp which was necessary to damp down the noisy clatter of the film passing through the gate. Sound recordists used a heavy Levers Rich tape recorder. In the 1950s even location documentaries were made with planned setups and filmed one shot at a time, with each shot carefully lit. This ponderous style carried over into early current affairs, with scripts prepared shot by shot. As 35mm film is very expensive, the aim was to shoot not more than five times more film footage than was actually used – a 5-1 ratio – which was very tight, especially when you consider that every shot must begin with a marker board and inevitably has a bit of overrun at the end. Anecdote has it that director Rollo Gamble was known for profligacy as his ratio sometimes went as high as 16-1. Interviews, too, were shot with a single camera. First the interviewee was filmed, then the camera was moved, the lighting adjusted, the interviewee went away, and the interviewer was filmed separately, asking questions, nodding, smiling and looking interested, so that the editor could assemble a fluent piece. These 'cut aways' and 'noddies' could potentially be filmed not only in another place, but also on another day (Magee 1966:48–51).

It was difficult for filming to become more flexible because of an agreement with the film technicians' union, the Association of Cinematograph Technicians (ACT) (which was adding 'television' to its name and becoming the ACTT round about now). The BBC did not recognize the union, which meant that *Panorama* had been able to adopt flexible crewing arrangements, but *This Week* and other ITV programmes were hampered by an agreement that put television items into the same category as full-length feature films. Reg Courtney-Browne argues that this anomaly was caused by a misunderstanding by Associated-Rediffusion's general manager, Tom Brownrigg, who had no previous knowledge of the film or television industries. He had retained his navy title, liked to be addressed as Captain Brownrigg, and 'was said to have commanded A-R as if it were a battleship' (Sendall 1982:117). The story went around that he had misinterpreted the word 'feature', which describes both a major fiction film and a longish news item (Courtney-Browne 1975:5). More plausibly, the agreement came about because A-R were negotiating to film at Shepperton Studios using well-established feature crews, whose union agreements were already in place (Darlow 2004:51). But it was to be an expensive misjudgement. For many years reporters and directors complained about the burden of having to use a crew large enough for a cinema production. When Bryan Magee joined the series in 1960 he noted,

> for a *This Week* interview the film unit consists of the film director and his assistant (always a girl – the only one in the group), the cameraman and his assistant, the sound man and his assistant; then, probably one or two electricians and another couple of men to drive the trucks (Magee 1966:52).

There were many jokes about *This Week* reporters arriving with their huge entourage.

Although the union included directors, producers and researchers, it was acutely aware that the expertise and job security of its technical grades needed to be protected from undercutting and downgrading of status. Membership was guarded. A closed shop was in operation in the ITV companies – in other words no one could be employed in an ACTT grade without union membership. At the same time membership was difficult to obtain and limited to those with experience. Employment was hedged around with restrictions and there were strict prohibitions on acting outside your job description. Relations with the ACTT and the other technicians' unions were to crop up again and again in the history of the series – and they frequently played a destructive role.

When the newly shot film came back from location, it first had to be developed at one of the specialized laboratories around London. If there was no time to make a print, the editor had to use the precious master negative, which meant that if a shot was scratched or lost there would be no way to replace it. More often a 'rush' print would be made, and the sound, which had been separately recorded on quarter-inch tape, would be transferred to magnetic film. Frequently these 'rushes' would only arrive on the day before transmission. Then the pictures had to be synchronized with the sound, viewed, and, following some high-speed editing, a version had to be ready by lunchtime on the day of transmission, so that the commentary could be written, recorded and matched to the picture. In the early days, A-R did not even have facilities to view the film, so the rushes were projected at ITN on the seventh floor of Television House.

But the electronic transformation of television was already at its shaky beginnings. Despite the dire financial situation of the company, Managing Director Paul Adorian had the foresight to authorize the purchase of two newly invented Ampex videotape recorders, which were demonstrated in the *This Week* of 26 June 1958, and Reg Courtney-Browne was sent to New York to investigate transmission by satellite (Telstar was launched in July 1962). As so often with new technology, there were worries and concerns about misrepresentation and manipulation. Viewers saw Michael Westmore perform a murder confession on audio tape – which was then edited so that it appeared to be a declaration of innocence (Courtney-Browne 1975:8).

Suez and Hungary

'The foundations of our world have been rocked,' declared Michael Westmore on 2 November 1956 when *This Week* had been on the air for barely nine months. He was right. Nineteen-fifty-six turned out to be a challenging year in which to have launched a programme that dealt with political and international issues. In October and November of that year, the two major fault lines, which in their different ways were to dominate global politics through the second half of the twentieth century and into the twenty-first, erupted into armed conflict. In the Middle East Israel invaded Egypt, Britain and France bombed the Suez Canal Zone, and British paratroopers landed in Port Said. The following day the Western confrontation with Soviet communism came to a head as Russian tanks rolled into Hungary, where a popular uprising had begun to reclaim precious freedoms.

In July, when President Gamal Abdul Nasser of Egypt had announced the nationalization of the Anglo-French Suez Canal Company, *This Week* had stirred the event into its usual eclectic mix. James Cameron had interviewed two MPs in a six-minute live discussion, and this was followed by a report of 'rock and roll riots' in the USA (following the release of the film *Rock Around the Clock*), Dick Lester at the piano, and an item on American playwright Arthur Miller, who had been charged with contempt by the UnAmerican Activities Committee while in Britain on honeymoon with film star Marilyn Monroe (27.7.56).

Despite the vilification of Nasser by the government and in the press, which created an image of 'a second Hitler' and a 'serious military and ideological threat to Britain and the free world', *This Week* went ahead with an interview with the Egyptian leader (24.8.56). Nasser took the opportunity to differentiate between the management of the Canal and the freedom of navigation. It was a rare occasion, since, as Tony Shaw's comprehensive study of Suez coverage shows, the British media almost completely overlooked Nasser's legal right to nationalize, and focused on the manner and implications of the act (Shaw 1996:12,190).

As in more recent Middle East crises, the media became subject to an intensive propaganda campaign by the British government. The independence of political broadcasting was still uncertain and the BBC was particularly susceptible to government pressure. Eden was exasperated by the Corporation's (weak enough) attempts at balance in presenting the Egyptian view, and also in their much contested decision to allow Hugh Gaitskell, Leader of the Opposition, a right of reply to his Prime Ministerial broadcast. Eden's secretary noted the Prime Minister's 'passion and determination to teach the BBC a lesson'. 'Are they enemies or just socialists?' he had demanded. Cabinet ministers were reported to be looking up the rules to see how they could bring broadcasting under control (Cockerell 1988:47–8; Shaw 1996:189).

Commercial television was less open to pressure. Kenneth Clark, chair of ITA reported,

> I was on my way to give a lecture on Raphael … when Eden asked me to see him at No 10. He asked me, in the national interest, to slant the news about Suez. … I told him it could not be done. We were working under an Act of Parliament which called for impartiality. I left and went on my way to give my lecture and never heard another word about it (Shaw 1996:132, 135).

This Week's interview with Nasser was remarkably well received by reviewers, who did not seem concerned that it was giving air space to a demonized enemy. For the *Star*, 'This Week has been growing in stature. ... Last night it leapt to manhood with its interview with Col. Nasser, the latest bogeyman, who put his case for the Suez snatch' (24.8.56).

The programme also took its film cameras out into the streets to do vox pops, and most interviewees disagreed with Eden's intervention because 'we've still got to move out in the end' (2.11.56). The nation was not united; opposition to the invasion was strong and showed itself in vociferous public demonstrations. The Labour Party came out against the attack, as did the *News Chronicle* and the *Manchester Guardian* (which called it 'hideously miscalculated and utterly immoral' (5.11.56)). A political programme such as *This Week* was able to maintain its balance by reporting the views of many individuals of standing who were opposed to the government. On 2 November, after that dramatic opening, Tom Hopkinson conducted studio interviews with newspaper correspondents and MPs. James Callaghan described the scenes in the House of Commons as being 'unparalleled in twenty years'.

On 9 November it was a map of Hungary that dominated the studio, with 'drum dramatics over'. This programme led with an item on the Soviet invasion, followed with one on the flow of refugees to Austria. Many journalists were based in Vienna, as it was a link point for the new Eurovision cable, and Hungary became the first foreign story the public could follow night after night. *Panorama* came live from Vienna and managed to get cameras into Hungary itself (17.11.56) (Lindley 2002:43). *This Week* could not compete, but it continued to report on refugees (16.11.56). All too predictably, in the following months, the tragic story of Hungarian refugees became transformed into a domestic story on asylum seekers in Britain. Refugees are being trained to be miners – 'our coal mines are 9,000 men short' – but will local people accept the Hungarians? Their English is bad etc, but they will do the more menial jobs. 'Only two or three chaps will go to each colliery so [in a typical 1950s *This Week* commentary twist] there's no danger of an increase in the divorce rate ...' (22.2.57).

On its 'worst day ... since it took office in 1951', under pressure from the USA, the British government agreed to withdraw troops from Egypt. Sir Anthony Eden, suffering from 'severe overstrain', left for an extended holiday. Once more, with the help of a studio map, *This Week*'s discussion broadened to consider the rise of Arab nationalism and the threat of Russian intervention (23.11.56). Experts on Islam and the impending Islamic revival were few, but the programme made the effort. His Highness the Aga Khan was interviewed on 'Moslem nations, what next', and Emile Bustani, Minister of Reconstruction in the Lebanon, was interviewed twice (14 and 28.12.56). The crisis in the Middle East had been a crisis of colonial confidence and of Britain's global role, but it was also a crisis of rising post-war prosperity. Western nations, and Britain in particular, were forced to recognize that world resources were not under their automatic control. As usual, balancing the light and the serious, *This Week* made many jokes about the possibility of petrol rationing, including a comic item on alternative modes of transport (30.11.56).

As well as being a watershed in modern global politics, Suez is widely thought to have revolutionized political television. Grace Wyndham Goldie commented that it was 'a salutary warning of the lengths to which a political party may go, when in power, to prevent the broadcasting of any opinions but its own'. She stressed the importance of 'maintaining procedures to which the broadcasting organizations can refer when refusing to submit to government pressures exerted at moments of tension when feelings are running high' (Goldie 1977:175–86, 208). The existence of ITV, a channel with a greater distance from government, itself had an effect. Suez had confirmed that broadcasters had the right to question political leaders on television, and, as Philip Purser wrote in the *Daily Mail*, 'more and more politicians are realizing that there is nothing to be feared from appearing on television and much to be gained' (Courtney-Browne 1975:16). *Panorama* claimed that, following Suez, television 'took root in the nation's mind as the place to hear what important people had to say' (Lindley 2002:47). There was a feeling amongst *This Week* journalists that they too should be moving towards greater political authority.

Following the crises of 1956, the television companies decided to ignore the infamous '14-Day Rule' – the ban on discussing issues coming before parliament within two weeks of a parliamentary debate. *This Week* had in practice broken the rule every time it included debates with MPs on contemporary legislation – but it had been a risk. Eventually the government suspended the rule, at first for 'an experimental period' then indefinitely (Goldie 1977:17–20).

Sobering up

The summer of 1956 had been difficult for Associated-Rediffusion, as Associated Newspapers withdrew from the company. Owing to the confidence of the powerful BET and to an agreement with Granada, which was designed to reduce the risks taken by Granada but which effectively gave A-R a share of that company's profits, the company hung on (Black 1972:103).

In that first year there had been a great deal of scepticism about independent television. Lord Beaverbrook's Express newspapers consistently criticized it, and on ITV's first anniversary *Illustrated* magazine published an attack headed 'A year of failure' together with a picture of a miserable family watching television. On *This Week* William Hardcastle interviewed the man in the picture, who turned out to be a model, unrelated to the woman and children shown. The family was proclaimed a 'fake'. Introducing the programme Jeremy Thorpe declared that ITV had, in fact, been a success. 'Six million people can now look at it. Almost every important advertiser uses it' (21.9.56). (The figure of 6 million was actually an extrapolation from the number of sets that could receive ITV, which was, at the end of 1956, just over 2½ million (ITA *Annual Report 1962–3*, quoted by Bartlett 1986:41).) As it happened, by the following winter, advertisers were rushing into television 'like a tidal wave', as the companies intensified their mixture of brashness, non-establishment regional appeal, a 'cult of personality' and unashamedly populist scheduling. Turnover went up 'at a rate that left the companies slightly embarrassed by the size of their killing. They were like men who had drilled for oil in their back gardens and found the largest gusher in the world' (Black 1972:169). In the notorious words of Roy Thomson of Scottish Television, they had gained 'a licence to print money'.

In December 1957 *This Week* switched from Fridays to Thursdays, and continued to experiment. For the first Thursday transmission the entire edition came live from Paris in co-operation with the French state broadcaster ORTF. ORTF would not allow commercial breaks, but the ITV network refused the programme without them, so the team made an alternative programme just for the network. The following week was the first edition to be produced entirely on film (19 and 26.12.57).

The hybrid programmes of these early years could be seen as a sort of experimental exuberance, with their animals in the studio, visual puns and sudden changes of register from high seriousness to the extremes of flippancy. But they were part of what Bernard Sendall, Deputy Director General of the ITA, would later describe – rather loftily – as the companies' 'retreat from culture' (Sendall 1982:326). It was partly this pressure that brought about a climate of change, but change in any case fitted in with what many of the journalists and producers on *This Week* had been thinking, particularly since the traumatic events of November 1956. Ludovic Kennedy, previously a newscaster at ITN, had joined *This Week* as a reporter and presenter in 1957, but moved to *Panorama* two years later, saying he had 'outgrown' the programme. 'It was a scrappy affair,' he wrote, 'with items of quite astonishing triviality.' Peter Black commented, 'he won't be the last to switch, so long as ITV stuffs its peak hours with thrills and giggles' (Kennedy 1989:249–50, 254–5). The general feeling was that the programme had run out of steam. At Christmas 1960 Desmond Wilcox reported on candlelit dinners from a pub in Middlesbrough while a new presenter, Brian Connell, displayed joke presents for people in the news. Courtney-Browne described it as, 'the last gasp of facetiousness and whimsy on *This Week*' (Courtney-Browne 1975:23).

Brian Connell had joined the series in 1960 as its main presenter, as part of an effort to give it more weight. Although *This Week* saw *Panorama* rather than *Tonight* as its direct rival, it had not been able to find a presenter to compare with Richard Dimbleby. 'Dimbleby *was Panorama*, its abiding style and authority,' said Michael Ingrams, 'very few in the *This Week* team underrated the importance of his formidable presence and professionalism' (Courtney-Browne 1975:22). The series had had a number of presenters, including producers Elkan Allan and Cyril Bennett, and journalists Ludovic Kennedy and Richard Goold-Adams, but Connell seemed to be the answer. He was a Fleet Street veteran with a neat naval beard who had been one of the first newscasters on ITN and ITN's foreign affairs reporter. His weighty presence and conservative influence were considerable, and for a while he was identified with the series.

But by the summer of 1961 criticism from the ITA was mounting and there was a real chance that *This Week* would lose its networked slot and the national prestige that went with it. Peter Hunt had built it up from its beginnings and had supervised it for five and a half years without even a summer break, and the strain was showing. So John McMillan, Controller of Programmes, turned to journalist Cyril Bennett and film director Peter Morley who had pooled their complementary talents to build up a reputation for substantial documentaries with political and international themes. 'You've had your fun in Japan and France – and now you owe me,' McMillan had told them. With Morley as hands-on Producer and Bennett as Editor, the brief was to revitalize the series, and, in McMillan's words, 'to make it sing again'. After six months, he said, they could go back to doing what they liked best (Morley 2005:97). They immediately made a break with the tabloid, magazine-style format of the past. 'Two subjects became the norm and one was frequent. The treatment was in depth, the style taut, and presentation tightly disciplined,' wrote Reg Courtney-Browne (1975:77). The stories behind the news were gaining priority and the question of audience strength began to be framed in different terms. Bernard Sendall of the ITA wrote that 'slowly, over a period of about three years, the programme (like A-R themselves) sobered up' (Sendall 1982:355). Flippancy, humour and glamour were on the way out, together with celebrity interviews, film reviews and April Fool jokes.

In 1961 David Hennessey (later to become Lord Windlesham) succeeded Peter Hunt as Head of Features.

A frivolous medium?

So was it true that television was, in its very nature, a frivolous medium? For those concerned with news and political programming, frivolity had been linked to the distractions – and attractions – of the visual. It was linked to the widening of entertainment values and an audience appeal which relied on easy emotion – whether laughter or amazement – as opposed to strenuous thought. The motives of commerce were also distrusted. In the early 1970s, Peter Black noted that many who had campaigned for commercial television for democratic, participatory reasons had been deeply shocked to find that the new audience seemed only too eager to lap up the crassest of game shows and the most vulgar of the big-money quizzes. And all these worries have recurred throughout the history of current affairs television.

In the late 1950s some were arguing that 'frivolity' and all that it implied must be eliminated from programmes that claimed to be 'serious', while others, including Donald Baverstock with his successful formula for *Tonight*, insisted that it should be accommodated. On *This Week*, the format in which the light-hearted and the serious were juxtaposed, was, by the early 1960s, judged to be inappropriate. The task was then to develop a form of journalism that would deal with the visual and play to the strengths of the medium in a way that avoided the more trivial of entertainment values.

2 THE PILKINGTONS TAKE OVER

Sobering up

Today we would rather be charged with not being topical than screen a scrappy uninformative programme. We do not chase the headlines. ... The time span covered in our search for topical elements has broadened. No longer is it from one Thursday to the next. Now it embraces the whole range of contemporary affairs (1966).

So wrote Cyril Bennett in 'Ten Years of TV Journalism', the publication that celebrated *This Week*'s first decade. The tone and approach could hardly be more different from Caryl Doncaster's assertion that the stories behind the news needed to be enlivened with humour and glamour, and from the urgency of that early wind-up line, 'For us, next week's edition begins thirty seconds from *now*!'

By the mid-1960s the cultural climate had changed dramatically. The very fact that the companies had become so prosperous meant that the ITA could insist that they widen their range, especially in relation to current affairs. At the BBC, Director General Hugh Carlton Greene (who was 'progressive, iconoclastic, liberal and naughty' according to his biographer (Tracey 1998: viii)) presided over the introduction of BBC2 and championed an agenda that took contemporary issues head on, with powerful dramas and strengthened current affairs, as well as an explosion of irreverent political satire which was all the more shocking following the deference of the early days. Apolitical frivolity had given way to a much more politicized critical humour. At *This Week* a new generation of programme makers was in charge, determined to bring a sharper intelligence to the series.

The decade had begun with a ringing endorsement of public values. In 1960 the Conservative government had set up a committee to 'advise on the services which should in future be provided in the UK by the BBC and ITA', and the Pilkington Report, published in 1962, had reverberations well beyond broadcasting. Pilkington 'judged the nation's culture', wrote historian, Jean Seaton (Curran and Seaton 1997:175). The report was highly critical of the ITV companies' populism and the 'triviality' of their output, and came out strongly in favour of public service and the responsibility of broadcasters to 'experiment, to show the new and unusual, to give a hearing to dissent' (para 53). Controversially it found that 'box office success' was incompatible with 'quality'. In sum, its judgement of ITV was damning (Sendall 1983:85–93; Pilkington 1962:paras 43, 199).

The Pilkington Report was heavily influenced by the views of committee member Richard Hoggart, whose book, *The Uses of Literacy*, had set out to explore the strengths of working-class culture in the post-war era, just as mass entertainment was challenging traditional alignments. Television cut across class and regional divides, but Hoggart was suspicious of the consumerist basis of the changes. For him, if culture was not deeply rooted in the texture of everyday life, it was mere 'candy-floss', immediately attractive but deceptive and insubstantial (Hoggart 1958:169–202). Yet the modern industrial world had improved the lives of working people precisely by making them part of a mass market and turning them into consumers. Their leisure was becoming as important to the economy as their productive work – indeed their purchasing ability was at the heart of post-war development. In the face of this dilemma, Hoggart insisted that popular culture could only find an authentic democratic presence outside the market. His ideas, together with those of the left-wing critic Raymond Williams, influenced a generation of academics who wanted to broaden the meaning of 'culture' and understand its political importance (Williams 1974). The popularity of television posed a problem for this way of thinking. Could it be part of an 'authentic' culture? Could it speak, in the words of documentarist John Grierson, to 'the common man' in 'the complex and intimate drama of his citizenship' (Grierson 1938)? Or does that approach imply a sort of patronizing intellectualism, just at the time when working-class culture was abandoning deference, developing a taste for entertainment and relishing its increased leisure hours? Through the Pilkington Report these rather esoteric debates were to have a lasting influence on UK broadcasting. (Almost half a century later, the debate over whether television should see its audience as 'citizens' as well as 'consumers' would take on a new dimension as the 2003 Communications Act came into force and UK broadcasting shifted uncomfortably into the multi-channel, digital age.)

The newly invigorated BBC presented its evidence to the Pilkington Committee very carefully, but ITV assumed that its huge popular audiences would be evidence in themselves. The Committee was dissatisfied with the independent companies' performance and also with the ITA's unwillingness to curb them, and proposed that a strengthened ITA should itself take over broadcasting and commission programmes directly. The tone of the report fed the prejudices of those who thought the medium was vulgar and frivolous – a goggle box watched by square eyes (O'Sullivan 1991:159). Pilkington's view that 'triviality' is a natural vice of television and 'more dangerous to the soul than wickedness' (para 102) appealed to elite traditionalists as well as those who wanted a non-commercial grounding for creative and innovative programming (Milland 2004). But television magnates were outraged. Roy Thomson of Scottish Television called the report 'completely biased, socialistic and unrealistic', while Peter Cadbury of Westward threw a party at which he ritually burnt 'a giant effigy of the report and six authentic copies (at 18 shillings each)' (Black 1972:134). Not surprisingly, the Conservative government did not implement all the recommendations, but it did accept that the next television channel should be BBC2 rather than ITV2, and that the Authority should be strengthened and should keep a greater distance from the companies. The 1964 Television Act gave the ITA power to require that certain types of programme should be made, and also the power to interfere in news and current affairs to ensure 'balance and impartiality'. In the view of the author of a later report, Noel Annan, 'The Pilkington Report changed the face of ITV' by ushering in stricter controls over its 'moments of excess' (Barr 1986:219). As time went on, these 'moments of excess' turned out to involve not only television's so called 'natural vice', triviality, but also attempts to create tougher, more challenging journalism.

But Pilkington had set the tone. With the coming of BBC2 in 1964,

> complementary programming as practised by BBC1 and BBC2 now took priority over competition as a goal. For another decade it remained the general view that competition for audiences and revenue would lead to a lowering of standards and was to be avoided (Isaacs 1989:3).

The people's eyes and ears or 'an unmannerly way of sneaking a stare'?

> The main task of the serious journalist [is to be] 'the people's eyes and ears ... the instrument associating people's government with people's opinion (*Guardian* 28.1.85).

wrote the celebrated journalist James Cameron, who contributed regularly to *This Week* in the 1960s. His words expressed a sense of responsibility to the public which chimed with what many journalists on the series were now thinking. Bryan Magee who joined the series in 1960 wrote, 'it's a good idea to let the sentinel of the public eye play to [a] problem' while not forgetting the need to appeal to the broader audience. 'We said to ourselves that we were making *Guardian* content available to a *Mirror* readership ... and we were sort of successful in that. ... All television figures were huge in those days, but we were watched by about a third of the population' (*Guardian* 7.6.03). However, when Cyril Bennett and Peter Morley took over in 1961, critic Peter Black proclaimed that 'Pilkingtons' were now in charge (*Daily Mail* 24.6.61).

The tone had, in any case, begun to change. There were fewer items where scriptwriters added the sort of cinema newsreel commentary that traded off puns and flippant remarks; journalists were more likely to be responsible for a complete item, and attention was paid to developing more up-to-date styles of interviewing in tune with a sense of accountability – the 'people's eyes and ears' – as well as the demands of the medium. 'The method of interviewing has sharpened up,' Peter Hunt had written, 'we now attach far greater importance to the close-up than we did in the early days' (*Television Times* 9.8.57). By 1963, when Prime Minister Harold Macmillan appeared on *This Week*, critic Maurice Wiggin wrote, 'Peter Morley's cameras roved and probed, coming in closer than any *Panorama* lensman would dare. I suppose it's all right, though I can't pretend to like it: it seems an unmannerly way of sneaking a "stare" which you wouldn't dream of taking face to face' (*Sunday Times* 13.1.63).

This Week interviewed Prime Ministers and Leaders of the Opposition as well as innumerable cabinet ministers, business-men, leaders of local councils and others in positions of authority who were themselves learning to perform for the cameras. And Macmillan had stood the test. 'In a few minutes he ran through affability, nonchalance, gaiety, a touch or two of sardonic humour and a moment of emotional gravity when he spoke of the Great War and the grim Teesside years. If this was acting it was in the knighthood class' (*Sunday Times* 13.1.63).

But interviewing major politicians brought its own prob-lems, including that of abiding by the ITA's rigid requirements for balance, and providing the Authority with a head count of how many politicians from each party had been used in features programmes every month, 'to ensure that we weren't giving numerical advantage to, particularly, either of the two major parties!' (Courtney-Browne 1975:33).

Two reporters who joined *This Week* in 1960 became notable interviewers in totally different styles. Bryan Magee summed up his experience in a book on television interviewing. He laid out in meticulous detail the intellectual command of the subject matter and the extensive preparation needed by a competent political interviewer (a question is 'a sophisticated product embodying a dozen considerations of which the viewer is unaware'). He was clear that the interviewer's views must never intrude. 'The job rests on the denial of one's personality; not on the expression of one's feelings, thoughts, principles and beliefs, but on their concealment'. His own reporting covered the gamut of topics from homosexuality to the economy, and he outlined the quite differ-ent techniques needed for more personal stories (the interviewee should be able to 'reveal his secrets in emotional security. ... He is in my hands. I can almost feel the waves of reassurance going out from me' (Magee 1966:38, 62)). But it was Desmond Wilcox who perfected the ability to delve deep into the emotional lives of his subjects, persuading them to speak to the camera – and to millions of television viewers – about difficult and often taboo subjects they may have kept hidden from their closest friends.

Wilcox had been chosen from 30 candidates in response to a

newspaper advertisement. He soon developed his deeply influential televisual style – intense, emotional, frequently near the knuckle, dealing with challenging and shocking subjects – which regularly led to controversy. These early examples of the culture of confession eventually burst the boundaries of current affairs journalism and led him to launch the long-running series, *Man Alive* (BBC 1965–81), which dealt with 'human affairs not current affairs, emphasising feeling and emotion not fact and opinion'. It developed the pregnant pause and the key question 'how do you *feel* about this?' (BBC2 30.8.93). But he was not the first. Dan Farson had earlier left *This Week* to set up the equally personal *People In Trouble* (ITV 1958–60).

Established journalists on the series still included many who had made their names in the Second World War and its aftermath, and who had honed their craft in the tradition of written journalism, with a precise adjective, a felicitous choice of words and a judicious wit. Prime amongst these was James Cameron, who delivered 'the lengthiest, most coherent, most sane, most sonorous series of sermons that modern journalism affords' (*Guardian* 28.1.85). His Christmas item on that most tangible symbol of the Cold War, the Wall that divided East and West Berlin, conveyed the bleakness of that 'haunted and horrible frontier' (19.12.63).

Robert Kee had worked on the *Observer* and the *Sunday Times*, as well as *Picture Post*, which was considered to be 'a model for aspiring television journalists' (Lindley 2002:73). He had been an RAF bomber pilot and a prisoner of war in Germany, and had reported for *Panorama*. In 1961, together with other *Panorama* journalists, he had set up an independent production company, Television Reporters International (TRI). But the time of the small independents had not yet come. TRI collapsed, and in 1963 Kee joined *This Week*. Other regulars included Russell Spurr, who had been working for Canadian Broadcasting in Delhi, Kenneth Harris, Paul Johnson, who was editor of the *New Statesman*, and ITN's political reporter George Ffitch.

As stories grew more substantial, the role of the researcher, who prepared the ground for the director and the reporter, became more rigorous, and was clearly defined as a recognized grade. From 1961 some of Rediffusion's annual intake of university graduates were allocated to *This Week* as trainee researchers. They included David Frost, who proposed various satirical items starring himself. But the days when raising a laugh was a priority were over for *This Week*, and Frost began moonlighting at the BBC in pilots for *That Was The Week That Was* (1962–63) (Frost 1993:40–1). Its 30 minutes of songs, satire and political subversion were a different take on the week – which would set the tone of the decade just as much as the newly sober current affairs.

A university background was creating a sort of fraternity amongst the newer generation of post-war journalists and politicians. Bryan Magee had been at Oxford with Robin Day, Jeremy Thorpe, William Rees-Mogg and Michael Heseltine – all of whom began their careers as television journalists.

> If you had told me that Jeremy Thorpe would be leader of the Liberal Party in his 30s, that William Rees-Mogg would be editor of *The Times* in his 30s and Michael Heseltine would be in the cabinet, I would have said 'of course'. It sounds horrible but that's the way we thought and it had a bearing on the way we conducted ourselves

wrote Magee some 40 years later (*Guardian* 7.6.03). In 1966 he had described the advantage the 'young Oxbridge television reporter' had over the average Fleet Street hack – as he was accepted by those in authority as a social equal (Magee 1966:106). Magee was more aware of social privilege than most, as he was a shopkeeper's son, brought up in Hoxton – at the time a highly disreputable part of London. *His* status was hard won through application and education (Magee 2004).

One observer described the *This Week* reporting team in the following terms, 'the gently reflective Magee, the ascetic Paul Johnson, the earnest, worried Desmond Wilcox and the bluff big hitter Kenneth Harris'. They were, he wrote, a match for *Panorama* and concluded, 'Gentlemen, you may now wear full colours' (*Daily Mail* 18.5.62). The university sports metaphor and the address of 'Gentlemen' are a clear give away. What was in one sense a broadening of scope – in intellect, energy, depth of reporting and professionalism – could also be described as a form of narrowing, excluding less professional attitudes, less educated backgrounds and, remarkably, women.

The role of researcher could be seen as a supportive one, and at least seven women researchers were recruited in the early 1960s. None of them became reporters or directors on the series. But when *This Week* advertised in 1961 'to strengthen its team of reporters/interviewers' it invited both men and women 'who know something about everything and everything about something' to apply (6.6.61). There were 500 responses, and 'This Week chose little Miss Judith Jackson, aged 25, not a journalist but an actress doing walk-on parts at the Old Vic. She's pretty and at her interview, so I hear, she handled a testing ordeal well' (Derby Evening Telegraph 6.6.61). Reg Courtney-Browne commented that it was 'something of an experiment in having a young lady reporter on the programme' and noted that she did not stay long (1975:23). (In fact Judith Jackson had a long career as a respected journalist.) Several women who had earlier contributed, such as Elaine Grand, Jeanne Le Chard and Sheila Gregg (who returned for a brief period in 1965), were hardly visible. (Director Jeanne Le Chard told me that her voice was taken off an item about the Race Relations Board (1.11.66) and replaced with that of a man.) The gesture towards femininity, which had come with Caryl Doncaster's evocation of 'glamour' in the early days of the series, no longer seemed appropriate. The generation of powerful women – such as Grace Wyndham Goldie – who owed their promotion to the absence of men during the Second World War, was now moving on, and the new generation were only in the early stages of a struggle for equality on their own terms.

Throughout the 1960s and into the 1970s there were very few women reporters or directors, and these were only briefly employed or were freelancers directing one-off programmes.

Life on *This Week*

The series continued to use a multi-item format, but, as well as studio interviews and plenty of pundits and men in suits, the longer filmed reports dominated. Six minutes had been considered a major slot in the early editions, but by 1960 items were down to two or three per edition, which meant that each one got around 12 minutes. Following pressure from Peter Morley and Cyril Bennett the commercial break in the middle was also removed. Advertisements which had alternated quite happily with the quick-fire items of the 1950s were now less in tune with the surrounding subject matter. In January 1962 the series finally settled into the Thursday slot it was to occupy until the end of its run.

The first two editions under the new regime of Morley and Bennett marked a watershed – two single-topic, multi-faceted programmes underpinned by economics, one on Iran and its links to British oil interests (23.6.61), the other on the crisis in Fleet Street (30.6.61). The edition on Iran included a discussion with Iranian students by Judith Jackson and an interview with the Shah by Jeremy Thorpe. Back in the studio Thorpe then interviewed Harold Macmillan. The edition on Fleet Street was triggered by the shrinking number of national newspapers. Judith Jackson and Desmond Wilcox reported on a printers' strike, speaking to strikers and their leader, Emily Garvey; in the studio Brian Connell interviewed Roy Thomson, who owned the *Scotsman* newspaper as well as Scottish Television, and there was a debate with the editors of the *Express* and *Daily Mirror*. Commenting on Morley and Bennett's approach, Maurice Wiggin later praised the 'technique of getting a quote in the living voice from people directly concerned in the news' which 'helped to give it great impact and immediacy' (*Sunday Times* 18.8.63). Morley had decided from the start that he would himself direct the live studio items each week. It would 'give me a chance to set a coherent style for the "on air" look of the programme'. At the same time 'This was my way of giving my adrenalin a weekly outing' (Morley 2005:98–9).

When Cyril Bennett and Peter Morley took over, a single edition of *This Week* cost only £1,500. The *Sunday Times* suggested that perhaps it should spend a bit more when 'a scrambled report from Belgrade … could not be heard' (3.9.61). And the pressure to produce items at speed continued. *This Week* was on the sixth floor of Television House, but facilities for sound transfer and dubbing – which gave priority to *This Week* – were on the eighth, and transmission was from the first floor, so there was a considerable amount of jumping into lifts and running up and down stairs with heavy cans of 35mm film (film editor Robin Marriott to PH).

World in Action

This Week continued to measure itself against *Panorama* (Morley (2005) describes how both series had a spy in the other camp), but in 1963 it gained a sharp new rival from Manchester. Granada's current affairs magazine *Searchlight* (1958–61) had been described as 'television's hardest hitting programme about social wrongs' (Black 1972:164). It was now succeeded by *World in Action* (1963–99). Under its dynamic editor, Tim Hewat, the new programme was even more punchy and assertive. Hewat had a profound disrespect for self-important journalists, and plunged in with an anonymous commentary representing the series, rather than named reporters. 'The first edition, about nuclear striking power, was too jazzed up, too brash and brassy in its presentation, for my austere taste', wrote Maurice Wiggin,

> This is only perhaps, another way of telling the Granada adventurers that they have succeeded in doing just what they set out to do. Doubtless there is a place in factual television for the stark, tough 'tabloid' technique, which is obviously what they are aiming at (*Sunday Times* 13.1.63).

Leslie Woodhead, who worked on *World in Action* in every capacity from researcher to series Editor, described the style developed by Hewat as 'hit you in the eye, tell them something in the first 12 seconds, then tell them it again and probably tell them a third time'. His visual sense was literal. 'People would say if the word "pigeon holed" came up, you would first see a pigeon then a hole' (talk 2004). *World in Action* could not be called trivial or frivolous, but it was to ruffle the feathers of the ITA and the establishment (Goddard et al 2001).

'Despite its pervading solemnity and occupational portentousness, [*Panorama*] keeps going with dogged stamina, jogging steadily down the middle of the road, glancing fearfully to left and right but generally managing to project a likeable sort of home-brewed, pragmatic reasonableness,' wrote Maurice Wiggin, and pointed out that the two ITV companies were now competing to rival the BBC not with more entertainment and distraction, but in styles of journalism.

> Granada would very much like to be the company producing *This Week*. ... They fancy their chance of putting *Panorama* in the shade. But Peter Morley has improved *This Week* so much that A-R are certainly not likely to give up now, after trying so long and so [hard] (*Sunday Times* 13.1.63).

From 1963, because of changing personnel at the top, A-R became plain Rediffusion.

The stain of a corpse

In 1963 the Cold War was at its most dangerous following the 1962 Cuban missile crisis; there were race riots in Alabama and, on

Friday 22 November, the West was shaken by the assassination of US President John Fitzgerald Kennedy. That evening Peter Morley and Cyril Bennett were due to be presented with an award for the best factual series by the Guild of Television Producers and Directors. Together with most of the senior personnel from ITV and the BBC, they were at the Dorchester Hotel when the news came over the ticker-tape machines. The ITV network, taken completely by surprise, showed no commercials for 90 minutes and held the 'interlude' cards, punctuated by news flashes. Working at high speed, the *This Week* team mounted a tribute after the late-night news.

The funeral was broadcast live by Telstar, and Anthony Burgess wrote in the *Listener*, 'we have seen everything now; that impartial eye has looked on murder; from now on there will always be the stain of a corpse on the living-room hearthrug' (*Independent* 18.11.2003).

In Britain, 1963 saw the scandal that rocked the political scene and fascinated the media, bringing the new hedonism of the 1960s together with a fascination with the lives of the upper classes, the covert world of espionage and the chill of the Cold War. War Minister John Profumo was revealed to have been part of a circle of call girls and upper-class libertines which also included an attaché at the Soviet embassy. Both of them had been having an affair with 'good-time girl' Christine Keeler. The fact that she was young, fashionable and highly photogenic gave an added flavour to reporting which took a salacious delight in this smashing of 1950s pruderies.

This Week made several programmes on the Profumo scandal. On 6 June, using the now well-established technique of approaching a topic from several different perspectives, reporters provided items which considered the history of the case, an explanation of the laws of libel and the political implications. The climax was a scoop interview with Keeler's friend Stephen Ward, in which Desmond Wilcox faced him with the accusation that he had been Keeler's pimp. The allegation was put with great tact by smoothy Wilcox, and Ward emphatically denied it. The interview was recorded in the afternoon at Television House, and the problem faced by the two researchers, Brian West and Jeremy Taylor, was how to keep Ward clear of the pursuing Fleet Street journalists between the recording time of 4pm and transmission at 9.15. Taylor gave the following account,

> The press had let down the tyres of the hired car which had brought him from his Mews to Television House, but Brian took him into the next door building, over the fire escape and out through the side entrance into Aldwych where I was waiting in a taxi. ... We went to the nearest tube station. Then a quick trip round the Circle Line and out at Notting Hill to a chauffeur-driven hired car which took Brian, Stephen Ward and I away to a quiet Buckinghamshire hotel known to Desmond. ... It was an uneasy meal; he wanted to see himself on telly. There was no television so they had to go into 'the servants quarters'. ... He simply said what a jolly good interview it was and could he take the car back to his home (Courtney-Browne 1975:28).

Within days Ward was on trial for living on immoral earnings, and four weeks later was dead from an overdose. The interview made the headlines and was described by the *TV Times* as 'a fitting retirement compliment to Bennett and Morley' who were coming to the end of their producership (6.8.63). They left the series after less than two years and the commentators sang their praises for 'raising the prestige of independent television in the field of current affairs'. They 'leave *This Week* at the highest point of its renown. Their enterprise has made it a feature not to be missed' (*Sunday Times* 18.8.63).

Bennett and Morley had only planned to stay for six months. After a year they became restless, but John McMillan wanted them to find a suitable successor before leaving. It took another year before they recruited Jeremy Isaacs, fresh from working with Tim Hewat at Granada. He was a dynamic and committed programme maker who was to build *This Week* into a substantial series and whose continued support – not only as Producer from August 1963 to October 1965, but also as Controller of Features (1968–74) and then Director of Programmes (1974–78) at Thames Television – was central to its reputation. He 'inspired a loyalty amongst programme makers who had worked for him unequalled, in my experience, by any other television executive in Britain,' wrote independent producer Michael Darlow (2004:213).

In 1963 Cyril Bennett became Head of Features at Rediffusion, taking over from David Hennessey, and Peter Morley went back to his illustrious career making special documentaries.

Jeremy Isaacs and the television medium

'We aimed to exploit the medium to its fullest potential, even if in a limited, mundane, half hour of television journalism,' Jeremy

Isaacs told Vicki Wegg-Prosser. (The following quotations are from that 1990 interview.)

When Isaacs took over, *This Week* gained its first Producer whose experience was solely in television. He was emphatic that the nature of current affairs should arise from the medium itself, and, in contrast to the excitement about 'liveness' which had characterized the 1950s, by the mid-1960s the cutting-edge programmes were the ones that got out of the studio and were made on film. Documentary formats were leading the trend, and the sort of studio reconstructions that Caryl Doncaster had cut her teeth on were definitely out of fashion. The look and feel of television was changing as the sense that the studio was a familiar base which links 'us' television people to 'you' the audience at home, gave way to a much more direct opening of a 'window on the world'. Isaacs described the studio as 'cold, unfeeling and alienating', and added, 'I had an absolute belief in the effectiveness of film to communicate life as it was lived, and that determined the choice of subject matter and the techniques.' Film could get out and about and would show rather than tell. It could reveal how people really lived and focus on the *effects* of political decisions rather than the decisions themselves. It could mount a 'crusade on behalf of the underdog'. This meant that programme makers needed 'a fusion of film-making skills and journalistic flair'. Journalists, who were still largely trained in the print medium, needed to become visually literate and aim for a marriage of image and sound.

Under the influence of experienced documentary makers like Peter Morley, current affairs was already developing a visual style and grammar of its own, clearly different from the brief reports that characterized the news, but also different from the studied aesthetic of the documentary tradition. *This Week* was led by the news agenda, but the developing use of film and of the single-item programme was bringing the genre much closer to the documentary mode. The distinction between current affairs and documentary has been one of those difficult fault lines that would be repeatedly negotiated over the years.

Those in authority versus 'our' concerns

'The *political* concerns those in authority, the *social* deals with "our" concerns,' writes media historian Paddy Scannell (1979).

At the BBC in the 1950s a clear distinction had developed between the Talks Department, which produced current affairs and political programming, and the Documentary Department, which looked at social topics and was explicitly 'not political' (Bell 1986). The institutional division helped to consolidate the cultural forms, but that sort of split could never be absolute. Paul Rotha, BBC Television's first Head of Documentary, described the 'story documentary' and 'documentary journalism' as 'two ends of the spectrum', and current affairs programming in the 1960s owed much to the pioneering work of documentary producers like Norman Swallow and Denis Mitchell, who developed a style that relied on location filming and social observation (Corner 1991:42). Swallow had declared that his series *Special Enquiry* (1952–59) was 'never political' – he called it 'actuality documentary'. Although it was presented by a reporter, Robert Reid, he acted as an 'ordinary person' searching for information rather than an expert commentator. The *Radio Times* called it 'an experiment in television reporting' (Bell 1986:161). (Although the Documentary Department tried to keep itself separate from the more political Talks, eventually it was absorbed into it – which was one reason why Caryl Doncaster moved to Associated-Rediffusion and started *This Week*.)

The distinction between current affairs and documentary has largely hinged on *styles* of journalism, contrasting the ability of documentary to allow the images to carry the meaning against the desire of current affairs to use the journalist's words to explore and explain. Despite some notable exceptions, the typical current affairs programme remains structured around the flow of the reporter's voice, punctuated in tone and texture by the voices of interviewees, witnesses and experts.

But at the beginning of the 1960s, a revolutionary new television journalism was pioneered in the USA, triumphantly announced as an 'alternative to reporter-led journalism ... a new form of truth' (BBC2 12.3.94). Robert Drew, a picture editor at *Life* magazine, had been asked to produce material for a cable television channel. Inspired by the work of photo-journalists, he recruited a group of collaborators who combined film-making skills with technical expertise. The cameras and sound equipment currently in use were too cumbersome for the flexibility they were after, so the team sought out lightweight 16mm cameras and zoom lenses that could probe into the very centre of an action. They also

evolved techniques for recording synchronous sound while on
the move, which meant that for the first time participants could be
overheard in conversation with each other, rather than being *interviewed* as they spoke formally to the camera. For Drew and his
colleagues, interviews were anathema. Commentaries, also, were
unnecessary. Rather than being led by a voice whose authority
was at best dubious, camera and recorder should act as the eyes
and ears of the viewers. The audience should feel as if they were
present at the scene; then they could make their own judgements
about what they were observing. In other words, Drew argued,
the traditional journalist was redundant. What was needed were
'film-makers' – alert observers, wielding a camera and a sound
recorder, able to report on an event because they were *there*, in
the middle of it. (At the time of writing, Robert Drew, Richard
Leacock, Albert Maysles and others of the original group still
vocally advocate this position at international festivals, in television programmes and at any other available outlet.)

Forty years on, an audience accustomed to undercover footage, webcasts, 24-hour video surveillance, miniaturized cameras
attached to birds, and news crews reporting live from the battle
lines, may not recognize the impact of these innovations. But
in 1960, when Drew Associates made *Primary*, which followed
Hubert Humphrey and John F. Kennedy as they fought for the
Democratic presidential nomination – eavesdropping on their
private phone calls, listening in as they whispered to their aides,
spying on their moments of relaxation and long waking nights,
close behind Kennedy as he walked through the outstretched
arms of the crowd – the effect was electrifying. In the heat of
the moment, careful framing and aesthetic images were simply
not appropriate. Instead the camera swooped and zoomed as it
probed in on the action.

In the UK many young directors and camera people pressed
for the introduction of the new techniques. At *World in Action*
Richard Leacock was invited to give talks and workshops, and
Jeremy Isaacs moved to *This Week* just as Rediffusion was beginning to replace its cumbersome 35mm equipment. But there was
strong resistance from technicians and laboratories. Isaacs says
it was extremely difficult to get some people to change their attitudes. This is hardly surprising, as such radical changes meant
more pressure and a much faster turn-around for everyone in a
long and complex chain, from filming through processing and

editing right up to transmission (Winston 1995:1). Many in the
technical grades were anxious to protect their status, which
depended on a specialized knowledge of equipment and a carefully honed ability to produce high-quality images and sound.
Traditionalists regretted the lower resolution of 16mm and the
loss of technical quality, as well as objecting to more casual filming techniques associated with balancing the camera on the
shoulder instead of keeping it steady on a tripod. Any erosion
of the distinction between technician and journalist was also
suspect. The deep divisions between the different activities in
the team were institutionalized in the employment structures of
the time and enforced by the ACTT, the technicians' union. But
Peter Morley had already introduced 16mm filming (although at
first the rushes had to be blown up to 35mm for the editing and
other processes), and as the 1960s progressed, hand-held cameras
became the norm for programmes that set out to get closer to the
lives of ordinary people and, in Isaacs's words, focus on the social
effects of politics, rather than the pontificating of politicians and
those in authority.

The move away from the studio also meant that the traditional
presenter was no longer seen as the audience's helpful friend,
but as someone who simply got in the way. 'What do *you* think?'
– Michael Ingrams's question from that very first programme,
accompanied by a direct gaze at the audience – no longer needed
to be posed in quite such direct terms. And as for *This Week*'s
established linkman, Brian Connell, the general impression was
that he spent too much time telling the audience what *he* thought.
The use of a studio anchor did not suit the more direct journalism
that Jeremy Isaacs wanted, and the situation was exacerbated by
the fact that he and Connell simply did not get on. It was a clash
of egos, and one of Isaacs's first actions was to get rid of Brian
Connell.

The 'irritating filter'

Brian Connell had been recruited for his gravitas and substantial
presence and as *This Week*'s answer to Richard Dimbleby. He was
dedicated to journalism: 'if you bring me in, I'll pull anything not
journalistic,' he had said (to VWP). Over the three years during
which he presented *This Week* he became more than a front man
and was actively involved in every edition, writing his own links,

conducting major interviews, reporting on important events and generally inflecting the series according to his views.

He had an urbane self-confidence. 'Brian Connell used to stroll across from Television House to the Waldorf and partake of half a dozen oysters. What style! What glamour!', wrote David Frost, at the time a junior researcher (Frost 1993:41). He was a committed royalist who reputedly kept a signed photograph of Prince Philip by his bed and was increasingly out of step with the rest of the team. Critic Philip Purser pointed out that being a right-wing royalist (and also an ex-naval man, no doubt) appealed to 'Capt T.M. Brownrigg CBE DSO Ret'd, who runs A-R' (13.10.63). But it was at odds with the group of radical journalists who were now working on the series – and particularly the new Producer, Jeremy Isaacs. Connell judged the team to be far more left-wing than it actually was. 'This was the period when the Trots joined the media,' he claimed, but added 'I had been in naval intelligence, and was not conned by the Trots.' He praised Peter Morley for being 'dedicated and gifted and not at all political', but judged that Cyril Bennett's views 'were very far to the left of the Labour Party'. It was hardly surprising that he found the weekly Friday morning meetings to be a disaster 'because of acrimony' and that he was usually in a minority of one. He was critical of the programme's choice of stories. 'This Week's items were not balanced, they were too anti-government.' 'Too many misery and ruin stories ... amounted to being subversive.' He felt that the management – David Hennessy, John McMillan and Captain Brownrigg – 'all thought the programmes were just displaying freedom of expression. I was fed up and glad to get out' (to VWP).

Relations with Jeremy Isaacs were strained from the first. Connell complained: 'I was asked to cut down or cut out my summings-up and I refused to do this – they were unscripted.' But the final break came with a programme on birth control, specifically the contraceptive pill (3.10.63). (The pill had been introduced in 1961 – the original trials were with married women, and only with the permission of their husbands.) Connell's catholic sensibilities were shaken and he wound up the programme by saying that he knew at least one mother of 14 who was happy with the Church's teachings. This was very badly received. Brian Connell resigned and Isaacs ensured that the resignation was accepted. Reg Courtney-Browne described the parting as 'not cordial'. Playwright Dennis Potter, never one to mince his words, wrote in the *Daily Herald* of the 'Missing link with no regrets. ... The programme did without any bland voice of introduction or even a concluding bromide. ... There was no irritating filter, Brian Connell had gone, the best thing to happen to the programme. ... Brian Connell was as boring as Richard Dimbleby' (18.10.63).

Morality and personal identity

The birth control item had included interviews by Desmond Wilcox with catholic women from Liverpool. One had eight children in poor health, and another had 14, one of them mentally handicapped. At a birth-control clinic a catholic mother agrees that she has broken her faith; a doctor says that the 'rhythm method' cannot work because of drunken husbands on Saturday nights, and Wilcox talks to Father O'Leary, who declares that 'contraception is against the natural law of God. Marriage is a sacred holy estate' (3.10.63).

The rigid moral attitudes of Britain in the immediate postwar period were under challenge from many sides. Bryan Magee had written of the 1962 Obscene Publications Act: 'Where there is public disgust it is a good idea to let the sentinel of the public eye play to the problem' (Magee 1966), and it would not be long before the clear Labour majority brought by Harold Wilson's 1966 election victory would enable even greater liberalization of the laws that dealt with sexuality and private life – including measures on homosexuality, divorce and abortion – as well as more public issues such as race relations, women's rights and poverty.

In 1965 Wilcox faced possibly the most contentious of these subjects – abortion (4.2.65). At the time it was all but illegal, and the context for the programme was the increasingly vocal campaign for women's right to control their bodies which culminated in the Abortion Act of 1967. (The Act was passed after 16 hours of debate 'and the longest continuous sitting for 16 years' (*The Times* 14.7.67).) Prior to the Act women of all backgrounds regularly used illegal 'back street' abortionists. As in the birth-control programme, practices which were absolutely common but whose existence was scarcely whispered, were openly discussed on the television screen. Director Stephen Peet described (to VWP) how the all-male team was shocked by the social and medical horrors revealed. There was the lack of aftercare, the dirty nursing home and the excruciating pain from a botched abortion, as well as terrified doctors who simply turned their clients on to the street following the illegal procedure.

The film vividly demonstrated the inconsistencies of the current law by intercutting the accounts of a south London mother of ten with a sick husband and an income of £13 per week, and a Chelsea housewife with two children, who felt it would be inconvenient to have another. (Stephen Peet called it *World in Action* style – a tribute to the Granada series' punchy approach.) The south London mother was recommended by her doctor, saw many specialists, but was ultimately refused. 'They said it was against the law.' The Chelsea wife contacted the Harley Street gynaecologist whom 'everyone goes to. He's the best and most expensive.' She saw two psychiatrists. 'You have to cry and they write it down.' The south London woman told Wilcox, 'I was in a terrible state. … I got some pills but they weren't any good. … If I had had £20 I could have had it done, but I didn't have the money.' 'Would you have had a back-street abortion?' 'Yes'.

The challenge was to reveal on peak-time popular television the existence of social practices which were a familiar part of women's lives, but which were both illegal and considered by many to be morally reprehensible. The programme faced the challenge head on, not with reasoned argument but with the unvarnished narratives of the women involved. Some were prepared to speak directly to camera, others were filmed from behind, with the camera resting on Wilcox's earnest, listening expression. When *This Week* returned to this theme ten years later, it was no longer considered acceptable for a man to question women on such a topic, but it would take protracted negotiations between producers, the company and the ACTT to ensure that the 1975 programme was made by an all-women team.

Race was an equally potent domestic issue, and it too could hinge on questions of sexuality. Desmond Wilcox wanted to end his programme 'The Negro Next Door' (19.8.65) with a challenge to the audience: 'would you let *your* daughter marry a negro?' The ending was not used, but the programme in which black and white neighbours were interviewed about each other, and then brought together in an awkward but revealing climax, was an early example of what is now described as 'reality television'. In the words of the great documentarist Jean Rouch, who arguably invented the genre, it was not so much 'life as it is lived, but life as it is provoked'. The dialogue speaks for itself. The following week an edition on Jamaica (26.8.65) showed the shanty towns of the really poor, the mundane violence of Jamaican life and the queue of those waiting to emigrate – girls in white dresses, boys in suits. It asks, what awaits them in Britain?

The race issue remained an on-going concern of the series, drawing out problems concerning housing, employment and voting. Nineteen-sixty-six saw an edition on the newly established Race Relations Board (1.11.66); Robert Kee fronted a programme on Sparkbrook, Birmingham, which concluded that the problem was poor housing, not colour (23.2.67); and in the run-up to the 1964 election, Desmond Wilcox looked at 'Coloured Voting' (24.9.64). A review by Martin Harrison in the *Sunday Times* criticized *Panorama*'s failure in this area: '*This Week* tackled the racial issue safely enough. Why could one channel handle it and not the other?' (27.9.64).

Jeremy Isaacs was encouraging the team to widen the coverage of social issues to questions of personal identity, and thought that the editions on homosexuality broke new ground. As with the women who had had abortions, in 'Homosexuals' (22.10.64) the identities of the interviewees had to be concealed. 'It seemed wrong then that anyone should be unable to make public so overwhelmingly important a truth about the self, or even to acknowledge that it was a truth,' he wrote (Isaacs 1989:133). This broadening agenda was not seen as a rejection of the political but an extension of it. The sort of topic that centred on social issues, and especially personal experience, which Norman Swallow had argued should be rigorously separated from political debate, was presented as casting a new light on the nature of the political itself.

Window on the world

Meanwhile, the British Empire was giving its last gasps as the African colonies gained their independence one by one – all too often leaving a trail of violence, such as the bloody war between Nigeria and Biafra, reported by John Edwards in a *This Week* special (29.7.68). In 1961 apartheid South Africa left the Commonwealth and in 1964 Nelson Mandela was sentenced to life imprisonment. The following year, Ian Smith of Rhodesia resisted democratization, declared unilateral independence (UDI) and his country slowly collapsed into civil war. News reports from America's escalating war in Vietnam were received with increasing horror; in the Middle East the simmering conflict between Israel and its neighbours spilled over into the 1967 Six-Day War, and Mao Tse Tung's China declared a 'cultural revolution'.

For *This Week* the actor Peter Finch spoke Nelson Mandela's inspirational speech to the court in a Christmas Eve item made with Amnesty International (24.12.64); Lewis Rudd and Godfrey Hodgson travelled to China posing as tourists (26.1.67); James Cameron made three programmes on Latin America; and there was extensive coverage of Rhodesia and Vietnam. ('The thing that most made me want to work on *This Week* when I was at BBC,' said David Elstein who joined the series in 1968, 'was a Robert Kee report from Rhodesia during UDI; it was absolutely crackling with atmosphere and significance and I thought, wow, this is the real McCoy (to PH).) By 1965 Monica Furlong could write in the *Daily Mail*, 'It has been a long haul, but *This Week* has steadily overtaken *Panorama* in the last year in the qualities of interest, courage and sheer common sense' (12.3.65).

Tenth anniversary

Jeremy Isaacs left to go to *Panorama* in 1965, which he also tried to turn into a single-subject programme 'but did not quite make it stick' (Isaacs 1989:4). He had created an atmosphere described as 'high-powered and stimulating, but much more controlled' than previously (Sheila Gregg to VWP). He himself says that he was keen to inspire order in the team, and that the management at Rediffusion had given him a great deal of freedom. Although his period as Producer of *This Week* had been relatively short, he remained a formative influence on the series and on many aspects of British television. Following his departure there was an unsettling period with four different Producers in quick succession, including the future Director General of the BBC, Alasdair Milne.

Nineteen-sixty-six was to be the year of swinging London, and in January *This Week* reached its tenth anniversary. The series had settled into the format it was to keep – with variations of stress and emphasis – over the next 26 years. Serious without being solemn, it was made up of single-item editions fronted by a team of known and trusted journalists, which interleaved filmed reports with studio discussions, and interviewed individuals from all walks of life as well as those in authority. It moved with ease in the back-street slum and in the highest reaches of power. As Peter Williams put it, 'We are privileged. We can go to those at the top and ask them what they are doing' (to PH). The privilege included the unquestioned right to move around the globe, to bring back that report and to provide the eyes through which the rest of us will see the world. John Edwards, who joined the series from ITN in 1967, remembered a 'freshness, excitement and surprise, seeing, for example, Africa for the first time' (*35 Years on the Front Line* 29.1.91). 'The world was a virgin and we had our way with her', was the rather less circumspect comment of Trevor Philpott of *Tonight* (Lindley 2002:77).

Together with the other current affairs programmes, *This Week* had created a relaxed, masculine, educated, urbane and compassionate view of the world. At the same time it was the sort of confident approach that can lead to deep exasperation from the uneducated, non-male, non-white deservers of compassion – whose cries for pluralism were just beginning to be heard and were occasionally surfacing in the series. They would bring unexpected changes by the end of the 1970s.

The series concluded its anniversary year with a Christmas programme that was rather different from previous Christmases. Fronted by a new reporter, Peter Williams, 'We Wish You a Merry Christmas' contrasted the Christmas of a rich family – extrovert publisher Robert Maxwell no less – and that of a poor one. Maxwell's party is filmed from high in the gallery of his substantial mansion. There are glamorous guests and lovely food, with Maxwell at the head of the table. Meanwhile the Frazer family in Paddington are coping with a sick father and a mother who cares for six children in a single room. She says it will be like any other day. Peter Williams had been anxious to make a programme about happiness for Christmas and pointed out that both rich and poor find happiness with their children (23.12.66).

The margins of television genres are never secure. In 1966 *This Week* spawned a second weekly programme which covered some of the subject matter which had been regular fare in the 1950s. Broadcast late on Mondays it was devoted to the arts, national and international. Robert Kee, Bryan Magee and Sheila Gregg interviewed personalities including the actor Laurence Olivier, the publisher Victor Gollancz and the conductor Malcolm

Sargent. Indeed from September 1966 there were no less than three weekly editions for the team to produce, since *This Week* itself went twice weekly. The experiment meant a great deal of rush and some scrappy items. The second programme was abandoned when Phillip Whitehead took over as Producer.

Jeremy Isaacs returned in 1967, not long before Rediffusion was replaced by Thames Television. He had not been happy at the BBC, and Cyril Bennett, now Director of Programmes, brought him back as Controller of Features. Isaacs invited Phillip Whitehead, who had worked with him on *Panorama*, to take over *This Week*. Whitehead had resigned from the BBC in sympathy with Isaacs, who, in his view, had been 'forced out' (to VWP). He was only 28 at the time, a dynamic young man with political ambitions – in 1970 he would become Labour MP for Derby. With characteristic energy he was married on 1 April and started work at *This Week* on the 2nd. It was a tumultuous time in which to take over a current affairs series and Whitehead relished the challenge. ('Phillip seems to act on the principle that there are at least two of him, and they can expend the energy of two people and be in two places at once,' wrote historian Bruce Cumings, who worked with him in 1988 (Cumings 1992:181).)

Nineteen-sixty-seven saw some remarkable programmes, amongst them a glimpse of lingering colonial attitudes at a time of declining British power. 'Aden: The Last Post' (7.8.67) was a depiction – which with hindsight seems rather indulgent – of the defiant Scottish regiment who imposed tough military control in the dying days of the Arab colony. 'For a brief moment of history Colonel Mitchell is lord of all he sees,' reported Llew Gardner over a landscape of romantic military mythology. The arrogant 'Mad Mitch' led his Highlanders, bagpipes swirling, down the dusty streets of the Crater district. He had become a media hero, set on avenging the deaths of ten ambushed British soldiers by dominating the area. 'The plan is to kill terrorists,' he declares in his classic military accent. 'Luckily we're allowed to do that.' There was no exploration of the views of the colonized. Four months later, after 128 years, the British withdrew and Aden became South Yemen.

An unpopular programme at a popular time?

By the mid-1960s 'commitment' and 'seriousness' in the Pilkington mode had won out over the aim to maximize audiences, a situation which suited both regulators and programme makers. The commercial owners of the companies had not abandoned their aim of maximizing profits, but were very satisfied with their monopoly over advertising. It was a secure settlement which gave confidence to those who wanted to develop social and informational programming. They could also point to considerable overseas sales.

Current affairs was now well established as a genre, with sophisticated formats for enlarging on the news agenda. But Independent Television News was also pressing to move beyond its brief bulletins. Despite the companies' reluctance, the ITA agreed, and in July 1967 ITN launched *News at Ten* as a substantial half-hour on the network, with the opportunity to explore topics at greater depth. The Authority was concerned that in response to this new prominence of informational material the companies might shuffle their factual series out of peak time, so it ruled that certain types of programme, which it considered to be essential for a balanced evening of television, were to be 'mandated'. This meant that they were given fixed slots and the time was laid down when they would be transmitted throughout the network. Mandated programmes included *This Week*, which was to be broadcast at 8.30 or 9pm on Thursdays, and *World in Action*, in mid-evening on Mondays (Sendall 1983:232–3). The move effectively underpinned the two series, protecting them against the more commercial impulses of their producing companies. John Freeman of LWT would later refer grumpily to putting on an 'unpopular' programme at a 'popular' time (Potter 1989:106). Although *This Week* had received a great deal of support from the Rediffusion management, the measure gave it even greater security. (The fact that 'Rediffusion backed its current affairs men with a fierce resentment of the Authority's right to interfere' (Black 1972:166) is not entirely surprising, as the Authority also represented restraint on commercial activities.) However, the new arrangement was a recognition that the genre had a significance for British society as a whole and should not be subject only to the economic judgements of its producing companies. Its duty to be 'the sentinel of the public eye' was recognized and protected.

The bitter conflicts between the Authority and *This Week* that developed during the 1970s should be seen against this background of protection as a 'mandated' programme in a mid-evening slot. Regulation enabled the genre to flourish, but, as the 1970s developed, the regulator became increasingly nervous of the degree of freedom demanded by independently minded journalists.

3 INTO THE 'GOLDEN AGE'?

Thames Television: the forced marriage

Many who worked on *This Week* remember the decade between 1968 and 1978 as its golden age. But it began in a state of confusion with the demise of Rediffusion as an independent company. In 1967 the Independent Television Authority had undertaken its first review of commercial television since its launch 12 years previously and it made the shock decision not to renew Rediffusion's licence to broadcast. 'It is hard to exaggerate the trauma of that moment,' wrote critic Peter Fiddick (1984:10).

At the time, Rediffusion was the largest and most profitable of the network companies and was widely viewed as the strongest, but the ITA's reshuffle paid little attention to strength and viability. The Authority forced Rediffusion to merge with ABC Television to form a new company which would broadcast to the London region on weekdays. Thames Television, with its evocative logo of the London skyline – St Paul's, Tower Bridge, the Houses of Parliament – rising up out of the river, was born of that forced marriage. The move shocked many commentators, but the Authority had aimed to put content and public service values above commercial considerations. It criticized Rediffusion because it had stuck with quiz shows and give-aways – *Double Your Money, Take Your Pick* – at a time when others were paying more attention to Pilkington's strictures. There was no programme maker on the company's board, and its general stance was that 'a public service should aim to give the majority of the public what the majority wants to see, and at the best time available' (Black 1972:194). The situation had been exacerbated by a conflict of personality between ITA chair Lord Hill (nominee of Labour PM Harold Wilson) and Sir John Spencer Wills, chair of Rediffusion, who was open about his purely business aims. Hill thought that Spencer Wills had behaved arrogantly, and the company lost its licence to broadcast (Sendall 1983:342–7). Peter Black argued that Rediffusion had a poorer public image than its record deserved and pointed out that as well as bailing out Granada in the difficult first months – and arguably saving the whole structure from bankruptcy – it had also been the first company to introduce a 'marvellous schools service' (1972:194, 200). The ITA's drastic reorganization shook up the whole structure, including dividing the North region into West and East (Granada and Yorkshire TV) and increasing the number of network companies to five.

From the beginning of ITV, regulation with non-commercial priorities and public service goals had moderated the view of television as a business, subject only to market principles. In 1967 the ITA saw themselves as protecting this remit, but the debate was by no means settled, and some very different decisions were to be made in future Broadcasting Acts.

Within the awkward alliance which made up Thames Television there was general dissatisfaction and a great deal of in-fighting between the two companies. Rediffusion's Director of Programmes, Cyril Bennett, had already left; he had become part of the successful London Weekend Television (LWT) franchise application. ABC gained overall control of the new company and Conservative MP Selwyn Lloyd, one of the foremost advocates of a market-based system, triumphed 'Labour's got Granada, we've got the rest' (Black 1972).

Phillip Whitehead had only been in place for a few weeks when the shock decision was announced. Together with the loss of Cyril Bennett it was a major blow to morale. The team was shattered, expecting the worst. But the turmoil of the transitional period died down remarkably quickly. The new managing director, Howard Thomas, had a long track record in broadcasting and had been running ABC since its launch. He was, in Whitehead's view, a 'very decent and modest man' who was able to play to the strengths of the two companies – ABC's drama and Rediffusion's current affairs. Thames was able to attract people with established records in all genres and 'started making fine programmes instantly' (Fiddick 1984:10). *This Week* continued with Phillip Whitehead as producer, firmly backed by the new Director of Programmes, Brian Tesler and by Jeremy Isaacs, who remained in place as Head of Features.

In early 1971 there was a change in the levy arrangements, which meant that the ITV companies were taxed on profits rather than advertising revenue, so it was now in their interest to plough more money into their programmes. 'The message was, push the boat out,' said Jeremy Isaacs. He instantly proposed his monumental 26-part *The World at War* (1973–74), a series which would become celebrated for its comprehensive account of the Second World War and the detailed rigour of its research. Thames allowed its political output to expand and launched two new series, *Something to Say* and *People and Politics*. The acute observer, Peter Fiddick, first editor of the *Guardian*'s media section, put it succinctly: 'Corporate cash and the creative drive [were caught] on the same upswing' (1984:11). It was an invaluable context for the flowering of *This Week*.

The series rapidly regained its momentum and an atmosphere of great confidence developed. The company supported its programme makers against interference from the strengthened ITA ('It's a great boost to … morale … to know that one is getting well argued backing from the top. The general view is that this is one of the more pleasant surprises in Thames TV,' wrote Phillip Whitehead to Howard Thomas (memo 24.10.68)). A new generation of journalists was given considerable freedom to pursue their interests and develop their styles, and the role of Jeremy Isaacs was pivotal. In 1974 he became Director of Programmes, which gave him an overview of the whole of Thames's output, and he used this powerful position to enable reporters and programme makers to follow their journalistic instincts with no worries about budgets or even the size of the audience. He told Peter Taylor, 'the ratings are not your problem. They're my problem. You must do what you feel you ought to be doing and do it the way you feel you ought to do it.' (Taylor commented, 'That's the last time I've ever heard that said. The priorities of television began to change' (talk 2003).) The atmosphere was very different from Caryl Doncaster's first *This Week* when 'everything was geared to the commercial element'.

In the view of the ITA, strengthened regulation together with autonomy for the ITV companies achieved 'a generally acceptable balance between freedom and control'. But tensions remained within Thames, particularly between Isaacs and the chairman, Sir Hartley Shawcross, over what was increasingly perceived as the programme's leftish political slant (talk by Jeremy Potter, author of volumes 3 and 4 of the official ITA history, 1999).

1968 and the Prague Spring

Just like 1956, the year of *This Week*'s birth, 1968, its first year with Thames, was a traumatic one in global politics. It was a time when many of the events could be interpreted – and, with hindsight, over-simplified – as left against right, the oppressed rising up against their oppressors. In Europe there was the 'Prague Spring' and its brutal suppression; in the United States, campaigns against racial segregation and the Vietnam War and the assassinations of Martin Luther King and Bobby Kennedy. In Vietnam there was the Tet Offensive and the impending invasion of Cambodia; in Africa, the Biafra War; while in the Middle East the aftermath of the Six-Day War was unfolding. In France the strikes and student demonstrations, which nearly brought down the de Gaulle government, pioneered a new style of impulsive, participatory political action, which linked anti-colonialism and support for global struggles with political analysis and cultural activism. The space race was speeding up, and the following year came the US moon landings. Phillip Whitehead organized an hour-long 'moonshot special' with ITN. *This Week*'s overseas programmes in the last years of the 1960s covered all of these events, and much of the reporting straddled the transition from Rediffusion to Thames.

From the Middle East, programmes included 'The Right to Exist', following the Six-Day War ('Robert [Kee] did the whole programme without autocue,' said Whitehead (6.7.67)), and from Vietnam, Kee reported on the Tet Offensive (22.2.68). There was a study of Martin Luther King, as news of his assassination came through (4.4.68) and the Black Panthers were filmed for 'Say it Loud I'm Black and Proud' (27.3.69). (In the same film, Jesse Jackson, leading the movement for black economic power and employment, asked the all-white *This Week* team to leave – since there were plenty of unemployed black film technicians available.) John Edwards monitored events in the United States and investigated the extraordinary events in the exclusive retreat of Martha's Vineyard, where Senator Edward Kennedy was involved in a late-night car accident in which his companion was drowned. His car had toppled into the water off Chappaquidick Island, and there was much cynical questioning of his account of diving to the rescue, then swimming back to his mainland hotel. John Edwards tested the account by doing the swim himself for the programme, which, like many others, was made at high speed. He flew out on Saturday, shot in Martha's Vineyard on Monday, got back on Tuesday, and the programme was transmitted on Thursday (31.7.69).

Seen with hindsight, many of these programmes of the late 1960s evoke a poignant moment before disaster struck. Edwards's account of Bobby Kennedy's presidential campaign was transmitted a month before his assassination; there was a view of Beirut before that elegant city was reduced to rubble; two programmes on the ethnic conflict in Cyprus; and John Morgan's lyrical and evocative portrait of Cambodia under Prince Sianhouk just before the US invasion. The Prince, with great charm, conducts Morgan around the royal palace; there's a Buddhist ceremony, a boat on the Mekong and fishing at twilight. Sianhouk points to dangers from all sides – Vietnam, Laos, Thailand. He advocates 'Buddhist socialism, a socialism of the spirit' (20.11.69). Ten years later Julian Manyon would give a horrific account of the slaughter in the country under the murderous regime of the Khmer Rouge (5.5.79). And there was the euphoric moment of the Prague Spring.

Phillip Whitehead's special interest was Eastern Europe. Despite Khrushchev's amelioration of Stalin's worst excesses (*This Week*'s enthusiastic coverage of Khrushchev's visit to Britain in March 1956 had been superseded by the horror of the Hungarian invasion), in the context of the Cold War, reporting from the Eastern Bloc remained virtually impossible. Anything that might be interpreted as sympathy towards Soviet communism remained beyond the limits of objectivity, and coverage tended to be of Soviet dissidents and Western defectors. However, in the libertarian mood of the 1960s many journalists and intellectuals believed that hatred of totalitarianism need not imply a complete rejection of socialist ideals, and in early 1968 the movement known as the Prague Spring provided inspiration for those who were arguing for 'socialism with a human face'. Communist Czechoslovakia was demonstrating its dissatisfaction with the hard-line regime, and 'the political scene looked as if whoever was manipulating the puppets had let go of all the strings' (Zeman 1969:13–14). For *This Week* John Morgan reported on the celebrations which marked the anniversary of the liberation from the Nazis (28.3.68). But on Wednesday 21 August, with no prior warning, Russian tanks rolled into Prague.

It was three weeks after Thames had taken over. Reporter Robert Kee (who had made an earlier documentary on Czechoslovakia) heard the news at 7am. He instantly telephoned Jeremy Isaacs. Isaacs gave the go-ahead, and soon after midday Kee had met up with freelance camera/sound man Erik Durschmied in Nuremberg. Durschmied, at that time based between Paris and a boat on the Thames, had built a powerful reputation for quick-footed filming in difficult conditions. He saw the world through his lens, and his technical expertise – single-handedly wielding equipment normally operated by at least four people – was unsurpassed. The aim was to produce a film for the following Thursday, which meant getting the material back to London in time for processing and editing. But when Kee and Durschmied attempted to enter Czechoslovakia they were thrown out, and the Czechs did not open the border until Sunday. Meanwhile Isaacs re-jigged the schedules to monitor the situation in two studio-based specials with politicians and experts (21 and 22.8.68). Robert Kee rushed back with his material and 'Prague No Surrender' was assembled at speed and transmitted as planned (29.8.68). Its lingering sequences of crowds in the streets – singing, whistling to drown out Russian loudspeakers, or simply watching and waiting; its evocation of passive resistance and black humour (the signposts are all painted out except the one pointing to Moscow), its restraint (casualties are spoken of but never shown) and the controlled determination of those who speak to the camera gave it a deep sense of humanity and involvement. (It won the Television General News category of the World Newsfilm Awards that year.)

Whitehead was keen to do a follow up. Reporting from Czechoslovakia had become very difficult, but he had an extensive list of Czech contacts. News agencies such as Reuters could be consulted, as well as academic specialists, Czech residents in the UK, and television personnel in Prague who kept in touch at considerable risk to themselves. European archives were contacted, visits were planned, researchers on previous programmes were asked for information on 'film archives, hotels, bars, currency touts and prostitutes [sic]'. In October director David Elstein travelled to Prague as a tourist. He hired local crews to film in the streets and smuggled the film out. The resulting compilation grew too big for a normal *This Week* slot and became a 53-minute special, 'Remember Czechoslovakia' (4.2.69). '*This Week* put more care into this film than anything else I have been involved with in my 18 months at independent television,' Phillip Whitehead told the press. When the programme became ITV's entry for the Italia prize, it was boycotted by the Russians on the jury. (The National Union of Students wanted a print to show at their meetings, but this was refused as ITV programmes could not be used for political fundraising.)

In March 1969 Whitehead visited Czechoslovakia himself, despite a crack down on foreign television crews and an increase in surveillance and phone tapping. (Even so, one student contact promised to introduce the crew to Gustav Husak's son in return for an annual subscription to *Melody Maker*.) Hard man Husak had taken over, and the pretext for the next programme was the proposal for a federal structure between Czech and Slovak areas. The real aim was to seek out signs of resistance, including memories of the student, Jan Palach, who burnt himself to death in protest at the Russian occupation ('Czechoslovakia: Hard Reality' 15.5.69). Czechoslovakia, with its reputation for moderation, resilience and humour, would remain the Eastern Bloc country that gained most attention from *This Week*, right up to the time when it finally shook off Soviet domination with the Velvet Revolution in 1989. Whitehead was unable to re-enter Czechoslovakia for seven years.

Life on *This Week*

As Rediffusion faded into Thames, a core group of reporters settled into the series. Some, like Bryan Magee and Robert Kee, had been with *This Week* for several years. Others included John Morgan, Peter Williams, John Edwards and Llew Gardner, who specialized in political interviews. Soon they were to be joined by the Thames generation, including Peter Taylor and Jonathan Dimbleby. Dimbleby had done a stint at the BBC and quotes a memo from Paul Fox, then of BBC Bristol: '*Another* Dimbleby wants to go into television. He's a bit short on height but he seems bright enough.' Dimbleby added that this was 'the only job in the world that I'd ever thought I really wanted to do' (talk 1995).

Television programmes are always the product of a team, and more so when the team is committed to a long-term weekly series. Phillip Whitehead took over Jeremy Isaacs's revolving schedule with a team meeting on Friday mornings. The aim was to plan three to four weeks ahead with director/reporter/researcher teams working on programme ideas. Cameramen, sound recordists and film editors would be allocated at a later stage, as would studio facilities when needed. But all *This Week* producers have prided themselves on their flexibility and ability to respond to current events. 'It is common for the team producing the programme to be continually reformulating their ideas, recalling crews from the middle of a location, scrapping film, scrapping interviews, or ringing people to say they will not be required for interview after all because events have moved,' wrote Bryan Magee. Even if a producer has a first-class programme

> shot on the other side of the world at immense cost ... [and] some major and wholly unforeseen news story breaks ... he must have the detachment and self-confidence to throw his entire programme in the bin, call his team to emergency stations, and mastermind a one-day crash operation that will scoop the screens that night (Magee 1966:97).

In this spirit, when John Glenn was launched into space, Magee left for New York on Tuesday night, filmed the following day, was back at London Airport on Thursday morning and presented the programme that evening. He needed no luggage, as he had only slept on the plane (1966:99). Such flexibility meant that the power to make expensive decisions must be in the hands of managers who are close to the programme makers. Robert Kee had been able to set off for Prague after a single phone call. Jeremy Isaacs, as Controller of Features, had given him the go ahead and had made space that same evening for an unscheduled programme. The 'short managerial structure' of ITV companies meant that this sort of decision making was possible, unlike the more cautious BBC where if 'one programme makes a mistake the whole of the BBC is under pressure', said David Elstein (quoted in Rosenthal 1981:115).

But high-speed working and last-minute changes in the

schedule demanded flexibility from the whole support network – editors, laboratory technicians, dubbing mixers as well as typists, studio managers, engineers and many others who did not work on the exciting front line, but without whom the programmes would not have been possible. A last-minute rush was a regular part of their weekly experience, and film editors in particular could find themselves working throughout the night. Overtime agreements with the Association of Cinematograph and Television Technicians and other unions meant that longer hours sent the costs of programmes rocketing.

Reporters and directors are unanimous about the problems caused by the ACTT's excessive efforts to protect its members – which were a severe limitation on the ability to produce effective programmes. The launch of the new ITV companies had meant negotiating a new agreement with the union, and at first this had led to deadlock. Consequently the ACTT blacked out Thames's first night, on 27 July 1968, for almost two hours, and at LWT the opening announcement 'We have ways of making you ...' never got as far as 'laugh'.

The agreement arrived at by Thames reaffirmed the 'closed shop' policy, which meant that only ACTT members could be employed and only they could operate the equipment. Regulations covered the size of crews. 'Filming Norman Mailer's campaign in New York we had to hire a stretch limousine to get them all in' (David Elstein to VWP), and special permission had to be requested for 'short crews' of six or less. All this artificially inflated the cost of programmes, since all flights had to be first class and breaches of the agreement carried financial penalties. These came into force if the overnight break of ten hours was not observed, if work began before 7am and if restrictions were ignored. The situation was particularly difficult when the team was working undercover or trying to film as tourists. Technicians on the whole welcomed the protection and the chance to share in some of the spoils of ITV's wealth, but reporters and directors are still unanimous about the problems caused. In the words of David Elstein, himself a union activist, it was bad labour relations, and the arrangement created 'pointless aggravation and made life a misery'. His view was that Thames Television became reluctant to put more money into programmes (despite the fact that 'the company's rolling in money, and is embarrassed by the amount of money it takes on advertising') because it was soaked up by the ACTT (Rosenthal 1981:130–1).

The ITV reshuffle also coincided with the arrival of colour. The BBC had been broadcasting experiments for several years using the higher-resolution image developed for BBC2 which used 625 lines as opposed to the original 405. The plan was to switch off the 405 signal when a significant proportion of the public had purchased the higher-quality sets, and this meant that the transition was slow. But the 1967 Wimbledon tennis championships were broadcast live in full colour, and by 1969 all channels switched to 625 and colour television had definitively arrived.

Most directors and producers were full of enthusiasm. Colour brought greater realism and wider aesthetic possibilities, although there were some doubts. David Attenborough, then controller of BBC2, was hesitant. 'We'll have to look hard to see if we can take that degree of realism,' he said. Vietnam was at its height, the first war to be graphically reported on television, and he worried about the disturbing intensity of full-colour images of the wounded. At ITV it was the sales departments that were pushing to move ahead, since colour was easier to market. Colour film stocks had been available for many years, but they had limited possibilities compared with black and white. In particular they needed much brighter lighting conditions, which made it virtually impossible to shoot at night or in dingy rooms without a whole panoply of electricians, generators and massive lighting set-ups. Now faster film stocks were becoming available. Cameramen were keen to use them and film editors went on special 'editing in colour' courses. The problem was that the ACTT demanded a 10 per cent pay increase which the companies were unwilling to meet. Within ITV its members went on what became known as a 'colour strike'. But colour was inevitable, and soon technical improvements meant that filmed reports could cover the same wide spectrum that black and white had begun to explore with such revelatory results.

The first *This Week* transmitted in colour was 'Cambodia: The Prince' in November 1969, described by Phillip Whitehead as 'a big investment' – and by the early 1970s, colour was the norm. An overseas report, such as 'Viva La Causa' on the strike by immigrant grape pickers in California, could begin with an evocative sunrise which gave it a sensuous filmic quality (28.8.69).

The Independent Broadcasting Authority

The regulatory Authority was another constraint and a major influence on *This Week* in the 1970s. With the launch of commercial radio in 1972, the Independent Television Authority became the Independent Broadcasting Authority (IBA), covering both media, but its approach and most of its personnel were essentially the same. According to Jeremy Potter, Sir Robert Fraser, the first director general, appointed in 1954, was thought to be too much under the thumb of the ITV barons from the entertainment world – Sidney Bernstein of Granada and Lew Grade of ATV – so when he retired in 1970, an educationist, Brian Young, ex-headmaster of the prestigious boys' public school Charterhouse, was appointed. Apparently Young had not even thought of applying for the job. (In the British tradition an important qualification for a place on the IBA was a lack of experience in broadcasting, commented Potter (talk 1999).) From 1967 the chair of the Authority was Lord Aylestone – the Labour politician Herbert Bowden – who was open about his preference for the lighter side of ITV, but he was succeeded in 1975 by the high-minded Lady Bridget Plowden, who had earlier chaired an influential committee on primary schools. The appointments brought a renewed emphasis within the Authority towards the 'serious' and the educational, and a strong awareness of public service commitments in the post-Pilkington mood. 'Independent Television had a headmaster and a headmistress at the same time,' wrote Potter (1989:91). For a period in early 1971 the Authority had allowed the companies to replace *This Week* on the network with repeats of *Whicker's World* – a move described by the *Daily Mail* as 'outrageous and indefensible' (12.2.71) – and one of the first moves of the new regime was to insist that it was reinstated.

The Authority saw itself as a beleaguered organization, criticized as a censor when it intervened, criticized by the puritans when it didn't. It was subjected to lobbying from bodies ranging from moral pressure groups to individual MPs and the government itself. Complaints from the public mostly concerned issues of taste and decency 'particularly nudity and the faintest mention of sex' rather than political issues, whereas the Authority itself was mostly concerned about its duty to monitor any broadcast that might lead to public disorder, and what Potter described as 'slanted documentaries' (talk 1999). Effectively this meant that journalism that challenged the 'official' view was likely to give rise to problems. In the following decade *This Week* would come into conflict with the Authority on both grounds. It challenged social morality when it broadcast programmes on abortion and sex education, and it offended politicians with 'slanted documentaries' and probing investigations. Journalists remained convinced that programmes that ruffled official feathers were an essential part of the current affairs agenda, and Jeremy Isaacs frequently complained that the Authority was moving beyond its brief and taking on an editorial role.

In fact, reprimands from the ITA marked the final *This Week* from Rediffusion and the first from Thames. The last programme under Rediffusion attempted to understand the criminal mind. It had to be withdrawn as 'not in the public interest' because it included an interview with a self-confessed criminal (*Guardian* 27.7.68). In the first programme for Thames the complaint was partisanship and left-wing bias. On 1 August 1968, John Morgan, brought up in South Wales, eloquent, passionate and a rugby aficionado, reported on the controversial tour of South Africa by the British Lions rugby team.

South Africa

The case of apartheid South Africa was one on which left-liberal opinion and the broader media consensus tended to be united. David Elstein was later to describe it as an issue in which 'the left has a lot of right on its side' (Rosenthal 1981:122). The regime was universally condemned as reprehensible; its excesses were deplored and opposition from the black majority was widely supported – although there were doubts about the armed resistance for which Nelson Mandela and eight others had been jailed four years before. The premise of 'The Afrikaner: Win at all Costs' (1.8.68) was that the white South African rugby team was engaging in unfair play that paralleled the unfairness of the regime. 'In this sporting war,' declared Morgan, 'the Afrikaner won, avenging defeat in the Boer War. And they were not too fussy about how they won.'

One viewer's letter attacked the programme as a 'stream of socialist propaganda', while another praised Morgan's 'fairness'. But following complaints from the South African embassy, the ITA told Thames's Managing Director that the 'programme could not be defended' and Howard Thomas wrote a letter of regret to the ambassador (Potter 1989:113). The uneasy relationship with the embassy was to collapse into overt hostility over the decade. Permission to film in South Africa was usually delayed and eventually withheld altogether. The ACTT banned all filming apart from news reporting, and successive *This Week* journalists remained determined to point the cameras in directions the South African government preferred to keep hidden. Over the years secret filming would alternate with reports that used various subterfuges to avoid official scrutiny. Struggling against official censorship to get across conditions in the black townships and 'homelands' was a continuous challenge.

In 1970 Phillip Whitehead won his parliamentary seat and Jo Menell, who had begun as a researcher on the programme, succeeded him as Producer. Menell was from a prosperous South African background and had a crusade to fight. He persuaded the embassy to permit filming in one of the Bantustans, the supposedly autonomous 'homelands' which had been set up to resettle urban Africans. Such a film, he argued, 'would draw attention to a fascinating and positive feature which has received all too little attention' (letter 11.2.70). The embassy set conditions: the programme would deal only with the homeland and no other stock material would be inserted, a representative of the Department of Information would supervise the filming and 'would satisfy themselves at all stages of production ... that you are striving to present a balanced view of the subject' (letter 18.3.70). In the event, Peter Williams went to the Transkei with director David Gill.

'The Black Experiment' (28.5.70) shows the opening of the Transkei parliament by a white commissioner. The Bantustans had been set up by an Act in 1951, but even the most advanced had only a minimal degree of independence. In the film, South African power is clearly visible as white 'advisers' sit behind the black assembly members. Mr de Villiers of the embassy gave the game away when he wrote, 'Certain things had been arranged for the team's benefit. For example, the staged session of the legislative assembly has seldom, if ever, been done before' (letter 27.4.70). Intercut with the assembly were sequences of men waiting for permits to travel, and children walking eight miles to school. The film was rigorously previewed by Jeremy Isaacs, Brian Tesler, Howard Thomas and Lord Shawcross. It was then shown to the

South African embassy who requested minor changes which were duly made. Peter Black in the *Daily Mail* described it as 'as effective a nailing of lying propaganda as television has given us' (29.4.70).

Despite its own careful supervision, the embassy was not pleased, especially as Menell had arranged for a second team, with Charles Douglas Home as reporter (he was later to be editor of *The Times*), to make a programme on white extremists. Not only did 'Whiter Than Thou' (23.4.70) implicitly compare Afrikanerdom with Nazi Germany – commentary over a gymnastic display refers to 'the threat to what they believe is the master race' – but it ended with a fight breaking out at an extremist Herstigte Nasionale Party (HNP) rally. As a result the crew were 'manhandled' when they tried to get in to another HNP meeting. Researcher Colin Martin argued that the commentary was justified. Menell told the *Daily Sketch*, 'The fact that we actually filmed this punch up was the last straw' (23.4.70).

The following day, the South African ambassador, H.G. Luttig, reminded Howard Thomas of the ITA's criticisms two years before, 'We are extremely perturbed that certain television producers seem intent on projecting the Afrikaner people as a bigoted, backward people.' The Johannesburg newspaper *Die Transvaaler* had done some research into Jo Menell 's background and discovered that his father was chairman of Anglo-Transvaal Consolidated Investment Ltd. In an extended correspondence, Menell challenged the editor to show the film to a general audience in South Africa, a challenge that the editor, Mr Noffke, seemed only too willing to take up. But Jeremy Isaacs wrote 'No' in the margin, in the heavy pen that he used for such notes.

As with other difficult and inaccessible parts of the world, current affairs programmes had to find unofficial ways to respond when reports of uprisings and their brutal suppression emerged. Under David Elstein's editorship, following the riots in the Soweto township, director Jon Blair (who was South African by birth) and reporter John Fielding travelled separately as tourists and interviewed the student leader, Tietse Machinini, who was on the run from the secret police (2.9.76). David Elstein was not told of his whereabouts, so could not help the furious South African authorities ('not that I would have told those likely to endanger his life if I had known'), and the team laid a false trail by telling the press that a corrupt customs officer had been bribed to allow the filmed material out of the country (DE to PH). A few months later the series purchased footage from a film by free-lance cameraman Erik Durschmied, who had spent two months making complementary portraits of black and white South Africans (19.5.77); and, following the death of the black activist Steve Biko in police custody, researcher Gordon Stephens obtained transcripts of the inquest, in which the white prison doctors denied seeing the blatant wounds which had led to Biko's death (8.12.77). Freelance director Michael Darlow directed a re-enactment, which was cast over two days and shot over two more. It was a new initiative for a current affairs programme, and had an afterlife as a stage production in London and off-Broadway in New York.

Ironically, in the mid-1970s a Thames technical team were acting as advisers to South African broadcasters, and Thames's engineering director, Stuart Sansom, left to work at the South African state-controlled television station, SABC (*Thames Review* 1974/75).

Mainstream journalism, oppositional radicalism and the counter-culture

The '1960s' have entered political folklore as a shorthand for irresponsibility, hedonism and licence – a heady mixture of unrealistic political idealism and cultural upheaval which stretched from the universities to the streets, from radical philosophy to underground drug culture. It was the age of the Beatles, the Rolling Stones and art-school chic, and some of the most responsible journalists turned up at work wearing kaftans. There was a general sense that the new generation was what mattered, and youthful irreverence went together with a relaxation of morals, sanctioned by the liberalizing legislation of the Wilson government. Back in 1960 a jury had found that D.H. Lawrence's highly literary novel, *Lady Chatterley's Lover*, was not obscene, but in the summer of 1971 the longest obscenity trial in British history centred on a strip cartoon drawn by a 16-year-old. In a dramatic clash of old and new cultures, the editors of the underground magazine *Oz* were prosecuted for the explicit sexual jokes and drawings in what it described as its 'Skoolkids Issue'.

Jonathan Dimbleby, who was soon to join *This Week*, sat through the five weeks of the trial in the public gallery. Such was the public interest that when the guilty verdicts were announced on a Thursday, the edition planned for that evening was scrapped and replaced with a studio discussion (5.8.71). Producer Ian Martin praised the flexibility not only of the unit 'but of the other departments on whom we depend'. (The verdicts were later to be overturned because Judge Argyll was ruled to have been openly partisan.)

Beyond the froth, the changes in cultural attitudes and social alignment were significant. The approach of Richard Hoggart and Raymond Williams, which had sought to radicalize a class society, was being replaced by a more diffused radicalism in which women, ethnic minorities, regional voices and diverse other social groups were pushing for recognition and a public voice. The strikes by the powerful National Union of Mineworkers, with its deep-rooted evocation of working-class solidarity, would lead to the downfall of Edward Heath's Conservative government, but effectively they marked the beginnings of a final flickering of class-based confrontations and of working-class self-confidence. *This Week* marked the 1972 strike with a sympathetic report from the Yorkshire mining village of Armthorpe (20.1.72). 'For those of us who lived through those stirring days, this film is a precious record of a world that has all but disappeared,' commented Welsh MP Kim Howells in 1991 (*35 Years on the Front Line* 19.2.91).

The thoroughgoing radicalism of the counter-culture posed a different challenge to current affairs, since it laid out a persuasive and carefully argued critique of conformity and the mainstream, whether in the media, politics or other cultural forms. Alternative ways of making films were emerging which did not accept many of the principles that current affairs had been at such pains to establish. A lively independent film-making culture grew up that reflected student activism, opposition to the war in Vietnam, feminism, and support for postcolonial and Third World struggles in Africa and Latin America. 'Alternative' film-making scorned balance and gave total commitment to an oppositional position, especially on issues such as Northern Ireland and South Africa. It did not accept the role of the journalist as a dispassionate observer, nor the well-established programme formats, nor the distanced professionalism of the television structures – all of which seemed rooted in establishment values. It was a critique that focused on ways of knowing, as well as on what is known. Some of its activists set up the Independent Filmmakers Association (IFA) in the autumn of 1974 which ran parallel to mainstream current affairs (Dickinson 1999). And, despite the differences, its mood affected mainstream series such as *This Week*.

At the same time, this was the period in which the series was building with great confidence on the committed journalistic ethos that had been consolidated under Jeremy Isaacs – an approach that was securely grounded in humanist, social democratic values, committed to truth, objectivity and a view of the audience as citizens with the right to be informed. When Jonathan Dimbleby joined the series he described 'a strong sense of people watching a great programme with a great tradition and great forebears' (to PH). The aim was to be at the political centre, rather than at the margins. So the two influences sat side by side: on the one hand, the challenge of the new social movements which were re-evaluating the marginal, and, on the other, a strengthening of television journalism as a mature and authoritative project, claiming the right to challenge those in power on the public's behalf, and to be, in the words of James Cameron, 'the people's eyes and ears … the instrument associating people's government with people's opinion' (*Guardian* 28.1.85). The two tendencies intertwined and influenced each other, but they were very different. The first argued for multiple voices and multiple perspectives. It was suspicious of authority, aligned with the dispossessed and mistrusted claims to 'truth', while the second aimed to speak with the secure voice of an objective commentator. This meant that mainstream current affairs came in for some swingeing criticism from radical academics as well as independent film-makers (e.g. Hall et al 1976).

Editions of *This Week* that directly addressed New Left politics and the counter-culture tended to be slightly awkward, trying to fit the ideas into a mould which they themselves determinedly refused. Two programmes set out to understand the massive demonstrations in Paris in the summer of 1968 and the threat they posed to the French government (23 and 30.5.68). 'Student Revolution' featured anti-Vietnam leader Tariq Ali and the students' sit-in at Hornsey College of Art in the run-up to a major demonstration in London (John Morgan concluded with a lofty judgement quoted from George Orwell, 'they play with fire without knowing that fire burns' (24.10.68)); and a special on censorship and the 'permissive society' showed nakedness on stage (26.6.69).

As the 1970s progressed, the new social configuration gained greater legitimacy, and eventually found an outlet in Channel 4, founded in 1982, which was explicitly required to give expression to diversity and commitment. Jeremy Isaacs became its first Chief Executive.

A slightly different challenge came from campaigning groups whose core members were established television producers. They too felt that the outlets provided by the BBC and ITV companies were too narrow and too restrictive. The respected director Michael Darlow was one of its main activists. He wrote,

> Within a few years of entering television I came increasingly to question how it was that some programmes got made and others did not, who got to make such decisions and how they got their authority, why some people were given the opportunity to make programmes and express opinions and some were not. ... Increasingly we came to believe that the whole system of control and funding in film and broadcasting was inappropriate to the needs and aspirations of the new age. [It] no longer adequately met the range of needs and tastes of the viewing public or of society at large (Darlow 2004:3).

Some of these producers were setting up independent companies to gain greater control over their own output. Some began to campaign about the structure of television as a whole. The Free Communications Group (set up in 1969) pointed to what they saw as the narrowness of programme content, and to unwarranted interference in creative work, particularly moral and political censorship. The 76 Group questioned what would happen after the ITV licences ran out in 1976. A fourth channel would then become available and there was considerable pressure from the commercial companies who wanted an ITV2 and a freer hand in broadcasting. Prominent members of both campaigning groups were *This Week* Producer, soon to be MP, Phillip Whitehead, and *This Week* director and future Producer David Elstein (Darlow 2004:36, 66).

Many programme makers moved between the different worlds, and *This Week* Producer Jo Menell was one of them. (The appointment of Menell as Producer was later described by Peter Williams as 'a mistake', because 'he was far left – the programme went through a bad period' (to PH).) During his brief tenure he initiated a group of programmes that explored the 'underground' culture of the times and topics that were considered marginal and morally suspect, including 'group marriage' (13.8.70), cannabis (12.3.70) and hippy politics in the USA (12.11.70).

The new mood also questioned the limits of objectivity. Reporting from the point of view of 'the enemy' has always been difficult territory. Protests against the Vietnam War were not always linked to support for North Vietnam, but there was scanty reporting of that country. Western journalists were not acceptable to the North Vietnamese, so when trade unionist Clive Jenkins went to Hanoi with a trade union delegation he was commissioned to make a film for *This Week* with Mike Fash as camera/director. His commentary asserts that since 1945 North Vietnam has wiped out illiteracy, health care has improved and death in childbirth has almost been eliminated. There is a sequence of Hanoi streets, a display of captured US bombs and mines, and shots of injured people. The editor of the main newspaper declares that they will not give in (8.10.70).

After a year, it was felt that Menell had gone too far, and he left. Thames's chairman, Lord Shawcross, wrote, 'I hear he has gone to advise the new president of Chile [Salvador Allende]. It seems a good place for him.' (Menell 's wife was from Chile and he had gone to help run the State Broadcasting Service.) Ian Martin took over as producer for a brief period in 1971, to be followed by John Edwards in 1972. In Chile, the democratically elected Allende was assassinated in 1973 and his government brought down by US intervention through the CIA. The country collapsed into dictatorship. When Jo Menell came back he made a film which consisted of images of penises, called simply 'Dick' (1989). It was so successful that he established an annual 'Dick Award' for the most innovative independent film.

In 1974 the Committee on the Future of Broadcasting, chaired by Lord Annan – originally set up in 1970 but then cancelled – was revived by the incoming Labour government. Phillip Whitehead, now MP for Derby, was amongst its members. The committee became the focus for campaigning from the independent producers' organizations, as well as from the ITV companies, who were strongly lobbying for an ITV2.

Women, sexuality and the personal

Amongst the memos for 'Remember Czechoslovakia' a researcher had given the name and address of a female contact in Prague along with the note 'a good screw. ... She's not exactly on the game but likes to be bought drinks.' That careless reference was symptomatic of the times. Women were decorative, useful as secretaries and 'a good screw'.

In the masculine, rationalist atmosphere of *This Week* in the 1960s and 1970s, there were problems around dealing with issues of importance to women. The series had been reclaimed from the feminized influence of humour and glamour and at the same time – and it is not clear whether this was a coincidence, certainly no one would admit to its being deliberate – women themselves had largely disappeared from the team, that is if you do not count the essential support workers, including PAs, secretaries and some researchers. Jenny Hughes directed a few programmes in 1969, Vanya Kewley had a brief period as director in 1972 and Judy Lever directed a programme on the shortage of kidney machines (6.10.77), but there were no regular women reporters or directors on *This Week* in the 1970s, and no women technicians. It fitted with a general pattern in which women were not welcome in 'serious' journalism (as newsreaders, political correspondents, war reporters), in technology (as engineers, camera or sound technicians) or in positions of power (heads of department, managing directors).

But feminism too was an important facet of the times. Nineteen-seventy was the year of Germaine Greer's *The Female Eunuch* and Kate Millett's *Sexual Politics*, with their searing indictment of gender inequality. Yet despite its assertion that the position of women was central to the political debate, feminism tended to be pushed to the margins of current affairs, together with other manifestations of left 'extremism'. Jo Menell had made a gesture. The Equal Pay Act was passed in 1970 (it would take effect from 1975) and it made a classic hook for a programme. He invited Juliet Mitchell, together with director Liz Kustow and researcher Lyn Gambles, to make a programme that would put forward an analysis of women's inequality. Mitchell was one of the editors of *New Left Review* and a member of the London Women's Liberation Workshop. Her book *Women's Estate*, published a few months later, was to become a classic. But Menell had to work hard to justify employing a team who were not *This Week* staff. All other directors are busy, he argued, Kustow and Mitchell are specialists in the field, and 'I think it extremely important that this film should be made by women, because past films of this nature have always suffered from a "male bias" when tackling this subject.'

At the time, independent women's film groups were evolving a thoroughgoing critique of conventional film-making, both in theory and in practice. They argued that traditional film styles could not reflect the reality of women's lives, since images of women are so often taken over by men for their own pleasure. Mitchell's film emphasized this point in a sequence using Page-Three-style pin-ups (and, as if to prove the point, Mitchell's own appearance was commented on at length by critics). The programme refused accepted definitions and dealt with the unpaid aspects of women's work as well as with women's employment. A four-part split screen showed different types of work, and there was a re-enactment of a registry office wedding ('It's a Woman's Life' 30.7.70). Mitchell caused a flurry of memos when she requested an extra £100 on top of her agreed fee of £500 (because the interviews had taken longer than expected) and claimed for new dresses and a haircut.

Despite campaigns around equal rights and women's paid employment, women's lives were still conventionally seen as confined to the personal sphere – homemaking, motherhood, sexuality. In contrast to the frothy 'humour and glamour' which had been thought to attract a female audience in the early days of the series, an approach that would take women's issues seriously, and would focus on topics such as the human body, personal and emotional relationships or the detail of everyday lives, seemed even more out of place in the tougher world of hard news and current affairs. Bringing such topics into public view might challenge conventions of 'taste and decency'. Desmond Wilcox had explored the territory with his programmes on birth control, abortion, homosexuality and the interpersonal relationships of race, but his intensely personal approach could not be contained within the current affairs format, and he had left to set up *Man Alive* (BBC 1965–81). However, rigid social mores had been shaken up by liberalizing legislation as well as feminist pressures, and it was in this atmosphere that *This Week* returned to the topics of sex education, birth control and abortion. At the same time, a high-profile backlash was gaining strength.

Mary Whitehouse and sex education

The new moral right had television in its sights. Mary Whitehouse had been campaigning to 'clean up TV' since the early 1960s, and in 1965 had launched the high-profile National Viewers' and Listeners' Association (NVLA). According to Whitehouse, 'pre-marital sex was being made acceptable by television'. Since outrage over television's excess always made good copy, the campaign set out to generate publicity, and used it to put pressure on the regulators to tighten up on issues of 'taste and decency' (Tracey and Morrison 1979). Whitehouse herself had been a sex education teacher, and when she complained to *This Week* about an edition on sex education she was invited to a follow-up debate (20 and 27.2.75). 'Sex and the 14-Year-Old' had been constructed around a class given by teacher Dr Elphis Christopher who asserted that information about sex is everyone's right. The tabloids grabbed the opportunity for a headline – 'TV sex lesson shocker', shouted the *Daily Mirror* (20.2.75) – and there was a bundle of letters from viewers, outraged by her frank approach. 'That disgusting, filthy woman doctor,' wrote one, 'how dare that jezebel corrupt our children.' Worst of all was the opening sequence in which Dr Christopher shows a condom to a class of teenagers. Now, in the 2000s, 20 years after the 1980s campaigns against AIDS, which made condoms on television as common as paper bags, it is difficult to imagine the shock generated by that image. Jeremy Isaacs previewed the film with Bernard Sendall of the IBA, who decreed that it should be transmitted at 9.30pm instead of the usual 8.30.

Aware that the press were keen to publicize any conflict, Isaacs had ruled that there should be no advance information when a programme was subject to IBA scrutiny – and he was not pleased when he found that the press had got hold of the notorious image of the condom. In fact Thames's press office had only been able to interest reviewers when they got wind of a dispute, and Producer David Elstein, who had strongly disagreed with the decision to move to a later time, had made the clip available to the *Mirror* whose reporter had been waiting around to hear the IBA's decision. And many viewers objected to the move. One wrote, 'What did we have in its place for younger viewers? *The Sweeney*, as nasty a combination of sex, violence and corruption as you'll get.'

After the following week's live debate and phone-in (with a

30-line exchange), several viewers compared Dr Christopher and Mrs Whitehouse, 'what a crazy mixed up person Dr Christopher looks. Mrs Whitehouse looked like a typical middle-aged mother with a greater knowledge of children'; 'Dr Christopher is not even pleasant to look at and she was quite rude to Mrs Whitehouse.' Some simply gave vent to their feelings, 'It was most disgusting. I haven't got over the shock of it yet.' To which David Elstein replied, 'I'm sorry our programme upset you so much. I hope by now you have recovered.' But many viewers supported Dr Christopher, 'I married at 16 and of course I was pregnant – no one told me about sex.' Elstein took the trouble to reply to all of them, and promised a second, longer programme 'as soon as I can persuade the higher ups'.

Five months later he kept his promise and, in a one-hour special, the complete lesson was transmitted, including questions and answers from the students (17.7.75). Despite the comments of many viewers that 9.30pm had been too late for young people to watch the programme, 'Learning About Sex, Part 2' (actually Part 3 if you count the studio discussion) was transmitted at 11pm, on a day when ITN's coverage of the Apollo-Soyuz meeting in space took the 8.30 slot.

Abortion

For feminist writers and film-makers the most personal aspects of women's lives should be treated with a seriousness that asserts that these issues, too, are part of the central political agenda. Researcher Jenny Wilkes was a member of the London Independent Women's Film Group and was determined that *This Week* should do a programme on abortion. It had been ten years since Desmond Wilcox had interviewed women in the run-up to the 1967 Act, and the issue was once more on the agenda, as James White's amendment came before Parliament. '[I] want to make sure we are not giving out abortion on demand,' he told a *This Week* discussion programme (3.7.75). The law had been liberalized, but the opposition remained powerful. Nevertheless the climate of opinion had changed. Mainstream magazines, such as *Parents*, carried explicit and sometimes graphically illustrated features on abortion, and in both France and the USA campaigners were publicizing self-help methods in publications and in films. Why should the process of abortion not be seen on UK television?

In the summer of 1975 Wilkes persuaded Professor Richard Beard of St Mary's Hospital, Paddington, to allow the process to be filmed. David Elstein backed her and gave the hospital a guarantee that nothing would be transmitted without their agreement. Wilkes argued that there should be an all-woman crew. The problem was that, at the time, there was no female camera operator in the ACTT, and the closed-shop agreement meant that only ACTT members could be employed. (Outside the mainstream, women film-makers, often working collectively, had been teaching themselves the technical grades of camera and sound, from which the rigid union regulations, as well as long-standing prejudice, had excluded them.)

However, Joan Churchill's ACTT membership was under consideration. An American who was an experienced camerawoman in the USA, she was teaching at the British National Film School and had been making frequent and frustrating applications to join. Elstein explained the situation to the union and listed Churchill's extensive credits. It was grudgingly agreed that no one else was qualified for the job, and she was given a six-week temporary work permit, which described her has a 'lady cameraman'. She found the Thames ACTT shop very hostile, 'I hated going into that building' (to PH). Union representative John White called it a 'new and completely unprecedented crewing arrangement' and took the opportunity to complain about other things as well, such as problems with meal breaks and general lack of liaison.

Unlike Desmond Wilcox's programme, which had been based on set-up interviews and disguised identities, this film followed several named women as they progressed through the clinic's sequence of consultations and medical procedures, from the first meeting with doctors and social workers, through the careful follow-up. Interviews with members of the medical team were done on the hoof, and social workers were observed discussing the pros and cons of supporting women through the process. Professor Beard relaxes from his work, turns to the camera and describes with great lucidity the social and personal benefits that justify abortion. He does not do abortions beyond the 20th week of pregnancy. 'The foetus is too near the point of independent survival for it to be morally right.' In all, three abortions are filmed – one with a full anaesthetic, and two with a local anaesthetic. After a shock opening, in which hospital doors swing open and a young woman is wheeled into the operating theatre, the process is followed with clinical precision in a classic observational piece, which eschews the analysis, argument and visual conceits of Juliet Mitchell's equal-pay programme.

The hospital was closely involved in the production and was concerned not to include scenes that would be too sensitive. When it judged that one interviewee had been too distressed to have given proper permission, the whole programme was reconstructed and some sequences were filmed again.

The programme was completed in July and the IBA were not happy. Lady Plowden felt that it showed 'women in a very undignified light going through an awful experience', but she held a screening for the female members of the IBA staff who voted to show it. Only then was it passed for transmission, with the proviso that it went out at 9pm instead of the usual 8pm and was moderated by a studio discussion (15.10.75). Significantly the Authority had accepted that the response of the women on its staff would be different – and in this case more relevant – than that of the men.

Thames's press release fuelled the controversy. 'The crucial area is the "balance of risk" clause in the 1967 Abortion Act. ... Is this consultant's interpretation of the Act correct?' it asked. But several important taboos had been broken, including that of a woman working as a camera person. It was undoubtedly a breakthrough, but it would be many years before that particular gender divide would become less rigid.

Nor would the issue of abortion go away. Indeed, disputes intensified. There was an innocence about those 1970s feminist demands – made with an awareness of centuries of suffering – which gained a greater complexity in the face of improved medical knowledge about the early development of the foetus, increasing awareness of the complexities of reproductive rights, and escalating attacks from religious fundamentalists who claimed that the unborn child's right to life must be respected above all other considerations. However, it would be another 12 years before *This Week* did another programme about abortion. In 1987 there was an all-woman production team without fuss, but a male camera person ('Eighteen Weeks?' 22.10.87).

The freedom to experiment

The 1970s saw a real sense of the freedom to experiment, pushing the series closer to the diversity of documentary, both in style and in content. Peter Williams was able to develop his deep concern with social topics and members of society who had tended to be overlooked. 'All Our Miss Steadmans' (15.10.70) spent time with a frail 83-year-old left to cope alone. A pair of remarkable programmes followed the difficulties of staff and children in care homes ('Other People's Children' and 'Take Three Girls' (1 and 8.2.73)), while 'Schoolgirl Prisoners' interviewed teen-age girls held in adult prisons (15.1.76). Williams also conducted explorations of the morality and subjectivity of those who commit crimes in 'Sweet as a Nut' (29.7.68) and 'You Only Do Life' (8.8.68), programmes that featured a contract killer and other convicted criminals who talk (anonymously) with sang froid about the ease with which a crime can be committed.

'Just One of Those Things' (13.2.75) was very different. Made with director Martin Smith it was based on an experiment with alternative approaches to crime and punishment, in which crimi-nals were brought into conversation with their victims. In June 1972 Peter Dallas had been wounded in a violent and unprovoked knife attack on a South London railway station. Bystander James Allen saw what happened, came to his assistance and was also severely wounded. Phillip Priestly of National Victims' Support arranged a meeting between them and the convicted assailant, Kevin McDermott, who had just been released after serving two years of a four-year prison sentence. Unlike the knowing and calculating criminals of Williams's earlier programmes, this was an exercise in denial. McDermott looks straight at the mild-mannered Dallas and declares ' I can't for the life of me make out what sparked off the incident. … I'm usually quite placid.' The programme offers no answers and makes for disorientating viewing. (One viewer, clearly accustomed to seeing the sort of challenging interview that was the convention in dealing with criminals, was not prepared to tolerate a different approach. 'It was conducted terribly. The ineffective interviewer built the attacker on a pedestal instead of trying to belittle him and treat him with the contempt he deserved.')

In 1974 Arnold Bulka, who had been Producer of *This Week* for barely five months, committed suicide, overwhelmed by the pressure of the job. David Elstein took over as Producer, at first on a temporary basis, and he conducted the series through the next tempestuous years until it was taken off the air in 1978. He took full advantage of Thames's prosperity and indulgence, pushing the limits of this 'golden age' – a time when 'you could cover dozens of different types of stories without being bound to a formula and without fear of competition' (to VWP). *This Week* continued to develop a great flexibility and widened the range of mainstream current affairs formats. As well as experimenting with new approaches to understanding crime, it used dramatic reconstruction in the Steve Biko programme (8.12.77) and in Richard Broad's imaginative speculation of how television would have covered a miners' strike in 1844 (21.1.75). And it conducted classic investigations, including one into the murder of a homosexual, Maxwell Confait, which succeeded in getting the innocent men who had been convicted out of jail (7.11.74).

David Elstein's own favourite programme had little to do with the mainstream agenda, nor with his stated intention to do harder, more political programmes. 'Nymphs and Shepherds' (19.6.75) traced the fortunes of some of the 200 working-class schoolchildren from Manchester who had taken part in a staggeringly successful recording of the song 46 years previously. 'When I suggested it they thought I was mad. ... I had to work hard to persuade director Martin Smith to do it ... but I liked the fact the series could be quirky' (to VWP).

4 MOMENTS OF EXCESS

Making sense, making judgements
and the passion of caring

If the job of a news service was to tell what was happening at any given moment, then the job of current affairs was to help us understand what was happening. They had to try to do that by reporting on situations which persisted over weeks, months and years, and which lay behind and gave rise to events that daily made the headlines. Current affairs has a duty to explain the background for what is going on (Jeremy Isaacs, quoted in Paulu 1981:211).

This Week reporter Peter Taylor put this same point very clearly in a letter to the public relations officer of the British army, when seeking permission to make a programme. The television audience, he wrote,

are now punch drunk with the nightly horrors they see on the news. There is no chance for analysis on these news bulletins, and no possibility to connect all these events in one piece to make sense of them. This is where we hope we can help and inform.

This rational aspiration to help and inform, to make connections and explain the background, is grounded in what the academic Barrie Gunter described as the 'moral disposition towards reporting' which goes along with the legal requirement for neutrality and balance on UK television (Gunter 1997:5). It places a great responsibility on the shoulders of the journalists and the produc-

tion team. 'The audience rely on us to exercise our editorial judgement,' said David Elstein, 'otherwise they wouldn't know what to
make of what's coming off the set' (Rosenthal 1981:123).

But a moral disposition may take several forms, and exercising
editorial judgement inevitably involves selection and interpretation. It rarely produces the sort of knee-jerk 'objectivity' that gives
equal weight to opposing points of view. For Jonathan Dimbleby,
'making a political judgement was a legitimate part of reporting'
(to PH), and at least one reviewer agreed. A programme which is
'scared of appearing to favour one side or another ... makes for
unhelpful as well as dull current affairs'. But Peter Black went on
to point out that 'this technique is more or less obligatory under
the Television Act' (*Daily Mail* 12.3.70). *This Week* was prepared to
push at the limits of the Act, especially under David Elstein, who
declared,

> I have never subscribed to the myth of objectivity in journalism
> or in television current affairs. I've always believed in committed
> programmes. That doesn't mean that people have to be overtly
> socialist or fascist or whatever it might be. It's just that the reporter,
> the interviewers, ought to have commitment. It can be the scan-
> dal of a cover up ... it can be the passion of caring about a subject'
> (Rosenthal 1981:121).

The ITA themselves were much exercised over the issue. Jeremy
Potter pointed to the 'acute problem' of programmes that follow the
One Pair of Eyes principle like the *This Week* made by Clive Jenkins
in North Vietnam. In fact the BBC's *One Pair of Eyes*, in which
reporters were open about their personal responses to a topic,
was a clear recognition of the limits of current affairs balance. But
personal journalism could easily become campaigning journalism, and the IBA made it clear that current affairs series were not
expected to produce either. 'Authored' programmes should not
appear in regular current affairs slots (Potter 1989:117–19).

While the 'passion of caring about a subject' was balanced
against the cool, rationalist drive to explain what lay behind
and gave rise to the headlines, current affairs continued to be
drawn towards documentary forms and approaches. Programme
makers were excited by the freedom of the documentary structure, the ability of documentary to construct a moving 'story'
around individuals and their experience, and by the power of the
image. Programmes on social and domestic topics such as 'All

Our Miss Steadmans' on an 83-year-old living in poverty (1970),
and on overseas topics, such as 'Viva La Causa' on a strike in California and its charismatic leader (1969), had strong visual impact
and a personal appeal. But influential voices within the television
industry itself were critical of both tendencies. *This Week* was to
be attacked on the one hand by those who argued that, in allowing the journalists to follow their personal preoccupations, the
series was becoming too committed and too serious, neglecting
its wider audience; and on the other by those who claimed that it
was not serious enough, and that documentary values were pushing out sober journalistic ones. Just as in the 1950s frivolity had
seemed an intrinsic part of the television medium, so these new
accusations of excess also arose from the nature of the medium
– journalism that was (too) persistent and (too) personal, and an
(over) reliance on the visual.

'The Unknown Famine'

When Jonathan Dimbleby joined *This Week* at the age of 27 in
January 1972, he was already interested in development issues,
but described his wariness in promoting them,

> if you pushed too hard [you] could very rapidly make people say
> 'Oh, he's just got an obsession'. I was very careful, therefore, to clothe
> my development curiosity within a much more traditional frame-
> work of 'here are major political issues at stake; here is a great drama
> taking place' (Harrison and Palmer 1986:44).

His very first report was from Rhodesia and about the work of
the Pearce Commission, which was attempting to broker a settlement in that country.

In June 1973, following up a brief newspaper report, he
persuaded Producer John Edwards to allow him to go to Senegal
to make a programme on the drought in the Sahel region
(28.6.73). The powerful images of dying animals and the caked
and fissured earth helped win an award for Ray Sieman's camera
work. Responses to that programme led him to Ethiopia and 'The
Unknown Famine'.

'The Unknown Famine' (18.10.73), directed by Ian Stuttard,
became the most acclaimed *This Week* of the decade, and it encapsulated all those qualities which could become suspect – a heavy
reliance on the visual, a deep emotional impact and the visibility

of a reporter advocating a cause. It opens with one of the most memorable sequences in current affairs television. Following a reminder of the earlier report on drought, a slow, relentless tracking shot moves along a queue of people squatting on both sides of a cracked and dusty path. Using a wide angle that includes both sides of the path, the camera takes the viewer between the rows, which are sometimes up to three or four deep. The waiting people are sparsely dressed in rags which have become the same light brown colour as the surrounding dust. Someone pulls a baby out of the way of the camera, someone flicks away a fly, but apart from that they are eerily silent and still. Whenever the queue seems about to end, another cluster of patient, painfully thin people comes into view and the shot moves inexorably on, lasting a full 2 minutes 25 seconds. Ray Sieman had simply walked between the long lines of exhausted men, women and children, his camera held low.

The commentary accompanying the shot is sparse. There are no words for 15 seconds – a long time in television terms. Then the first sentences, 'This is a queue for food. These people are Ethiopian peasants. Once they had cattle, land and houses. They sold them all to buy food. Now they have only their rags. They're destitute,' are followed by another pause. This is how the rest of the commentary goes:

> Here they receive two meals a day. The food: two handfuls of boiled wheat in the morning and a piece of bread in the afternoon. It keeps them from death, no more.

Seven seconds' pause.

> Last year these people were strong, fit and active. They had known hardship, of course. They had suffered several years of drought. But a year ago, when the rains failed utterly, their crops failed too. This spring the rains failed again. By April this year they were starving. They dragged themselves exhausted into the towns, many of them dying on the way. They have been like this now, surviving not living, for six months.

Six seconds' pause.

> There has not been enough food for the last six months. In Wollo alone at least 60,000 and possibly more than 100,000 have died from the famine.

Ten seconds' silence. The shot dissolves to the next.

The words provide a re-contexting of the image. The visual dynamism of the moving shot – which multiplies and depersonalizes tragic bodies, one after the other – is matched by another verbal dynamic which directs our attention to the invisible history of the people we are shown. We are invited to revise our initial impression, to see a process rather than a state. These people were 'strong, fit and active', but circumstances have brought them to this condition. They are *not* examples of timeless suffering.

The film had a massive press coverage and huge repercussions. Headlines demanded 'Let's *do* something!' and by Christmas it was estimated that £1.5 million had been raised in aid to Ethiopia. Jonathan Dimbleby has written, spoken and been interviewed about the programme many times (e.g. Harrison and Palmer 1986). He has frequently pointed out that although he knew of the ongoing political situation which helped to turn the effects of drought into a disastrous famine, he decided not to refer to it, as it would have distracted from the main message about the desperate situation in which the people found themselves.

The film caused a deep sense of shock within Ethiopia itself, since the government had covered up the seriousness of the situation. The terrible images were repeatedly shown on local television and at anti-government rallies, and were re-edited to make a new film, 'The Hidden Hunger', in which the shots of starving people were interspersed with shots of extravagance and ostentation amongst the rich and powerful, including a wedding cake flown in from London at the cost of £1,250. The image of starvation, used in this very different context, became a political weapon and was instrumental in bringing to an end the repressive rule of the Emperor Haile Selassie (Harrison and Palmer 1986:61–2; Dimbleby in the *Independent* 8.12.98).

Contamination: an unhappy marriage and a bastard genre

The seductive drift towards documentary, partisanship and personal reporting provoked criticisms from influential voices. Two years after 'The Unknown Famine', in a series of celebrated articles in *The Times*, John Birt, at the time Head of Current Affairs at London Weekend Television (LWT), together with economics journalist Peter Jay attacked current affairs programmes for their 'bias against understanding'. They do not give specific examples, but the phrase was to become infamous, as was the authors' recommended alternative, the 'mission to explain'. The arguments were to have a marked influence on the history of current affairs, as Birt and Jay put their principles into practice with their own austere LWT series *Weekend World* (1972–88), and then at the BBC when Birt became first deputy, then Director General, aiming to 'take over the journalism' and issuing rigid guidelines to current affairs programme makers (Lindley 2002:321–2; Tracey 1983).

Less often remembered than their criticisms are the reasons they gave. The 'bias against understanding', claimed Birt and Jay, was a consequence of a 'bastard' genre, born of an 'unhappy marriage between newspapers and film'. For them it was the film ethos that was to blame, 'contaminating … not only the choice and treatment of the stories, but also those members of the team on whom the directors rely for their journalistic input – the researchers and reporters'. Birt and Jay describe current affairs 'films' – pejoratively – as 'polished and ambitious', in which 'film imperatives override journalistic concepts' and where 'the aim is to make a film not to produce a report' (*The Times* 30.9.75). This leads current affairs to focus on the emotive areas of crisis, outrage and disaster. 'A constant emphasis is placed on society's sores by television feature journalists with little or no attempt to seek the root causes or discuss the ways by which the sore may be removed' (*The Times* 28.2.75).

This warning against the 'contamination' of the journalistic enterprise from the high-principled field of documentary, as opposed to populist frivolity, nevertheless contains the familiar suspicion of the contaminating power of the medium itself. It implies that the visual nature of television may hinder the verbal attempt to explain, and that an emotional concentration on 'society's sores' always discourages a cool attempt to account for those sores. Such concerns echoed the practical disputes that have taken place on many a current affairs location shoot. 'If a director insists on a beautiful shot … an argument may start up for the 100th time about truth values versus entertainment values,' Bryan Magee had written. The reporter wants to 'get the proportions right, to show truthfully how various elements in a situation are related to each other', whereas 'most other people connected with the programme [want] to highlight what is striking or unexpected or entertaining'. His example was that dull homosexuals in suits are more representative than the dyed hair and leather that make exciting television (Magee 1966:79).

The implication that if visual values are allowed to predominate then the core values of journalism may be lost, echoes a long-standing antipathy to the visual amongst intellectuals. Philosopher W.J.T. Mitchell begins an influential book by admitting that his 'intention of producing a valid theory of images became a book about the *fear* of images' (Mitchell 1986:3). Even the first Director of Television at the BBC, Cecil McGivern, had mistrusted 'the glittering, empty showbiz formula that appealed only to the eye' (Black 1972:17). A similar antipathy can be detected in the everyday language of television professionals, for whom visual elements can become 'talking heads' or 'moving wallpaper'. Yet, despite a long history of suspicions – or, perhaps, in a strange way borne up by those suspicions – the creative energy of television journalism has lain precisely in the tension it brings into play between the pressures of the visual and the imperatives of the verbal – a tension that is clearly illustrated in the opening sequence of 'The Unknown Famine'. Television journalism gains its particular strengths from the interplay between the flow of images of varying power and intensity, and the construction of verbal sense which plays against that imagery (Holland 2001b). Jeremy Isaacs described it succinctly as 'a fusion of film-making skills and journalistic flair'.

Yet, as this book demonstrates, antipathies, including a fear of the visual, have connected a network of ideas and attitudes which, over the history of current affairs, have been thought to threaten the integrity of the genre. As well as frivolity and emotion, they include 'tabloidization', feminization, unreliability and a 'displaced hostility to those who participate in and enjoy mass culture' (Mirzoeff 1999:10–11). As we have seen, such fears and suspicions have had real effects and have brought about major changes in programme policy and shifts in the ways in which programmes are produced and in their approach to their audience.

An aside on imagery

While recognizing the potent interplay between word and image, it is important not to dismiss too easily arguments such as those made by Birt and Jay. Some of their doubts and worries about the visual, and particularly its emotive qualities, can be shown to be justified. After all, Jonathan Dimbleby made it clear that

he deliberately ignored the politics behind the Ethiopian famine
so as not to reduce his programme's impact. The overwhelming
strength of such imagery means that however meticulously words
are matched to pictures, several things may happen. First, when
the completed film is shown, the powerful impression given by
the visuals may overwhelm that of the words. Viewers may forget
that they are also listeners and simply ignore what is being said.
Secondly, at a purely material level, the image may easily be separated from its sound. Shots such as the opening track from 'The
Unknown Famine' have been frequently re-used in other films,
for other purposes and in different contexts. Thirdly, the image
will almost certainly remind viewers of and refer them to similar images with which they are familiar, and which help them
to interpret – or possibly misinterpret – this one. They certainly
influence its meaning. Finally, as the image gains currency, viewers and critics may specifically reject any verbal information as
distracting, and even regret that it spoils the emotional impact.
If the image of a starving child outrages, the sense of outrage
may, in a perverse way, be relished for itself. Viewers may take
pleasure in being stirred to action and be unwilling to debate
the complex whys and wherefores, or to question whether that
action is appropriate. The emotional reaction may indeed obliter-
ate the rational one. Viewers may not want their emotion to be
diluted by qualifications, explanations or doubts. Newspaper
coverage of 'The Unknown Famine' demonstrated something of
this response. (The writer Alex de Waal even argued that a closer
knowledge of the situation would have shown that the rush to
give aid was actually counter-productive (de Waal 1989).)

'The Unknown Famine' appeared at a time when images of
destitution in the Third World, and particularly in Africa, were
becoming widely available – through photo-journalism in the
recently launched Sunday colour supplements, and through fundraising campaigns by the aid agencies. Even though the famine
in Ethiopia was (more or less) unknown in the West, a framework for making sense of its imagery was already set. Pictures of
starving children, desperate mothers, and people who are nothing more than a bag of skin and bones in an arid landscape were
already reflected back and forth across the media. 'The Unknown
Famine' contributed to this set of images. Stills from the film
appeared in newspapers, and sequences were extensively used in
educational programmes as well as in programmes which dealt

with the history of Ethiopia and of current affairs journalism. By the 1980s, photographers and commentators, as well as many within the aid agencies, were regretting the cumulative effects of such imagery and arguing that it created the impression of an Africa filled only with starving and incompetent people with no history, culture or political organization (e.g. *Ten*:8, No. 23, 1986). The General Assembly of European NGOs eventually adopted a new code of conduct on images, 'portraying poverty and dependence as the norm is not accurate … [those who are pictured] risk "exploitation by camera" if their identity or opinions are excluded in the promotion of development issues' (Benthall 1993:182–5; Holland 2004:148–59).

In the early 1970s Jonathan Dimbleby had been caught up in the horror of the famine and thought, 'if I could report the reality of what I had seen, something would happen'. (He also admitted to contradictory reactions, including pride because he was aware of the huge impact the programme would make (*An Ethiopian Journey*, ITV 1998).) Later he came to question the effectiveness of a television report. 'There is something faintly absurd about young men and women trailing around the globe in what we have now come to call disaster tourism' (talk 1995). The dilemma was – and remains – how it is possible to report disasters and distress in the face of what sociologist Stanley Cohen has described as 'states of denial', and the constant recuperation of the imagery into stereotype, tradition and aesthetics (Cohen 2001).

The Middle East

Although many journalists on *This Week* had special interests, such as Jonathan Dimbleby's concern with development issues, they were not employed as specialists but were expected to turn their hand to any of the topics in the current affairs spectrum. This was slightly at odds with the expressed aim 'to explain the background for what is going on', and to 'report on situations which persisted over weeks, months and years', since each of the complex situations that flared into open warfare or major crisis carried their own body of detailed political and historical knowledge, as well as more pragmatic up-to-date information and lists of essential contacts. The Middle East, with its interlocking conflicts, was one example of an area of great sensitivity and labyrinthine complexity. Robert Fisk, who reported for *The Times* from Beirut for 13 years from 1975 and whose understanding of situations which persisted over the years was unrivalled, has pointed out the danger of over-simplification, to which, he wrote, 'television journalism, with its dependence on the image, its subordination of words to pictures, contributed' (Fisk 1990:430).

On *This Week*, David Elstein was a Middle East specialist. He later wrote to a viewer who had doubted his qualifications,

> I have studied the politics of Israel and the Middle East for 15 years. I have a double first in history and I have specialised in the period covering the British Mandate in Palestine. I've been to Israel many times. I was the first television journalist to enter East Jerusalem in the 67 war. I was the first television journalist to film on the Golan Heights in the 73 war. I may be stupid but I'm not ignorant.

In 1968 Elstein, then aged 23, had been due to join the series as a director after working at the BBC, but, as Thames took over, he was held up because the ACTT were ensuring that existing Rediffusion and ABC staff were redeployed first. In between jobs the ACTT asked him to help film a picket outside Television House – 'including filming my new Producer, Phillip Whitehead, crossing the picket line!' (to PH). In 1969 he was in Israel with reporter Llew Gardner, who had himself reported many times from the region.

The politics of the Middle East, and Israel in particular, drew on deep emotions, collective mythologies and long-standing antagonisms. In 1948 the foundation of a Jewish state in Palestine – the territory which Britain was controlling under a League of Nations Mandate – had recognized the horrors suffered by the Jewish populations of Europe, but appeared to the Arab world as a consolidation of Western power in their region. Thousands of Palestinians had been displaced by the incomers, many of them accommodated in refugee camps in the neighbouring territories. Since 1948, conflict between Israel and its neighbours had alternated between major wars and low-level skirmishes. In June 1967, in what became known as the Six-Day War (reported by Elstein for *Panorama*) Israel extended its borders by capturing the Gaza Strip and part of the Sinai peninsula from Egypt, part of the Golan Heights from Syria, and the West Bank of the Jordan River from Jordan. In 1969 Elstein and Gardner were reporting on the Israeli announcement that it would keep most of these captured territories (16.1.69). Producer Phillip Whitehead had telexed them to 'onpush swiftest' as *Panorama* was researching the same topic. In the event the BBC scooped *This Week* with an interview with Israeli General Moshe Dayan.

Although David Elstein was later to describe the Palestinian cause as one where 'the left has a lot of right on its side', the team was aware of the need to tread a delicate line between prejudices – dramatically reflected in the huge post-bags they received. To one particularly forceful writer Phillip Whitehead pointed out that it was the programme's duty to consider all sides. 'Letters such as yours which simply refuse to consider that it is a complex question are no help at all. It distressed me very much to read it.'

This Week broadcast a total of 22 editions on the Middle East between 1968 and 1978.

In those last years of the 1960s, a new generation of Palestinian exiles was becoming more bitter and their actions more extreme. As guerrilla groups began to stage aeroplane hijacks and terrorist attacks, *This Week* researcher Martin Short set up an interview with 'a heroine of the revolution ... an entirely new phenomenon in Islamic womanhood', hijacker Leila Khaled. (With hindsight it is surprising that there was, apparently, no question about the legitimacy of interviewing a 'terrorist'.) In the autumn of 1969 Short spent six weeks in Lebanon, where the increasingly militant Palestinian presence and the indiscriminate Israeli retaliation (including bombing Beirut airport) was exacerbating a situation in which rival interest groups were already close to civil war. However, his telex reflected the sort of pressures that could lead to the over-simplification later criticized by Robert Fisk,

> It seems quite out of proportion that what is happening here should be such front page treatment in London. Anyone would think that some people wish chaos would ensue and mean to talk in such a way as to create it. To us this is quite unethical conduct on the part of pressmen ... even [if] other crews have to justify their presence here by partly exaggerating action. A few tanks and shells mean nothing, especially when landing in an empty field.

Phillip Whitehead replied, 'No wish to create mythical situation but accurately report situation as you find it with reference to 1. dilemma of Lebanese political leaders who we will interview, and 2. ambitions and aims of leaders of Arab struggle against Israeli expansion.' He thought that film of militant Palestinians training in the refugee camps would be an essential component, so Short

suggested that half of the team should go to Syria to meet them.
The ACTT would not allow the crew to split, so reporter Robert
Kee and director Udi Eichler left him to hold the fort in Beirut. He
was desperate that they would not get back in time for the crucial
interview. In the event, they made it, and 'Lebanon, The Road to
War' (13.11.69) was completed.

The film was in colour and shows a Westernized Beirut with
elegant streets and cosmopolitan centres. But the restaurants are
empty, and Leila Khaled explains that the hijacking exploits were
planned to discourage tourism. Kee points to the way the world's
press had exaggerated the fighting, and to prove it travels by taxi
from one side of the divided city to the other. But 'The West is
making a Vietnam of the area, with Israel as Saigon.' The refugee camps have become militant camps as young Palestinians do
military training.

In September 1970 the Palestinians were driven out of Jordan
and consolidated their strength in Lebanon. By 1973, as the rival
factions began open warfare, Jonathan Dimbleby made his first
programme on the Middle East. He was convinced of the need for
progressive socialist movements around the world and argued
that 'the security of the Palestinian revolution' was at odds with
Lebanese sovereignty. He outlines the history of the refugees,
which he was to re-tell many times. 'Lebanon: The Last Refuge'
(17.5.73) begins with an air fight over Beirut as Arab kills Arab
and the Lebanese army attacks Palestinian commando units.

Later that year, as he was filming in Ethiopia, Egypt and Syria
attacked Israel, aiming to win back the land occupied in 1967. It
was Yom Kippur, one of the holiest days on the Jewish calendar.
In Addis Ababa a delay was announced as Dimbleby boarded
the plane. Knowing the Ethiopian government would be deeply
unhappy about his material, he had concealed the film cans in his
hand luggage for the flight back to London. At first he was sure
he had been detected, but the delay was due to the Yom Kippur
War. The USA backed Israel, and in protest the Middle East oil
states imposed an embargo and raised their prices, overturning
the normal negotiated system. Unlike the Suez crisis in the 1950s,
This Week did not respond with jokes about petrol rationing.

David Elstein became *This Week* Producer in 1974, and the
series continued to monitor the escalating conflict in Lebanon.
With its warring clans, rival religions and interference from the
US, Israel and Syria, even Robert Fisk later wrote 'how little we

had understood in 1976' (Fisk 1990:50). In 'The Agony of Lebanon' (22.4.76), made when the civil war was at its height, camera
Teddy Adcock and sound Eric Brazier get frighteningly close to
the skirmishes in the Beirut streets, and follow the Palestinian
militia as they ride shotgun through the deserted quarters. The
film does not flinch from the brutality and the carnage of the
conflict. Unidentified corpses dumped after an attack on a shanty
town are filmed in all their horrifying detail, defying the taboo
on showing the dead on television.

In his introduction Jonathan Dimbleby reports on the armed
militias of 'at least six groups'. Even so he describes the conflict
as a clash of class rather than of religion. For him the right-wing
Christian factions represented the wealthy Lebanese, opposing the refugee Palestinians and the mainly Muslim poor. 'The
society created the slums and ignored their poverty. ... This is a
war between right and left, rich against poor, a war about class.'
Reviewer Chris Dunkley wrote of 'the personal opinion of the
reporter and how compassion is used to enable it' (*Financial Times*
28.4.76). Dimbleby was later to make a television series and to
write a book on the plight of the dispossessed Palestinians.

The war was temporarily settled as the Syrian army invaded,
backing the right-wing Christian militia. 'Lebanon, The Final
Solution' (14.10.76) took up the story and included equally horrific
images. It was the Syrians who seemed ready to impose the final
solution. They destroyed a refugee camp where 60,000 people had
lived. The skulls and bodies of 3,000 casualties were left on show
for six weeks. Dimbleby points to support for Syria from Israel
and the USA. 'The battle in Lebanon is really a Palestinian fight
for a stake in the Middle East.' Neville Clarke, senior programmes
officer at the IBA, passed on a complaint from a viewer disputing
the claim that Israel was supplying tanks, guns and training to
the right-wing Christian guerrillas. Elstein replied that Dimbleby
and the crew had seen the equipment, had been told about it
by the Christian leadership, and that it had been reported elsewhere.

Some of the fattest files of letters that poured into the *This Week*
office, and the greatest expressions of outrage, were reserved for
programmes about the Middle East, particularly if they implied
any criticism at all of the Israeli position. Many viewers criticized
Jonathan Dimbleby's 'total lack of objectivity ... anti-Israeli lies',
'Mr Dimbleby's father would have turned in his grave', as well

as Elstein's role, 'As a Jew I implore you now that we are such a small minority in this country, use any influence in your power you may have to *help* Israel in the future.' And they could get personal: 'Are you the David Elstein who went to school with my children? ... They, like all citizens of Israel, are aware that at the moment it seems fashionable to "beat the Jew".'

Elstein replied to all the letters; there were replies to his replies, and he engaged them with some relish. To one persistent writer he said, 'I enclose a transcript in case you would like to write to me again in an attempt to persuade me.' He makes it clear that 'we will be making a programme from the Israeli point of view' and adds, 'I can assure you we do not make programmes about the Middle East to improve our ratings. For some reason I cannot fathom our audience seem less fascinated by the problems of the Middle East than is my production team.'

Several taboos had been broached in the Middle East coverage. Speaking to terrorists, showing dead bodies and expressing partisan views – all had seemed justified by the extremity of the events reported on.

Downie and Dimbleby

Jonathan Dimbleby argued that his first programmes about famine in Africa helped to open up long-term development as an issue. Rather than waiting for dramatic events, 'people could now go to other areas of the world and make a film about the predicament of this or that place' (Harrison and Palmer 1986:63). In the words of Jeremy Isaacs it was now more possible to report 'on situations which persisted over weeks, months and years, and which lay behind and gave rise to events that daily made the headlines'.

Dimbleby made five more films about Ethiopia before being banned from that country by Colonel Mengistu who had replaced Emperor Haile Selassie. At first he made no secret of his admiration for what he saw as a socialist revolution. A dramatic scene in 'Revolution is Declared' (31.7.75) shows tribesmen galloping in from the countryside with streaming banners and all the euphoria of a medieval pageant. 'I naively thought here was something that might work,' he said later.

But when he travelled to Asmara, capital of the disputed province of Eritrea, which had been viciously attacked by Ethiopian forces, he linked the continuing shortages with the long-term civil war which Ethiopia continued to wage. The team had a heavy Ethiopian government escort and there was no way to contact the Eritrean resistance ('War and Famine' 7.8.75). However *This Week*'s next programme on the region penetrated deep into rebel territory. At considerable risk to their own safety, journalist Gwynne Roberts and camera Nicholas Downie filmed independently in Eritrea for three months. They offered *This Week* their film, 'The Savage War', which revealed deserted villages, refugees living in caves and the Eritrean Liberation Front training guerrillas, including women and young boys. Despite the rarity of such footage, the ACTT were dubious about using the work of a freelance cameraman. David Elstein, now playing two roles as Producer of *This Week* and union activist, pointed out that the enterprise was too hazardous for an ACTT crew. As a compromise the footage was incorporated into 'War in Ethiopia', introduced by Jonathan Dimbleby (1.4.76). It was the first of several remarkable reports by Nick Downie from the front line of war zones, including the Western Sahara (21.4.77), Rhodesia (28.9.78) and Afghanistan (10.1.80), all of which won Royal Television Society awards.

As a self-sufficient freelancer Downie was prepared to share the risks with the subjects of his films. Indeed, he was often closer to the action than the fighters he was filming – so close that his collaborator and sound recordist, Richard Cecil, was shot dead as they filmed in Rhodesia ('Front Line Rhodesia' 28.9.78). He was himself a soldier, 'an ex-SAS man who had changed his rifle for a camera', whose knowledge of war and the dangers to which he was exposed was often superior to that of these untrained guerrillas. He described himself as a modern scientific soldier filming medieval wars.

Downie's work gave *This Week* an insight that was not possible for its regular teams. He spent many months with the people he was reporting on, and the results show the danger of trying to impose too much sense on the jumbled and dangerous confusion of low-level, long-running conflicts. His films show close-range killing in scrub, bush and desert. They include unblinking shots of dying fighters, blood oozing from impossible wounds, a head smeared on to the ground. In 'Front Line Rhodesia', Richard Cecil is briefly visible as he helps to carry a mortally wounded man to a truck only minutes before he himself is killed. There is a heart-stopping moment when a soldier points his gun at a rustle in the undergrowth, hesitates for a second, and a terrified woman emerges clutching a child by the hand. Downie's commentary speaks of the difficulty these fighters will have in re-adjusting after the brutality and violence of their experience, 'it is doubtful if they will ever adapt to the routine and comparative boredom' of everyday life (35 Years on the Front Line 7.5.91).

When publicity-minded Mike Townson took over the series in 1978, Nick Downie became a selling point. A photograph showed him bearded, resting his hand on his camera. 'He loathes war', ran the rather overblown publicity 'but understands the mud-splattered men who pull the trigger.' Despite the risks he took he had difficulty in making ends meet. Although he kept the rights to his material, he claimed that he regularly had to pawn his equipment to fund his next project. He blamed the closed shop and the 'cartel operated by ITV and the BBC' (Darlow 2004:200).

In Ethiopia, Jonathan Dimbleby documented the changed atmosphere and exposed the 'Red Terror' of 1977 and 1978 (23.2.78). Mengistu was now an autocratic ruler, whipping up hatred against neighbouring Somalia as well as Eritrea, while in the capital, Addis Ababa, 'a reign of terror rules'. 'Murder has become a common act, and there are summary executions.' A Mengistu supporter declares 'red terror is not assassination. It kills white terror.' The film ends with a graveyard. This was the film which brought Dimbleby into disrepute with his one-time friends in the Ethiopian government and he was banned from the country. 'I was accused of being an agent of Western imperialism' (to PH). He returned ten years later, after Mengistu's downfall, also for This Week, to make two programmes which, once more, concentrated on political as well as long-term development issues (4 and 11.2.88). (He was now a prominent television figure and much was made of his return. Some on the series criticized him for megalomania, as the programmes included the hiring of a helicopter – possibly an unnecessary expense.)

During the 1970s Dimbleby continued to be optimistic about what he saw as socialist change in many of the trouble spots he reported from. In 'Tanzania: The World is One' (3.3.77) he praised ten years of that country's co-operative experiment, despite Julius Nyerere's single-party rule. He went to Peru, Brazil and Bolivia, and made a number of reports on natural disasters around the world, including floods in Bangladesh (19.9.74), the cyclone that devastated parts of Andra Pradesh (12.1.78) and the earthquake in Guatemala (11.3.75). In these films, a close and moving observation of human misery is placed in the context of longer-term issues. From the human perspective, people are always named and interviewed respectfully, the disruption to their daily lives and the details of their living conditions are meticulously demonstrated. And the immediate disaster creates an opportunity to make longer-term points. 'When the earthquake happened in Guatemala and Jonathan Dimbleby went out there we consciously said, the story's not the earthquake, the story's Guatemala and what kind of society it is … and we'll never get another chance to talk to our audience about this place … so use this moment and use it well' (Elstein in Rosenthal 1981:120–1).

Dimbleby linked the underdevelopment of that country to its neglect, and hence the exceptional vulnerability of its buildings to natural disaster. 'These people need an earthquake in their minds to escape the misery of their lives,' he had said, pointing out that while the shanty towns were wrecked, the banks in the centre were unharmed. He was called to book by the IBA. 'It was because I had been tough on the Americans,' he told me.

Thames Television and life on *This Week*

In 1975 Thames Television appeared to be flourishing. It had studios at Euston and at Teddington, which were undergoing re-development. A subsidiary, Euston Films, had been set up in 1971 to make filmed dramas such as *The Sweeney*, and the company was proud of its commitment to serious programming. Two *This Week* specials, 'Five Long Years', on Northern Ireland (12.8.74), and 'The World's Worst Aircrash', an investigation into the DC10 disaster (19.2.75), had both been given additional time on the network at the expense of entertainment programmes. Current affairs took up 8 per cent of its 56 programme hours per week, and *This Week* itself was gaining a substantial audience. The BBC did not compete against it and it was regularly in the top 20 with 10 million viewers. Despite all this, Thames's Managing Director, Howard Thomas, was concerned about the company's situation. The 'exchequer levy' had been changed to a levy on gross advertising revenue, which meant that pouring funds into a critical success like *The World at War* was no longer feasible. (£500,000 had been committed for that series in 1971. Its final cost was £1,000,000.) Profits were not rising and Thomas described the year 1974/75 as a time of economic depression. The system of licence renewal through the IBA was also causing problems, as Thames's contract only ran to 1979 (the crucial date of 1976, targeted by the 76 Group, had been delayed), which meant that long-term planning and investment were problematic (*Thames Television Review 1974/5*). The Annan Committee was looking at the future of broadcasting, and, remembering the results of the Pilkington Committee and the ITA's 1967 review, it is hardly surprising that Thames was feeling insecure.

On *This Week*, a regular and predictable output, which viewers and production team alike could rely on, gave the series dependability. Its heroic moments and major conflicts made the headlines, but the weekly programme and the never-ending work of the support staff continued with regularity. David Elstein kept the Friday meetings going and ensured that the film editors attended 'to soften the intellectual backbiting that could go on'. (Llew Gardner, in particular, he said, could be very critical.) Having 'measured the strength of the ideas' in the morning, Elstein would see individual reporters and directors and take decisions on Friday afternoons. As had become the established pattern on *This Week*, longer-term projects (such as the two-part investigation into the mysterious disappearance of the Hull trawler, *The Gaul* (16 and 23.10.75) – for which associate producer Brian Haynes took a special course in planktonology – and an extended edition on the black market in Range Rovers, traded across Europe (13.6.78)) were balanced against quick reactions to immediate events and extensive political interviews at election times. Budgets did not change much over the 1970s, but a 1,000-mile restriction on travel remained in place. (Elstein pointed out that this meant everyone knew how far Rome was from London and so on.) As before, a longer overseas trip needed to cover its high cost by delivering at least two programmes.

Self-regarding journalists and politicized reporting

John Birt and Peter Jay had criticized current affairs for being too much like documentary and not political enough, but from a quite different perspective *This Week* was being criticized for being *too* political, dominated by the obsessions of its journalists and paying no attention to the interests of its audience. These were points made by Mike Townson, who was to edit *TVEye*, the series which replaced *This Week* in 1978. In Townson's opinion pursuing themes and structures, as opposed to responding to the events of the moment, led to reporting that was overly politicized. It was 'issue led', following the interests of the journalists, rather than 'story led' to engage the audience (to PH). Such criticisms grew sharper through the various crises that led to *This Week*'s abolition and its replacement by *TVEye*.

During the 1970s it had been generally accepted that, in David Elstein's words, the most effective current affairs programmes were made by 'the kind of people who are interested in investigating society, in challenging subjects, in asking is the status quo acceptable', and it was this determination to investigate and challenge that ruffled the feathers of those in power (Rosenthal 1981:122). There were inevitable accusations of left-wing bias, but the considered view of the IBA was that there was little justification for this. 'Rather it detected amongst the programme makers a fashionable middle-class guilt about social conditions, identified as "soft centred liberalism"' (Potter 1990:60). It was a tolerant judgement which echoed the consensus of the times. But the political mood was changing and confrontations between the Authority and the programme team became more abrasive as the 1970s progressed.

Ultimately, the work of two very different journalists helped to bring the series to breaking point, not because they neglected journalistic principles, but because they followed them with too great a dedication. Both Jonathan Dimbleby and Peter Taylor were criticized by the IBA for pushing their own agendas. As well as the somewhat safer overseas reports, Dimbleby had brought his critical style to the many programmes he made on poverty and disadvantage in Britain. These included 'Liverpool 8' (17.8.72) and 'Blackhill', which dealt with the slums of Glasgow (12.6.75). Once more, a humanitarian concern was an acceptable – and, indeed, an expected – element of the series, but when such UK-based topics drew overt *political* conclusions they appeared partisan and the critics were quick to pounce.

Early in 1977 the IBA Board instructed its Director of Television to write to the Director of Programmes at Thames 'to let him be in no doubt about the strength of feeling amongst members of the Authority about the intrusion of the personal views of the presenter/reporter Jonathan Dimbleby in *This Week* programmes' (Potter 1989:114). ('I was called up in front of my old headmaster,'

Dimbleby told me. Brian Young, Director General of the IBA, had been head of Dimbleby's old school, Charterhouse.) The specific occasion was a complaint from Conservative MP Ian Sproat about 'A Lady Wrote to Me ...', which dealt with social security abuses (20.1.77). Sproat was well known for his views on 'social security scroungers' and had been filmed making a speech in his Aberdeen constituency. He complained that his views had been distorted by selective editing, virtually calling him a liar, and the programme was generally 'an attempted hatchet job on myself'. 'The closing minutes of the programme were surely straight, personal editorializing by Mr Dimbleby in a way that should be totally unacceptable – whatever his views happen to be' (Potter 1989:114). Although the IBA did not accept that he had been deliberately misled, nor that his views had been distorted, it did accept that Dimbleby's closing remarks had been out of place. Those remarks were,

> Social security is not a fringe benefit. It was established out of common humanity to protect the deprived. The poor can't fight back. Can't remind us that their scroungers cost the state only nought point one six per cent of the Supplementary Benefit budget. Cannot remind us of the millions they don't claim, theirs by right. Cannot remind us either of another world, a world where money is manipulated, tax evaded and avoided, where expense accounts are indulged on friends and family, but charged to the company. Where there are bosses who pay their workers below the rate set by law. A world where many more millions of pounds are stolen from the state, but a world without rhetoric or slogans or scroungers. No wonder New Year's Eve is bleak in Salford.

Dimbleby himself commented that by pointing to heavier losses suffered by the treasury in tax dodging he had legitimately set allegations of social security scrounging into context. 'We thought, let's see how hurtful it feels if you are not a scrounger to be described as if you were.' The IBA demanded a balancing programme, 'and it kept coming up at meetings, "what's happening about the Sproat answer-back"', which never actually got made. Director of Programmes Jeremy Isaacs told Dimbleby to 'ease off', but David Elstein backed his reporter. 'I was delighted we did the programme and it brought a lot of comfort to people who are very downtrodden' (JI to VWP; Rosenthal 1981:122).

Peter Taylor was also criticized by the IBA, both for his campaigning programmes on smoking and health, and for following the Northern Ireland conflict with a persistence that became uncomfortable to successive governments set on secrecy and heavily influenced by their military and intelligence advisers. At one point it was suggested that *This Week* should 'use another reporter' (Curtis 1984:59).

Viewing the programmes on smoking and health is an uncomfortable experience, but they exude a tangible sense of freedom from artificial balance in dealing with such a generally accepted worthy cause. Taylor's cool, meticulous reporting was quite different from Dimbleby's impassioned and personal style. He nevertheless took a confident stance in the four programmes, driven, as he explains in his book, *Smoke Ring*, by his concern for his wife (herself a researcher on *This Week*) who had been a heavy smoker (Taylor 1984:xiii). 'Dying For a Fag' (3.5.75) became notorious for its extended sequence of clogged and cancerous lungs preserved in bins in a hospital lab ('Under here we have buckets of them. This is what the statistics mean'). 'Licence to Kill' (10.5.75) intercut a review of the tobacco industry and its advertising with a gruesome operation on a cancer patient. 'Ashes to Ashes' (11.9.75) followed four of the estimated 200,000 viewers who had declared they would give up smoking, and monitored the progress of Bill Orris, a lung cancer sufferer who died before the programme was completed.

Tobacco manufacturers refused to be represented in the programmes. The cameras were turned away from an Imperial Group shareholders' meeting, but Taylor had bought a £1 share and challenged the chairman on audio-tape before being escorted out. However, after much negotiation, Phillip Morris, manufacturers of Marlboro cigarettes, were persuaded to co-operate in a fourth programme. 'Death in the West' (9.9.76) compared the rugged outdoor image of the cowboys in the advertisements with the ill health of six generic 'cowboys' who had been heavy smokers. Their doctors stated that in their view, their patients' conditions had been caused by cigarette smoking. Phillip Morris reacted with fury, accused Taylor of deception, and sought an injunction against the programme – prompted by the news that *60 Minutes*, CBS's legendary current affairs programme, was keen to network the programme in the USA. Phillip Morris's disingenuous legal argument hinged on whether the company had granted use of their library material for more than one UK transmission. In an out-of-court settlement, Thames agreed never to show the programme again and to keep only one copy in the archives. Later an NBC affiliate in San Francisco (KRON Channel 4) took the risk. They screened 'Death in the West' in full, and then included extracts in a special on smoking (11.5 and 9.7.82). Researchers for that programme followed up Thames's original interviewees and found that five out of the six had died, and the sixth 'isn't in very good shape' (*Broadcast* 9.8.82). The programme had such an impact that a special 'Death in the West' curriculum was devised to be used by schools throughout the Bay area. Pirated copies were used as teaching aids by teachers and doctors across the USA and elsewhere, most notably Australia. 'Death in the West' became part of the global campaign against the tobacco industry.

In a rare glimpse of industry pressure on journalists, Lord Robens, President of Incorporated Society of British Advertisers, wrote to Howard Thomas, Thames's Managing Director, that 'people in industry … are affronted' at the way Dr Treasure, who had represented the advertising industry, was treated in 'Ashes to Ashes'. He also wrote to Lady Plowden, Chair of the IBA,

> Not only was the greater part of his argument removed, leaving disjointed and incomplete segments, but the other side had clearly been given advance notice of Dr Treasure's arguments without according the same right to Dr Treasure. … It is important that senior people in industry and commerce should be willing to appear in television and radio programmes to discuss, explain and sometimes defend the attitudes, decisions and policies of their companies. There has been a reluctance to do this which, has I believe, led to a widespread misunderstanding of the role of industry and of its position and responsibility in society.

The good days have gone?

The very qualities that most journalists on *This Week* valued were those that contributed to bringing the series to an end – or at least mutating it into *TVEye*. Jonathan Dimbleby and Peter Taylor were both in their different ways pushing at the possibilities of the genre. When Dimbleby reported on the earthquake in Guatemala and on social security 'scrounging' he had made challenging political judgements which had gone well beyond the more personal reactions he had expressed in 'The Unknown Famine'. Taylor's relentless probing in his programmes on smoking and health upset business interests. Even more seriously, he upset the government with his Northern Ireland reporting. *This Week*'s coverage of the province became highly embarrassing to the authorities, and Northern Ireland became the programme's breaking point – as it would be again with 'Death on the Rock' ten years later.

In August 1978 Thames's current affairs series was relaunched as *TVEye*, with Mike Townson in charge. Jeremy Isaacs left the company 'half resigning, half being pushed' (Bolton 1990:36). (Jonathan Dimbleby remembers a tearful farewell in the car park. Jeremy Isaacs said, 'Get out, dear boy, the good days have gone' (to PH).) David Elstein was in any case in trouble with the management, as he was actively campaigning against the fourth television channel being awarded to ITV (Darlow 2004:193). He was 'shunted to documentaries' before becoming an independent producer. Many of the *This Week* reporters and directors stayed on for only a brief period.

In the year of the Queen's 25th Jubilee, a threat to broadcasting the celebrations got Thames Television into the headlines. 'Queens' Big Day Blacked Out by the ITV Girls', cried the *Daily Mirror* (4.5.77). 'ITV will be unable to screen the Jubilee celebrations. Production Assistants and other members of the ACTT held an all-day meeting at Teddington Studios today.' On *This Week*, the edition on the Queen's Jubilee visit to Northern Ireland would cause even greater outrage.

It is worth looking at *This Week*'s coverage of Northern Ireland in some detail, partly because it includes some of the most remarkable programmes made by the series; partly to demonstrate the detail, consistency and thoroughness of the coverage, and to illustrate the daily problems – and dangers – faced by journalists and production teams who needed to steer a course between sharply divided factions; but perhaps most importantly because it strained to the utmost relations between investigative journalism, television regulation and the government itself in the reporting of a low-level, post-colonial conflict which was dangerously close to home.

Director Peter Tiffin and camera Teddy Adcock filming in Belfast
for 'The Soldiers', 1972. Courtesy FremantleMedia.

5 *THIS WEEK* AND NORTHERN IRELAND, PART 1: FIVE LONG YEARS

There's lots of deaths in Northern Ireland. A thousand deaths: Strabane, Belfast, everywhere. Everyone's suffering. But what for? It hasn't brought anyone anything.

Do you think that people who live in the rest of the United Kingdom, who don't live here, understand what a thousand deaths mean?

No, no. I don't really think they do. It's those who lost that really understand what a loss is to them. ... There's a lot more to it when you've lost someone of your own.

(Evelyn Bogle speaking to Peter Taylor in 'Remember Strabane' 11.4.74)

The Irish bog

Northern Ireland burst on to the current affairs agenda with the civil rights marches of 1968. Prior to that, the British public had received little or no information about the province, its violent history and the undemocratic nature of its partially independent regime. In 'Five Long Years', a *This Week* programme of 1974, Michael Stewart (Home Secretary 1965–66) described Northern Ireland in that period as 'a police state' which 'equipped the executive, the police and government with powers over the liberty of the individual, powers of arrest and detention that we should regard as intolerable over here, except in time of war' (12.8.74).

Northern Ireland was part of the United Kingdom but could be rejected as incomprehensibly different. Politicians and television executives alike had tended to share James Callaghan's view: 'The advice that came to me from all sides was on no account get sucked into the Irish bog' (Callaghan 1973:15).

The island of Ireland had been partitioned in 1921 after a guerrilla war against the British occupiers led by the Irish Republican Army (IRA). When the largely catholic south became independent, the northern statelet – six counties with a protestant majority who fiercely defended the union with Britain – gained a pro-union government based in Stormont Castle outside Belfast, and continued on the margins of the body politic of the United Kingdom. Usually referred to as Ulster (one of the ancient provinces of Ireland) it posed a challenge to the meaning of both British and Irish identities. After the shock of 1968, Northern Ireland proved the sticking point for consensus current affairs in the British media, bringing journalism to the limits of the sayable. It lost people their jobs and brought programmes to grief, including, on two occasions, *This Week*. As terror became a regular part of domestic British politics, Northern Ireland became the focus of the greatest government pressure on television journalism. It brought the most overt acts of censorship and the only example of a ban on a political party which prevented an elected MP from speaking on the airwaves.

In its first ten years, *This Week* had not neglected Ireland, but had taken it in its stride, one issue amongst many. The 1950s had seen some light-hearted items that poked uncritical amusement at the *Irishness* of the Irish, but issues of discrimination and civil rights in the North were hardly addressed, although some reporters, including Robert Kee, did their best to get the province on to the news agenda (Kee 1976). Violence inevitably draws media attention, and when the IRA launched a bombing campaign against the North in 1956, its former officer was interviewed on *This Week* (21.12.56). However, when Michael Ingrams planned to interview the current IRA chief of staff (albeit with his back to camera), there was a foretaste of the many confrontations with the authorities, as the ITA forbade the broadcast (*Daily Herald* 2.2.57). In 1962 the IRA renounced violence for political action and the issue faded away once more.

Most programmes about Northern Ireland were not transmitted in the province itself, as Ulster Television (UTV) had a 'natural anxiety about allowing certain programmes to be shown' and frequently exercised its right to opt out of networked programmes (*Irish Times* 24.11.71). UTV had been set up in 1959 as part of the ITV network, and was solidly run by Northern Irish protestants. It was owned by a group headed by the Earl of Antrim, whose extensive business interests included the Loyalist protestant paper the *Newsletter*. UTV's Managing Director was Brum Henderson, whose brother ran the paper. Effectively this meant a black-out of any independent or critical view – a situation that was tolerated by the Independent Television Authority. Looking back, it seems amazing that no investigative programme had seriously taken on the massive denial of civil and political rights which was the lot of catholics in the province. However, from 1968 the situation could no longer be hidden from the outside world and television itself became part of a struggle for propaganda advantage.

Northern Ireland and current affairs

As the crisis escalated, it posed a serious challenge to current affairs television, which was repeatedly forced to consider which topics could legitimately be brought into the public arena for discussion, and to ask who had the right to add their voice to that discussion and who might define its terms. At issue was the relation between broadcasters in a regulated public service system and the democratic state itself. After 1968, both the BBC and the ITA scrutinized reports from Northern Ireland more consistently and rigorously than any other topic, and the right to define the agenda became a matter of dispute between reporters in the field, programme editors and executives, the producing companies, the regulating authorities and successive governments. The BBC was at the centre of some spectacular rows, and the independent companies were frequently involved in open dispute with the ITA/IBA. At the heart of the disputes was the question of objectivity between the government and those whom it defined as its enemies – in this case, the IRA. Should broadcasters accept the definitions of the government of the day without question? Did journalists have a *right* to report the activities of violent oppositional groups? Did they have a *duty* to explain them to the public at large? Events in the province were shocking in an unprecedented way. Their raw violence, their closeness to home and the sense that this was the culmination of a history hardly recognized by the media put them in a class apart.

Much has been written about the way Northern Ireland has been reported, inevitably stressing the major confrontations and the biggest rows. There has been much trenchant criticism of censorship, bias and misrepresentation (Curtis 1984; Miller 1994). What I plan to do here is to supplement those accounts by highlighting some themes which emerged through *This Week's* coverage over the 1970s, and the ways in which these pushed at the limits of, and, in my view, ultimately strengthened, the current affairs genre. I want to include an account of the routine programmes that could take as much effort and careful work to set up as those that were subsequently seen as important. The themes I shall explore include: relations with the regulatory body and tensions between the journalists on the ground and executives and regulators; definitions of 'the enemy' and the legitimacy of broadcasting the views of 'the enemy' – specifically the IRA; the views of 'ordinary people' caught up in the conflict and how they could be heard; and finally the question of history and how immediate events could be interpreted within a longer historical context. As time went on, judgements made in earlier programmes were revisited and re-assessed, and the accumulation of programmes over the decade – most of them by the reporter Peter Taylor, who became a specialist in the area – demonstrated the strength of a secure, long-running television series with a regular team committed to a long-term view.

Writing in 1983, Philip Schlesinger and his co-authors surveyed a decade in which images and narratives of terrorism played a major role in the British media (Schlesinger et al 1983). They identified four underlying perspectives, which have themselves gained a new resonance as an apocalyptic fear of terrorism grips the early 2000s. The 'official' perspective on terrorism de-politicizes 'terrorist' acts, and tends to be held largely by the government and the forces of law and order – the army and police; the 'populist' perspective takes the 'war against terrorism' at its face value and insists that an armed reaction is legitimate. The 'oppositional' perspective is taken by those who support what are defined as 'terrorist' acts. It justifies the use of violence for political ends and denies the legitimacy of the democratic state. Finally, the 'alternative' perspective claims that the explanations offered by 'terrorists' should be listened to, if not accepted, and should be interpreted within their own context of understanding. This is the view that tends to be held by civil libertarians, liberal academics and many journalists. Discussing the interplay of television forms – news, current affairs, comedy and drama – within which these perspectives interweave, Schlesinger and his colleagues argue that the relatively 'open' form of current affairs allows programmes to explore alternative explanations that are not always acceptable to the authorities. Over the decade of the 1970s it was current affairs that distanced itself most from the 'official' position.

The Authority and the authorities

Over the summer of 1968, *This Week*'s young editor, Phillip White-head, was concerned with global events – from the uprising in Prague, to major wars from Biafra to Vietnam. Northern Ireland was one issue amongst many. However, in October, shocking images of peaceful civil rights demonstrators, including MP Gerry Fitt, ferociously attacked by baton-wielding police, were transmitted in news bulletins across Britain. Over the following months the situation in the province rapidly deteriorated, threatening the devolved government. For *This Week* John Morgan conducted an exclusive interview with Northern Ireland Prime Minister Terence O'Neill, as his relatively liberal policies were challenged from within the Unionist ranks (6.2.69).

From 1969 the ITA ruled that all programmes on the province had first to be checked with them. The Television Act of 1954 required 'due impartiality' on matters of public controversy and forbade the inclusion of anything 'likely to encourage or incite to crime or to lead to disorder or to be offensive to public feeling'. The Authority now interpreted this as a duty to view and assess a programme before it was completed. Chairman Lord Aylestone remarked that 'he who carried the can had the right to feel the weight of it' (Potter 1989:93). Programmes about Northern Ireland must also be approved by the Authority's resident officer in Northern Ireland and by the Managing Director of UTV, the redoubtable Brum Henderson, who was to remain in post until 1983. In what Anthony Smith described as a 'panic reaction' to the political crisis, UTV had decided to 'limit its reporting to hard news and not go out of its way to solicit comment'. The ITA was anxious that UTV sensitivities should be respected. It always scrutinized programmes with the Northern Ireland audience in

mind and cautioned ITN that the 'dividing line between information and incitement was difficult to draw' (Smith 1978:120).
Although it preferred to negotiate with the programme controllers to sort out any problems quietly behind the scenes, the aim
to reach a cosy consensus did not always work. In the early 1970s,
Granada Television and *World in Action* took the brunt of the critical scrutiny and were at the centre of some very public rows. The
Authority's relations with *This Week* and Thames deteriorated
over the decade.

In 1972 the devolved parliament in Northern Ireland was
abolished. The UK government set up its Northern Ireland Office
instead, and began to regard the media as part of its Northern
Ireland policy. Through the Northern Ireland Information Service, it provided briefings and produced its own propaganda
which it hoped would point journalists in what it saw as a positive direction (Miller 1993). The army, too, provided highly selective information – from time to time revealed as misinformation
– for journalists (Curtis 1984). *This Week*, like other news organizations, needed to maintain careful relations with these powerful institutions, as well as the Northern Ireland police force, the
Royal Ulster Constabulary (RUC). Essential as sources, their attitudes changed when they themselves became the subjects of a
report. As institutions with authority and as arms of the state,
they claimed the right to define their own terms and to shield
themselves from inconvenient probing.

In addition to this external sensitivity, it was necessary for
the Producer of *This Week* to discuss programmes on Northern
Ireland with programme controllers within Thames Television
itself. Northern Ireland was a topic for which the Managing
Director and sometimes the company Chairman took personal
responsibility, and reporters and directors were subject to what
seemed like endless interference. Jeremy Isaacs became Director
of Programmes in 1974 and was always supportive, but Howard
Thomas, Chairman from 1974, and others in management grew
increasingly nervous when the official line was questioned.

Two halves of the decade

The 'marching season' has always been the time of greatest
tension in Northern Ireland. The 12th of July commemorates the
Battle of the Boyne in 1690, when the protestant King William of

Orange (King Billy) defeated the catholic James II who had been deposed in England and was trying to gain a foothold in Ireland. The 12th of August commemorates the lifting of the siege of Londonderry, the walled city that had held out against James in 1689. Three centuries later, in their annual triumphalist marches, Loyalist organizations, headed by the Orange Lodges, continued to express their contempt for defeated catholics. In August 1969 catholics attacked a march in Derry, and protestant retaliation led to what became known as the 'Battle of the Bogside', when barricades went up to defend catholic areas and CS gas was used for the first time. In Belfast protestants burned hundreds of catholic homes. MP Gerry Fitt, of the mainly catholic Social Democratic and Labour Party (SDLP), phoned Home Secretary James Callaghan appealing for the British army to protect the catholic population. 'I remember Jim Callaghan saying, "Gerry, it may be an easy thing to get the British army into Northern Ireland, but it's going to be much more difficult to get it out"' ('Five Long Years'). The army arrived in August 1969 and the media followed.

There was a freshness about the programmes of the early 1970s in content as well as style. It seemed possible to put everyone on television, from paramilitaries to army sergeants, from bereaved relatives to politicians, as well as 'ordinary people' from all 'sides'. These programmes document events as they unfold, recording a sense of horror and disbelief that is difficult to recapture nearly 40 years later. The second half of the decade, from 1974 to the cancelling of *This Week* in 1978, was harder and more bitter. The IRA began a campaign of bombing on mainland Britain which brought public revulsion, especially after the killing of 26 uninvolved civilians in pubs in Guildford and Birmingham. Just as programme makers on *This Week* argued ever more forcefully that the explanation of contemporary events lay in the political history of Ireland, government policy, followed by most of the press, focused on the present moment and the unreasoning criminality of the brutal terrorists. The policy of the 1974 Labour government was to 'Ulsterize' the conflict, keeping the British army in the background, and to 'criminalize' those involved in terrorist acts, removing the cachet of 'political activist'. The public spotlight fell less on the communities and more on the government's measures and their consequences. The Prevention of Terrorism Act (1974) brought increased restrictions on the media, and the government felt able to put overt pressure on the IBA as well as the BBC.

Ordinary people

Reginald Maudling, visiting Northern Ireland when he became
Home Secretary in 1970, 'left feeling this was a very difficult
country where, on the whole, people were determined to disagree
with one another' ('Five Long Years'). Yet *This Week* programmes
returned again and again to the theme of common humanity,
searching beyond sectarian prejudice. Following 'What Was Lost,
What Was Won?' (21.8.69) the *Guardian* congratulated the series
for 'setting out to establish a new concept of journalism: that
good news is *real* news' (22.8.69). The ACTT had agreed to a crew
reduction and 'war zone' insurance for that first film made in the
unaccustomed circumstances of armed conflict on the streets
in the United Kingdom. Llew Gardner's commentary placed it
as 'the latest battle in a 300-year-old religious war'. Although he
set out to be even handed between catholics and protestants, the
programme implicitly took the position that was rapidly established across the British media, that both sides were to blame but
the IRA were the underlying culprits. Although catholics burnt
out of their homes deny they want revenge, Gardner responds,
'You say you are all innocent, but there is an IRA slogan on that
wall there.' It was only towards the end of the programme that it
became clear that most of the 400 homes destroyed had belonged
to catholics. Even so, the message from UTV was that the phone
calls were 'fast and furious' and the switchboard was jammed.
All but one of 50 calls thought that this type of programme did
nothing but inflame the passions of extremists on both sides and
that further disorder could result.

Yet many programmes illustrated the communality of death
and distress, including several directed by a young freelancer,
David Hart. 'Death in Belfast' was a slow, contemplative film
about three men who had died in the riots (2.7.70); in 'Belfast, No
Way Out' (2.4.70) catholics and protestants demonstrate together
when faced with eviction because of non-payment of rent. James
Henry and his wife, who is deaf and dumb, live by gas and candlelight; the roof of Mrs Ditty's house has collapsed – although she's
a mother of ten, she's not eligible for a council house. Her children play in the street and one was run over and killed. Later,
Peter Taylor and director David Gill filmed children from the
two communities on holiday together (21.9.72). The humanitarian
approach was not without its political implications, since it tacitly

reinforced a sense that agreement is human and natural, making disagreement seem the more puzzling and inexplicable. Stressing the incomprehensibility of the situation was to become part of the government line, and to suggest that violence has its root causes and its own rationale was seen as tantamount to advocating it. When programmes stressed the theme of common humanity, the links between the 'men of violence' and the communities in which they were rooted remained hard to discern.

The British army

As the British army took up its duties in Belfast, *This Week* made 'The Men in the Middle' (18.9.69), a remarkable piece of raw observation in the verité style. The situation seems visibly puzzling to soldiers whose unfamiliar job is to persuade the local population – mainly catholics – to take down their makeshift barricades and accept instead a 'peace line' erected by the army. The bemused Sandhurst accents of the officers contrast with the Northern Irish vowels of catholics and protestants at either end of Dover Street. There is a problem over No. 87. In the civil war of 1921 there had been a machine gun outside this house. Now the locals are in hot debate with the soldiers, who offer its resident access through a special 'one woman corridor'. Children play at being soldiers, clambering over the piled-up vehicles and barbed wire; protestant schoolboys offer reporter John Edwards copper, lead and brass looted from abandoned catholic houses. A colonel and a major reminisce about Aden and complain that they can't tell the difference between catholics and protestants. Eventually the barricades come down. 'The kid glove technique had worked,' concludes Edwards. 'In Northern Ireland the moderates are always being asked to stand up to be counted … but until that day arrives, the army will remain the only effective force for moderation.' Twenty-five years later, interviewed by Peter Taylor, the same corporal who had been earnestly trying to convince the locals, reflected on how 'pissed off' he had been feeling at the time (BBC2 7.8.94).

There was a natural affinity between journalists and soldiers. 'The media's identification with the troops was instant and total,' wrote *Guardian* correspondent Simon Winchester (1974:124). They shared a masculine camaraderie and both 'would moan about the ills of Ireland' (Curtis 1984:25). The soldiers in 'The Men in the

Middle' and in subsequent programmes such as 'The Soldiers' (21.12.72) are not portrayed as the local people saw them – sometimes as uniformed protectors, often as armed occupiers with the power to search, harass and intimidate – but as 'ordinary people' themselves, caught up in events they were unable to understand. They could best make sense of their experiences by comparing them with other colonial wars. At first they were the men in the middle, but it was not long before the ordinary soldiers in particular began to make sense of their situation by defining the IRA, and frequently the catholic population as a whole, as their enemy. In August 1970, troops conducted a ruthless house-to-house search for arms in catholic West Belfast. For local priest Canon Murphy, their conduct 'lost' the women of the community, many of whom had previously been working for peace. 'They were embittered, and God knows it would be very hard to blame them. In those little homes with their children and the gas coming in. They couldn't get out; they weren't allowed out, and if they stayed in, the gas still got them' ('Five Long Years'). The women protested with dustbin lids while protestants cheered on the house searches. It was 24 years before this action could be discussed critically on television. Interviewed by Peter Taylor in August 1994, soldiers frankly remember tearing the houses apart with no respect for feelings or property. One described ripping the tiles off a roof, then pausing to think – what right have I to destroy someone's property? (BBC2 7.8.94). Through such programmes, which are able to review events from many perspectives, history on television has acquired a complexity beyond the mere document or the eyewitness account. It has become layered with tellings and retellings, revealing the depths of conflicting viewpoints as well as adding new insights. A critical examination of the army's activities was both more difficult to conduct and more difficult to conceive of in 1970.

The enemy

The biggest dilemma faced by all current affairs programmes over the decade concerned the reporting of paramilitary organizations. The 1967 Criminal Law Act (Northern Ireland) had imposed a duty to give the police information likely to secure, or assist in securing, the apprehension of any person who had committed an arrestable offence (Potter 1990:207). The question of whether the IRA was a political organization whose violent tactics were the only means of expression open to them, or whether they were simply brutal individuals bent on violence for its own sake, was repeatedly asked. In 1969, despite the graffiti noticed by Llew Gardner, the IRA was considered a spent force. Its Official wing had even got rid of its weapons. However, a split in the organization was formalized in December 1969, and in 'IRA: Arms and the Men' (20.8.70) the leader of the breakaway Provisionals, John Kelly, described the situation. In their 'hour of need,' he said, when 400 houses were burnt in Belfast 'the people were left defenceless'. The IRA had precisely 12 weapons, mostly obsolete, and the graffiti that decorated the catholic communities taunted them with 'I Ran Away'. He and his associates had travelled the six counties in search of arms. 'As one man put it to me, two weeks before August 15th, had someone offered him a revolver he would have run ten miles from him. But after 15 August he lay in bed wondering where the man was who'd offered him the revolver.'

The interview with Kelly was broadcast in a pair of programmes on the paramilitary organizations, as serious rioting was taking place on the streets of Belfast and Derry. First Llew Gardner had reported on the militant Orangemen (23.7.70), then Peter Williams looked at the resurgence of the IRA and the fears that the Irish Republic would be persuaded to arm them (20.8.70). 'For the first time,' claimed the press release, 'the military leaders of the IRA speak out on television.' This was not quite true. *This Week*'s 1957 interview had, indeed, been banned, but in 1956 Norman MacKenzie had interviewed a former IRA officer. In 1970 the sight of refugees fleeing over the border, the shock of the outrages perpetrated against the catholic community and the legitimacy given by the possible involvement of the Irish government led to this extensive interview. Peter Williams asked John Kelly, 'Do you have any conscience about operations which may involve loss of life?' Kelly replied, 'This must be balanced against one's convictions and one's beliefs. ... It has been the tradition in Ireland that we achieve at least a partial independence by the use of physical force, physical violence.' The strength of community support for this view was indicated by the 5,000 people who were filmed following the coffin of veteran IRA man Jimmy Steele.

Reviewing the programme Peter Black spoke of the confusing effects of hearing from those one would rather dismiss as being beyond the reach of rational dialogue.

> One peculiar effect of TV news is that, although the public are better
> informed than any other generation has been since time began, the
> impression left by the stream of information is that all situations are
> too difficult and complex for the ordinary person to be able to do
> anything about ... to know more is to be confused more.

Rather than being *told* about John Kelly you must make up your
own mind from watching and hearing him for yourself. 'You had
to admit at least the probability that on the evidence shown, Kelly
... is not a villain in any of the ways with which the TV's fictions
have made us familiar. The shading of right into wrong and back
again must have left a deep sense of helplessness' (*Daily Mail*
21.8.70). That was a message the British government, the army
and the RUC were to take to heart as pressure to isolate the IRA
grew.

A turning point in the history of ITV

In the first half of 1971 the attentions of the *This Week* team, under
producer Ian Martin, were largely elsewhere – on the anniversary
of the My Lai massacre in Vietnam, on Rhodesia after UDI and
on the referendum on the Common Market. But events in Northern Ireland were dramatic. In February Gunner Robert Curtis
became the first British soldier to be killed in Ireland in 50 years,
and in July the army shot two men dead, claiming they were
armed. In August the government introduced internment without trial and 340 catholics and two protestants were detained.
The mainly catholic SDLP withdrew from the Stormont government and John Hume, its deputy leader, was interviewed by Llew
Gardner in the first *This Week* on the province for ten months
(26.8.71). Later Hume recalled, 'I have never experienced the feeling that existed in the streets of my own city at that time. The
sheer violent reaction of the people, the intense emotion against
the actions that had taken place that morning.' The demand to
join the IRA was such that the organization didn't have the facilities to handle the number of recruits that started to come in ('Five
Long Years'). Internment was also to bring about what Anthony
Smith described as 'a turning point in the history of Independent
Television' (Smith 1978:123).

Now that the situation could be convincingly described as
a conflict between the British army and terrorist insurgents, it

seemed not unreasonable for the government to ask the broad-casting organizations to set limits on their reporting. The BBC was at the forefront of the ensuing dispute. Leader writers in the right-wing press chorused that since there was a war on, the BBC must show itself to be on the side of the 'nation'. Jak in the *Evening Standard* produced a cartoon showing a television producer asking British troops, one of whom lay wounded, to expose themselves to fire once more for the benefit of the cameras (Curtis 1984:9). Tory backbenchers complained that the government was 'losing the propaganda war'. In November, Christopher Chataway, Minister of Posts and Telecommunications in the 1970 Conservative government, declared that broadcasters were not required to strike an even balance between IRA and the Stormont government, nor between the British army and the 'terrorists'. He reminded them that they exercise their editorial judgement within the context 'of the values and the objectives of the society they are there to serve', hence ensuring the 'double mechanism of continuing political pressure and routine internal self-censorship' (Schlesinger 1978:211–12). Home Secretary Reginald Maudling had a private word with both Lord Hill of the BBC and Lord Aylestone of the ITA. Hill reassured him that 'as between army and gunmen the BBC is not and cannot be impartial'. He was echoed by Aylestone: 'As far as I'm concerned Britain is at war with the IRA in Ulster and the IRA will get no more coverage than the Nazis would have in the last war' (Schlesinger et al 1983:122)

The BBC obediently set in place stringent guidelines that gave management an unprecedented degree of control over programming decisions. In consequence various programmes were curtailed or banned (Curtis 1984:151). Jonathan Dimbleby was at the time presenter of the BBC's *World This Weekend* and was due to move to *This Week* in January 1972. In December 1971 he wrote an unsigned article in the *New Statesman* detailing BBC restrictions – for example, reporters had been instructed to present all interviews with released internees 'as sceptically as possible' (31.12.71).

The ITA escaped much of the direct attack, but in Liz Curtis's words it 'panicked autonomously', becoming more stringent in its supervision. From September 1971 it began to discourage the practice of allowing UTV to opt out of programmes, since 'that was in some sense a public admission of failure' (Smith 1978:121).

This meant that all ITV programmes became subject to the tighter requirements of the Ulster company. And UTV remained endlessly touchy. Brum Henderson complained that the appearance of John Hume on a *This Week* programme was followed by 'a spate of telephone calls which were in the main both abusive and insulting' (11.11.71). When the ITA backed him up, Jeremy Isaacs wrote to the Director of Programmes, Brian Tesler,

> interference by the Authority in our editorial decisions as to what we should transmit when, is growing to such a ludicrous extent that it may be necessary to make a public stand against it. ... The fact is that those who make programmes – that is us – are the only people in this sort of situation who can judge what to put in them. It is not a job for bureaucrats. I shall be grateful for your support in saying so.

The ITA's interference was at first directed at Granada rather than Thames. *World in Action* had planned a programme on the pressures on the Republic of Ireland caused by the crisis in the North. 'South of the Border', due to be shown in November 1971, included speeches by IRA Chief of Staff Sean MacStiofain and Sinn Fein President Ruairi O'Bradaigh, balanced by southern Irish politicians Conor Cruise O'Brien, known for his strong opposition to the IRA, and Garret Fitzgerald, who said that the British army's tactics had contributed to the deteriorating situation in the North. Possibly upset by Fitzgerald as much as the IRA, Lord Aylestone claimed the programme was 'aiding and abetting the enemy' and it was not allowed to be shown (Potter 1990:209). There was speculation that the ban was at the instigation of Brum Henderson, and that the ITA had been 'got at' by government ministers (*Sunday Times* 7.11.71). Lord Aylestone had in fact been called to the Home Office 'where the Home Secretary informed him of the fears of some MPs about television coverage of events in Northern Ireland and expressed his own concern that television news teams were too aggressive in interviewing soldiers' (Potter 1990:209). There was much comment from the right-wing press on the fact that 'we' are at war so we must support 'our' soldiers uncritically. Yet many television journalists felt that reporting would not be properly impartial if they did not also give space to those the government had defined as 'the enemy'.

In what Anthony Smith described as the 'rumpus that ... was a turning point in the history of Independent Television', several hundred reporters and producers met at the Institute of Contemporary Arts in London and declared that 'we deplore the intensification of censorship ... and pledge ourselves to oppose it'. This angry response was part of an escalating critique expressed by radical academics and leftish publications. The organization Information on Ireland was launched and the journal *Index on Censorship* began publication. Writing in its second issue, Anthony Smith argued that broadcasting 'can only operate in that neutral way when the receiving society as a whole accepts a common set of standards' (Smith 1978:123, 106–7). In relation to Northern Ireland, those common standards simply did not exist.

The ITA issued a statement saying, 'there is no truth whatever in reports that the ITA has imposed a blanket ban on programmes about Ulster or is practising political censorship against views opposed to those of the British government' (Potter 1990:209). But in his *New Statesman* article Jonathan Dimbleby declared,

> The censorship and restrictions placed on reporters and editors make it practically impossible for them to ask the question 'why?' Why do the catholics now laugh openly when a British soldier is shot down and killed, when a year ago they would offer the army cups of tea? Why do the catholics refuse to condemn the bombings and the shootings? Why do they still succour the IRA? (31.12.71)

In this argumentative and difficult climate Dimbleby joined *This Week* and so did Peter Taylor from Thames Television's regional *Today* programme. Taylor had made two programmes for the series in the previous year when his interview with black activist Angela Davis in prison in the United States had been a worldwide scoop. (The interview took place behind a glass screen with Davis's face barely visible under her huge afro wig (4.11.71).) From January 1972 John Edwards took over as series producer, and Peter Taylor has described the sense of excitement and creative energy under his editorship. He 'ran the programme like he ran the cricket team'; it was 'a sort of roller coaster, when no one quite knew what was going to happen the following week' (to PH).

Bloody Sunday

Almost at once, events in Northern Ireland took a turn that was to shape the feelings of the catholic community for decades to come. On what became known as Bloody Sunday, 30 January 1972, 13 people were killed when a British army unit opened fire on an anti-internment march in Derry's catholic Bogside district. Eyewitnesses were there in abundance, including *This Week* researcher David Tereshchuk. That same afternoon John Edwards sent Peter Williams and the newly appointed Peter Taylor with directors Vanya Kewley – one of the very few women on the programme in the 1970s – and David Gill. It was Peter Taylor's second programme on the *This Week* staff. His first had been a moving report from the Yorkshire mining village of Armthorpe at the heart of the strike that was absorbing much domestic reporting at the time (20.1.72). In the Bogside the two crews filmed eyewitnesses, and Peter Williams became the only reporter to talk to the NCOs of the First Battalion Parachute Regiment, the soldiers who actually took part in the shooting. The teams, including camera Ian McFarlane and sound Brian Rendle, 'worked all hours of the day and night' (memo from Peter Taylor).

There were only four days before transmission the following Thursday (3.2.72). Processing and editing times were cut down to a minimum and the typists who transcribed the voice tapes worked through the night. However, in an unprecedented move, the government announced a judicial inquiry into the events to be conducted by Lord Chief Justice Widgery, and the Downing Street Press Office warned that anything that anticipated his findings could be interpreted as contempt. A solution was worked out between Jeremy Isaacs and David Glencross, the ITA's senior programme officer (who described it as 'the best kind of pre-transmission consultation'). They agreed to broadcast two ten-minute rolls of unedited film, linked by John Edwards in the studio. The clapper boards were left on the front of each roll to show that nothing had been added or omitted and no editorial slant was put on the material. In Glencross's opinion the programme 'was an original step forward in an area (i.e. of contempt) which is pretty well uncharted in television journalism'. Isaacs pointed out that such full consultation with the regulator was due to 'the very unusual nature of the programme' and not something they could always promise (letters: 7 and 9.2.72).

The two sequences consisted of Peter Taylor speaking to James Chapman, a Welsh ex-soldier whose flat in the Bogside overlooked the scene, and Peter Williams's interview with the NCOs. Grouped together in the sergeants' mess, the soldiers, obviously tense, speak of the danger they felt they were in and their impression that they saw men with guns. Several described a gun battle. 'We came under fire from at least five positions'; 'I fired three rounds at him and the man went down.' Another defended his unit with conviction, 'It's because they're so bloody professional in this unit that there's only 13, and every one of those 13 was a rebel. They either had a nail bomb or a weapon of some sort otherwise they wouldn't be up there dead.' The RSM had 'No regrets whatsoever'. Several spoke with bitterness, as the 47th soldier had been killed that night. 'We're here, we've got to take their bullets and because we hit back on the onslaught against us there's got to be an enquiry against us, the British soldiers.' Mr Chapman's appalled reaction was in striking contrast, 'I watched them shooting indiscriminately into the fleeing crowd of several thousand people.' *This Week*'s transcripts and film were made available to the Widgery Tribunal, whose report was widely regarded as a whitewash (Curtis 1984:49–51).

The programme had been simple, and mediation was reduced to the minimum, but the surrounding media climate was dominated by the accounts put out by the army in the aftermath of the shootings. The popular press in particular were only too willing to publicize loudly the claim that the soldiers were firing in response to an attack. But the memories of the event were to be re-explored in the media many times as the fifth, tenth, twentieth and thirtieth anniversaries of Bloody Sunday came round. In 1992 Peter Taylor himself literally went over the ground again in a programme for the BBC (*Inside Story* 28.1.92), and in 2002 the events were reconstructed in two major dramas, which drew on the news footage and eyewitness accounts of the time (ITV 20.1.02; C4 28.1.02). But the truth is still in dispute. Twenty-six years later, a new judicial inquiry was set up under Lord Saville which reviewed *This Week*'s material once more, including an unbroadcast interview with the commanding officer of the Provisional IRA's Derry Brigade, which remarkably had survived. (Called to give evidence to that inquiry, Taylor was pressured to reveal his sources under threat of subpoena, but felt that, even long after the event, his promise of confidentiality was sacrosanct.)

The reverberations of Bloody Sunday changed the mood in both Ireland and Britain. Northern Ireland catholics hardened behind the IRA; there was a renewed call on the mainland to withdraw British troops; the Provisionals gained many new recruits and launched a bombing campaign; and the MP John Laird, interviewed by Peter Williams, justified the rise of the ultra-Unionist Vanguard movement (23.3.72). That programme

kicked off with the Provisional IRA Chief of Staff, Sean MacStiofain, interviewed in Dublin, wearing a patch over one eye where
he had been injured by a parcel bomb. He reiterated the IRA's
three demands: the British government to withdraw troops and
recognize Irish people's right to self-determination; amnesty for
all 'political prisoners', 'not merely the internees'; and the abolition
of the Northern Ireland government at Stormont Castle. 'Things
are at an all-or-nothing stage.' The interview was given no pre-
publicity and Sean Day Lewis in the *Daily Telegraph* called it a
wise precaution. 'If it had been stopped by advance public outcry,
the only gain would have been by the IRA itself.' In contrast to
Peter Black's earlier judgement on John Kelly, Day Lewis's view
was that 'MacStiofain was revealed as a sort of obsessive robot
with no discernable saving grace. … His voice suggested a total
inflexibility and absence of human feeling' (24.3.72). Two days
later Stormont Prime Minister Brian Faulkner resigned and
Edward Heath imposed direct rule over the province from Britain. Protestants saw the move as a concession to IRA violence.

Learning about Northern Ireland

Peter Taylor was new to Northern Ireland as well as to *This
Week*, and found himself learning rapidly. His next programme,
'Busman's Holiday' (6.4.72), followed a process of discovery
which in some ways paralleled his own. The idea was to take an
ordinary couple to see for themselves. And when Tom and Doris
Edmondson, a bus driver and his wife from Hull, compared their
direct experience of Belfast with the television portrayal they had
become accustomed to, it was the gap between the image and
the real life contact that struck them most. 'You've got to see it,'
said Tom. 'Television doesn't show you this, does it? This picture
won't show what we can see, stood here – it won't, it can't.' With
Taylor they drive through West Belfast, shocked by the closeness of the army presence. They question the soldiers who check
their car, and talk to kids who look older than their age. Tom
chats to a bus driver who regularly risks hijacking, and they are
appalled by the sight of a shop bombed only an hour before and
by the matter-of-fact way in which the disaster is accepted by
those around. In catholic Andersonstown they meet Mr and Mrs
John McDonnell, whose son was interned, as was John himself
in the Second World War. The McDonnells explain why they

changed their minds about the British army presence. For them the IRA are patriots. Nearly 20 years later, when this programme was retransmitted, the British public were not allowed to hear the McDonnells' concluding opinions because of the 1988 ban on broadcasting any support for an organization that advocated terrorism (*35 Years on the Front Line* 26.2.91).

The men in Tom's depot had heard about the maliciousness of the invisible enemy, 'women go around with hat-pins and stick them in the testicles of the British troops'. They think that the hands of the army are tied by politicians, and when they do stand firm, as on Bloody Sunday, 'they never hear the end of it'. The general feeling, shared by Tom, was that 'the Irish should be left to sort themselves out'. But, because 'you get a lot more truth off the camera than you do on it', Tom admits he has completely changed his mind. Without the army 'you're letting people in for a bloodbath, a lot of death'. 'You'd have to be a very callous man, more callous than I could be I'm afraid, to desert them. ... Absolute reversal of opinion to what I had, I think.'

Behind the barricades

Through *This Week*'s programmes it is possible to trace the hardening of opinions on both sides, as the protestant backlash against direct rule built up. In the Bogside the Republican barricades had become a permanent fixture, creating Republican 'Free Derry', and the policy of British troops was to keep out and observe. The challenge to reporters was to reach the whole spectrum of authentic opinion, despite the public revulsion at the use of violence and the increasing haze of propaganda.

'I was particularly anxious to clear up the rumour you had mentioned to me on the telephone that a *This Week* team had staged an incident in which the contents of a house had been destroyed,' wrote Peter Taylor to Keith McDowell, Head of Information at the Northern Ireland Office,

> I give you my word that we never filmed such an incident let alone staged it, and I hasten to add that we are not in the habit of making television programmes in this manner. I would be most interested to hear where the story came from, as I am sure you will appreciate, such rumours reflect unfairly on our professional conduct and make your job more difficult than it already is (June 1972).

Republicans and Unionists vied for propaganda advantage. Taylor filmed an IRA roadblock – motorists are stopped by men with guns and faces covered by balaclavas – and also the hooded leader of the paramilitary Ulster Defence Association (UDA), which claimed 20,000 members. Taylor described the IRA as staging 'propaganda for the benefit of press and television to prove to the world that the IRA are in complete charge', while the UDA explain that their barricades are to provoke the army into dismantling the Republican ones (25.5.72). *This Week* was the only team filming from inside the protestant barricades. The only films made inside Free Derry and the other catholic enclaves were by independent film-makers who allied themselves with the Republican cause (Dickinson 1999:266).

During 1972 MI6 had been in touch with the IRA. The Provisionals declared a ceasefire 'provided a public reciprocal response is forthcoming from the armed forces of the British crown'. Sean MacStiofain, Martin McGuinness and Gerry Adams came to Chelsea to meet William Whitelaw, Northern Ireland Secretary, who said he found 'no sign … that they really were prepared seriously to contemplate the political realities as they are' ('Five Long Years' 12.8.74). The ceasefire ended within 48 hours of the meeting, and two *This Week* teams were there when it was broken in a tense confrontation between army, the IRA and groups of catholic and protestant families.

'The Lenadoon Incident' (20.7.72) demonstrated the ethnic cleansing of the early 1970s, as families previously living in mixed areas of Belfast abandoned their homes and clustered into separate communities. In July homeless catholics had been allocated some abandoned houses in what had been the protestant end of Lenadoon Avenue. Protestants were reluctant to let them in, but the IRA forced the issue and the catholics marched down the hill towards the empty houses. Both groups accused the other of intimidation. As the crew filmed, an army Saracen rammed the furniture lorry. Rubber bullets were fired and the IRA interpreted this as the end of the ceasefire. Peter Taylor was at the bottom of Lenadoon Avenue with the protestants, Jonathan Dimbleby at the top as the catholic estate was abandoned by its inhabitants, who claimed that they would only feel safe in an exclusively catholic area. As the army moved in to take over the houses as billets, a priest, Father Jack Fitzsimons, led all 3,000 residents to camp in a nearby sports field. Dimbleby described it as 'the evacuation of ordinary people by ordinary people'. Taylor interviewed Seamus Twomey of the Provisional IRA, who suggested that the ceasefire should be monitored by an outside body. 'It would have to be proposed to the people Mr Whitelaw got in contact with before.' On 31 July 1972 the British army launched 'Operation Motorman' and 12,000 troops, supported by tanks and bulldozers, smashed the Free Derry barricades.

After an initial seven months on *This Week*, which had included 'Bloody Sunday', 'Busman's Holiday', 'The Protestants Say No-go' and 'Lenadoon', and having interviewed IRA and UDA leaders, as well as politicians, soldiers and many ordinary people, Peter Taylor, who had started with no particular interest in Ireland, found himself drawn into the subject through a mixture of horror at the events he was witnessing and the need to understand and clarify. He was to make 26 more programmes on Northern Ireland for Thames Television, before moving to the BBC in 1979 and continuing to investigate and monitor events in the province, as well as the broader issues of security and terrorism.

The soldiers

Following Bloody Sunday, when its actions came under unprece-dented scrutiny from journalists and television cameras, the army was much more aware of public perceptions. Its 1972 manual declared 'Every local mention of the army affects its image. ... Every effort must be made to forestall or counteract accusations when through mishap, misdeed or misunderstanding, a unit may find itself the subject of press interest which could lead to adverse publicity.' It began to train officers in how to appear on television (Curtis 1984:75, 233).

At the same time, Peter Taylor was negotiating with the army's Public Relations Department to make a Christmas programme with the troops in Northern Ireland, and, for the first time since direct rule, he was granted unrestricted access to ordinary soldiers and the freedom to talk to them about their feelings and attitudes. Back in Lenadoon Avenue he found soldiers billeted in a living room just like those *This Week* had filmed only five months earlier as they were abandoned by their tenants. Members of the audience who had followed *This Week* programmes would have had a clearer knowledge of the background to their presence than the soldiers had themselves. But these men had suffered more

casualties than in any operation since the Second World War and
lived in constant fear of being shot, bombed or mortared. The
Green Howards in Lenadoon saw their operation purely as a war
against the IRA. They cannot be neutral, they say, and 'want to
get back at the IRA as much as the IRA want to get at us'. They
find that the protestants are friendly, whereas the IRA are 'from
the Republic', hence they are foreign. A debate develops. 'You
can't go bombing into the streets and punching the fuck out of
some Paddy, because they'll start creating and it's bad publicity,'
said one. 'No matter how bad they are, you've still got innocent
people over here,' said another. Even so, the consensus was that
the gunman had an unfair advantage. 'Everyone helps him, the
women, the children, the dogs, all the workmen in the streets,
they all help him get away' (21.12.72).

Despite the insistence on the IRA as their enemy, their justification for staying is still that there would be a bloodbath between
the two sides if the British pull out. The frankness about brutality which emerged much later in Peter Taylor's 'A Soldier's Tale'
(BBC2 7.8.94) could, at this point, only be read between the lines.
Following the programme, Brigadier J.W. Stanier of Army Public
Relations wrote to thank Producer John Edwards, adding 'I do
hope we shall have some further opportunities of helping you in
the future.' Counter-terrorism expert Richard Clutterbuck later
wrote that 'having someone like the boy next door' on the screens
will 'help counter the "jackboot" image which hostile journalists
will try to project about the army or police' (Curtis 1984:234).

Power sharing and community

During the autumn and winter of 1973, *This Week*'s attention
moved away from Northern Ireland. Peter Taylor travelled
secretly to Czechoslovakia to film dissidents there, accompanied
by researcher Sue McConachy, who later became his wife, and
reported on the Glasgow firemen's strike. The most remarkable
This Week of the year was Jonathan Dimbleby's 'The Unknown
Famine'. In Northern Ireland, a power-sharing Executive, in
which catholics would be guaranteed seats, was due to take office
in January 1974, but was immediately disrupted by Ian Paisley's
Ulster Unionists. A *This Week* team was outside on the first day
as it was 'reduced to an unworkable shambles as hardliners
protested vigorously at protestant sharing power with catholics.

... Unionists spat at Unionists, the mace was seized and passed from hand to hand and police forcibly removed the Rev Ian Paisley' (*The Times* 22.1.74).

In two programmes, Peter Taylor looked at the power-sharing initiative from the different perspectives of the two communities (24 and 31.1.74). In the first, directed by Peter Tiffin, against a background of graffiti in the Shankill Road, he comments that the protestants 'live in a state of siege more imagined than real'. In the heated atmosphere of the clubs they assert, 'We must stand up and fight. As protestants we're proud to be British.' Although a ceasefire was in force, UVF men wear masks and carry guns.

The second programme, directed by the late David Gill, switched to life in one of the poorest catholic ghettoes, the Divis Flats in West Belfast. For the first time the army is seen with something of the fear they inspire in those they consider to be their enemy, as a children's rehearsal for a New Year's party is intercut with soldiers searching along the dingy walkways. The tenants of the Divis are delighted that for the first time in 50 years they have political representation. 'The Provos have lost support here, but all the kids have seen violence and their houses have been regularly raided by the army.' From the army's point of view even the children are suspects and potential IRA recruits. (In 'A Soldier's Tale' a soldier admits that he 'hated those people with an intensity that made him sick' (BBC2 7.8.94).) This film is much slower paced with fewer sequences than would be the practice in later years. It is shot in an observational style, not packed with facts, but concerned to explore people's opinions and give some sense of the climate in which those opinions evolved. The two programmes together achieved a real insight into the links between power and decision making at the top, and consciousness on the ground. They did not, for once, seek out people who could somehow remain outside the conflict, nor did they treat violence as irrational and meaningless behaviour.

While established journalists were concerned about their inability to report the IRA and other paramilitary groups, many independent film-makers in Britain and in Northern Ireland pointed out that the least represented of all perspectives was that of the ordinary catholics, like those in the Divis, and particularly the women. These were people who were neither terrorists nor prominent activists, but embedded in the experience of their separate community. They had lived with deprivation and discrimination and made sense of their experience with an account that was at odds with the official view. There was a continuum rather than a clear-cut distinction between the views of the IRA, Sinn Fein and 'ordinary catholics', even when those 'ordinary catholics' were deeply opposed to violence.

On the 25th anniversary of the arrival of British troops, Peter Taylor revisited the Divis (BBC2 1994). Mary – who had clattered her dustbin lid on the ground in protest in 1971 – spoke of her continued Republican commitment but felt she would not see a significant improvement in her lifetime. Both the earnest young boy who had sworn not to get involved, and his perky friend who at the age of 11 was prepared to die for Ireland, had, by 1994, done time in prison.

At the beginning of 1974 *This Week* like the rest of the country was preoccupied with the State of Emergency and the Three-Day Week imposed to deal with the power shortages caused by the miners' and power workers' strikes. The consequent general election, called in February 1974, came at the worst possible time for the politics of tolerance in Northern Ireland. The Loyalists fought it on their opposition to power sharing and won 11 out of the 12 Northern Ireland seats. Merlyn Rees became Northern Ireland Secretary in a new Labour government with just a toe-hold on power and a majority of four.

In May 1974 the protestant Ulster Workers' Council organized a strike in opposition to the Sunningdale Agreement, which had set up the power-sharing Executive in the North and a Council of Ireland to strengthen relations between North and South. It brought power cuts and food shortages, and set up street barricades manned by protestant paramilitary groups. But the British army avoided confrontation. 'You can't take the harsh sort of measure. You can't go round shooting people because they want to do a certain thing,' said General Sir Frank King ('Five Long Years'). *This Week* addressed the topic with a studio discussion (23.5.74). There was no support for Brian Faulkner and his fellow members on the Executive. On 28 May 1974, they resigned and Faulkner gave the first interview to Peter Taylor (30.5.74). It included a bitter attack on PM Harold Wilson for a speech that had hardened the resolve of protestant extremists opposed to power sharing.

'Five Long Years': the decision makers

'We take issue by issue and very rarely impose a perspective and I'm not too happy about that,' David Elstein told an interviewer, 'when you actually see it in some sort of context it is astonishing and revelatory.' It was now five years since British troops had been sent to Northern Ireland and the time seemed ripe to 'see it in some sort of context' (Rosenthal 1981:124–5). Peter Taylor suggested a major retrospective 'not so much through the eyes of all who suffered as in "Remember Strabane", but through the eyes of those politicians and soldiers who took the decisions that led us along the path to our present impasse.' Such subjects ought not to be the prerogative of the BBC, who were themselves planning a major review. 'I'm sure the IBA, if not the network, would agree' (memo 16.4.74). In the event Elstein became the director and the team put together a remarkable collection of interviewees for a 90-minute programme, 'Five Long Years' (12.8.74). There were major political figures from Britain and both parts of Ireland, three British generals, three Loyalist politicians and three acting or former IRA chiefs of staff. (The team were driven by Republican 'minders' to a remote farmhouse for their interview with David O'Connell, one of the most articulate spokesmen for the IRA.) All the interviewees were told beforehand that the IRA were to be included, but only Ian Paisley refused to participate (Rosenthal 1981:126). Belfast journalist and political activist Eamonn McCann made an energetic and graphic contribution. It was he who recalled the most memorable line, 'We don't want to fight,' said a young man before the Battle of the Bogside, 'but if we have to fight, let us fight like peaceful men.'

The BBC retrospective presented by Martin Bell scooped it by two weeks, but 'Bell is a very straight-laced reporter of the news, and *This Week* are past masters at the art of background painting,' wrote Patrick Stoddart in the *Evening News* (12.8.74). Reviewers noted the complexity of the problems and the lack of easy solutions. The *Mail* concluded, 'A cheap and easy comment would be that this careful survey told us more than we wanted to know. Not more than we needed to know, however' (13.8.74).

But the mix of interviewees and the multiple perspectives were never to be repeated. The army, which had at first appreciated the programme and used it for in-service training, would soon change its position and refuse to appear with paramilitaries

(Rosenthal 1981:126).

In 'Five Long Years' representatives of the paramilitary groups appeared as legitimate spokespeople with clear-cut aims and a coherent – even when reprehensible – strategy. And the broadcast was not unique. When David O'Connell had been interviewed for LWT's *Weekend World* by its regular presenter Mary Holland (21.1.73), the IBA had not objected and had issued a paper to all independent companies entitled 'Programmes about criminals', affirming their liberal position,

> The fact that assorted groups and individuals choose to act outside the properly constituted democratic machinery does not in itself render their case unworthy of attention, however horrifying their actions may become. It cannot be denied that the IRA and the UDA are factors in the Northern Ireland situation just as much as the SDLP and the Ulster Unionists. An understanding of why they act in this way is essential to any attempt to report and explain the Northern Ireland crisis. It is for this reason that there are occasions when interviews with illegal organisations are justified. The main problem is how to report accurately without giving the platform which most politically motivated groups seek (Potter 1990:210).

This approach would soon be overturned by the Prevention of Terrorism Act.

An influential view amongst counter-insurgency experts was that terrorism was a form of 'theatre' and that terrorists were interested only in publicity. Deny them a public voice and the security forces could easily mop them up (Schlesinger et al 1983:148). It was a view that underlay much right-wing comment, and the case was strengthened when, in the climax to their mainland bombing campaign, the IRA exploded bombs at a Birmingham pub, killing 21 (21.11.74). The bombing came four days after *Weekend World* interviewed O'Connell for a second time, and the two events were linked by newspapers and politicians. Television, once more, was accused of succouring the enemy and even of creating a channel through which O'Connell could communicate with his agents. In a panic reaction, the Prevention of Terrorism Act was rushed through parliament, outlawing the IRA as an organization involved in terror. Jeremy Potter describes 'an exchange of strong and conflicting views' at a meeting of the IBA as to whether this meant that to allow IRA spokespeople to appear on television would, in itself, constitute a criminal act.

But

> the Authority was advised that this did not significantly change
> the legal position as far as broadcasters were concerned. ... It was
> resolved to pursue the same pragmatic policy of judging each case
> individually on its merits, while requiring from the companies the
> earliest possible intimation of any similar programme item in future,
> and an assurance that approval for it had been obtained from the
> company's chief executive (1990:211).

Thames's Director of Programmes, Jeremy Isaacs, was equally
circumspect. In a memo to all in the Current Affairs and Documentary departments he wrote,

> The law in this country has changed. I am advised that it is illegal to
> interview on television members of organisations proscribed under
> the Prevention of Terrorism Act. So far the schedule of proscribed
> organisations consists of only one, the IRA. It is also plain now, that
> bombs on our own doorsteps mean that to broadcast the views of the
> bombers risks infringing the provisions of the Television Act which
> prohibit items 'offensive to public feeling'. This risk must be balanced
> in the future as in the past with our journalistic responsibility to
> provide our audience with information to which they are entitled,
> including the views of their enemies. However, from now on, it is
> imperative that no approach be made by any of you for an interview
> with any member of a terrorist organisation in this country without
> prior consent of the Controller of Current Affairs and Documenta-
> ries, John Edwards, who will obtain my positive approval before
> giving permission to go ahead (11.12.74; published in Campaign for
> Free Speech on Ireland 1979:27).

At *This Week*, Arnold Bulka, who had been producer for only
five months, tragically committed suicide, and David Elstein,
who had directed 'Five Long Years', took over the running of the
series. Backed by Jeremy Isaacs, he held fast to the principle that
the audience are *entitled* to information that includes the 'views
of their enemies'. The IRA themselves announced a temporary
ceasefire.

Over this first period, *This Week* had followed what Schlesinger
and his colleagues describe as an 'alternative' approach to reporting terrorist activity, in which the explanations offered by 'terrorists' are listened to, if not accepted, and are interpreted within
their own context of understanding. Programmes had trodden
a delicate path between the desire to seek out 'ordinary people'
who would be distanced from the conflict, but also recognized

that the commitments and prejudices of many ordinary people may well be unpalatable. Keeping largely to the consensus agenda meant that the British army was seen as a neutral force, and it was often the pivot of the report. Programmes sought to maintain a 'balance' between catholic and protestant, even while recognizing the asymmetry of their situations and the inappropriateness of an even-handed view. Space had been given to paramilitaries, but this was always framed in a 'hostile' interview. In these first five years, both government and the IBA had been working out their own positions, and *This Week* had not been unduly limited. However, in the second half of the decade, as policies hardened, the strengthening of the IBA's controls was to have dramatic repercussions on Northern Ireland reporting, which continued to be 'more than we wanted to know, but not more than we needed to'.

6
THIS WEEK AND NORTHERN IRELAND, PART 2: MORE THAN WE WANTED TO KNOW

Interference and censorship

> Reporting Northern Ireland has never been easy – not just because the issues are complex and literally involve life and death – but because the political climate in which journalists operate often conditions their reporting and what their broadcasting organisations are prepared to transmit. … All governments enlist the media as their ally when terrorism threatens the state and the pressure can be unrelenting (Peter Taylor to PH).

Pressure on *This Week* built up over the second half of the 1970s as the series came into conflict with the authorities with increasing frequency and acrimony. The 1974 Prevention of Terrorism Act (PTA) carried definite warnings for the media. In the House of Lords, Lord Hailsham and the former Northern Ireland Prime Minister Lord Brookeborough claimed that David O'Connell had used his *Weekend World* interview to 'communicate with troops on the ground' and by implication to initiate the Birmingham bombs. Some Conservatives attempted to strengthen the Act by making a broadcast or any other 'publicity' which might 'support, sustain or further the activities of a proscribed organisation' punishable by fine or imprisonment (Curtis 1984:160). Home Secretary Roy Jenkins was evasive when Peter Taylor asked him, in a *This Week* programme, whether journalists were liable to be prosecuted if they were to interview an IRA member, 'I believe in independent broadcasting … but … in my view, in the new circumstances … a

repeat of the O'Connell interview would be entirely inappropriate' (12.12.74).

The new measures contributed to an atmosphere in which
fewer public attempts were made to understand the background
to the problem. The sense of panic created a climate for major
miscarriages of justice, as the wrong people were arrested for the
Birmingham bombings (strikingly revealed in a long-running
campaign by Granada's *World in Action* ('Who Bombed Birmingham?' 28.3.90)). Terrorism seen in isolation from its social origins
could only remain puzzling and violence could never be anything
but 'mindless'. In his interview Jenkins made much of the irra-
tionality of the IRA. To say that hanging would deter them, he
insisted, would reinforce the impression that they are rational
human beings. On the contrary, 'They love martyrs and would
be happy to have martyrs.' He agreed that the powers given to
the police by the PTA – power to detain suspects without charge
for seven days and to exclude persons from Great Britain – did
involve a 'certain interference with civil liberties which would
not be justified in normal circumstances'. Rumours that the six
men arrested for the Birmingham bombings had been assaulted
in custody were already circulating.

Almost as a challenge to the new regulatory regime, Taylor's
next programme featured the fundraising activities of southern
Irish Sinn Fein Councillor John Joe McGirl, released that year
from internment. 'Hands Across the Sea' (8.5.75) begins with
what could well be taken for an IRA ceremony at the grave of
a dead hero. Berets are worn and a rifle salute is fired. In fact
this is Philadelphia USA and the grave is that of Joe McGarrity,
a prominent Irish-American who had financed the IRA since
the 1916 uprising. The programme follows McGirl to New York's
Irish bars, where they sing 'The men behind the wire' about
the internees held in Long Kesh detention centre. For him, IRA
volunteers 'were not self-seekers, they've all been dedicated and
honourable', and he issues a clear warning to Britain, 'She'd better
not play cat and mouse with the IRA, because our bomb could
again burst in their faces.' The Noraid organization had been
started in 1969 by veterans of 1916 who had escaped to the USA,
and fed on generations of bitterness from those whose parents
and grandparents had been forcibly deported or starved out of
Ireland in the mid-nineteenth century. Legally it was a registered
charity which supported the families of interned Republicans.

But the film shows a consignment of guns seized in Baltimore, as Taylor demonstrates that it also helps the IRA. The programme highlighted a neglected aspect of the conflict – the long-standing Irish-American dimension.

The IBA made it clear that they were disturbed by the portrayal of fundraising for the proscribed organization and the open expression of views by a 'terrorist', particularly as the scheduled transmission date was 1 May 1975, the day of the election for the Constitutional Convention in Northern Ireland. Producer David Elstein pointed out that McGirl was at that time a county council member in the Irish Republic, and that polling in Northern Ireland closed at 8pm, half an hour before transmission time. The Authority viewed a rough version of the programme, but later regretted doing so, since they were determined not to allow transmission on polling day (Potter 1990:211).

At *This Week* the decision was seen as outright censorship. The entire team, 14 journalists, directors and researchers, wrote to Lord Annan, chair of the Committee on the Future of Broadcasting, currently looking into the division of editorial responsibility between the ITV companies and the IBA. 'The IBA decided to ban the programme last week *without even seeing it*. ... We still do not know the reason for the ban.' They were determined that Lord Annan should get the letter that day and dispatched a researcher to deliver it in person. Noel Annan replied, 'Your emissary duly tracked me down and handed me the document at 7.30. She deserves a pat on the back for her endurance!' The Authority stated in a press release that even though the programme would have been transmitted after the polls had closed 'it would still be election night when feelings in Northern Ireland could still be running high'. And the pre-publicity may have caused problems.

By chance the AGM of the ACTT's Euston shop was on 1 May. As well as being Producer of *This Week*, David Elstein was active in the union. He proposed a motion deploring the IBA's decision, which,

> creates a precedent in relations between the IBA and the ITV companies, as this is the first programme to be banned without being seen – indeed while it was still being shot. This shop declares that it has no confidence in the competence of the IBA any longer to exercise judgment on the suitability for transmission of current affairs programmes.

ACTT head office went even further and threatened to black out any alternative programme – a threat which was averted at the last minute (Potter 1990:211 n20). Elstein thought it was important for the union to get involved in issues of journalism and to take a stand against censorship, but his actions did not please Thames management and he was severely rapped over the knuckles.

The incident was well publicized in the newspapers, and the IBA described it as 'exactly the wrong way to conduct IBA/company dialogue' (Potter 1990:59–60). In a letter to Lord Annan, Lady Plowden, the new Chair of the IBA, complained, 'A "ban" which makes a good headline can make an action sound unreasonable, even when it is a carefully considered matter of timing.' UTV, she added, had 'considerable reservations' about whether the programme should be shown at all. Her conclusion was rather ominous for programme makers: 'If some responsible members of the public' think that a programme item has contributed to the risks of civil disorder or crime, the Authority must take this into account, 'whether this is factually so or not'. In the next few years she was to have frequent personal contacts with 'responsible members of the public' such as Northern Ireland Chief Constable Kenneth Newman. She concluded that 'the Authority and its staff must be prepared to exercise a measure of editorial control that may go beyond specific requirements spelt out explicitly in the fourth section of the Act'.

Educationist Bridget Plowden had joined IBA's Director General, ex-headmaster Brian Young, to make a team that Jeremy Potter described as 'formidably worthy but unbalanced'. 'They were seen apprehensively as missionaries come to convert the native ITV viewer from the worship of frolicsome light entertainment to the true god of solemn adult education' (Potter 1989:91). That judgement was rather at odds with that of the journalists on *This Week*, who saw the IBA as limiting their commitment, not so much to anything frolicsome, but to a more challenging view of education and public service. Indeed, on taking up her job, Plowden had declared that 'television is not the right medium for investigative journalism' (Fiddick in the *Guardian* 12.4.75).

'Hands Across the Sea' was transmitted a week late on 8 May 1974 and was received as a programme highly critical of the IRA. On 1 May its replacement had been preceded by a caption stating that the original had been postponed at the request of the IBA. The incident initiated an abrasive period in the relations between the Authority and *This Week* which, as we have seen, was not confined to programmes on Northern Ireland.

Peter Taylor was also involved in other controversial programmes, including those on smoking and health and on sex education. In June 1975 he made a trip to Rhodesia to report on the growing emergency there, and his next programme on Northern Ireland was rather less dramatic. 'Ulster, the Loyalists Say No' (18.9.75) came from UTV studios in Belfast and dealt with the split in the Loyalists' vote on the latest power-sharing initiative. At this point the ACTT had imposed a ban on working in Northern Ireland because of a dispute over insurance. This meant that Taylor had no researcher and little time to prepare his interviews. He spent his time rushing between William Craig and Ian Paisley, the heads of the two factions, persuading them to appear in the studio with each other, and only just arrived in time for the live transmission. Not surprisingly John Edwards, now Head of Features, thought the programme was substandard.

The IRA had declared a ceasefire in 1975, which seemed to increase the bloodshed rather than end it. The UDA responded by escalating murders of Republicans. On 4 January 1976, gunmen walked in to a country farmhouse in South Armagh and shot three brothers while they were watching television. Two were killed instantly. Despite the family's appeal for no revenge, the following night 11 protestants on a local mini-bus, also including two brothers, were gunned down by local Provisionals. On 7 January the government sent troops from the elite SAS, 'the army's cloak and dagger operation', into the 'Bandit Country' of South Armagh. Peter Taylor and his crew spent three days in the area to make 'Massacre of the Innocents' (8.1.76). This time the crew had war zone insurance. The events were a turning point in the escalation of Loyalist violence, although at the time the majority of the media focused on the even more violent Republican reaction. And the 'cloak and dagger' SAS introduced a new element into the narrative.

Irish history

'Five Long Years' had given an account of the British army presence in Northern Ireland, but, as events progressed, Peter Taylor began to introduce his programmes by looking further backwards and suggesting explanations in the longer context of Irish history. Many journalists were aware that ignoring the history of a problem meant that its present reverberations could not be fully examined. Taylor's introduction to 'The Choices for Ulster' (29.1.76) spoke of the Tudor invasion of Ireland and its consolidation under William of Orange, 'Thus it was England that created the problem of Ulster.' Ruairi O'Bradaigh of Provisional Sinn Fein asserted that their aim remained British withdrawal. Bernard Sendall of the IBA wrote, 'I do not think it could have been done better within the limits of half an hour' (letter to Jeremy Isaacs). Peter Taylor was 32 at the time, on a salary of £8,500 pa.

Yet history itself was a pawn in the contest, and reactions to his next programme were not so sanguine. Its working title was, in the circumstances, rather provocative, 'IRA, 60th Anniversary'. Ultimately called 'Men of Easter' (29.5.76), it marked the Dublin uprising of 1916 which eventually led to the establishment of the Irish Free State and the partitioning of Ireland in 1921. But the anniversary was now of more significance to beleaguered catholics in the North than the rapidly modernizing republic in the South. A heroic tale of insurgency and martyrdom helped to make sense of their predicament and the Provisional IRA's chosen strategy of terrorist violence. Although the programme in no way glamorized the IRA, by giving it recognition and allowing those associated with it to discuss strategy and internal differences, it was given a human face – and that was unwelcome in the light of government policy. The story was presented through the eyes of Sean McEntee and Tommy Merrigan, 86-year-old veterans of the Easter Rising. Although the title 'Provisional' refers to the illegal Provisional government of Ireland set up in 1918, McEntee is anxious to distance the men of 1916 from the Provos of 1969. 'It's blasphemous to mention the names of Pearse [the poet hero of the 1916 uprising] and the Provos together.' David O'Connell, who had completed a jail sentence for IRA membership and was now Vice President of the political Provisional Sinn Fein, thought differently. 'They fought the fight we fight. ... We continue that fight.' Charles Haughey, who, in 1970 had been charged with gun running to the North, and was later to become Irish Prime Minister, declared that he saw 1916 as unfinished business.

The programme did not go down well with the Irish government, who were not happy to be reminded of their own violent past, and deplored the space given to O'Connell. Since 1972, a ban had been in place in the Republic forbidding the broadcasting of members of proscribed organizations – effectively the IRA and Sinn Fein. This gave rise to the odd situation in which viewers in the South could only hear some of their own politicians' views if they watched British television broadcast from the North. The Irish Minister of Justice, Mr Cooney, had threatened legal action against the organizers of this anniversary demonstration, and was reported to have blamed British television for 'allegedly bolstering up the Provisional IRA'. He described as outrageous the decision by Thames to screen the interview, describing it as 'validating what is essentially invalid, unlawful, illegal and evil'. To broadcast it indirectly condoned it. Those who have 'exaggerated hang-ups about press freedom ... fail to recognize a battle being fought for democracy. They cannot stay on the sidelines.' He went on to criticize the British government for meeting the paramilitary groups, 'even to acknowledge their existence is to concede that the gun can get as far as the table where talks take place' (*The Times* 29.4.76).

In the first three months of 1976, the IBA had refused permission to use IRA spokesmen on ITV on three occasions, but had agreed to an ATV programme, 'Death of an Informer', on the grounds that 'a public row about the suppression of the programme would have been more damaging to the public interest' (Potter 1990:211). David Elstein, John Edwards and Jeremy Isaacs had given various undertakings to Bernard Sendall of the IBA, that the *This Week* programme on the Easter anniversary 'would be a properly critical examination of Irish republicanism 60 years after the Easter Rising and it would attempt to set the Provisional IRA into the context of Irish politics'. Isaacs agreed not to publicize it until it was viewed by the Authority and that it would not 'contain an incitement to violence or a contribution from an illegal organisation as we together define it'. A handwritten note added, 'in case of insoluble difficulty, we shall be in a position to mount an alternative' (memos). The definition of 'illegal organisation' had been teased out over 'Hands Across the Sea' when John Joe McGirl was allowed to appear because he was a southern Sinn Fein councillor and not a current member of the IRA. It was thought that to have been a member of a proscribed organization *before* it was proscribed would not disqualify a speaker. An outline of 'Men of Easter' was sent to Bernard Sendall on Tuesday, 27 April 1976. The Authority approved the programme and it was transmitted two days later (Potter 1990:212). Peter Lennon wrote that it 'walked sure footed through more than delicate territory' (*Sunday Times* 2.5.76). Shaun Usher commented that 'tradition and legend have much to answer for' (*Daily Mail* 30.4.76).

Later that summer Jonathan Dimbleby took part in a wide-ranging BBC discussion on television's achievements over 25 years, and took up the issue of Irish history and its absence,

> because it is a very delicate, politically sensitive issue which is very difficult to do adequately on television, and therefore the job has been baulked. ... The reason why it is baulked is because of the political institutions, BBC, IBA, British government, British opposition, who don't wish us to know too much too well about Northern Ireland.

For him, a historical approach should move beyond the limits of 'objectivity' as currently defined, like the American Morley Safer's groundbreaking 1965 report that documented the brutality of US troops in Vietnam. This had been 'very honest, very outspoken, had nothing to do with impartiality and nothing to do with neutrality. He was approaching as close as he could to an objective assessment, but had a human, subjective response to what he saw.' On the IRA, 'I want to report its case. It doesn't make an assumption about there being a rational case. I want to be able, and I want other reporters to be able, to report that case, that's all' ('What do you think of it so far?' BBC2 28.8.76, transcribed in Campaign for Free Speech on Ireland 1979:6–7).

Peter Taylor, too, pressed for a series on Irish history, although he himself had many other things on his plate during 1976, including his continuing investigation into cigarette smoking and health, the Middle East, and another visit to Rhodesia. 'Northern Ireland will still be with us in 1981,' he wrote in a memo to Jeremy Isaacs. In the event, as 1981 approached, Thames Television was to make an extremely thorough, carefully researched, five-part history, *The Troubles* (1981) (Downing 1989), and Isaacs moved to the BBC and mounted a substantial series fronted by historian and ex-*This Week* reporter, Robert Kee (*Ireland: A Television History* 1980–81).

Allies or recorders?

On 5 April 1976, James Callaghan succeeded Harold Wilson as Prime Minister. In September Merlyn Rees became Home Secretary, and, in a significant appointment, Roy Mason took over as Northern Ireland Secretary. Rees had been open to negotiation and had held talks with the Provisionals. Mason was, in Peter Taylor's words, 'a man hewn from rougher rock', a former defence minister who was much more inclined to see things from the army's point of view. 'Under Mason journalists were more than ever counted as allies in the war, not recorders of it' (Taylor 1979:22). Indeed, Mason suggested that a news blackout on 'terrorist activities' in Northern Ireland would help, 'an idea that was dropped only after his civil servants had convinced him of its impracticality, most notably that such restrictions could not be used to muzzle Dublin newspapers' (Schlesinger et al 1983:118). In the province itself Kenneth Newman had become Chief Constable and was initiating a tougher regime on the part of the police.

During the autumn of 1976 *This Week* was negotiating with the army for another programme on their role in the province. 'The Soldiers' (21.12.72) had been well received, and the projected programme would take a similar tack, speaking to soldiers of all ranks about their progress and difficulties, avoiding questions of a political nature or ones that might cause a breach of security. The aim was to start filming in October when Peter Taylor got back from Rhodesia. David Elstein also proposed including spokesmen from the IRA and UDA, interviewed on their military capacity rather than their politics. The army would have two-thirds of the programme and 'their enemies' the remaining third. But there were strong reservations. Brigadier Martin Farndale wrote that it would be 'irresponsible to have members of the armed forces in uniform in the same programme as men who are wanted by those forces' (1.10.76). Elstein wrote to Neville Clarke of the IBA that a programme solely devoted to the army's activities 'would create a dangerous precedent'. Their rejection of 'a perfectly normal and proper proposal' indicated 'a significant shift of opinion within both the Northern Ireland Office and the Ministry of Defence'. The precedent set by 'Five Long Years' was no longer acceptable. Instead, when Taylor returned from Rhodesia, with researcher Peter Denton, with whom he had made most of his Northern Ireland programmes, he went to Lenadoon Avenue for the third time to record what he described as 'the biggest forced transfer of population in Europe since World War 2' (28.10.76). 'Ultimately it is the paramilitaries who decide where people live.'

Alleged links between broadcasts and terrorist incidents were a routine part of the pressures on the media. But the most serious development was the declared antipathy to television in general and the BBC in particular of Roy Mason, the new Northern Ireland Secretary. At a dinner at the Culloden Hotel, Belfast, to celebrate the opening of new BBC studios there, he launched what was described as the 'second battle of Culloden' (Curtis 1984:161). He told the assembled BBC dignitaries that their organization was 'disloyal, supported the rebels, purveyed their propaganda and refused to accept the advice of the Northern Ireland Office on what news to carry'. His threat involved their Charter and income and he called for a three-month blackout on the reporting of 'terrorist activities'. The BBC reaffirmed its commitment to open reporting but the general climate was definitely more hostile (Bolton 1990). Peter Taylor described 1977 as 'the year when political pressure was most intense'. Of the ten current affairs television programmes made about Northern Ireland in that year, six came from *This Week*. As well as the brutal killings, which by now had become almost routine, 1977 saw the fifth anniversary of Bloody Sunday, escalating protests in the prisons, increasing accusations against the Royal Ulster Constabulary for their treatment of suspects under interrogation, and a second intimidatory Loyalist strike. It was also the year in which the United Kingdom was supposed to come together to celebrate the Queen's Jubilee.

Memory and archive

'The trouble with the English is that they never remember. And the trouble with the Irish is that they never forget,' said John Hume in 'Derry: Time to Remember' (3.2.77), which marked the fifth anniversary of Bloody Sunday. Film researchers and archivists were making an increasingly important contribution as the years of the Troubles wore on. This programme used film clips of the Bloody Sunday shootings that had by now become familiar to regular television viewers – images that would continue to be reviewed many times and were later re-created for two television dramas. There were the scattering crowds, the soldiers running between their tanks and the priest waving his blood-stained handkerchief as he helps carry a dying youth out of the line of fire. This is the unique knowledge of a television age. By 1977 the people in those pictures were no longer the anonymous figures they had originally been – Father Edward Daly was now the catholic Bishop of Derry and the anonymous young man was named as Jack Duddy.

Recorded history rubs differently against different memories, and the walled city continued to represent the struggle for
both communities. Even though by 1977, as the programme made
clear, the gerrymandering which had given protestants an automatic majority had been abolished; elections for the council were
fair; catholics were properly represented and women from the
two communities were working together in the peace movement.
Yet protestants still remembered the siege of 1689, and catholics,
whose protective barricades were demolished in 1972, saw an
ongoing battle. The British army still maintained an intimidating
presence – Bishop Daly says it had never recovered the confidence
of the people. The programme weaves the familiar current affairs
collage – a peace movement meeting, a wreath-laying ceremony
and a Sinn Fein rally at which the speaker calls for 'one last push'
to force the British out of Ireland. And it was that phrase that
caused the problems. Calling for 'one last push' was considered
by the IBA to be an incitement to violence under the Prevention
of Terrorism Act, and a breach of the undertakings given them by
David Elstein. Despite feeling angry, Peter Taylor compromised
by lowering the sound for that part of the speech and replacing it
with commentary (Taylor 1979:23).

The programme was shown in the week that Geoffrey Agate,
head of the American-owned Dupont factory in Derry, was assassinated. Targeting industrialists was a new departure for the
IRA, undermining Roy Mason's economic strategy of building up
employment through overseas investment (Taylor 1980:158). As
so often, the viewers who phoned or wrote in deplored what they
saw as anti-British bias. The duty officer's handwritten note of
the telephone calls recorded, 'Snarls, protests; it was biased, one
sided, disgraceful; is the IRA paying for programmes, is there
a member of the IRA on the *This Week* team'. To a viewer who
asked, 'Why do you show the British soldier in the worst light?'
David Elstein replied sourly, 'I'm afraid the conditions they seek
to impose before agreeing to our filming them are unacceptable
to us and until the army's attitude changes I doubt if we would
be able to include them in programmes about Northern Ireland.'
To another correspondent he replied, 'It's no job of ours to conceal
what's going on.'

Strikes, prisons and the police

The Labour government was aiming to achieve something like a normal system of justice in Northern Ireland, with the British army playing a secondary role to the police, the Royal Ulster Constabulary. So when, on 2 May 1977, the Loyalists called a strike, pressuring for tighter security and a return to protestant control, the RUC was in charge. Mindful that the Loyalist strike of 1974 had brought down the power-sharing Executive, David Elstein replaced the scheduled programme with a debate, live from UTV (5.5.77). The protestant community was polarized. It was 'protestant working class against working class. Cars were ripped, brake fluid thrown on the bodywork and there were slogans scratched.' Harold McCusker, MP for Armagh, was beaten up by strike supporters as he came to the studio. But the strike did not succeed. In 1974 the army had stood back. Now the RUC clamped down mercilessly and Paisley himself was arrested. Peter Taylor's portrait of him (26.5.77) was an insight into the world view of the fundamentalist protestant community who saw themselves threatened from all sides. 'Our message to Roy Mason,' roars Paisley, 'is no surrender.' (Taylor was criticized in some quarters for making his subject look human – not least when Paisley offered an ice cream to the film crew.)

It was during the security clampdown following the strike that Peter Taylor heard increased accusations of the ill treatment of suspects by the police, especially at the Castlereagh interrogation centre in Belfast. Following recommendations from Lord Justice Diplock, the 1973 Emergency Provisions Act had set up a system by which alleged terrorist offences could be heard by a single judge sitting without a jury, and with the power to convict on the accused's confession alone. It was no secret that the methods used to obtain confessions were, to say the least, intimidating; the Act actually permitted any means short of 'torture or inhuman or degrading treatment' (Taylor 1980:180–2, 29–37). It defined terrorism as 'the use of violence for political ends', but, at the same time, it abolished special treatment for 'political' prisoners.

Since 1972, those held under the policy of internment had been described as 'special-category prisoners' rather than criminals, and they had certain privileges, such as wearing their own clothes. But from March 1976, they became ordinary criminals who could no longer claim any privileges, and the change in policy was to have far-reaching repercussions. It resulted in the 'blanket protest' in which prisoners refused to wear prison clothing, preferring to remain naked, wrapped only in a prison blanket; the 'dirty protest' when they refused to slop out and were prepared to smear their faeces over the walls of their cells; and the hunger strikes which brought the deaths of ten catholic prisoners.

'Political' internees had been held in a makeshift camp just outside Belfast known as Long Kesh. It looked for all the world like a Second World War prisoner-of-war camp with prisoners living in wire compounds, known as 'cages'. Although it was being rebuilt as a permanent prison for the new influx, those imprisoned before 1976 retained their special status and continued to live in the 'cages'. Here they not only wore their own clothing, but were able to organize according to paramilitary discipline. In the summer of 1977 *This Week* was contacted by Loyalist prisoners, offering the use of 8mm home-movie-style film footage which showed drilling and paramilitary training. Researcher Alan Stewart was assigned to the project and travelled to Belfast to bring back the film, even though there was a strong suspicion that it had been shot especially to pass on to the media (*Guardian* 22.9.77). At the time, Stewart was proposing a programme on housing associations and their paramilitary connections in Northern Ireland. As always, many more ideas were floated than actually got made, and the housing issue did not reach the screens.

'In Friendship and Forgiveness?'

Nineteen-seventy-seven was the year of the Queen's Jubilee: 25 years on the throne. In what Peter Taylor described as a 'triumph for the Chief Constable and the Secretary of State', a royal visit to Northern Ireland was arranged on a particularly sensitive date (Taylor 1980:199). The 11th of August was in the middle of the marching season, between the Battle of the Boyne celebrations on 12 July and the Apprentice Boys' march on 12 August. John Hume's view was that the timing 'identified the Queen with the most triumphalist section of the Loyalist tradition'. Taylor and Stewart were preparing the film about special-category prisoners as the Royal PR machine swung into place. When the Queen arrived in Northern Ireland on the Wednesday, 10 August, Taylor phoned David Elstein and suggested a quick programme for the following night which would look at the cosmetic coverage by the rest of the media and show something of what she, and by implication the British public, was prevented from seeing. For example, in *Republican News* an ominous cartoon was captioned, 'We'll make your visit go with a bang.' Later Taylor described the television news coverage as 'brilliantly orchestrated'. 'It presented a picture of a province almost pacified, with grateful and loyal subjects from both sections of the community taking the Queen and her message to their hearts.'

Director Ian Stuttard was in Belfast with a crew for the prisoners' programme and had already filmed the angry street demonstrations that marked the anniversary of the introduction of internment. Stuttard had joined *This Week* in 1972 and had worked with Jonathan Dimbleby on several of his programmes on Africa. Since mid-1975 he had directed many Northern Ireland programmes and made no secret of his republican sympathies. He was keen to make a film that showed the Queen's visit against a background of unresolved conflict, shown while she was still in the province.

David Elstein decided to go for the normal *This Week* time the following Thursday (18 August), which still entailed working at speed. By Saturday the crew had finished filming, the editor worked over the weekend, and by Tuesday an assembly was ready. On Wednesday the 17th, the day before transmission, the crew went to Yorkshire to film the funeral of Private Harrison, who had been shot dead in the week of the filming. At 6.40 the same day a 45-minute rough cut was relayed to the IBA. Lines to Belfast closed at 7pm so UTV only received the first part of the programme.

The title, 'In Friendship and Forgiveness?', put a question mark after the concluding remarks of the Queen's address in Coleraine. 'People everywhere recognize that violence is senseless and wrong,' she had said. 'If this community is to survive and prosper, they must live and work together in friendship and forgiveness.' In the film, the speech is intercut with the 'regular Sunday pastime' in Northern Ireland, throwing stones at soldiers. The programme seethes with anti-British activity. While discreet crowds are welcoming the Queen at Hillsborough Castle and ultra-Loyalists are sounding their support, in the catholic Falls Road a demonstration with dustbin lids and whistles echoes those bitter days when internment was introduced. Graffiti reads 'Lizzie the leech' and marchers carry black flags and banners saying 'Queen of Death'. Taylor's opening commentary reminded his audience that 400 years ago Elizabeth I sent troops to Ulster to crush 'those who have rebelliously taken arms', while today Provisional Sinn Fein are preaching rebellion against the army of Elizabeth II. To emphasize the point, Sinn Fein's Andreas O'Callaghan, up from Dublin for the occasion, delivered a resounding call to arms, and the Provisional IRA, armed and masked, set up a roadblock. 'More propaganda than military exercise,' commented Taylor, 'perhaps for our benefit, perhaps as a morale booster for their supporters.' This was the side of Northern Ireland the Queen did not see. 'The visit made both sides more sharply aware of their heritage.' The programme marked two deaths. The army shot and killed 16-year-old Paul McWilliams, claiming he was carrying a petrol bomb, and the Provisional IRA shot 20-year-old Private Lewis Harrison in retaliation. 'The events of the week drew to a close not on the streets of Belfast but in the lanes of a Yorkshire mining village. … Private Harrison died, not because the Queen visited Ulster, but because the power she represents still remains in that part of Ireland.'

After their viewing, Neville Clarke of the IBA phoned David Elstein. The Authority was not happy with the filming of yet another IRA roadblock, and they would not accept the speech by Andreas O'Callaghan. 'While there is a British army in occupation on our streets,' O'Callaghan had cried,

> any Irishman who has it within his means, meaning any Irishman who can get his hands on a gun or weapon, he has the duty not to keep that gun in cold storage or even less to use that gun against the people who are fighting the British army. Let them get out and fight the British army themselves. As long as there's one British soldier in any part of Ireland, there will always be people who struggle, there will always be people who will resist (Taylor 1979:23).

The IBA's objection caused anger amongst the *This Week* team. Stuttard argued that they should return to the studio, explaining that a sequence could not be shown (*Guardian* 27.8.77). Thames's solicitor thought the IBA were over cautious but agreed to seek counsel's opinion. A few hours before transmission was due, Hilary Heilbron QC advised that O'Callaghan's words might breach the rulings on incitement (in the Broadcasting Act 1973) but they could be turned into reported speech. The team went ahead with the compromise and lowered the sound on O'Callaghan's speech. The direct reference to guns was left out and instead the commentary stated that O'Callaghan 'urged Irishmen to carry on the fight against British soldiers in Northern Ireland using whatever weapons they could lay their hands on. It was an open call to arms.' By 6.30 the new soundtrack was ready, and the programme was played back to the IBA while the commentary recording was being finished. But the Authority still objected, and five minutes before transmission told Thames that the programme could not be shown. Taylor and Stuttard were in Isaacs's office, and in Taylor's words, 'Jeremy hit the roof. He said it was absurd that we as programme makers are not also publishers' (to PH). Taylor's earlier report on drinking and driving was repeated instead.

But David Elstein and Jeremy Isaacs were not prepared to leave it at that. They consulted another QC, Michael Sherrard, who disagreed with the IBA. 'Having regard to the careful way in which it is presented', he thought O'Callaghan's speech was unlikely to incite violence. Although such an effect might be *possible*, the Authority was required to consider what was *likely*. As for the roadblock, he was satisfied there was no question of the team having set it up and pointed out that the Broadcasting Act was concerned with the *effect* of a film, not with the manner in which it had been procured. In his view the programme 'complies with the requirement for a news feature to be presented with "due impartiality and accuracy"' and there was no reason not to transmit (*Guardian* 27.8.77). His six-and-a-half-hours' work cost Thames £432. Commentary emphasizing that the crew had been tipped off about the roadblock was added to the sequence and this time the IBA accepted the QC's view.

At first the Authority had also objected to Taylor's concluding commentary. In their view 'it presented an incomplete picture of the problem, there being no mention of religion, of catholics and protestants and the army keeping them from each other'. But for Taylor, its sentiment, however politically sensitive, was historically accurate. After much discussion, his words were allowed to stand and Thames was able to broadcast the programme, together with its concluding reference to British colonialism. But it was not transmitted in *This Week*'s usual networked slot. In London it went out on the following Friday at the less popular time of 6pm, and then at staggered times across the network, in slots that ranged from Friday teatime to Monday lunchtime and nearly midnight on UTV. Once more the timing had been an issue as well as the content. Peter Taylor had wanted the programme to be seen while the British press was lapping up the set pieces arranged for them by the Northern Ireland Office and army PR machines. By the following week the topicality was gone and the challenge to the cosmetic presentation was less obvious.

The right-wing newspapers monitored the row with some excitement, torn between their instinctive opposition to censorship, their pathological hatred of terrorists and their even greater antipathy to television journalists who refused to accept the consensus view. The liberal broadsheets remained suspicious of the Authority and what they saw as its arrogant stance. 'We have total power,' the *Guardian* quoted a spokesperson, 'we are the broadcasters' (19.8.77). W. Stephen Gilbert in the *Observer* thought that the programme was 'the best, most even handed and most informational piece on Northern Ireland that *This Week* have produced for a long time' (28.8.77). A Northern Ireland Office official told Peter Taylor he thought it 'stank' (Taylor 1979:24).

Behind the wire

At the end of August 1977, Peter Taylor, Alan Stewart and Ian Stuttard went back to the programme that had been sidetracked by the Jubilee. 'Life Behind the Wire' (22.9.77) was planned around the 8mm footage shot by Loyalist internees, showing them parading in paramilitary uniform. Taylor pointed out that this in itself 'highlighted the conflict between the government's insistence that the prisoners were common criminals lacking political motivation, and the inmates' view of themselves as political prisoners.' In response to a request for an interview, Roy Mason, Northern Ireland Secretary, said, 'Let it be known that the Northern Ireland Office would like the (comparative) peace and quiet reigning both inside and outside the wire to continue.' 'By spotlighting anomalies of the current penal system we would be stirring up a hornets' nest which is only emitting a low buzz just now,' wrote Stewart to David Elstein (memo 21.7.77). The NIO had suggested he make a profile of Roy Mason's first year in office instead (Taylor 1979:24). The prison officers had even greater reason to be cautious, as, over the last 18 months, six of their colleagues had been murdered. 'We have paid for devotion to duty with the life blood of some of our members,' said Desmond Irvine, Chief Officer of the Northern Ireland Prison Officers' Federation. After long discussions two prison officers agreed to be filmed; one was unnamed and shown in silhouette, but Irvine himself made the courageous decision to face the camera.

The completed programme began with a sight guaranteed to shock the audience,

> Hundreds of men in paramilitary uniform parade, drill, undergo weapon-training and political indoctrination, take orders from their own commanding officers and maintain military discipline, all under the eyes of gaolers who may not even speak to a prisoner without the permission of his commanding officer – a fellow prisoner (programme publicity).

The flags and uniforms of the UDA parade were all made from materials available in the prison. Special-category status had been achieved in 1972 by a hunger strike of internees, claiming that they were political prisoners, not criminals. It was granted by the Home Secretary of the time, William Whitelaw, who now, five years later, thinks the decision was 'utterly, wholly and entirely wrong'. When this programme was made, 650 prisoners still qualified for special-category status, with privileges including the right to wear their own clothes, receive food parcels, visits and letters, and to organize classes. The programme included stills of IRA prisoners doing weapons practice with dummy guns made in handcraft classes, conducting lessons on bomb making and even digging tunnels. Desmond Irvine confirms the situation, 'It's frowned on, but it's impossible to stop it.' When Roy Mason abolished special-category status in March 1976 he had stated, 'People who may once have claimed an ideal, are thugs and gangsters.' But at a Falls Road demonstration in support of the 'blanket men' – the 160 Republican prisoners who had been convicted since abolition and were refusing to be classed as criminals – the mother of Michael and Jackie MacMullen is unequivocal, 'They're at war. They never fought for their own gains, they fought for love of their country.' Prison officer Desmond Irvine himself recognized the history of Irish prisoners refusing to wear prison clothing. 'They do it because it is their belief … there must be a certain measure of respect which you give to them.'

In her review of the programme, Nancy Banks Smith echoed

his view, 'There is the pride of the devil about their attitude which is not without a hellish dignity' (*Guardian* 23.9.77). A *Guardian* 'staff reporter' attributed a hellish logic to them, too, 'An observer in Belfast [code for RUC?] says the IRA might be aiming to provoke a crackdown in security inside the prison which could provoke continuing support for them.' Desmond Irvine wrote to Peter Taylor congratulating him. 'Your superb handling of a very delicate topic and the manner in which it was presented resulted in praise from staff and prisoners.' He added,

> I believe the programme will ease the burden borne by my members. To be told by the spokesman for the Provos that they respected my frank answers to questions and would act in a reciprocal manner, gives me grounds for believing we are entering a new phase where co-operation between staff and prisoners will improve (Taylor 1979:24; *Guardian* 5.12.77).

Micky McMullen, the 'blanket man' whose mother had been interviewed, wrote to Alan Stewart: 'I was convicted for killing one British soldier, but am I not like other soldiers in time of war with one purpose in mind, kill before you are killed?' He argued that the rules of war, rather than those of law and order, were appropriate, and he elaborated his conviction that the 'war' must be taken to England.

> Unfortunate because of what war entails, especially a war like this, but we must be more cold blooded than our enemy. In this case it is a very difficult task to be more cold bloodied than the English as they have been at it now for hundreds of years (letter 19.8.77).

In this clash of definitions, Conservative Northern Ireland spokesman Airey Neave understood the attitude of the IRA prisoners and deplored it. He called for 'the most immediate action to stop the flow of Irish terrorist propaganda though the British news media'. Taylor had described the programme as 'real Colditz World War Two stuff'. It was an unfortunate analogy, as Neave had himself been in Colditz and had escaped in 1942. For him Taylor's words were an 'insult to the men who were honourable prisoners of war'. He protested to the IBA about perpetuating the 'myth that the terrorists in Northern Ireland are heroic and honourable soldiers' (*Daily Telegraph* 23.9.77). The IBA had had no objections to the programme, but Airey Neave was not the only politician to leave them in no doubt that their judgement was deemed unsatisfactory. Roy Mason wrote to Lady Plowden,

'I regret very much indeed the lack of concern for the possible effects of the programme. ... [It] is at best unbalanced and at worst positively harmful' (letter 29.9.77).

In Northern Ireland, Chief Constable Kenneth Newman had launched his own campaign. On the evening of transmission, he had issued an instruction telling every policeman that their lives were now in greater danger. In the event it seemed that his worst fears were realized, as eight days after the broadcast, prison officer Desmond Irvine was shot dead. The Provisional IRA had gone back on their earlier declaration of respect for his position. They now stated, 'Mr Irvine was consciously aware and fully recognized that jailed Republicans were prisoners of war. Despite this he and his colleagues continued to implement Mason's policy of classifying political prisoners as "criminals". In these circumstances and for these actions they can expect to be attacked.' In the wake of the killing, one Belfast journalist rang Peter Taylor and asked him how he felt about having blood on his hands. Taylor went to Irvine's funeral and seriously considered ending his coverage of Northern Ireland (to PH). ' "Putting lives at risk" and "responsible reporting" took on a new dimension,' he wrote (Taylor 1979:24).

Roy Mason's next complaint referred to all three recent *This Week* programmes. He deplored the

> tendentious language and caption material ... the presentation of allegations as if they were facts; and the clear impression given by those involved in the production that they believed in the case they were presenting ... a snide and distorted view. ... Incalculable assistance given to those who are interested in building up a case against the RUC (Potter 1990:212).

The Authority passed on these concerns to Thames, mentioning the 'cumulative effect of its programmes, all of which appeared to have a starting point which was critical of, if not actively hostile to, majority opinion in Ulster'. The employed staff at the IBA were more reluctant to jump to the government's support. They wrote to the members of the Authority observing that reactions to many programmes about Northern Ireland did

> little more than reflect the existing deep divisions within the community. Until those divisions show real signs of reconciliation it is not to be expected that our programmes will receive general approval and commendation, least of all from ministers and others who have the

unenviable responsibility for trying to achieve reconciliation and genuine progress (Potter 1989:212).

The matter of responsibility for Desmond Irvine's death was discussed between Roy Mason and Lady Plowden and the IBA agreed that the programme was not culpable.

That is not what one expects of responsible commentators

While this high-level row was taking place, Peter Taylor and Alan Stewart had begun looking into one of the darkest of Northern Ireland's corners – the allegations of ill treatment of terrorist suspects during interrogation by the Royal Ulster Constabulary. Taylor later described his sense of shock as he began to realize that these were not just allegations, but 'allegations with substance' (to PH). *This Week* was not the first to address this sensitive topic. On 2 March 1977 the BBC's *Tonight* had raised a political storm by broadcasting Keith Kyle's interview with schoolteacher Bernard O'Connor, who gave a detailed account of the treatment to which he had been subjected. His claims of being kicked, punched, humiliated and nearly suffocated were well documented and were checked many times by the BBC before the programme was committed to the air. Roy Mason and Airey Neave had both attacked the BBC as irresponsible and damaging to the morale of the police (Taylor 1980:167). Once more the programme was seen in the context of a 'propaganda war' in which any criticism of 'our side' meant that 'we' were losing. 'A review of present attitudes to media freedom is needed therefore, to take account of the present emergency. ... The BBC have given the impression they are not really on the side of civil power in Northern Ireland,' declared Neave (Curtis 1984:54–5). That programme, too, had been accused of causing the death of a law officer, as Constable Brown of the RUC was shot dead by the IRA a fortnight after transmission.

As the allegations of brutality continued, the RUC issued a press release,

> Some months ago the RUC publicly predicted that the campaign of propaganda against the Force would intensify. ... The volume and nature of the allegations should be interpreted not as a worrying indication of police misconduct but as a barometer of growing police success. ... There is now clear evidence that not only are allegations

being manufactured but that some prisoners are going to the extreme
lengths of injuring themselves so as to throw blame on the police.

And there followed a warning to those who would publicize such
allegations, 'allegations of torture and brutality are the spurious
"justification" put forward by terrorists for the murder of police
officers. … A heavy responsibility rests on all those who publicly
discuss this subject to measure their words and consider the
public consequences.' The statement asserted that despite 'human
frailty' no evidence has been produced 'to justify a prosecution
against any police officer for alleged ill-treatment' (RUC press
release 24.6.77). It was a difficult climate in which to work. Both
political parties and almost everyone in any position of authority were strongly opposed to any critical comment, and oppositional sources were by definition discredited. 'Journalism to be
effective, needs allies within the state apparatus, and these are
only forthcoming if there are internal conflicts of interest,' wrote
media researcher Philip Elliott, reflecting on the situation in 1979.
'To get the authorisation necessary to license an accusation or
opinion in public, journalists have increasingly had to rely on
institutions outside the British nation state, the European Court
of Human Rights and similar supra-national bodies' (Campaign
for Free Speech on Ireland 1979:37).

Medical evidence was the only objective confirmation that
brutality had been used, and it later emerged that several prison
doctors who had responsibility for examining the suspects before
and after their interrogation had been deeply concerned at what
was going on. But at the time they maintained a strict silence.
Dr Irwin, who the following spring agreed to be interviewed
by Mary Holland on *Weekend World* (11.3.79), did not reply to
Peter Taylor's hand-delivered letter, and the medical officer of
Castlereagh, Dr Page, put the phone down on him. Many GPs
refused to comment, but Dr James O'Rawe, a catholic whose practice drew patients from both communities, was prepared to help.
Taylor also learned that members of the Northern Ireland Police
Authority, including the protestant Councillor Jack Hassard, had
been making representations within the police service for several
months. He agreed to be interviewed anonymously. It was only
after 'lengthy and confidential discussions with senior members
of Northern Ireland's legal profession and judiciary' that the team
decided to proceed with their investigation (Taylor letter to *Daily*

Telegraph 1.11.77). There was speculation that Taylor's consultants may have 'included the Lord Chief Justice himself' (*Broadcast* 7.11.77).

But to make a credible programme, Taylor would need to persuade some of those making the allegations to speak to the camera. Since many suspects who had been interrogated were reluctant even to complain to their doctors – afraid they would be taken back for more of the same – this was extremely difficult. However, Dr O'Rawe introduced him to a protestant who had been interrogated for three days as a suspected member of a Loyalist paramilitary organization. Taylor saw him four days after he had been released.

> He said he had been spread-eagled against a wall and beaten, been bent across a chair in a crab position and punched in the stomach; been made to squat with his back to the wall for an hour, as if he were sitting on an imaginary chair; had his wrists bent and his fingers pulled (Taylor 1980:220).

'Inhuman and Degrading Treatment?' (27.10.77) eventually documented ten cases of ill treatment, confirmed by medical evidence.

The RUC strongly opposed the making of the programme, at first refusing any co-operation at all. Then, a week before transmission was planned, Chief Constable Kenneth Newman suggested he would grant an interview, provided he saw the whole programme first and had 'equal time'. Taylor telexed the script and details of the ten cases to the RUC press office, Elstein offered a five- or six-minute interview and there were high-level discussions between the RUC, the IBA and the senior management of Thames (*Guardian* 29.10.77). The day before transmission Newman refused an interview but proposed a five-minute statement to camera instead. *This Week* producer David Elstein agonized over the decision, tempted to take what seemed like a courageous stand and say 'no interview no programme', but Thames's new Head of Current Affairs, Peter Pagnamenta, fresh from the BBC, decreed that the ultimatum should be accepted (Bolton 1990:34). Peter Taylor felt seriously compromised. On the morning of transmission he flew to Belfast to film Newman's statement. 'I stood there while he did it, just itching to ask him a supplementary' (to PH).

Kenneth Newman's statement denied brutality and explained

the injuries observed by the doctors in several ways. Some prisoners come to police stations already bruised, some deliberately inflict injury on themselves, and some attack the investigators and provoke a situation where they must be restrained. In his conclusion, Taylor emphasized that this was not an interview, that *This Week* still believed the allegations to be correct, and called for an independent inquiry. In television circles it was noted as a 'very important and possibly dangerous precedent' to include 'an unchallenged statement of denial by an establishment body like the RUC who have a very serious case to answer' (*Broadcast* 7.11.77).

Ulster Television agreed to transmit the programme after discussions which lasted several hours, but, despite his victory, Newman was 'clearly very angry'. He warned RUC officers that the Provisional IRA might make the programme an excuse to attack them in their homes, and a few hours before it was due to go out, he put his men on 'red alert' (*Guardian* 27.10.77, 3.11.77). He was said to be consulting police lawyers about the possibility of prosecuting Thames, and on the day of transmission invited Lady Plowden, chair of the IBA, to lunch at his Belfast HQ and complained that the programme 'lacked balance'. ('Whose fault was that?' commented Peter Taylor (Taylor 1979:25).) The IBA was now the centre of a storm of protest, both public and private, and faced demands that they exercise their power of censorship. The Northern Ireland Office issued an unprecedented statement, specifically attacking Peter Taylor and the *This Week* team,

> It is significant that the producers and the reporter of this programme have produced three programmes in quick succession which have concentrated on presenting the blackest possible picture of events in Northern Ireland. After the last programme on prisons, a prison officer who appeared on the programme was murdered, and last night's programme may well place police officers, who deserve all support, at even further risk. That is not what one expects of responsible commentators (Curtis 1984:58–9).

But attacks from the NIO and the RUC 'were mild compared with the outrage evident in every line of Airey Neave's reaction', according to Derek Brown of the *Guardian*. 'In a statement of extraordinary virulence,' he declared the programme was 'reckless and arrogant and clearly designed to create prejudice and innuendo against the RUC and discredit the Chief Constable' (29.10.77). The

Daily Telegraph leader was headed 'Lethal television' and was an open call for political censorship. 'This is the third go the producers and reporters of *This Week* have had against the forces of law and order in Ulster. ... If the IBA will not stop this homicidal irresponsibility, the government must step in' (29.10.77). Responses from Ireland North and South were less heated. David McKitterick wrote in the *Irish Times*: 'Hardly anyone in Northern Ireland believes that members of the RUC do not rough up suspects. The only things in question in the minds of most people, are whether it is sanctioned at top level, and whether it is justified' (28.10.77).

When asked in the House of Commons by ex-*This Week* Producer, Labour MP Phillip Whitehead, if he would investigate the allegations, Roy Mason took the opportunity to express his views in no uncertain terms. The programme was 'irresponsible and insensitive' and he was sorry the IBA had allowed it to go out – a comment that Peter Taylor described as 'ominous, in view of later events' (Taylor 1980:222). Mason asserted that a prison officer was murdered 48 hours (as opposed to the correct length of time, which was eight days) after a *This Week* film had been transmitted, and the statement was repeated in the House of Lords. 'The official records of both Houses now carries a myth in the making,' wrote Peter Fiddick 'with the clearly intended implication that *This Week* is culpable in the death of Mr Desmond Irvine' (*Guardian* 5.12.1977).

Government anger was to be the downfall of *This Week*. From Jonathan Dimbleby's attack on MP Ian Sproat to Peter Taylor's persistent investigations of the tobacco companies, none of this was acceptable. But Northern Ireland remained the biggest irritant. Peter Taylor had been presenting programmes on the province with a consistency unusual for a current affairs series. At *This Week* different reporters tended to deal with the same topic and the same reporter with many different topics. Indeed Taylor had concurrently been engaged on what he described as one of the most enjoyable of his programmes for the series, spending nearly a year investigating the black market in Range Rovers across Europe and the USA (13.6.78). Nevertheless, in the 1970s a tendency to specialize had developed amongst strong and committed reporters, making the series more than usually 'reporter led'. With the backing of David Elstein and Jeremy Isaacs, Taylor pursued his interest in Northern Ireland into 1978, despite official disapproval. 'The pressure didn't come to me directly, it came from government through the IBA through to Thames and through to me – although in fact it didn't have much effect' was how he put it later (to PH). An IBA officer told David Elstein to 'lay off Northern Ireland' and to 'use another reporter' (Curtis 1984:59).

Premature at any time

But the regime was changing at Thames. In October 1977, George Cooper's contract as Managing Director came to an end and he was replaced by Bryan Cowgill, who had been Controller of BBC1 since 1974. He and Jeremy Isaacs did not get on. Isaacs sought reassurances that he, as Director of Programmes, would retain total responsibility for programming and scheduling, but in the end felt 'not able to breathe' (Potter 1990:64). And Peter Taylor did not give up his concern about the mistreatment of suspects. *This Week*'s documentation was passed to Amnesty International who were planning a visit to the province. The team was given more facilities than *This Week*, but denied access to the most important documents of all, the prison doctors' confidential reports. Even so, they confirmed the allegations of brutality, and concluded, 'Maltreatment has taken place with sufficient frequency to warrant a public enquiry to investigate it.' Taylor described it as a 'devastating document' (Taylor 1979:25).

On 28 May 1978 Roy Mason wrote in confidence to Nick Oosting, Deputy Secretary General of Amnesty International, asking him to postpone publication and await the government's comments, expected by the end of June. But the report was leaked to the *Guardian* and the *Irish Times*. On Wednesday 7 June, the BBC's *Tonight* programme commented on it, and Peter Taylor flew to Belfast to prepare a *This Week* for the following night. Since the previous reports had brought no obvious changes, Councillor Jack Hassard, who had been interviewed anonymously, was now prepared to face the camera and be named. He was open in his claim that both the Chief Constable and the Secretary of State had known all along what was happening (Taylor 1980:297).

> I'm here as a Councillor and a JP. ... I've been hiding behind offi-
> cialdom and banging my head against a stone wall for years. I don't
> intend to continue doing that for much longer. ... There are people
> who've been tortured and ill treated. ... The police force as a whole
> will never be acceptable while we have those villains behind the

scenes – villains who have gone unnoticed.

To Taylor's question on whether it was possible for the Chief Constable to be simply unaware of what appeared to have been happening, he replied,

> If the Chief Constable is naive enough to expect people to believe that well, listen, I tell you he's not with it at all. Because the blind and the stupid know what's happening so why should the Chief Constable not know what's happening? At least I have informed both the Chief Constable and the Secretary of State often enough.

The five minutes of filmed interviews were to be followed by a studio discussion involving Enoch Powell, John Taylor and Patrick Duffy. David Wheeler in the *Listener* commented, 'Aficionados of the way the box covers Northern Ireland will recognize this as straight-down-the-middle stuff, balanced almost to the point of anaesthesia' (15.6.78).

On that Thursday morning the IBA happened to be meeting. They took the opportunity to consider the programme planned for that evening and ruled that 'discussion of the report should be postponed until it is public, thereby giving those involved and the general public a chance to study it in detail'. There was no invocation of clauses in the Broadcasting Act and no discussion of possible amendments. And the decision was taken by IBA members against the advice of their own staff. David Glencross, Deputy Director of Television, criticized it in a note of protest to the Director General (Potter 1990:213). (Peter Taylor did not know of Glencross 's role. Later that summer he sat next to him on the Edinburgh shuttle, on his way to take part in a discussion on censorship at that year's television festival. He was still angry about the decision, and had sensed that Glencross was 'slightly uncomfortable' (to PH).)

The fury at Thames was huge. This time the management backed the programme makers and issued a statement regretting the IBA's decision. Throughout the day Thames tried to get the Authority to change its mind, especially as Roy Mason released the text of the government's response that very evening. The announcement caught the 6 o'clock news, in time for the Authority to be aware that the report was definitively in the public domain. In a final bid, Bryan Cowgill phoned IBA headquarters, where the only person who had not gone home was Director General Sir

Brian Young. He made it clear that he could not countermand a decision of the full Authority, and the programme was cancelled. The hope of reversing the ban meant that the potential contributors were not informed until the last minute. Enoch Powell had already arrived at the Belfast studio. 'If it's premature now it's premature at any time,' he said, and walked straight out through the revolving doors and was not seen again that night (DE to VWP). This time the ACTT carried out its threat to blank the screens and refused to transmit the comedy show put forward as an alternative ('with utter tastelessness', commented Liz Curtis (1984:62)). Instead there was a caption that read, 'The advertised programme at this time has been cancelled.' The National Union of Journalists supported the action, and legend has it that the blank screen got a reasonable rating.

When John Stapleton of BBC Television's *Nationwide* phoned the following morning to ask if his programme could show the pre-filmed sequences that Thames had not been allowed to transmit, Director of Programmes Jeremy Isaacs, who had steadfastly backed the *This Week* team over the previous year, agreed. The film was sent across London in a minicab to the BBC who showed it at 6.30 that evening with the caption, 'the film the IBA bosses will not let you see' (Taylor 1980:299).

Why can't we broadcast the truth?

The debate around Northern Ireland and the limits of responsible journalism continued. In March 1978 Jonathan Dimbleby assumed his most radical position yet, arguing that it was necessary to break away from the official framework and regard Northern Ireland as a colonial issue,

> If you can't see that the British army might be perceived by the catholic population as an army of occupation, then you can't see how the catholic population reacts to the IRA. If you can't see how the Irish catholic population reacts to the IRA, then you can't understand the British security problem in dealing with the IRA (quoted by Curtis 1984:150).

And for David Elstein, whose time as Producer of *This Week* had been marked by confrontations with the authorities, the duty of broadcast journalists 'is not to Westminster, but beyond, to the public at large, who are entitled to be informed, even if this embarrasses the politicians'. 'Why can't we broadcast the truth?'

he asked,

> What the public knows nothing about at all is the most sophisticated process of self censorship. That is when the 'brave' producer carefully stakes out the ground he thinks worth defending against institutional assault; and thereby concedes all ground which is never put in contention, and so is defined as untenable. By playing the game the producer endorses the rules.

For these reasons, the actual rows may seem 'narrow and somehow trivial' (Campaign for Free Speech on Ireland 1979:14–15).

At the other extreme, the right-wing Institute for the Study of Conflict criticized the content of all the main ITV current affairs programmes, *This Week*, *World in Action* and *Weekend World*. At a conference in 1978, 'pointed questions were asked about the political affiliations of those connected with the presentation of the programmes'. In the Institute's view the populist medium of television was not suitable for political debate. 'The mass audience tends … to lack independent criteria for judgement. … By definition, the leaders of society – whether in politics, industry, business or administration – are people who have the means of critical judgement' (Schlesinger et al 1983:144). In a curious echo of their view that the public at large are better off if they do *not* know what is going on, David Elstein had remarked, 'In ITV, producers are slowly coming to the conclusion that the most honest response to censorship of programmes about Northern Ireland is simply to stop making any.' *TVEye*, under Mike Townson, did not stop making programmes about the province – but their number was greatly reduced (ten editions in the eight years of *TVEye*, as opposed to 43 in the decade between 1968 and 1978).

The public mood was clearly changing, and not only at Thames Television. The report of the Bennett Commission, set up by Roy Mason in response to the Amnesty International report, was so deeply unsatisfactory to Gerry Fitt, SDLP MP for West Belfast, that for the first time in his political career he felt unable to support the Labour government in a vote of confidence (Taylor 1980:331). It was that motion, lost by a single vote on 28 March 1979, that opened the way for a general election and Margaret Thatcher's victory, ushering in a decade in which the sort of radical politics voiced by David Elstein and Jonathan Dimbleby in the 1970s came to sound naive and unrealistic.

7 PASSION OR SENSATION: *TVEYE*

Tabloid style and values

> The debate over the future of television should include more voices
> to oppose those who confuse serious current affairs with sterility,
> repetition and predictability. ... Current affairs should be driven
> by the desire to communicate to as many people as possible about
> the subjects that matter most to them (Mike Townson in *The Listener*
> 4.1.90).

This Week's Northern Ireland coverage had been highly controversial, but that was not the only factor that led to the shift in
policy that took the series off the air. 'No-one minds controversial programmes,' said Mike Townson, Editor of the replacement *TVEye*. He thought *This Week* 'had got into one of its boring
phases' (to PH). Paradoxically becoming 'boring' seemed to be
linked to the energy with which the series had pursued the issue
of Northern Ireland, which was not a popular topic with the
mass of viewers. By engaging with the central commitment of
current affairs, its duty 'to the public at large, who are entitled to
be informed, even if this embarrasses the politicians', it had been
pushing the boundaries of current affairs, and those boundaries
were contested in several ways. Politicians were anxious to spare
themselves embarrassment by declaring certain areas to be out
of bounds for pragmatic reasons associated with policy decisions
and national security, but a dangerous extension of that argument was that the public at large, the 'mass audience', was in any

case incompetent and 'tends … to lack independent criteria for judgement' (Institute for the Study of Conflict, quoted in Schlesinger et al 1983:144). The dilemma that underlay *TVEye*'s desire to broaden the audience by returning to a more populist style was its complicity in this downgrading of the audience's capacity to understand.

The reassertion of a more commercial imperative and the return to Caryl Doncaster's original concern for 'audience strength' implied a move away from political engagement – and it was a move which would please both the authorities, who were deeply unhappy about public criticism, and those whose chief concern was Thames Television as a business. The change in emphasis was part of a wider shift in company policy. In October 1977 Thames had gained a new managing director, Bryan Cowgill, and designated itself a 'company on the move' with a greater stress on entertainment and building the audience.

The launch of a new series was a rush decision, supported by the new Head of Current Affairs, Peter Pagnamenta, and against the wishes of David Elstein. Pagnamenta approached Mike Townson, editor of *Tonight*, who left the BBC at 24 hours' notice (Bolton 1990). The decision to change the name of the series was also taken at the 11th hour (DE to VWP), but a new name signalled a new direction – a different organizational style and a different approach to the audience. It was 'a change in the feel of the programme which was more than just a change in name' (PT to PH). Townson was brash and direct, opposed to pretensions and intellectualizing. In place of a relaxed masculine urbanity (problems were 'tiresome', colleagues were 'dear boy', production assistants made the tea), the atmosphere became less collegiate, more oriented to simply getting out there and doing it. Perhaps by coincidence, several women producers, including some who had worked with him at the BBC, joined the new series. Writing of Townson's time at *Tonight*, Roger Bolton – who became Editor of *This Week* when it returned in 1986 – paints a vivid picture of the man whose nickname had been 'Tiger'. He was scruffy and overweight and called people 'cock', but he 'had taken [*Tonight*] by the scruff of the neck, and by working 17 hours a day infused it with great energy'. Bolton described him as 'grafting tabloid style and values on to broadsheet journalism' (Bolton 1990:31).

There were many paradoxes in these shifting positions. Although Townson took the view that Northern Ireland was 'boring' to the public, under his editorship *Tonight* had broadcast many significant items on the province – notably Keith Kyle's interview with Bernard O'Connor who had been subjected to illegal interrogation techniques by the RUC (Kyle 1996:113–15). Yet he remained suspicious of the sort of journalistic 'commitment' and the 'passion of caring about a subject' that Elstein and Isaacs had encouraged. 'Why is so much current affairs approached as if the nation is being summoned to prayer?' he later demanded (*Listener* 4.1.90).

He shifted the emphasis away from long-running, slowly developing investigations that set out to be agenda-setting stuff to the more immediate concerns of the moment and human interest. For Townson current affairs is about the *now* and programmes should respond to events as they occur. They should not seek to be remembered for their special qualities, nor should they be designed to be seen more than once. They should concentrate on 'stories' rather than issues and avoid the politicized context that caused so much trouble. For him the most memorable *TVEye* programmes were the ones that gained a response from the press and the viewers. He was proud of freelancer Joan Shenton's 'Shanghai Surgeons' (24.4.80) on extraordinary techniques in Chinese surgery and of 'Here Comes Cruise' (27.10.83) in which *TVEye* built a fake cruise missile launcher and drove it from the American base at Greenham Common through the Berkshire lanes to gauge local reactions. Current affairs, he said, should aim for 'the same surefootedness which *Coronation Street* or *Match of the Day* show in their field' (to PH).

The 'passion of commitment', which involves an unflagging, long-standing interest, and an attention to detail which may not always be apparent on the surface, stood to be replaced by a politics of sensation – more concerned with a momentary excitement and with something eye-catching and immediate – which just might be less meticulous (and all those accusations were levelled at *TVEye*). The different approach to programming was received with dismay by many of the existing *This Week* team. 'I would have found it impossible to work on the programme,' said Jonathan Dimbleby (to PH). Within months of Townson's taking over the editorship, members of the team composed a memo accusing him of being unable to distinguish between 'what is significant and what is sensational' (*Daily Telegraph* 22.12.78).

Significant or sensational?

But for critic Chris Dunkley the first *TVEye* was '*This Week* with a new title and a new Editor. ... Their normal tight and polished product was loosened up and fuzzed out' (*Financial Times* 8.9.78). In some ways the loosening and fuzzing was a coincidence, since the first programme had been in preparation for a considerable length of time, but it certainly encroached into territory where, although there was no doubt about the importance of the event, celebrity and sensation had a hand in driving the agenda. 'To Mrs Brown a Daughter' (7.9.78) was a good populist story with medical and human interest, which seemed absolutely right to start the new series. A one-hour special followed the conception and birth of Louise Brown, the first 'test tube' baby. Reporter Peter Williams had been in touch with the surgeon, Patrick Steptoe, since making a *This Week* programme with him ten years earlier ('A Child of Your Own' (8.5.69)) and had followed Louise's parents through the process of in vitro fertilization and up to the birth. The government agency, the Central Office of Information, filmed the actual birth, and there were complex copyright agreements between the Associated Newspaper Group (ANG), who had purchased Mrs Brown's story for £300,000, and various other agencies which had rights to exploit the event. Thames negotiated a world exclusive on its programme and on the syndicated stills. All film trims, transcripts and other material were to be kept under lock and key for one year, and only one colour transparency could be borrowed for use in the *TV Times*. ANG even suggested that the Thames staff should sign a confidentiality agreement. Even Mr Brown, as he describes being taken to see his new born daughter, recalled that 'all I could see was police and security guards'.

The wheeling and dealing was already being described as 'squalid commercialism' (*Daily Mirror* 28.7.78) and it contributed to the scepticism with which the broadsheets received the programme. 'Money changed hands. The film does not challenge the morality or otherwise of the doctors' actions' (*Sunday Times* 3.9.78). 'A woman had her innards splattered all over television to help two doctors get rich,' wrote Julian Barnes – although it should be noted that he added with equal cynicism, 'This is the time of year when the permacrease safari suits come back from Sketchleys minus a few medal-like stains and investigative reporters prepare for another stint in the Ethiopian desert and up country guerrilla hideouts' (*New Statesman* 15.9.78).

Cynicism aside, the role and authority of current affairs journalism was certainly under question, and there was more to it than sensational splattered innards versus significant safari suits. As it happened, it would be Jeremy Isaacs, who had left Thames as Mike Townson was appointed, who went on to demonstrate, as Chief Executive of Channel 4, that, as well as a drive towards populism, there are other ways to widen the spread of voices contributing to the public debate.

Stories or issues?

For Jonathan Dimbleby the essence of *This Week* was that it had been a reporters' programme which focused essentially on issues. When, soon after Townson had taken over, he travelled to Nicaragua and gained an exclusive interview with the military dictator, General Anastasio Somoza (19.10.78), 'I made it clear it was *my* programme, not his programme' (to PH). But Townson had introduced changes that centralized control and gave the reporters less independence. He changed his own title from 'Producer' to 'Editor' – a more distant and less hands-on appellation – and upgraded 'directors' to 'producers'. The description gave them more status and stressed their organizational and hierarchical role. Peter Taylor said that Linda McDougal, who had joined the series from *Tonight*, had been 'told to keep an eye on me' when he made his next Northern Ireland programme, about the prisoners' 'dirty protest'. She was asked to call the office regularly when they were on location (talk 2003).

Townson believed that the self-indulgence of reporters had alienated the series from a wider audience, and argued that the producers should readjust that balance. 'There should be two reporters,' he said, 'one a visual reporter.' It was an interesting assumption about the relation between the visual and the verbal. John Birt and Peter Jay had deplored the way that visual values undermined verbal explanation, but for Townson reporters could be harnessed in their excessive pursuit of 'issues' by the construction of a visual 'story'. ('I'd like the film to look as sexy as possible,' he telexed a crew in Los Angeles. 'It's a unique chance in a *TVEye* run for a film which is visually a delight. All the tricks.') As well as stressing visual values, constructing a 'story' means engaging the audience's interest by structuring a programme around well-tried devices such as character and conflict. It implies a narrative shape which poses a dilemma to be solved and winds up with a satisfying conclusion. The renewed debate about the appropriateness of such structured 'stories' for current affairs echoed Bryan Magee's account of the tension between reporters who want to 'get the proportions right, to show truthfully how various elements in a situation are related to each other', and directors who want to 'highlight what is striking or unexpected or entertaining' (Magee 1966:53, 79).

Ironically *TVEye*'s change in emphasis did not give rise to filmic programmes in which reporters were less prominent. Instead it lent itself to a current affairs style in which they became *more* visible, but in a different way. 'It should be an "I" script with a touch of breathlessness about it (it *is* his own adventure story!)' wrote Townson of a *TVEye* edition that featured freelancer Gwynne Roberts trekking through the remote mountains of Kurdish Iraq to find the British hostage Michael Powell (28.1.82). A more populist approach also meant that celebrity could become an acceptable part of the mix. A reporter's personality could feature in a programme, their emotions and visible reactions could become part of the 'story' – even if their carefully argued political judgements remained unacceptable.

There was some nostalgia for *This Week* – and not only from those on the left. According to Philip Purser of the *Sunday Telegraph*, it was 'an extremely responsible and effective programme … give or take a couple of programmes on Northern Ireland, when it played into the hands of the thugs.' He concluded, 'I once said that it made the middle of the road a respectable place to be, which, on reflection could have been what finally disheartened David Elstein, Peter Taylor and Jonathan Dimbleby. To be accused of fairness was the last straw' (17.8.78). A few months later he wrote 'Let them bring back the name *This Week* with all its implications and scrap the present tatty, catch-penny designation and its sneaky promise of a keyhole view of some issue' (21.1.79).

But perhaps a patriarchal solemnity, secure in the rightness of its views, does not take sufficiently into account the sort of criticism Townson was making when he argued that the debate over the future of television should include a wider range of voices. Wanting the series to be more audience friendly was one way to

reach beyond its educated and politically aware circle of understanding. However, for many of the existing *This Week* team,
tabloid values meant an unwelcome compromise. It meant that
the audience were not to be pushed beyond what they *wanted* to
know, to be told what they *needed* to know. Jonathan Dimbleby
left, and before long Peter Taylor and Peter Williams also left.
Patrick O'Neill wrote in the *Daily Mail*,

> Mike Townson ... has made a few enemies inside television and a
> lot of friends outside with his 'televise and be damned' policy. He
> has developed a hard hitting, occasionally sensational but always
> watchable style for television current affairs. 'I don't intend to make
> programmes nobody watches,' he said (14.12.78).

It is easy to exaggerate the changes in order to make points and
spot the beginning of trends, but in retrospect it is clear that the
changes in mood and shifts in ideology were radical and irreversible, and they had as much to do with the political and economic
climate as with internal changes on the series.

Townson took over as industrial relations in the country were
deteriorating. 1978–79 saw the 'winter of discontent', with strikes
across the public services, and *TVEye* dealt with these conflicts
in the most traditional way. In February Llew Gardner interviewed the Chancellor of the Exchequer and scooped the BBC
for an extended interview with Prime Minister James Callaghan,
in which he admitted that his government had 'stumbled this
winter' (18.1 and 8.2.79); a Tory audience was invited to question trade unionists Clive Jenkins and John Edmunds (25.1.79)
and there was coverage of two weeks in a strike-bound hospital
(15.2.79). In May 1979 Margaret Thatcher was elected, determined
to introduce her own brand of economic and social radicalism,
and, in the late summer of that year, ITV itself was blacked out by
an 11-week strike (10 August–19 October 1979), causing millions
of pounds to be drained from the network in revenue (Potter
1990:68).

Mike Townson was to be the longest-serving editor of Thames's
main current affairs series, remaining with *TVEye* throughout its
eight-year run (September 1978–July 1986).

Increasing the drama

From the beginning *TVEye* covered an impressive range of international topics and, perhaps surprisingly, some of the accusations of sensationalism and prioritizing exciting 'stories' over exacting journalism were provoked by overseas items. Townson was keen to achieve some journalistic 'firsts' and in Julian Manyon the series gained a reporter with a reputation for ruthlessness and persistence in dealing with dangerous assignments ('it was pointless locking the door to him, he would walk right through it,' wrote Roger Bolton (1990:192)). Some producers on the series distrusted him and refused to work with him because of his uncompromising methods (to VWP). He had begun his career in Vietnam as a radio reporter, and in his first 18 months on *TVEye* travelled to Cambodia, where he revealed the full horror of Pol Pot's murderous regime; to Los Angeles where he reported on police tactics; to Rhodesia, as the civil war escalated; and to Iran. He and the teams who worked with him were prepared to take risks, and the dangers of many of these assignments were considerable.

'The Shah Versus the Mullahs' (14.12.78) was Manyon's first overseas programme for the series. It documented riots against Iran's pro-Western but autocratic ruler, and interviewed victims of torture. *TVEye*'s publicity machine was much more active than *This Week*'s had been, and the risks and vicissitudes of reporters in their quest for information became a feature of programme publicity. In Teheran, Manyon and director Norman Fenton were arrested at bayonet point while camera Royston Halliday narrowly escaped being fired at. The *Daily Mirror* quoted Manyon,

> We had to sit on the ground for half-an-hour while six soldiers trained their rifles on us. It was the worst moment in my life [Manyon was to live through a lot more worst moments]. Fortunately they never found the film, because it was hidden under the car bonnet. This is the film you will see tonight (14.12.78).

Within months the Shah was overthrown, and as Ayatollah Khomeini returned to establish a theocratic state, the *Sun* praised 'Julian Manyon who has been dodging bullets in the streets of the Iranian capital'. Press officer Mike Rhind managed to change the billings at short notice for Manyon's programme, 'Priest's Move' (1.2.79), and much was made of the drama of the change.

In November 1979 followers of the Ayatollah burst into the

US embassy in Teheran and held hostage more than 100 staff and marines. Manyon was able to win the trust of the armed students guarding the compound by showing them a video of his earlier programme on the Shah's atrocities. Although they did not let the crew in, they made an audio tape of the hostages' answers to Manyon's questions ('Talking to the Hostages' 6.12.79).

Between his programmes on Iran, Julian Manyon became one of the first Western journalists to get into Cambodia, which had become cut off from the outside world under the control of the Khmer Rouge. In the aftermath of the Vietnam War, this militant group had launched a regime of mass executions and population clearances, forcing hundred of thousands of townspeople out of their homes and into the countryside. Guided by Thai villagers, Manyon, producer David Mills, camera Ian Killian and sound Trefor Hunter walked through the booby-trapped border from Thailand and made a film that revealed atrocities on an almost unimaginable scale (5.5.79). A second programme showed the plight of the thousands of refugees who had fled across the border into Thailand and found that many had been forced back into Cambodia (17.5.79). When several viewers wrote that the programme had been unfair to the Thai government, Mike Townson replied 'to the best of my knowledge the facts reported are not in dispute and it was therefore correct to focus on them. We were reporting (not commenting).' Ten years later, Manyon accompanied a young widow, Var Hong, seen suffering from anthrax in the earlier programme, as she went back to Cambodia to trace her relatives (18.1.90).

In August 1980 news was coming through of a dramatic strike in the Polish shipyards at Gdansk. The previous year *TVEye* had angered the Polish embassy with a film on catholicism (22.3.79) – forbidden in communist Poland – and the team had been arrested for filming a village priest. Although it had not had much success with the critics ('The bedraggled crew were finally released, alas, for they brought back a load of droning religious material best left in the dungeons of the Polish Police,' wrote the *Daily Mirror* (23.3.79)), the embassy had warned that it might not co-operate with Thames in the future. Journalists were flocking to Gdansk, but there were prevarications over *TVEye*'s visa request. Although Mike Townson later admitted that they had not been formally turned down, he decided to turn the delay to their advantage, so Julian Manyon travelled as a tourist and the film was shot with an amateur 8mm camera. The resulting programme conveyed a real sense of urgency and presence as the Solidarity union won unprecedented recognition from the communist government. 'Seven Days in Gdansk' (4.9.80) won a Royal Television Society award and Manyon became 'reporter of the year'.

The Polish embassy were even angrier than before, arguing that 'the refusal of the official visa never took place, therefore I must assume it was a deliberate decision of the *TVEye* team to break the rules of decent journalism. ... They used cheap and unprofessional tricks to increase the drama of the subject covered.'

TV Lie?

The line between 'increasing the drama' through a stylistic device and misleading the viewers with an outright lie is not as clear-cut as it may seem, nor has experimentation with programme styles ever been confined to a few controversial reporters. At issue is the authority of the journalist's speech, the authenticity of the imagery and the interaction between the two. The device of the home movie, with its casual filmic style, had given an added power to 'Seven Days in Gdansk', and it had been interpreted as implying that the crew had been denied permission to film – an implication that was questionable. In 'The Last Round Up?' (25.5.81), Julian Manyon's programme about Czechoslovakian dissidents, reconstruction and clandestine filming were part of a major complaint whose reverberations echoed for more than a decade. The programme was widely debated in the press and Manyon became the centre of a long-running dispute in which Cold War politics, double dealing and espionage crossed with accusations of populism and sensationalism. It was also a test for the newly established body, the Broadcasting Complaints Commission (BCC).

Partly influenced by the extensive campaigns by Mary White-house and her National Viewers and Listeners Association, the BCC was set up by the 1980 Broadcasting Act with a brief to respond to those who felt they had been wrongly treated by broadcast programmes. Many condemned it as a state-sponsored censor and it was described by QC Geoffrey Robertson as a quango with 'dangers unmitigated' (*Listener* 13.11.80). However, the Commission could only rule on 'unjust and unfair treatment' of individuals who had participated in programmes or who had 'a direct interest in the subject matter'. It opened its doors for business on 1 June, and the Czech émigré Jan Kavan became its first complainant. The intensely political issues raised by 'The Last Round Up?' were at the limits of its remit and far from Mary Whitehouse's moralistic concerns.

Across the media many journalists and left-wing intellectuals had retained a particular empathy for the plight of Czechoslovakia, which, long before its Velvet Revolution in 1989, had seemed to pose a possible socialist future balanced between centralized Stalinism and rampant capitalism. *This Week*'s long-standing interest in the country had resulted in its moving programmes on the 1968 'Prague Spring' and the Soviet repression that followed. In 1981 Jan Kavan was respected as a democrat in exile. Based in London, he ran a publishing company, the Palach Press, named after the student Jan Palach who had burned himself to death in protest at the Soviet invasion. The organization imported printed materials from Czechoslovakia, and distributed – undercover – publications that were banned in that country. In April 1981 Kavan contacted *TVEye*, together with photographer Ivan Kyncl who had secretly filmed dissidents in prison in Czechoslovakia. He suggested slipping across the border to do some interviews. While a possible programme was under discussion, a van loaded with Kavan's materials, driven by two French sympathizers, was stopped at the Czech border and the drivers were arrested. Although they were soon released, the Czech authorities stepped up arrests amongst dissidents. Kavan had previously told Manyon and producer Norman Fenton that there had been documents hidden in the van, listing the names and addresses of dissidents who were to receive the materials. The link seemed obvious: the incident with the van would make a centre for the story and the arrests became the 'Last Round Up' of the title. The crew went off to Czechoslovakia via Vienna and Rome, and filmed a meeting with the volunteer drivers in Paris.

(There were several sub-plots to this story. One concerned the working hours of the electrician on the shoot. A memo from Vic O'Brien of the electricians' trade union, complained that the hours were 'appalling'. Producer Jon Blair, who had taken over from Fenton, replied, detailing night filming and flights between Rome, Paris and Vienna. 'I'm sorry if his hours were "appalling" but that also happens to be a fair summary of my views on the current EEPTU/ITCA agreement.')

The filming was done, including a reconstruction of the van being loaded in Paris and a distant shot of Kavan and the drivers in a café. But a problem arose. Kavan began to hint that he did not want a link made between the van and the arrests and suggested that there had been no list. (According to Manyon these were not clear assertions, as 'Kavan is the most opaque person, certainly in Europe and possibly on the planet' (to PH).) Manyon considered fudging the commentary but Mike Townson was convinced that the link should stay. So, when they screened the almost completed programme for the press with Kavan present, Manyon deliberately omitted the crucial claim about the list. The programme was duly transmitted – with the line about the list in place.

Kavan's response was an angry letter now stating categorically that there had been no list. He said it was untrue, unnecessary and had put the dissidents in further danger. Later he swore an affidavit to this effect and put in a full-blown complaint to the BCC. His other charges included: that he had not agreed to the meeting in Paris being filmed, that the programme had implied the drivers were paid agents and they were not, and that Palach Press was not given a final say over a film that could put people in danger. The fact that Manyon had inserted the line of commentary after Kavan had seen the film appeared to give credibility to the complaint.

It was a major crisis for *TVEye* and the issues for responsible journalism were huge. Effectively the question to be answered was, who was lying – the Czech dissident struggling against an oppressive government or the pushy reporter with a reputation for ruthlessness? It was possible that the team had been set up, but many saw the complaint in the context of Townson's reputed aim for popularity at the expense of meticulous research and Manyon's reputation for crashing on regardless. However, Thames's management backed them up and Townson responded to the complaints: Kavan *did* know he was being filmed and had even agreed a signal, and the Palach Press had *not* been promised a final say.

Although this was the shadowy territory of Cold War politics where false trails were part of the scenery, Kavan had considerable support amongst radical journalists – and the attacks on *TVEye* came from the *New Statesman*, the *Sunday Times* Insight team and *Private Eye*. The *Sunday Times* Insight article, spread across eight

columns, was headed 'TV Lie' (29.11.81). It alleged that a deliberate journalistic untruth was tolerated to make a better story and
that this had endangered the dissidents. But, interestingly, Insight
also added comments on the film-making style. 'Some of the
facts were doctored to give the film what its makers describe as a
"Starsky and Hutch" quality', and the article was illustrated with
a photograph of Manyon whose bushy hair-style did make him
look rather like Paul Michael Glaser as Starsky. Not only was the
sequence in which Kavan meets the drivers filmed without the
consent of the participants, claimed Insight, but the commentary
gave the impression that it was filmed as it actually happened,
which 'gave it a compelling authority'. The word 'reconstruction'
only appeared on the screen as the van was being loaded. Thus
the accusation of a 'lie' was backed up by quoting filmic techniques. For the writers, the central charge was 'that facts were
changed to make a more entertaining programme'. They went
on to point out that this 'provides the first major test of the effectiveness' of the new Broadcasting Complaints Commission. But
'neither the company nor the Commission is properly equipped
to deal with a complaint that is so bitterly disputed'.

Manyon and Townson sued the *Sunday Times* for libel and
obtained an injunction preventing the BCC from investigating
while the action was pending. The procedure was muddied by
the problem of Norman Fenton's expenses.

In another of the sub-plots to this affair, Norman Fenton, the
first producer allocated to the story, was, by 1984, in dispute with
Thames. After eight years' service – producing many distinguished programmes, often in extremely dangerous circumstances, as in Afghanistan and Argentina – his rolling contract
had not been renewed owing to the size of his expenses, which
were, in Manyon's words, 'of a historically generous nature' (to
PH). Management claimed that £13,000 in a single year needed to
be accounted for. The ACTT took up Fenton's cause and argued
that this was unfair dismissal as it was not clear that the expenses
were invalid. Especially in a war zone, the union claimed, money
has to be paid out in circumstances where receipts are not available. Thames did not accept that the ACTT had any standing in
the case and in consequence the union blacked out *TVEye* on 12
January 1984 and threatened the transmission of Thames news.
When the company finally accepted the ACTT's role and took
the dispute to the conciliation service ACAS, the ban was lifted

(*Broadcast* 20.1.84). But Fenton was in no mood to co-operate with Thames. He refused to confirm his original statement of his and Manyon's first meeting with Kavan, and at one point even threatened to give evidence for the *Sunday Times* (JM to PH).

The suit was eventually settled out of court, and in March 1984 the *Sunday Times* won costs. They accepted that Thames management did not knowingly put out untruths but they did not withdraw their allegations. Hence the blame was put on Manyon personally. When the libel action was over, the BCC went back to the case, but was hindered by its lack of ability to collect evidence. Fenton was not available to be questioned and the Commission had no powers to call witnesses, nor to deal with the political complexities of the complaint (*Broadcast* 19.3.84).

When the BCC finally delivered its judgement in November 1985, in order to remain within its remit, it needed to ensure that the personal interests of the complainant were the subject of 'unjust and unfair treatment' or that he had had 'a direct interest in the subject matter' – which meant that the conclusions were somewhat tortuous. But it criticized Manyon and upheld three out of the five complaints (BCC Adjudication 17.9.85). These were that Manyon had claimed untruthfully that Czech campaigner Jiri Ruml was trying to set up a workers' movement, increasing the danger he faced; that Kavan had been given insufficient opportunity to comment on the script; and that the claim there was a list of names and addresses constituted 'unjust treatment' which directly affected Kavan. The filming of Kavan in Paris did not constitute unfair treatment, as he should have known that filming was likely to take place.

The BCC had guidelines on investigative journalism. For example, 'individuals should normally have the opportunity to make representations on material to be shown which is critical of them' (Fourth Report), and this is what they referred to in their judgements about Kavan's right to hear the commentary. However, significantly, they too commented on the language and tone of the programme: to describe the group of friends who organized the activities as a 'secret organization' 'had somewhat melodramatic overtones', the choice of words was 'unfortunate'; the Paris filming was an 'inaccurate presentation of the facts' (by which, presumably, they, like the *Sunday Times*, meant there was an implication that this was not a reconstruction, but contemporary filming).

Following this damning ruling Julian Manyon offered his resignation, but it was not accepted by Barrie Sales (Director of News and Current Affairs). Thames Television continued to stand by him and *TVEye* continued to insist that the programme was made in good faith. A three-minute apology was transmitted, in which the NUJ insisted that the staff involved were named so that other Thames journalists were not implicated. Norman Fenton complained that the BCC had failed to take his evidence into account, and Jan Kavan stated that 'Thames has violated the fundamental rules of journalism' (*Broadcast* 22.11.85).

Julian Manyon continued to make hard-hitting programmes for *TVEye* and for *This Week* when it returned in 1986 (including the most notorious programme of all – 'Death on the Rock'). But it was the early 1990s before he finally managed to clear his name. When Czechoslovakia was freed from communist rule, the new Czech Republic put in place a process called 'lustration' to search the files of the secret police in order to root out collaborators and double agents. Documents were published which showed that Jan Kavan *had* in fact been an informer. Manyon decided to go to Prague personally to track down the files of the police operation when the van was searched back in 1981. 'I had to take a photocopier as hand luggage and spent eight hours in a darkened room photocopying 500 pages of STB [secret police] documentation, page by page' (to PH). Amongst the documents was a typed list of 500 names and addresses.

For the first time in its history, the BCC overturned a judgement:

> It is now established, and indeed accepted by Mr Kavan, that there were in fact uncoded names and addresses in the van, including those of the intended recipients of some of the literature in it. ... He knew that this was so, and ... he did not inform the Commission. The Commission do not accept his explanation that he was justified in withholding this information by reason of the need to protect others (5.3.92).

In yet another twist to the story, after a lengthy process in the Czech courts, Jan Kavan was cleared of being a collaborator (*Independent* 26.2.04).

Channel 4 and journalistic authority

Two critiques of the established current affairs style had been running in parallel through the 1970s, and both came to fruition in the 1980s. Mike Townson was amongst many who challenged the single-minded commitment to investigate and report come what may. His views echoed a populist position, which evoked a democratic rhetoric but implied that television journalism, just like other television genres, depends for its authority on audience numbers. If a substantial number of viewers do not watch, the argument goes, then arrogant journalists, pursuing their own agenda, have no right to take up space on the airwaves. But television journalism had also been challenged from an 'access' perspective, from the point of view of many who felt they had been excluded from a mainstream which was far too narrow. From this perspective the assumption by skilled professionals of an authoritative right to speak and to define a situation on behalf of others, excludes alternative meanings and involves an implicit exercise of power (Hall 1977). Although knowledgeable in its own terms, such journalism is based on a form of ignorance – ignorance of the lived reality of those who are part of the situations reported on and of the frameworks within which *they* create their own meaningful interpretation of their lives.

The Annan Committee on the Future of Broadcasting had reported in 1977. It asserted that there were important gaps in the attitudes that current affairs, and indeed UK television as a whole, had taken for granted. It concluded that, instead of an ITV2, the nation needed a new *type* of channel, which would address diversity and seek to satisfy minority tastes and interests (Negrine 1998:29–34). Consequently it adopted Anthony Smith's proposal for an Open Broadcasting Authority, which would 'celebrate difference rather than consensus' and would set out to please 'everyone some of the time, no-one all of the time' (Darlow 2004:168, 213). The channel would not make its own programmes, but act as a publisher of other companies' productions. Although this was seen as a leftish proposal, it had not been immediately accepted by the Labour government. So, with the arrival of the Conservatives in 1979, some campaigners evoked the new voguish language of Thatcherism and stressed that a channel of this sort would encourage small businesses and be part of the enterprise culture (Darlow 2004:202–3). Channel 4 was launched in

1982, strongly supported by the Conservative Home Secretary, William Whitelaw. Jeremy Isaacs became its Chief Executive, and Mrs Thatcher admonished him, 'Stand up for free enterprise, Mr Isaacs, won't you?' (Isaacs 1989:107).

As it happened Isaacs presided over a ground-breaking experiment that explicitly recognized the need for different forms of journalistic authority and had an acute sense of the voices pressing at the edges of the mainstream. As a non-commercial broadcaster Channel 4 was free to set its priorities according to cultural and democratic ends – and indeed was required to do so by its licence conditions (Harvey 1994:111–17; Bonner 1998:28). Isaacs's first actions in relation to current affairs were to commission two companies run by women to balance what had been a remarkable absence in the history of the genre, and to create outlets for frankly *unbalanced* treatments of current events, many of which ditched the traditional reporter and invented their own dynamic formats using the full range of techniques from animation through to hectoring captions and dramatic reconstructions (Blanchard and Morley 1982).

The new channel aimed to expand current affairs beyond the narrow circle of the educated and the politically aware, but unlike Mike Townson who was trying to reach a bigger, more general audience, Channel 4 set out to appeal to many distinct constituencies. Jeremy Isaacs stated his aim to 'make programmes of special appeal to particular audiences; ... to provide platforms for the widest range of opinion in utterance, discussion and debate'. If the audience for each programme was small – and some of the audiences for those early programmes hardly registered – the idea was that when added together they would represent a far more diverse spread of the UK population (Bonner 1998:29–30). The coming of the fourth channel changed the UK broadcasting ecology. The 'Channel 4 remit' became an important fact of the British broadcasting scene and the new perspective posed definite challenges to *TVEye* and other current affairs programmes. It extended the range of possibilities, in styles of programme making and in the *type* of authority a journalist could evoke.

But 'the restraints of a Channel 4 budget ... and a future dependent on an almost annual renewal of a profitable commission do not create the perfect conditions for risk taking,' wrote one journalist (Hird 1985), and the more radical of the experiments did not last. By 1987 the channel's regular current affairs output had settled down under the title *Dispatches*, and that series joined *Panorama, World in Action* and *This Week* as a major peak-time strand, dedicated to the breadth and balance of the main-stream agenda. But unlike the other three series, *Dispatches* was commissioned as single, one-off programmes, each from a different production company, so was not able to build a regular team working together over the years.

And the enterprise culture was having other effects. The growing strength of the independent sector, virtually created by Channel 4, was to lead to cost cutting, casualization and a loss of job security within the ITV companies. Paul Bonner, who was Jeremy Isaacs's deputy at Channel 4 from 1981, later wrote that it had the effect of 'channelling an originally left-wing aspiration for independent production into a reality which was to give an important extra lever to the free-market right' (Bonner 1998:34).

Margaret Thatcher and 1984

Mike Townson was fond of what he called the 'block buster' approach, in which several reporters contribute material on a topic from different locations, and, despite the accusations of populism, *TVEye* programmes continued to cover the broad sweep of the established current affairs agenda, alternating over-seas, domestic, social and political editions. The series continued the current affairs commitment to revealing the plight of the underprivileged, and, when Denis Tuohy reported from a street in Birkenhead where no adult over 20 had a job – apart from a blind man who, ironically, worked in the benefits office – he made a clear link with politics, since the local authority's privatiza-tion initiatives had brought about many redundancies (28.11.85). The stories of resignation and lack of hope were the obverse of the 1980s obsession with money making and enterprise. As it happened *News at Ten*, which followed the programme, dramati-cally reported on the 'success' of the government's privatization initiatives.

Peter Gill, who had been South Asia correspondent for the *Daily Telegraph*, had continued to pursue the interest in devel-opment which had been given such a public face by Jonathan Dimbleby's programmes. He has described his aim to fill in the context of global politics, including the politics of international aid (Gill 1986). In the summer of 1984 it was becoming apparent to the Ethiopian Relief and Rehabilitation Commission and to the international agencies that there was likely to be a recurrence of the dreadful famine of the 1970s, and Gill was the first journalist to receive a visa. The report from Michael Buerk of BBC News has stuck in the public consciousness as encapsulating the unimaginable despair in the north of Ethiopia at that time, but in 'Bitter Harvest' (25.10.1984) Peter Gill starkly illustrated the connection with global economics by intercutting the famine with the European grain mountain. The film was held up by a technicians' dispute at Thames and its impact was weakened, as it was transmitted a week after the non-political BBC story had broken.

Peter Gill followed up his investigations of the aid business with 'Does the Giving Help?' (8.11.84) and wanted to back it up with a book. He says that Thames management were 'singularly unenthusiastic' (Harrison and Palmer 1986:138), but the book eventually became *A Year in the Death of Africa* (1986), which powerfully reveals the wheeling and dealing behind the scenes at the UN agencies. The theme was later taken up in Gill's 'Mr Famine' (5.11.87) made for the re-instated *This Week*.

Peter Gill and Norman Fenton had also followed the disastrous Soviet invasion of Afghanistan, and became the first British crew to go to that country after the Western media were expelled (16.7.81). Later, as the Soviets withdrew, Gill made a moving programme on the young Russian soldiers who had found themselves caught up in a seemingly endless guerrilla war to which they had no commitment (14.4.88). But it was Nick Downie who had conveyed the sense of being in the midst of that dangerous and disorganized conflict. He had spent four months with rebel tribesman fighting Afghan government forces in the run-up to the invasion. Writing to a viewer who had been concerned at the sight of dead and dying men, Downie describes a ten-day battle that resulted in hundreds of casualties. 'Terrible things happen in war, and if one is to retain one's sanity as an outsider then you have to distance yourself emotionally from what is going on. ... I am a journalist ... and I regard it as my absolute duty to report what I see, not to interfere in events or try to influence them in any way' ('Afghanistan: With the Rebels' 10.1.80). Two years later, as the resistance dragged on, he was back, making the 500-mile journey from Pakistan through inhospitable mountainous terrain partly on foot, carrying his heavy camera gear ('Challenging the Russians' 14.1.82).

In April 1982 Argentinian forces sailed towards the Malvinas Islands just off the Argentine coast. The islands were a British possession, inhabited by people of British descent who knew them as the Falklands, and they had long been a thorn in the flesh of Argentinian nationalism. The brutal military dictatorship that had been in power since 1976 now decided to distract from its own unpopular rule and profit from the patriotic support that would follow from recapturing the islands. British Prime Minister Margaret Thatcher instantly dispatched a naval Task Force, amidst a blaze of publicity and nationalist fervour – at least on the part of the tabloid newspapers. Reporting from the ships of the Task Force was heavily restricted (Harris 1983), but Julian Manyon's hectic life now took him to Buenos Aires, together with producer Norman Fenton, camera Ted Adcock and sound Trefor Hunter – a team that had worked together on many other risky assignments. Despite the war situation, a number of UK journalists and crews, as well as international news agencies, based themselves in the Argentinian capital. Margaret Thatcher was, of course, outraged at any breach of patriotic solidarity. Denis Tuohy later wrote 'the British government, if it could, would have dispatched us all to the Tower' (*Scotsman* 17.12.92). For five weeks *TVEye*, fronted by Tuohy, interleaved reports from the enemy capital with reports on diplomacy and assessments of the lead-up to the war. Then, in an extended edition on 13 May, it was reported that Manyon and the crew had been kidnapped. The extraordinary circumstances led to a scooped interview with the Argentinian military President, General Galtieri.

As the crew were driving to their hotel, their car had been blocked by another, and Manyon, Adcock and Hunter were grabbed by armed men. 'I had no idea who or what they were, military police, soldiers or just plain death squads' (Bolton 1990:136). With a gun at their heads they were driven to a remote field, told to remove their clothes and walk away from the kidnappers who were pointing rifles at them. They heard the rifles being cocked and thought their time had come, but the next sound was of the cars driving away. The three were left stranded and terrified in their underpants. Fortunately Fenton had managed to slip away and they were eventually rescued with the help of the Argentinian Interior Minister. He sent a car to collect them, and invited them to grab some clothes and to join him at the headquarters of the armed forces where the top brass were celebrating Navy Day.

Fenton was already there with an ITN crew. Amazingly Galtieri emerged from the gathering and Manyon grabbed the only interview with the enemy head of state.

The war was over within the month, and, flushed with her success, Mrs Thatcher now declared herself ready to destroy what she described as 'the enemy within'. Nineteen-eighty-four was to see a decisive confrontation between her radical free-marketeering government and a militant trade union representing a solidly working-class industry which still had iconic status – coal mining. The strike was widely believed to have been provoked by a government determined to break this bastion of union power. That self-confident working-class self-awareness which had given a sense of identity to the new television audience in the early days of ITV was radically transformed by the miners' strike of 1984, and the year-long confrontation between Thatcher and the National Union of Mineworkers under its charismatic leader Arthur Scargill.

Remembering the strikes of 1972 and 1974, *TVEye* interviewed Scargill (29.3.84) and Ian MacGregor of the National Coal Board (24.5.84) and reported from the first colliery to stop work – which had found itself 'besieged by police and inundated with camera crews' (5.4.84). The villagers claimed that the media had 'capitalized on their drama, distorted the situation and blown up events out of all proportion' (*Broadcast* 25.5.84). Julian Manyon looked at the highly contentious police tactics (3.5.84) and at the intimidation of miners who refused to strike (31.5.84). Finally he reported from the North East as the winter dragged on and the strike began to peter out (6.12.84).

As politics became increasingly personalized, the figure of Margaret Thatcher came to dominate the media. The Falklands adventure and the miners' strike consolidated her image as the Iron Lady, and her remarkable fortitude and obstinate courage was admired even by her enemies when she narrowly escaped assassination as an IRA bomb devastated her hotel at the Conservative Party Conference that same year. And there was careful attention to her image – her hair, her voice and every detail of her appearance and manner. Encouraged by her publicity chief, Gordon Reece, she began to give interviews to the 'softer' tabloids rather than the more 'serious' media. She had complained about a live interview by Llew Gardner in early 1982 (18.2.82). Despite – or perhaps because of – his long experience (and despite a special chair being flown in from Sweden for the Prime Minister to sit on), Gardner's abrasive style did not please her and she refused to be interviewed by him again (Cockerell 1988:268; Cockerell et al 1984:192). Further interviews for *TVEye* were pre-recorded.

Fashion and corporate accident

The late 1980s was the time of high Thatcherism. The Falklands War had been fought and won, the miners had been defeated and there was a decisive shift in attitudes towards a free-market ideology, with its celebration of consumerism, financial success, entrepreneurism and a new management culture. The government's council house sales and the privatization of public utilities set a mood that was reflected in the increasingly expensive and colour-saturated advertisements that interleaved ITV programmes.

'Our television journalism is more vulnerable to fashion and to corporate accident than it should be,' wrote critic Peter Fiddick in a 1984 *Tribute to Thames Television* (p. 12). On the one hand the new audiences sought by Channel 4 were made up of diverse social groupings based on ethnicity, gender, sexuality, disability, locality – anything, it seemed, other than social class. And on the other hand, across the Independent Television network there was pressure to give priority to an undifferentiated mass appeal. Partly as a consequence of this more overt commercialism, a current affairs enterprise rooted in journalistic independence with no regard for taste or fashion and aspiring to accurate and persistent reporting, was looking even more fragile. Although the major companies, including Thames and Granada, continued to see the prestige of quality current affairs as an essential part of the mix, Thames was now on shakier ground. In 1985 it was the subject of a take-over bid which was blocked by the IBA.

8 MORE DRUMS: DEATH AND THE ROCK

This Week again: more drums

In 1985 Thames's abrasive Managing Director Bryan Cowgill was replaced by Richard Dunn. Now aged 42, he had joined the company as an assistant to Jeremy Isaacs in 1978, and by 1981 was on the Board of Management as Director of Production. Dunn invited David Elstein back to Thames as Director of Programmes and suggested that he should re-launch *This Week*. 'Nothing could do more to restore our status than to replace our current flagship with something more like a battleship or cruiser,' he wrote (DE to PH). To emphasize the change, the Karelia music was brought back in a newly recorded version – with more drums.

The new Editor was Roger Bolton, more in the Jeremy Isaacs than the Mike Townson mode, even though Bolton had been deputy to Townson on the BBC's *Tonight*. In 1978 he had taken over as *Tonight*'s Editor, and then had become Editor of *Panorama* where he set out to 'lead the public debate as opposed to reflecting it'. As he took over from Townson, once more the emphasis was to swing the series away from *TVEye*'s 'stories', prioritizing audience appeal, back towards 'issues' that might well be, in his own words, 'important but less easily accessible' (Bolton 1990:53, 178). He had a reputation for high seriousness and had already weathered some major political rows, especially over that most dangerous of topics, Northern Ireland. There were to be three Irish stories in his first year at *This Week*, including the very first edition. Jonathan Dimbleby, now an influential television figure, rejoined the programme with a sense of some unfinished business. His approach chimed with Bolton's and he became the face of the series, introducing each edition from the studio.

As with previous changes of name and direction, there were many continuities, not always achieved without some internal tensions. 'I was steering the programme through an agenda which Jonathan Dimbleby and I agreed on but some of the rest of the team did not,' wrote Bolton. 'Eventually I changed direction a little and mixed in more popular subject matter' (Bolton 1990). So the 1987–88 season began with three cultural/social signs of the times. John Taylor, in his first report for the series, went to Majorca to talk to the 'bonking, boorish Brits' on holiday, including interviewing one young man in prison. The *New Statesman* reviewer wrote, 'if you didn't see it, get a tape' (17.9.87). The following week, Margaret Jay reported from Holland on euthanasia and the moral questions raised in the light of AIDS (24.9.87), and in the first week of October came 'The Battle for the Bottom' (1.10.87). Peter Gill reported on the *Daily Star* newspaper's plunge down market. 'The Star is vulgar,' proclaims its editor, Mike Gabbert, as he flicks through pictures of topless pin-ups. 'Vulgarity is a very good thing. It's not pornography.' Philip Purser wrote that 'the best ideas in current affairs television just now are all in *This Week*' (*Daily Mail* 2.10.87).

In 1987 the series moved back to its 8.30 slot. David Elstein had wanted the earlier, more popular time of 7.30, but Bolton argued that that would make it a different type of programme (DE to PH). But the writing was on the wall. By the late 1980s debates within Thames had less to do with the importance and democratic role of current affairs than with sheer survival. The question of audience appeal and audience numbers was taking on a political significance and a new urgency.

A fundamental theoretical break

With its high-spending, stroppy unions and a regulatory body that had power to intervene in market decisions, ITV did not fit Margaret Thatcher's model of an efficient industry. As Director of Production at Thames, Richard Dunn had already begun to address the criticisms and had cut costs in the company. This had provoked a series of strikes and at one point he had organized a 'management emergency service' to keep transmission going. In 1985, three months after he became Managing Director, there was an attempt to take over Thames by a company in a much more rapacious entrepreneurial mode. Carlton Communications was run by Michael Green, a profit-focused millionaire who was to gain the ear of Margaret Thatcher and who wrote briefing papers on broadcasting for her (Davidson 1992:5, 33). He had made his money through technical facilities and production companies and had ambitions to add a broadcaster to his empire. Thames's long-standing shareholders, BET and Thorn EMI, accepted his offer, but Dunn appealed to the IBA on the grounds that Carlton had no track record in public service broadcasting. The Authority blocked the bid (Davidson 1992.32). Instead Thames was floated on the stock market. BET and Thorn EMI retained 56 per cent of the shares and the rest were widely spread amongst the public, including the staff.

However, in its confident second term, the Conservative government had run an energetic programme of privatization of public utilities and was turning its attention to the public services. Long-established institutions, including the National Health Service and education, were coming under scrutiny. Broadcasting, too, was part of the manifesto, and the aim was to 'free' the commercial companies from the 'burden' of regulation and public service responsibilities.

The BBC was a particular irritant to the government since it was funded by a licence fee and was outside the commercial market. A committee was set up under economist Alan Peacock to reconsider its funding, including 'securing income from the consumer other than through the licence fee'. The market basis of its report, published in 1986, 'was a fundamental theoretical break with all previous official reports on broadcasting in Britain,' wrote Paul Bonner in the official history of the IBA (Bonner 1998:78). In historian Paddy Scannell's view, the report's 'stringent economic approach ... completely shifted the grounds of the discussion' (Scannell 1990:21). But although the Committee treated broadcasting as a private commodity rather than a public good, it did list programmes that would be 'suitable for public patronage' and these included current affairs as well as news and documentaries. Such a separation meant that the traditional diverse mix which had juxtaposed audience appeal with serious journalism, and had led to such a productive interaction between the two, was likely to be challenged under a market regime.

Although the report was concerned with the BBC, Peacock threw in the suggestion that the ITV franchises could be auctioned to the highest bidder, rather than allocated by the regulatory Authority in its current, rather arcane manner (described, rather contemptuously, as a 'beauty contest' (Goodwin 1998:115)). In 1987 Thatcher herself chaired a cabinet committee on the future of ITV, and the government set about drafting a new Broadcasting Bill. The climate for the sort of current affairs that would be an integral part of a commercial channel, but would remain independent of commercial pressures, was becoming increasingly chilly.

In 1988 Richard Dunn became chair of the Independent Television Association (ITVA), the body that represented all the ITV companies, in charge of negotiating with the government and liaising with the IBA over the provisions of the Bill.

Dangerous assignments

Meanwhile Roger Bolton was moving away from populism. He was acutely aware of the danger of media spectacle, which could provoke more excitement than insight. 'We are all too often summoned by the sound of gunfire,' he commented, and aimed to investigate issues of public interest *before* they reached flashpoint. Yet current affairs would always need to engage itself with the striking events of the day – and these have included major wars, massacres and coups, as well as innumerable low-level conflicts that might otherwise have escaped the notice of the international community. Many overseas assignments of this sort entailed hardship and carried considerable dangers for reporters and crews. *This Week* and *TVEye* crews had been arrested or threatened in parts of the world ranging from Poland, Iran and Argentina to Northern Ireland. They had filmed unpredictable conflicts between heavily armed youths who were a law unto themselves in Lebanon, Ethiopia and Belfast. The risks taken by cameraman Nick Downie in Rhodesia, Afghanistan and Western Sahara had been huge and his collaborator and sound recordist, Richard Cecil, had been shot dead by his side. Roger Bolton's editorship began with a similar tragedy. A *This Week* team consisting of reporter Peter Gill, producer Alan Stewart, camera Ian Killian and sound John Heasman were travelling in Southern Sudan with some other journalists and local helpers. They had just completed a film on the relation between famine and the civil war which was raging in that country, when one of their trucks ran over a landmine. The explosion threw the vehicle off the track, killing Alan Stewart and seriously injuring Ian Killian. They were in a deserted area, eight hours' drive from the Kenyan border and the nearest Red Cross post. Peter Gill describes rescuing the battered cans of film (to PH), and 'Where Hunger is a Weapon' was transmitted on 6 November 1986, concluding with a tribute to Alan Stewart.

Promotional culture?

'Vulgarity is a very good thing,' Mike Gabbert of the *Daily Star* had declared, and it was a message from the 1980s that would seep from the popular press on to the television screens of the 1990s and 2000s. Led by newspapers such as the *Sun* and the *Star*, 'tabloid' communication was coming to mean not so much popular attractiveness and accessibility, as the more questionable qualities of salaciousness and titillation. In the mood of the late 1980s this could be seen as amusing rather than shocking, part of a fascination for style, dazzle, stories, jokes, minor amusements, posing and performance, which was reflected in glossy magazines like *The Face* and *Esquire* as well as television gossip and the burgeoning advertising industry. 'The most efficient industries of the 1980s have been the lie manufacturers, where lying and mythmaking are not just isolated, haphazard events ... but systematic and structural,' wrote commentator Max Arundale at the end of the decade, when the 1990 Broadcasting Act made advertisements, together with the rest of the commercial television output, subject only to complaint rather than initial scrutiny (*Guardian Weekend* 14–15.7.90). Politics and politicians were themselves increasingly concerned with image and presentation, and enthusiastically participated in a promotional culture in which public relations played a key role (Cockerell 1988:234–5).

However, despite the obsession with the superficial and the cynical, by the mid-1980s UK television was broadcasting a more comprehensive and diverse coverage of contemporary events than ever before. Outlets were multiplying as the extension of viewing hours brought early-morning television with the commercial *TV-AM* (1983–92), which was at first committed to serious news and current issues, and *Breakfast Time* on the BBC (1983–). Channel 4

launched a number of series given over to specific areas of interest – including *Africa Express*, and *Europe Express*, edited by Peter
Gill – and introduced innovations in scheduling, which included
'themed evenings' and 'seasons' on particular topics. Across the
television output there was a real expansion of political and international topics, including specialized series, such as *The Money
Programme* on economic issues, BBC's *Rough Justice* on crime and
criminality, and Channel 4's *Hard News* on the press. Television
could be seen as a distraction from everyday life, but it was also
finding new ways to explore the world around it. Many innovations showed that the two trends could benefit each other.

This Week itself got a new logo, which kicked off each edition
with the dramatic impact and the visual sparkle of the times.
Created with the special-effects facilities which were now an
essential part of television production, huge metallic letters
moved across the screen to form the words THIS WEEK, allowing sequences from the coming programme and from previous
programmes to be constructed into a montage behind them.

Programmes and issues

Plenty of editions of the new *This Week* dealt straightforwardly
with 'issues', even when their material was disturbing. 'We will
discuss sexual behaviour with an openness some of you might
find disconcerting,' warned Jonathan Dimbleby in his introduction to 'AIDS, the Last Chance' (23 and 30.10.86) The explosive
AIDS epidemic was challenging accepted taboos on public speech.
At first the condition had been labelled a 'gay plague', seen almost
as a judgement for irresponsible sexual behaviour, but before long
a serious commentary on AIDS was contributing to a climate
in which sexual language and explicit sexual depictions were
commonplace. A new vocabulary came into public circulation as
topics which had previously been completely forbidden or had
aroused a storm of controversy – such as *This Week*'s sex education programmes of the 1970s – were forced into the open. For a
brief moment there was a thoughtful, multi-faceted debate across
the British media on issues that involved sexuality, sex education, sexual practices and sexual abuse. This may sound remarkably naive to viewers accustomed to television of the 2000s where
programmes with titles such as *101 Embarrassing Sexual Accidents*
and *The Sex Inspectors* are regular fare (C4 26.7.04; C4 23.11.04), but

in the mid-1980s it came as a surprise that the image of a teacher holding up a condom was no longer considered gratuitous and provocative.

In 1985, as the scale of the AIDS epidemic became clear, reporter Peter Prendergast had talked to sufferer Bill Ayres on how the gay community was learning to cope (*TVEye* 28.2.85). On the reinstated *This Week*, a new reporter, Margaret Jay, interviewed young people who echoed those who had spoken to Desmond Wilcox about abortion back in the 1960s, telling of the pressures for promiscuous sex. Her two programmes provoked 6,000 telephone calls. Jay came to specialize in the subject and later headed the National AIDS Trust, because 'I wanted to be involved in a directly hands-on way in something I'd been interested in as a commentator' (*Evening Standard* 14.12.92).

Most programmes on the new *This Week* eschewed sensation and drama, reaching out to the understanding of the audience rather than seeking to provoke emotional reactions. They included careful expositions of a social or political controversy, and explanations of changing legislation, and they regularly used televisual techniques, including superimposed text and increasingly sophisticated graphics to clarify points. Some relatively random examples include, 'For the Sake of the Children' (24.5.90) which laid out the contradiction between the Race Relations Act which forbids discrimination on the grounds of race or religion, and the Education Act which offers parental choice. How is this contradiction resolved, asks reporter Margaret Gilmour, when parents want to reject a school because the majority of the students are muslim? In 'Letter to Gorbachev' (26.5.88), as the Cold War was thawing, Lorraine Heggessey and Ann Burns travelled as tourists to Latvia, despite the risks of the heavy Soviet presence in that country. Filming with amateur cameras they spoke to nationalists campaigning covertly for independence; and these sequences are interleaved with archive footage and an exposition of Baltic history. And there was an exploration of the mind-set of protestants in Northern Ireland, when, once more, the history of that province was clearly outlined (10.11.88). These programmes prioritized clarity and factuality and were fronted by modest reporters who were rarely visible. Even when Heggessey and Burns were travelling in a potentially dangerous environment, they avoided playing up the drama of their personal situation. Such programmes demonstrated the routine, thorough, informative approach that a secure weekly series was able to deploy.

It is notable that a significant number of women were now acting as reporters and producers, and many of them went on to develop influential careers. Lorraine Heggessey became the first woman to head BBC1 (2000–2005), and, as Baroness Jay, Margaret Jay became leader of the House of Lords under the 1997 Labour government. In 1997–98 she ran the government's Women's Unit. 'Women's issues are no longer social and political death, inviting ridicule from the world of men. That is progress,' wrote journalist Polly Toynbee. 'But,' she continued, 'the dread F word is still one step too far.' Margaret Jay had declined to call herself a feminist (*Guardian* 10.11.98).

'There are certain areas of the British national interest that you shouldn't get involved in'

Roger Bolton estimated that about one in five editions under his Editorship could be labelled 'investigatory' – and investigation could be explosive.

The late 1980s were a prelude to the television turmoil of the 1990s. The 1990 Broadcasting Act would bring a dramatic change in direction for British television, fuelled by the ideology of the Thatcher government, and it was *This Week* that provided what Labour leader Neil Kinnock described as 'the fuse' (*This Week* 17.12.92). Once more the sensitive question of Northern Ireland would drive the series to breaking point and become the focus of a maelstrom of political currents. 'Death on the Rock' (28.4.88) was estimated to have been seen by 6.5 million viewers. It led to the biggest row of the decade and its reverberations shook the television world. The programme was in the traditional mode of investigatory journalism and it provoked in Margaret Thatcher a reaction that was 'much deeper than furious' (*Sunday Times* 10.2.91).

Backed by careful research and presented with well-honed clarity, the programme challenged the official version of the foiling of a bomb plot and the killing of three IRA members by British soldiers of the undercover SAS in the British territory of Gibraltar. It outraged the government by daring to raise questions about the legality of their tough – and covert – measures against terrorism; it renewed basic questions about the scope of current affairs and its right to investigate sensitive areas and to push at the political agenda rather than simply report it; and crucially, it contributed to the intensifying debate about the public service role of commercial television in the UK.

A lightning conductor for intense feelings

> The national interest is no holy grail in the exclusive guardian-ship of the government of the day. ... Freedom to publish is itself a fundamental and enduring part of the national interest. So too is the power of the press and broadcast media to act as a curb on the abuse of power or maladministration.

commented Lord Windlesham and QC Richard Rampton in their report on 'Death on the Rock' (Windlesham and Rampton 1989:13). The report had been commissioned by Thames Television management in a mood close to panic as it was battered by criti-cism from the government and a hostile and immoderate press. They did not consult the production team who at first threatened not to participate. 'It looked to me like a process of intimidation,' wrote Roger Bolton (1990:270). But in the event the report turned out to be a thoughtful analysis of the programme in the context of an informed review of the current affairs genre and its qualities. Its judgements hinged on a crucial distinction. 'Producers need to have a clear idea of a programme's purpose: is it to expose wrong doing, or is it to postulate questions that are capable of more than one answer? ... Confusion of purpose at this stage can lead to misunderstanding and recriminations later.' It concluded that 'Death on the Rock' pointed to one 'possible' explanation of events rather than a 'single' conclusion (Windlesham and Ramp-ton 1989:17, 143).

The cool consideration of issues is less attractive than passion-ate advocacy, but for Windlesham, as well as 'the thoroughness with which [Death on the Rock] was made', it was the 'vividness with which it was presented' that made it a 'lightning conductor for ... intense feelings' (p. 143). In the event it was the lightning conductor that won out. The careful consideration, the balance and the vindication of the programme counted for little in the wider political context.

A citizen first and a journalist second?

Did the SAS men have the law on their side when they shot dead Danny McCann, Sean Savage and Mairead Farrell who were unarmed at the time? Were the soldiers acting in self-defence or were they operating what has become known as a 'shoot-to-kill policy', simply eliminating a group of known terrorists outside the due process of law without arrest, trial or verdict?

asked Jonathan Dimbleby in his preamble to 'Death on the Rock' (28.4.88).

Roger Bolton had already lived through two major confrontations with the Conservative government. Margaret Thatcher had come to power determined to clamp down on terrorists and to make sure that no media report could in any way be deemed to be giving them legitimacy. (An aide told Roger Bolton, 'the media have got to decide ... whether they are going to join the human race or not. ... You have to be a citizen first and a journalist second' (Bolton 1990:40).) Just before the 1979 election Thatcher's close friend and adviser, Airey Neave, had been assassinated, and she had been appalled when, under Bolton's editorship, the BBC's *Tonight* had interviewed an anonymous member of the Irish National Liberation Army – the group responsible for the killing (July 1979). She had asked the Attorney General to consider legal action, and when, only two months later, Bolton, now editing *Panorama*, produced an item that involved filming an IRA roadblock she publicly attacked the BBC and demanded that it 'put its house in order'. Pressure was put on the Corporation to find a scapegoat, and Bolton was temporarily removed from his job. (He tells the story vividly in his memoirs, *Death on the Rock and Other Stories* 1990.) The police used the Prevention of Terrorism Act to seize the untransmitted copy of the film and the BBC governors insisted that the projected programme was abandoned. The Corporation tightened its procedures and effectively it became impossible to interview members of groups responsible for atrocities and hence to gain any sort of insight into their motives and mind-set (Schlesinger et al 1983:127). Now that 'fundamental clash of principle' between a government that claimed the right to define the national interest, and broadcasters responsible to a diverse democratic public, which Bolton had first witnessed over Northern Ireland in the early 1970s, was coming to a head again, and he would find himself once more on the receiving end of the 'Number 10 flame throwers' (Bolton 1990:21; *Observer* 4.3.90).

In Northern Ireland itself, the 'blanket' protest in the prisons had developed into long hunger strikes in which ten Republican prisoners had starved to death, including Bobby Sands, elected as Sinn Fein MP for Fermanagh and South Tyrone. They were greeted as martyrs by the catholics, and the bitterness between the communities and the British army had increased. A resolution seemed further off than ever. In 1984 Margaret Thatcher herself had been targeted, and narrowly escaped death when her conference hotel in Brighton was bombed. The British hardened their approach, using informers, covert action and operations by the undercover SAS. Thatcher wrote in her memoirs that 'force is the only thing they understand', and there were accusations of a 'shoot to kill' policy. 'If you are getting into SAS country you are saying the end justifies the means,' a Thatcher colleague told Roger Bolton (*Observer* 4.3.90).

On 6 March 1988, two years into Bolton's editorship of the new *This Week*, the Gibraltar shootings took pace. The first reports asserted that an armed IRA group had been tracked to Gibraltar from Spain and had planted a car bomb, targeting a popular parade by the Royal Anglian Regiment. ITN reported 'a fierce gun battle'. However, the following day Foreign Secretary Geoffrey Howe told the Commons that the three were 'found not to be carrying arms' and that no bomb had been found. Roger Bolton writes of his growing puzzlement about the press accounts of the deaths (Bolton 1990:191). Many questions seemed unanswered. Why were the IRA members shot dead if unarmed? Why were they not arrested as they crossed the border from Spain? If the authorities believed there was a bomb in a car, why was the area not cleared? Most importantly, had the soldiers been operating within the law? Bolton asked Julian Manyon and producer Chris Oxley to investigate. They had been on the point of leaving for Japan for a story on the car industry, but Oxley went instead to Gibraltar to look for witnesses while Manyon went to Spain where he gained detailed information on the Spanish police operation that had monitored the IRA group at the request of the British. Bolton himself tried – unsuccessfully – to get an account from the Ministry of Defence and Downing Street. Researcher Eamon Hardy travelled to Belfast, and a second researcher, Alison Cahn, joined the team in Gibraltar. She did what the local police had apparently not done, and knocked on around 150 doors, trying to speak to everyone who lived within sight of the petrol station where the shootings had taken place. The team met witnesses who had already spoken to the local press, and despite encountering considerable reluctance to become involved ('with the IRA on one side and the SAS on the other, what would you expect?' was how one contact put it) they tracked down some new ones. These included Mrs Carmen Proetta, who agreed to speak to the cameras, and 19-year-old Kenneth Asquez, who was not willing to meet them but submitted a written statement to a lawyer.

Bolton negotiated a 45-minute network slot with a break in the middle for commercials, and the programme was introduced and rounded off by Jonathan Dimbleby. While 'Death on the Rock' was being completed, Dimbleby himself made another Irish 'Easter' programme. He visited West Belfast to gauge the mood of the Republican community on the anniversary of the 1916 uprising in the aftermath of the Gibraltar shootings and the attacks and counter-attacks that had accompanied the IRA members' funerals. His film showed dramatic murals which turned the three into martyrs; he met an unemployed youth of a pipe band who declared support for the IRA; he filmed Martin McGuinness of Sinn Fein telling a rally that the conditions created by the British 'have made armed struggle inevitable' (7.4.88). It was inflammatory stuff, but unlike the call for 'one last push' a decade earlier, it did not draw particular comment. That was left for 'Death on the Rock'. Meanwhile, *This Week*'s researcher Eamon Hardy was warned by the IRA to get out of Belfast (Bolton 1990:220).

'Death on the Rock' began by reminding viewers of the horrors of the IRA campaigns, with a moving sequence on Ronnie Hill, who was still in a coma following the bombing at Enniskillen the previous year. It then detailed the movements of the IRA members through Spain, and, with the assistance of the Spanish police, reconstructed the surveillance operation as they were trailed across the Costa del Sol to the border with Gibraltar. It showed the actual location of the bomb – discovered two days after the shootings in an underground car park in the coastal resort of Marbella.

For all the uproar which was to follow this programme, there was no criticism of the technique of reconstruction, which had been so vigorously criticized in 'The Last Round Up?' only seven years earlier. It was now an accepted part of the current affairs repertoire, and the reconstructed sequences with the Spanish police and the terrorist leaving the bomb were carefully shot and clearly labelled. (Roger Bolton had also wanted to blow up a car to illustrate the damage that a bomb would have caused, but the Ministry of Defence refused to co-operate.)

The second half of the programme featured the interviews with witnesses. None of them had heard the soldiers give challenges or warnings. Carmen Proetta, who had the best view, said she had seen Farrell and Savage putting their hands in the air rather than making threatening gestures, and two witnesses said that shots had been fired into the bodies when they were on the ground. In what turned out to be a massive understatement, Manyon's commentary introduced Proetta's statement as one which 'would cause great controversy'. In the final section the eminent QC George Carman called for 'a full examination of what actually occurred'.

Roger Bolton has pointed out that the usual way to end such a programme and to maintain balance is to include a response from the government, but 'we encountered a lack of co-operation from the authorities which was unique in my experience' (*35 Years on the Front Line*). Despite frequent requests, the Ministry of Defence refused to comment before an inquest took place, even though no date had been set. Even so this meant that the programme could be criticized for its timing, and even seen as a contempt of court, which might prejudice the inquest. At least that was the line taken by Foreign Secretary Geoffrey Howe, who personally telephoned Lord Thomson, chair of the IBA, two days before transmission was due, to demand that it should be postponed. The Authority took advice, previewed the programme, and David Glencross, Director of Television, responded that it had been approved 'at the highest level' (Bonner 1998:72–3). After all, the inquest would take place in Gibraltar where the events had already received considerable publicity. But on the day of transmission Howe renewed his request and publicized it at a press conference. In Glencross's view, if the government had not intervened, drawing attention to those very issues it wanted to hush up, the programme would have been quickly forgotten (to VWP). As it was, questions on 'trial by television' were asked in the Commons, Margaret Thatcher described her feelings as 'much deeper than being furious' and the press went on the attack.

The *Sun* called the programme a piece of IRA propaganda and described Roger Bolton as being 'lower than a snake's belly'. ('I'm not sure what that means,' Bolton commented, 'but I'm sure the *Sun* has been there' (*Observer* 4.3.90).) The *Sunday Times* Insight team set out once again to undermine *This Week*'s research. They predicted, 'What started as trial by television may yet become a trial of television.'

But this was not the left-leaning Insight team of the early 1980s. In 1988 the editor of the *Sunday Times* was Andrew Neil, who, as a former Northern Ireland correspondent, had good contacts with Ministry of Defence personnel and was doubling as Chairman of Rupert Murdoch's satellite television company, Sky TV. Murdoch also controlled *The Times*, the *Sunday Times*, the *Sun* and the *News of the World* and had wider television ambitions. Regulations about cross ownership of the media prevented him from controlling a terrestrial channel, although he had earlier bought shares in LWT. He was consequently using his newspapers to campaign against the regulated public service structure of British television. So it was not surprising that when the press set out to discredit the programme, the production team, the witnesses and the IBA into the bargain, the *Sunday Times* and the other Murdoch papers were in the lead. The fact that Julian Manyon still had an outstanding Broadcasting Complaints Commission judgement against him did not help. Worst treated was Carmen Proetta who was smeared as a brothel keeper. The *Sun* called her 'The Tart of Gib' and her picture was on most front pages. The *Sunday Times* alleged that she had lied about the British because she hated them, and her family, including her young daughter, were pestered for information about her. She eventually won libel awards against the *Sunday Times* as well as the *Sun* and the *Daily Mirror* (*Independent* 1.3.90).

Later some *Sunday Times* journalists complained publicly that their work had not been accurately used because it 'contradicted the official line', and the *Sunday Times* NUJ chapel called for an inquiry (Bonner 1998:75).

This Week had just settled into its autumn season when the Gibraltar inquest began, and the team had a distinct sense that they, too, were on trial, particularly when the headline in the *Evening Standard* was 'I lied for TV's Death on the Rock'. Kenneth Asquez had withdrawn his evidence and accused Thames of pressurizing him and offering him money. This was, in Bolton's words 'more than a crisis. This was a disaster' (Bolton 1990:1). In the event the retraction was retracted. But the coroner advised the jury against an open verdict and they consequently decided, with a majority of 9-2, that the three IRA members were killed lawfully. The programme's credibility had been challenged. 'The government and its supporters in the press claimed total victory and turned on *This Week*. ... There will be no further inquiry into the shootings. ... There was to be an inquiry into the programme makers, however,' wrote Bolton (*Observer* 4.3.90). Thames's new Chair, Sir Ian Trethowan, had had experience of these things, as he had been Director General of the BBC at the time of the INLA episode. On behalf of Thames he invited Privy Councillor Lord Windlesham to lead an inquiry into the circumstances around the making of the programme. Windlesham was a former Conservative leader of the House of Lords and a former minister in the Northern Ireland Office who also happened to be a good friend of Foreign Secretary Geoffrey Howe. It was a rather unpromising start. The newspapers reported that investigative journalism was on trial, and that its future, the future of Thames Television and of the Independent Broadcasting Authority itself hung on the outcome. 'The IBA will meet its end with Gibraltar as its epitaph,' wrote *TV Week* (Bolton 1990:14, 272).

However, Lord Windlesham had some experience of current affairs television. As David Hennessey, he had himself once been in charge of *This Week* as a Director of Programmes at Associated-Rediffusion (1961–63) and he was the author of several books on public service broadcasting. In *Broadcasting in a Free Society* he had written, 'a politically independent system of broadcasting is an essential element in a free society, and should not be taken for granted' (Windlesham 1981:41–2). By the winter of 1988–89, public concern about government interference over 'Death on the Rock' was mounting, and, in the event, the Windlesham/Rampton report vindicated the programme, making only minor criticisms concerning the way the witnesses had been introduced. Geoffrey Howe attacked it as being 'about television, by television, for television' (*Observer* 4.3.90). The programme won a number of industry awards.

It was later revealed that Home Secretary Douglas Hurd had disagreed with Geoffrey Howe and had felt it was not appropriate for the government to intervene in 'Death on the Rock' (Bonner 1998:78). However, just as the Windlesham/Rampton Inquiry was getting under way, he announced an even more restrictive measure, one which had long been advocated by right-wing politicians and newspapers such as the *Daily Telegraph*. This was a ban on the broadcasting of voices of individuals belonging to certain organizations linked to terrorism, even if they were elected representatives. It followed a similar ban which had been in place in the Republic of Ireland since 1972, and, of course, the organizations most affected were the IRA and their political wing, Sinn Fein. But only the *voice* was illegal. Broadcasters' attempts to subvert the ban gave rise to the ludicrous situation whereby spokespeople for Sinn Fein, including party leader Gerry Adams, who was an elected MP, were frequently *seen* on television, but their voices were replaced by those of actors. The strange, dislocated effect of these floating voices was deliberate. It would have been possible to synchronize a new voice perfectly, but the point would have been lost. Even so, the ban meant that an important political constituency could not be properly represented. The government had 'declared impartiality illegal', stated the Controller of BBC Northern Ireland, Dr Colin Morris (Baker 1996:122). 'The freedom to report was being reduced again,' wrote Bolton (*Observer* 4.3.90). The ban remained in place for seven years.

Margaret Thatcher was deeply outraged by the audacity of *This Week*'s journalism. For her, it was, quite literally, treachery to question the actions of the security services. An eminent Conservative peer told Roger Bolton that he hoped the experience of the Inquiry 'would put us and other television teams off making such programmes'. He was also told by a vocal critic of the programme, 'Of course there was a shoot to kill policy in Gibraltar, just as we had in the Far East and in Aden. ... But its none of your business. There are certain areas of the British national interest that you shouldn't get involved in' (*Observer* 4.3.90).

Thatcher was already determined to shake up what she saw as the cosy duopoly that controlled television in the UK, and 'Death on the Rock' strengthened her resolve. Her government's dislike of investigative reporting was paradoxically in line with its free-market principles. It was the powerful television regulator, the IBA, that had protected *This Week*, and the existence of that Authority hampered the operation of the market in commercial television. 'If the IBA had a chance of influencing the White Paper [on broadcasting] it lost it with the row over "Death on the Rock". Privately Thatcher had resolved that the regulator had to go' (Davidson 1992:16).

Broadcasting Act 1990

'There is a direct link between "Death on the Rock" and the Broadcasting Act,' claimed Neil Kinnock, Labour leader at the time (*This Week* 17.12.92). It was an exaggeration no doubt, even, according to the official history of the IBA, a 'myth' (Bonner 1998:77). But it was one that was widely believed. The changes to UK television introduced by the 1990 Act were to be even greater than the introduction of the commercial channel which had provoked such a heated national debate in the 1950s. Margaret Thatcher had been re-elected for a third term with her radical vision of privatization and economic liberalization undimmed, and the Act would push this project into broadcasting. Under its provisions, the Independent Broadcasting Authority was to be replaced by an Independent Television Commission – a new regulator with a 'light touch' and reduced powers – and the 'auction' suggested by the Peacock Report would take place, meaning that television companies must put in a financial bid for the right to broadcast. It was a measure that many thought was designed to punish companies that had made life uncomfortable for politicians by making programmes with priorities other than audience appeal.

The multi-channel era, heralded by satellite and cable channels, was already bringing new commercial competitors for ITV, and it was clear that the companies would soon lose the monopoly on advertising that had underpinned their prosperity and confidence. The Act decreed that Channel 4 was to sell its own advertising, and a fifth terrestrial channel, also to be funded by advertising, was mooted. 'There will be enough competition to the ITV stations to satisfy the most demanding free market proponents,' wrote Thames's Chair, Ian Trethowan, in the company's 1990 Annual Report. It was a situation that gave rise to new questions about the role of current affairs as part of a broad public service commitment. If ITV had more competition and less regulation it would be less likely to find space for innovative informational programmes, let alone politically risky ones.

Along with increased competition went a different conceptualization of the audience. Thames now sought out 'younger and more upmarket viewers' to attract their advertisers, and there was an increase in institutional, industrial and corporate advertising. 'The development of programme "brands" – programming designed to have a demonstrable appeal to a specifically defined audience segment – will be essential in maintaining the company's competitive edge' (*Annual Report* 1990). Maintaining the competitive edge was essential as the franchise round was looming, and it would be conducted under the new rules established by the Act. The licences would be up for sale and entrepreneurs who saw television solely as a lucrative business were jockeying for position.

Historian Andrew Davidson described ITV as a 'a Jekyll and Hyde outfit in the 1980s, a push-me-pull-you of conflicting values that produced £300,000-a-year executives embracing mammon and the quality-before-ratings-ethic as easy bedfellows' (Davidson 1992:274). The double imperative – to attract audiences *and* to put over challenging information – had been held in balance by the powerful concept of the television medium itself as a public service. But the Broadcasting Act was to change all that. No more easy bedfellows. Instead, wrote Michael Cockerell, it was likely that 'the highest bidders would have the lowest brows' and the new Independent Television Commission (ITC) would not have the right to protect current affairs by ensuring that it was transmitted in peak time (*Sunday Correspondent* 14.12.89).

Faced with such changes, programme makers who had raged against the restrictive hand of regulation began to value the regulators as protectors against the cruder market instincts of their employers. In late 1988 a group of producers at Granada set up a Campaign for Quality Television, which sent an open letter to the Prime Minister, suggesting that the proposed measures would involve a 'narrowing of real choice for the viewers'. The Campaign renewed the argument that ITV, although a commercial broadcaster, was effectively part of a diverse public service *system* in which the licence-fee-funded BBC and the commercial ITV engaged in a healthy competition for quality and innovation, rather than audience size and profits. As a result of their lobbying, and that of the ITV Association led by Richard Dunn, clauses in the Act ameliorated its market orientation and required franchise bidders to show their commitment to programme quality, as well as their ability to provide certain programme strands, including current affairs. In what were described as 'exceptional circumstances' bids of a higher quality could win over higher financial offers (Davidson 1992:25). David Elstein told a journalist, 'We've suffered in the last years from a vicious promotion of market forces at the expense of other things ... but if quality is to become more important now, it's hard to see how we'll be ejected' (*Observer* 1.4.90). His optimism was misplaced.

In 1989 Roger Bolton was promoted to Controller of Network Factual Programmes at Thames, and Elstein chose Jack Saltman to be his successor at *This Week*. Saltman was an ex-*TVEye* producer who had worked closely with Mike Townson. Bolton was not keen on the appointment nor on Saltman's more cautious approach.

An almost voyeuristic approach

'Increasingly during the 1980s,' wrote Jeremy Tunstall, following interviews with numerous television producers,

> journalists disputed as to whether the weekly current affairs programme had a future. ITV programmes lasting only 25 minutes and scheduled at 8.30pm, were increasingly seen as outdated: how could 25 minutes on Russia or Romania add to daily 10 and 15 minute live interviews, film packages and analysis from the same locations? (Tunstall 1993:60).

Advancing technology was bringing a different kind of competition, which could be exploited by the wealthy BBC, with its army of journalists and numerous outlets on radio as well as television. In 1987 John Birt had become BBC Deputy Director General with a brief to overhaul its news and current affairs. The 'Birt revolution' centralized and rationalized BBC journalism, with carefully costed budgets, more subject specialization and more money invested in journalism across the Corporation. It also brought Birt's 'mission to explain' – which involved pre-planning and advance scripting of current affairs programmes – an approach that many – including Paul Woolwich, who would be the last Editor of *This Week* – found stifling. ' [It] didn't suit my kind of journalism' (Tunstall 1993:58).

By contrast, at the ITV companies the focus was on the franchise round and the pressure from advertisers. In the autumn of 1989, Thames set up a Programme Development Unit to research into audiences' responses to some of its series, including *This Week*. Significantly, the Unit's Controller, Pamela Reiss, drew conclusions about content and style which renewed the assertion that 'stories' not 'issues' are needed to grab an audience's attention. It was a debate that had recurred many times over the history of the series, but this time the recommendations came not from journalists and producers, but from a Unit whose sole aim was audience maximization.

Reiss's language drew on the researcher's vocabulary of social psychology and emotional response. 'Empathy' and 'reward' are the key concepts, she argued. An audience will respond to 'an issue that affects *my* world ... an issue *I* can change'. For the viewer to gain a 'reward' from watching a programme there is 'a desire to find some resolutions ... so the viewer might share in some notional success. Open-ended topics – Ireland, the Middle East, the Common Market – confronted the viewer with a need to make a decision himself [sic], rewarding for a few but not many.' And 'the way that you do it' is as important as 'what you do'. For more difficult topics, 'an exciting, adventurous, almost voyeuristic approach with lots of film and very little studio discussion will get results,' she wrote in her report.

Many of the previous changes in programme style had followed from different *conceptualizations* of the audience. Reiss argued that there should be studies of *actual* audiences – after all 'the consumer is king'. Her Unit previewed nine pilot topics for *This Week* programmes with eight focus groups made up of 'floating' – or occasional – current affairs viewers. Following their report (although the *This Week* team insisted it was not *because* of the report) three of the ideas were dropped – on Northern Ireland, on the Solidarity organization in Poland and on defence spending. The most 'consistently appealing' idea was found to be 'The Toxic Time Bomb', on the disposal of toxic waste, which, in the event, was given two full programmes (26.10 and 2.11.89). Both achieved audience numbers and audience appreciation indexes way above the average for the series – audiences of 7.1 and 6.2 million viewers respectively, against an average for the autumn season of 5.2 million.

Overall, *This Week*'s performance was not considered very impressive, and many commentators thought the series would be allowed to quietly fade away. In the industry magazine *Broadcast*, LWT's Barry Cox judged the edition on the marketing of footballer Paul Gascoigne to be 'soft and – in places – silly' (1.11.90) and gave the following week's report from Northern Ireland 'nine on the "so what?" scale'. November 1990 was, of course, the month in which Margaret Thatcher resigned, and in Cox's view, *This Week*'s coverage – mostly interviews with Tory activists – was 'the most unsatisfactory' of the three main series. It was a harsh judgement, which concluded 'there seems to be a real absence of editorial grip or vision at Euston at the moment' (*Broadcast* 7.12.90).

However, early 1990 saw a change of direction as David Elstein brought in Roger Bolton's choice, Paul Woolwich, to replace Jack Saltman. Woolwich saw the situation as a challenge, and was determined to breathe new life into the series by combining a drive for popularity and bigger audiences with hard-hitting journalism. He had been producing *Hard News*, a witty and topical commentary on the press for Channel 4, and as far as he was concerned a tabloid approach was as good as any other, 'the world is grey, tabloids make it interesting'. He had a tough, argumentative streak, which came out in the weekly meetings (he was nicknamed the Headmaster), was constantly on the look out for scoops, and was a fierce publicist, making sure the press got copies of every programme and circulating reviews to the team. A good programme should make the newspaper headlines or, even better, get an associated feature article. He was able to give the impression that the topics of his programmes really mattered.

The caring, social topics were less Paul Woolwich's style than hard-hitting investigations and scandals: British Airways were playing dirty tricks on Richard Branson's Virgin, using bribes and other underhand ways of getting Virgin passengers to switch (the title 'Violating Virgin' was objected to by the women on the team, but it stayed (27.2.92)); British Rail was not servicing its trains properly, many had faulty doors and several passengers had fallen to their deaths as the doors swung open while the train was at high speed (Woolwich claimed that this programme forced a change of design (21.5.92)). Another 'Toxic Time Bomb' (1.10.92) looked at houses built in environmentally unsafe areas. Reporter Debi Davis stood in a suburban back garden and presented damning research commissioned by the series. It emerged that homeowners preferred not to discuss the dangers that were revealed in case their properties were blighted. A moving, if somewhat voyeuristic programme on 'cot death' – the sudden death of very young babies for no apparent reason – was fronted by the well-known presenter Anne Diamond, whose own baby had died only six weeks earlier. In 'Every Mother's Nightmare' (31.10.91) Diamond went to New Zealand and reported on measures that had halved cot deaths in that country. It was all good headline-catching stuff, which balanced corporate wrongdoing with consumer outrage and aimed for the middle-of-the-road viewer, with little challenge to political beliefs or social attitudes.

This Week programmes were now confident and stylish, with skilled directors drawing on the full range of available resources. The rather plodding alternation of interview and illustrative sequence which had all too often characterized routine current affairs, had given way to a mixture of styles which were much more image-conscious. Increasingly sophisticated computer-assisted graphics, fast-cutting montages, and reconstructions that looked for all the world like mini-dramas, with carefully composed and dramatically lit sequences, matched the expensive élan of the advertisements that surrounded them. Earlier doubts about the validity of drawing on filmic devices such as reconstruction, mood music and eye-catching imagery in a journalist-led series had, to a large extent, been swept away as programmes set out to be more dynamic in audience appeal by exploiting the full resources of the medium.

The opening sequence of 'The Enemy Within' (15.10.92), transmitted at the height of the IRA mainland bombing campaign and only weeks after the City of London had been devastated, began with a sequence shot at night, in dramatic chiaroscuro, reconstructing a police surveillance of IRA plotters importing bomb-making materials. Producer/reporter Martyn Gregory gave the mundane location of a London lorry park all the glamour and suspense of a thriller, with feature-film quality and tension-building music on the soundtrack. This visibly crafted style retells events that took place prior to the making of the film, in stark contrast to the nervous, amateur movie or concealed camera style, in which the investigators seek to reveal wrong-doing as it happens – in 'Violating Virgin' hidden cameras spied on British Airways agents as they lobbied Virgin customers.

Paul Woolwich refused to accept the thesis that the genre was out of date and engaged in a spirited defence of his series wherever he could. 'ITV's current affairs programmes are trouncing all their competitors,' he announced to *Broadcast*.

Thames loses its franchise

The results of the franchise round, run according to the new principles of financial bids for licences, were announced in October 1991. 'Quality has won on this occasion and the viewers will win,' claimed George Russell, head of the newly established Independent Television Commission (Davidson 1992:226). Despite its reputation and its track record, Thames had lost out to Carlton Communications. Carlton proposed running the London franchise as a publisher/broadcaster, commissioning programmes from independent companies rather than producing its own, and this was one reason for its higher bid. Thames would have needed to make substantial cuts to compete, so the management, led by Richard Dunn, had decided to rely on the 'exceptional circumstances' clause in the Broadcasting Act. The gamble had not worked, and the press unanimously assumed that the company was being punished for 'Death on the Rock'. Carlton, run by entrepreneur Michael Green, now controlled a substantial amount of ITV, with a stake in Central, GMTV, Meridian and ITN as well as its technical services and production companies.

For its final 18 months, *This Week* knew it was under sentence of death, but the debate around the future of current affairs became, if anything, more intense. 'The proof of the pudding will be in the ratings,' Pamela Reiss had concluded, and now, instead of questions of what sort of people might make up the audience, the focus was on sheer numbers. Instead of arguments around the protection of current affairs within the schedule, the question was whether programmes could 'earn' their peak-time position. 'Some ITV eyes are fixed on 1993 and the chance to ditch current affairs in peak time,' wrote commentator Peter Fiddick (*Guardian* 23.12.91).

'*This Week* blamed for ratings fall'

'*This Week* blamed for ratings fall,' announced the industry magazine *Broadcast*. 'If you have a mass audience at 8pm you don't waste it by handing it over to a less than popular current affairs programme.' That was the stark opinion of Dawn Airey, Director of Programme Planning at Central TV. 'The ratings rot sets in at 20.30 with *This Week*,' she wrote, 'and we have the devil's own job getting our audience back.' All in all, current affairs had a 'disastrous effect' (*Broadcast* 19.6.92). And the files contain numerous memos and charts that make it clear that whatever time the series was scheduled for, it shows a drop in ratings from the previous programme.

At the BBC Glenwyn Benson, editor of *Panorama*, set out the opposite position. 'It wouldn't even matter,' she declared, 'if only five people watched. ... It's a symbol to the country that the BBC considers that the subject we're covering is important.' Her views were quoted with derision by those who felt that programmes with few concessions to the audience had no place on peak-time television screens (*Independent* 25.11. 92).

The tension between 'adding to the democratic debate' and pleasing a sizeable audience had been set out when *This Week* was launched back in 1956. They had rarely been taken as mutually exclusive options, but, as we have seen, the precise balance between them had been argued over and worked through in many different ways over its 36 years. But the early 1990s was a moment in current affairs history that was fraught with anxiety. In the uncertain future it seemed possible that the self-consciously 'serious', which was characterizing John Birt's regime at the BBC, would be divided off from an unashamedly populist approach taken by a restructured ITV. Carlton's contribution to the debate was a flat rejection of any social purpose. It was expressed by Paul Jackson, the company's Director of Programmes. No programme that gets a regular audience of less than 6 million, he stated bluntly, deserves a place in the peak-time schedules. 'You may not like it but under the new licences ITV is mandated to be a popular channel that gets an audience, earns revenue and sustains a business,' he told an assembly of television professionals at the Edinburgh Television Festival, adding, 'those who argue for current affairs to stay in peak time are not just accepting things as they are' (*Guardian* 1.9.92).

The last programme

The final *This Week* punned with death. The regular Christmas edition on poverty and homelessness was reported by Margaret Gilmour and followed the bleak funeral of a man who had lived and died on the streets (10.12.92).

In his valedictory review, critic Hugh Herbert echoed another of the debates that had reverberated across the 36 years,

If current affairs programmes like the invaluable and doomed *This Week* have a fault it is that the nature of television demands constant changes of image and a repetitive stream of visual evidence, when it ought to give a few more seconds to beating ministers over the head with supplementaries.

As programme makers struggled to balance the increasing hysteria of such competing demands, the near universal judgement of commentators on the end of the old regime was that 'the nature of television' – that frivolous medium which had dismayed the highbrows in the 1950s – had somehow won out. And Herbert went on to express the fears of many, 'The danger now is that this will be only the first of the flagship current affairs programmes to be axed, or cast into the darkness of late night television where they will frighten only the insomniacs' (*Guardian* 11.12.92).

It was not quite *This Week*'s last word. A one-hour retrospective recalled that moment in January 1956 when Michael Ingrams looked the eager new ITV audience in the eye and demanded 'what do *you* think'? It celebrated the drive to provoke thought by drawing on the full resources of the medium, whatever the risks. And, for the first time in 36 years, the Intermezzo from Sibelius's Karelia Suite was played by an orchestra fully in vision (the London Symphony Orchestra at the Barbican in London, conducted by Colin Davis) – with plenty of drums (17.12.92).

It is tempting to note, as several commentators did in January 1993, that Carlton Television launched itself with a package of programmes in which the *Good Sex Guide* figured prominently. But, of course, things are never quite that simple.

NEXT WEEK: CITIZENS STILL?

What to nurture in the future

'Without understanding what went right and what went wrong in the past, we cannot know what to nurture in the future,' said Paul Bonner, the official historian of Independent Television and a distinguished programme maker and executive (talk 2004). Hopefully, the history of *This Week*, and of the dilemmas and problems which have routinely beset current affairs on a commercial television channel, will have pointed to a particular need for nurture as UK television rushes into its uncertain future.

Ten years after *This Week*'s demise, and nearing the 50th anniversary of its launch, a new Communications Act (2003) gave a further radical shake-up to the television landscape. It set up yet another new regulatory body, Ofcom, the Office of Communications. This organization is quite different from earlier television regulators, as it supervises a diverse bunch of media, including radio, cable and telecoms, and its prime function is to 'promote competition in relevant markets'. Regulation is described as a 'burden' which it is committed to remove. This has meant that Ofcom legitimized and hastened those changes to ITV that began with the 1990 shake-up, and allowed the network to move further away from its public service commitments. By 2005 ITV was no longer a network of regional companies, but a single, trimmed-down entity formed by a series of mergers, which had virtually abandoned current affairs in the traditional mode. Although the Communications Act also required Ofcom to 'maintain and strengthen' public service in broadcasting, Ofcom identified 'public service' as a consequence of 'market failure', defined as what the market does not provide. Ofcom therefore argued that 'public service broadcasting' – including current affairs programmes – must be supported *separately from* the market. The productive interchange between information and entertainment, commerce and public commitment has all but disappeared.

But even in the early 1990s, as *This Week* was drawing to a close amidst waves of nostalgia, irreversible developments in technology, shifts in political ideology and economic realities were already leading to a clear readjustment of priorities.

Back in 1993

Back in 1993, Sky Television had already swallowed up its domestic competitor, British Satellite Broadcasting. Sky was a globalized media organization with no statutory public service obligations and its Astra satellite was beaming channels devoted to cartoons, football and Hollywood movies – forms of entertainment that a growing section of the population were prepared to pay good money for. It provided growing competition for ITV, which was beginning to come under pressure from all sides. Channel 4 was now competing for advertising, and Channel Five was in the pipeline. ITV itself was partly centralized so that schedules were decided through a Network Centre instead of being negotiated between the separate companies, and current affairs was no longer protected in a mid-evening slot.

ITV could have continued to commission *This Week* – together with other programmes from Thames Television, negotiated by David Elstein – but they decided against it. In Elstein's view 'The loss of *This Week* was not to do with Thames losing its franchise, but with ITV not wanting it' (to PH). Instead Carlton commissioned a small independent company, Twenty Twenty Television, to provide a short-run current affairs series, *Storyline*. Twenty Twenty was headed by Claudia Milne, who had co-produced one of the first Channel 4 current affairs strands ten years earlier. This meant that, in the early 1990s, all three main series were headed by women – a situation unthinkable ten years before. *This Week* had never been run by a woman since Caryl Doncaster moved on in the late 1950s. Now Milne inherited *This Week*'s mantle at Carlton, Dianne Nelmes edited *World in Action* for Granada and Glenwyn Benson headed the BBC's *Panorama*. The unquestioned involvement of women in positions of authority, responsible for the broad scope of the current affairs agenda, was a significant development.

Claudia Milne was clear that, for her, current affairs was gender neutral. She wanted *Storyline* to be as hard hitting and mainstream as *This Week* had been, and she declared that, as the title implied, there would be a strong commitment to 'stories' that would capture the interest of a wide audience (to PH). The reviewers judged that she had succeeded. 'This programme was a good deal more substantial than anyone probably expected' (*Daily Mail* 8.1.93), but, as critic Chris Dunkley pointed out, *This Week* had been a long-running series which had supported six programme teams, all working simultaneously (and he could have added that, for much of its life, it had had secure backing from Thames management). There was no way that a small independent could match those resources with any consistency and ensure that 'at any time a crew could be on the next flight out of Heathrow to cover any trouble spot in the world' (*Financial Times* 16.12.92). *Storyline* was scheduled for 7.30, not a particularly advantageous time and one which Roger Bolton had earlier argued would completely change the nature of the series, opposite the BBC's most popular programme, *EastEnders*.

Also in 1993, John Birt took over as Director General at the BBC, and David Elstein became Head of Programming at BSkyB, because 'that's where television's future lies'.

The gap between the BBC and ITV grew wider as Birt continued to stamp his austere style on the Corporation's current affairs output. Programmes had to be meticulously researched and planned in detail before filming began, leaving no space for chance and no opportunity for stories to get out of control or develop unexpectedly during the filming process (Lindley 2002:321–5). The method was deeply unpopular amongst journalists, who argued that it led to conformity and predictability – and it was quite at odds with the increased drive for populism at ITV.

Programmes and the current affairs project

The new ITV companies reviewed their current affairs output in the climate of regulation with a 'lighter touch'. Central Television publicized its highly successful foot-in-the-door *Cook Report*, in which reporter Roger Cook waylays wrong-doers and challenges them face-to-face on camera ('more to do with … embarrassment television than with current affairs', judged Chris Dunkley (*Finan-*

cial Times 16.12.92)); at Granada, *World in Action* reached its 30th anniversary amidst much trepidation and some dire predictions of imminent demise. Despite their brief and their 'lighter touch', the ITC were themselves concerned about the direction things were taking and criticized 'the burgeoning of "infotainment programmes, given over to crime and disasters" '. Series such as the ambulance-chasing *Blues and Twos* (Carlton 1993) pushed for drama and excitement above all else. But despite their evacuation of explanation and context, it could be argued that they brought a different kind of energy to the current factual genre. 'It depends which end of the telescope you look down,' said Stuart Prebble, founder member of Campaign for Quality Television, now Controller of Network Factual Programmes (*Guardian* 10.1.94). But the wider condemnation was of 'dumbing down'.

As always, it is easy to exaggerate the negative impact of changes, and to treat innovation and any move away from high seriousness with suspicion. To a certain extent, the decline of mainstream current affairs across the 1990s was compensated for by many one-off programmes and forms of scheduling that mounted seasons of programmes on a single topic and gave over whole evenings to subjects of urgent contemporary interest (such as *Bloody Bosnia*, Channel 4, August 1993, and *Broke: Poverty Answering Back*, Channel 4, 1996). What could be described as a current affairs *project* was spread more widely across the schedules as part of a search for accessible formats which would not indulge simply in cynical populism. In many ways, the early 1990s saw a flowering of imaginative factual programme making that explored the expanding resources of the television medium.

Newer styles did not respect established distinctions between the 'serious' and the 'popular'. They ranged from a more personal style of journalism and the use of celebrities and 'ordinary people' as reporters, to drama documentaries and the incursion of comedy into the political arena (Holland 2001b). Even the 'social experiments' of the early 2000s, such as *Back to the Floor* in which managers become workers in their own enterprise, had the potential to enhance democratic understanding. Wars and global events – from the Balkans to the 9/11 attacks on New York and the wars in Afghanistan and Iraq – posed a new challenge for programme makers and schedulers, as technology expanded the possibilities for instantaneous reporting and 24-hour minute-by-minute coverage. One of the most remarkable insights into the war in Bosnia was the extraordinary four-minute nightly broadcast from a single street in Sarajevo throughout the siege of that city (BBC2 1993–94). In some ways traditional current affairs series lagged behind this output. They seemed out of date and many feared they were disappearing altogether, especially on ITV. A 1999 report from the Campaign for Quality Television chose the uncompromising title *A Shrinking Iceberg Travelling South*, and concluded, 'the genre is in crisis, possibly in terminal decline' (Barnett and Seymour 1999).

The shrinking iceberg

Although it was several years before the full effects of the changes were felt, the shift to a more commercial ITV did indeed lead, as many had predicted, to the disappearance of long-running mainstream current affairs on the ITV network. Yorkshire Television's *First Tuesday*, launched in 1983, ended in 1993; *Storyline* was revamped as *The Big Story* – charged with responding to the 'big story' of the week, rather than engaging in (arguably riskier) longer investigations – and ran until 1998; *World in Action* eventually ended in 1999 and ITV's main current affairs output was taken over by *Tonight With Trevor McDonald* (1999–) which began, just like *This Week* in the 1950s, as a lightweight magazine series, and continued to cover stories that reflected the agenda of the tabloid newspapers with a focus on celebrity and sensation. Its popular style was lively and informative, but it had few pretensions to review the scope of the global, domestic and political agenda as *This Week* had done.

Current affairs producers interviewed for the Campaign for Quality Television report complained about falling budgets, a lack of commitment from management and the difficulty of protecting journalistic values in an environment that was now ferociously competitive. They argued that the need to attract audiences overrode journalistic values, and led to 'dumbing down' and a shift towards 'manufactured journalism' made up of 'hype, entertainment, infotainment values, in which investigation takes the ... stunt approach' (Barnett and Seymour 1999:20, 29).

Yet, throughout this book, my contention has been that, although the project of current affairs has been challenged by many factors – including stunts, hype and infotainment – it has been at its most creative when it has been able to make use of and derive value from these things, *while at the same time* maintaining a space for consistent, persistent and disrespectful reporting – such as *This Week*'s coverage of Northern Ireland. The genre has been at its most challenging when it has set out to address a wider audience, and at its weakest when a gulf is created between programmes that are declared to be 'public service' – happy to speak only to a narrow circle of understanding – and those that are seen as mere entertainment for the uneducated. The idea and practice of a public service *system* has implied cross fertilization and a situation in which the 'popular' and the 'serious' constantly challenge each other. As the history of *This Week* has shown, this delicate balance has been achieved by strong regulation which has created a climate in which the commercial companies, too, have recognized their public service responsibility.

'The job of current affairs is to help us understand what is happening,' declared Jeremy Isaacs, and no democratic society can flourish without such understanding. We still badly need that angry buzz.

REFERENCES

Books and articles

Baehr, H. and Spindler-Brown, A. (1987) 'Firing a broadside: a feminist intervention into mainstream TV', in Helen Baehr and Gillian Dyer (eds) *Boxed In: Women and Television*, London: Pandora

Baker, K. (1996) 'Reporting the conflict', in Martin McLoone (ed) *Broadcasting in a Divided Community: 60 Years of the BBC in Northern Ireland*, Belfast: Institute of Irish Studies, Queen's University

Barnett, S. and Seymour, E. (1999) '"A Shrinking Iceberg Travelling South". Changing Trends in British Television: A Case Study of Drama and Current Affairs', London: Campaign for Quality Television

Barr, C. (1986) 'Broadcasting and cinema 2: screens within screens', in Charles Barr (ed) *All Our Yesterdays*, London: BFI

Bartlett, K. (1986) *British Television in the 1950s: ITV and the Cult of Personality*, paper presented to the International Television Studies Conference, London

Bell, E. (1986) 'Origins', in John Corner (ed) *Documentary and the Mass Media*, London: Arnold

Benthall, J. (1993) *Disasters, Relief and the Media*, London: I.B.Tauris

Black, P. (1972) *The Mirror in the Corner: People's Television*, London: Hutchinson

Blanchard, S. and Morley, D. (eds) (1982) *What's This Channel Fo(u)r? An Alternative Report*, London: Comedia

Bolton, R. (1990) *Death on the Rock and Other Stories*, London: W.H. Allen

Bonner, P. with Aston, L. (1998) *ITV in Britain, Vol 5: The Old Relationship Changes 1981–92*, London: Macmillan

Briggs, A. (1995) *The History of Broadcasting in the UK, Vol 5: Competition 1955–1974*, Oxford: Oxford University Press

Butler, D. (1995) *The Trouble with Reporting Northern Ireland*, Aldershot: Avebury

Callaghan, J. (1973) *A House Divided: The Dilemma of Northern Ireland*, London: Collins

Campaign for Free Speech on Ireland (eds) (1979) *The British Media and Ireland: Truth, the First Casualty*, London: Information on Ireland

Cardiff, D. and Scannell, P. (1987) 'Broadcasting and national unity', in Curran et al (eds) *Impacts and Influences: Essays on Media Power in the Twentieth Century*, London: Methuen

Cockerell, M. (1988) *Live from Number 10: The Inside Story of Prime Ministers and Television*, London: Faber and Faber

Cockerell, M., Hennessy, P. and Walker, D. (1984) *Sources Close to the Prime Minister: Inside the Hidden World of the News Manipulators*, London: Macmillan

Cohen, S. (2001) *States of Denial: Knowing about Atrocities and Suffering*, Cambridge: Polity

Corner, J. (ed) (1991) *Popular Television in Britain*, London: BFI

Courtney-Browne, R. (1975) *History of This Week*, unpublished paper

Cumings, B. (1992) *War and Television*, London: Verso

Curran, J. and Seaton, J. (1997) *Power Without Responsibility*, 5th edition, London: Routledge

Curtis, L. (1984) *Ireland: The Propaganda War*, London: Pluto

Dahlgren, P. and Sparks, C. (1991) *Communication and Citizenship: Journalism and the Public Sphere*, London: Routledge

Darlow, M. (2004) *The Independents Struggle: The Programme Makers Who Took on the TV Establishment*, London: Quartet

Davidson, A. (1992) *Under the Hammer: Greed and Glory Inside the Television Business*, London: Mandarin

Dickinson, M. (ed) (1999) *Rogue Reels: Oppositional Film in Britain 1945–90*, London: BFI

Downing, T. (ed) (1989) *The Troubles: The Background to the Question of Northern Ireland*, 3rd ed, London: Thames/Channel 4

Fiddick, P. (1984) *Tribute to Thames Television*, New York: Museum of Broadcasting

Fisk, R. (1990) *Pity the Nation: Lebanon at War*, London: André Deutsch

Frost, D. (1993) *An Autobiography Part 1: From Congregations to*

Audiences, London: HarperCollins

Gill, P. (1986) *A Year in the Death of Africa,* London: Paladin

Goddard, P., Corner, J. and Richardson, K. (2001) 'The formation of World in Action', in *Journalism,* Vol 2 (1), London: Sage

Goldie, G.W. (1977) *Facing the Nation: Television and Politics 1937–1976,* London: Bodley Head

Goodwin, P. (1998) *Television Under the Tories,* London: BFI

Grierson, J. (1938) 'Censorship and the documentary', in *World Film News,* November

Gunter, B. (1997) *Measuring Bias on Television,* Luton: University of Luton Press

Hall, S. (1977) 'Culture, the media, and the "ideological effect"', in J. Curran, M. Gurevitch and J. Woollacott (eds) *Mass Communication and Society,* London: Arnold

Hall, S., Connell, I., Curti, L. (1976) The "Unity" of current affairs television', in *Culture and Domination: Cultural Studies 9,* Birmingham: Centre for Contemporary Cultural Studies

Harris, R. (1983) *Gotcha! The Media, the Government and the Falklands Crisis,* London: Faber and Faber

Harrison, P. and Palmer, R. (1986) *News out of Africa: Biafra to Band Aid,* London: Hilary Shipman

Harvey, S. (1994) 'Channel Four Television: From Annan to Grade' in S. Hood (ed) *Behind the Screens: The Structure of British Television in the Nineties,* London: Lawrence and Wishart

Hird, C. (1985) *Different But Not Too Different? Current Affairs in Channel Four,* unpublished paper

Hoggart, R. (1958) *The Uses of Literacy,* Harmondsworth: Penguin

Holland, P. (2001a) 'Spectacular values: the pleasure of the text and the "contamination" of current affairs television', in *Visual Culture in Britain,* Vol 2, No. 2, London: Ashgate

—— (2001b) 'Authority and authenticity: redefining television current affairs', in M. Bromley (ed) *No News is Bad News,* London: Pearson Education

—— (2004) *Picturing Childhood: The Myth of the Child in Popular Imagery,* London: I.B.Tauris

Isaacs, J. (1989) *Storm Over 4: A Personal Account,* London: Weidenfeld and Nicholson

——(2006) *Look Me In the Eye,* London: Little Brown

Kee, R. (1976) *The Green Flag,* 3 vols, London: Quartet

Kennedy, L. (1989) *On My Way to the Club,* London: Collins

Kyle, K. (1996) 'Some personal recollections 1969–80', in Martin

McLoone (ed) *Broadcasting in a Divided Community: 60 Years of the BBC in Northern Ireland*, Belfast: Institute of Irish Studies, Queen's University

Laing, S. (1986) *Representations of Working Class Life 1957–64*, London: Macmillan

Leman, J. (1987) 'Programmes for women in 1950s British television', in Helen Baehr and Gillian Dyer (eds) *Boxed In: Women and Television*, London: Pandora

Lindley, R. (2002) *Panorama: Fifty Years of Pride and Paranoia*, London: Politicos

Magee, B. (1966) *The Television Interviewer*, London: Macdonald

—— (2004) *Clouds of Glory: A Hoxton Childhood*, London: Pimlico

Milland, J. (2004) 'Courting Malvolio: The Background to the Pilkington Committee on Broadcasting, 1960–62', in *Contemporary British History*, Vol 18, No. 2

Miller, D. (1993) 'The Northern Ireland Information Service and the media: aims, strategy, tactics', in John Eldridge (ed) *Getting the Message, News, Truth and Power*, London: Routledge

—— (1994) *Don't Mention the War: Northern Ireland, Propaganda and the Media*, London: Pluto

Mirzoeff, N. (1999) *An Introduction to Visual Culture*, London: Routledge

Mitchell, J. (1971) *Women's Estate*, Harmondsworth: Penguin

Mitchell, W.J.T. (1986) *Iconology: Image, Text, Ideology*, Chicago: University of Chicago Press

Morley, P. (2005) Unpublished memoirs

Negrine, R. (1998) *TV and the Press since 1945*, Manchester: Manchester University Press, Documents in Contemporary History series

O'Sullivan, T. (1991) 'Television memories and cultures of viewing 1950–65', in John Corner (ed) *Popular Television in Britain*, London: BFI

Paulu, B. (1981) *Television and Radio in the United Kingdom*, London: Macmillan

Pilkington, H. (1962) *Report of the Committee on Broadcasting 1960*, London: HMSO

Potter, J. (1989) *Independent Television in Britain, Vol 3: Politics and Control 1968–1980*, London: Macmillan

—— (1990) *Independent Television in Britain, Vol 4: Companies and Programmes 1968–80*, London: Macmillan

Rosenthal, A. (1981) *The Documentary Conscience: A Casebook in*

Film Making, Berkeley: University of California Press

Scannell, P. (1979) 'The social eye of television 1946–55', in *Media Culture and Society,* Vol 1, No. 1, London: Sage

—— (1990) 'Public service broadcasting: the history of a concept', in Andrew Goodwin and Garry Whannel (eds) *Understanding Television,* London: Routledge

Schlesinger, P. (1978) *Putting 'Reality' Together: BBC News,* London: Constable

Schlesinger, P., Murdock, G., Elliott, P. (1983) *Televising Terrorism,* London: Comedia

Sendall, B. (1982) *Independent Television in Britain, Vol 1: Origin and Foundation 1946–62,* London: Macmillan

—— (1983) *Independent Television in Britain, Vol 2: Expansion and Change 1958–68,* London: Macmillan

Shaw, T. (1996) *Eden, Suez and the Mass Media,* London: I.B.Tauris

Smith, A. (1978) *The Politics of Information,* London: Macmillan (includes "Television coverage of Northern Ireland', reprinted from *Index on Censorship,* Vol 1, No. 2, 1972)

Taylor, P. (1979) 'Reporting Northern Ireland', in Campaign for Free Speech on Ireland (eds) *The British Media and Ireland: Truth, the First Casualty,* London: Information on Ireland (reprinted from *Index on Censorship,* Vol 7, No. 6, London 1978)

—— (1980) *Beating the Terrorists? Interrogation in Omagh, Gough and Castlereagh,* Harmondsworth: Penguin

—— (1984) *Smoke Ring: The Politics of Tobacco,* London: Bodley Head

Thumim, J. (ed) (2002) *Small Screens, Big Ideas: Television in the 1950s,* London: I.B.Tauris

Tracey, M. (1983) *In the Culture of the Eye: 10 Years of Weekend World,* London: Hutchinson

—— (1998) *The Decline and Fall of Public Service Broadcasting,* Oxford: OUP

Tracey, M. and Morrison, D. (1979) *Whitehouse,* London: Macmillan

Tunstall, J. (1993) *Television Producers,* London: Routledge

de Waal, A. (1989) *Famine That Kills,* Oxford: Oxford University Press

Wegg-Prosser, V. (2002) '*This Week* in 1956: the introduction of current affairs on ITV', in Janet Thumim (ed) *Small Screens, Big Ideas: Television in the 1950s,* London: I.B.Tauris

Williams, R. (1974) *Television: Technology and Cultural Form,*

London: Fontana

Winchester, S. (1974) *In Holy Terror*, London: Faber and Faber

Windlesham, Lord (1981) *Broadcasting in a Free Society*, Oxford: Blackwell

Windlesham, Lord and Rampton, R. (1989) *The Windlesham/Rampton Report on Death on the Rock*, London: Faber and Faber

Winston, B. (1995) *Claiming the Real: The Documentary Film Revisited*, London: BFI

Zeman, Z.A.B. (1969) *Prague Spring*, London: Penguin

Television programmes

This Week. Editions are referred to by date, from 6.1.56 to 17.12.92

35 Years on the Front Line, Flashback Productions for Thames Television ITV. *This Week* retrospective, 15.1.1991 to 28.5.91

also

Bloody Sunday, Granada for ITV, 20.1.2002

Can I Ask You a Personal Question? BBC2's 1960s Evening, BBC2, 30.8.93

An Ethiopian Journey, Dimbleby Associates for LWT, ITV, 1998

Ireland: A Television History, 13 episodes, BBC2, 2.12.80–24.2.81

Remember Bloody Sunday, Inside Story series, BBC, 28.1.92

A Soldier's Tale, BBC2, 7.8.94

Sunday, Channel 4, 28.1.02

Theatre Without Actors, Arena Series, BBC2, 12.3.94 (about Robert Drew and direct cinema)

The Troubles, five episodes, Thames Television for ITV, 5.1–2.2.81

Who Bombed Birmingham?, World in Action series, Granada for ITV, 28.3.90

Written in Blood, 25 Bloody Years Season, BBC2, 21.8.94

Talks

Paul Bonner, *Screen Symposium,* 2004

Jonathan Dimbleby, *Sheffield Documentary Festival,* 1995

Jeremy Isaacs and Peter Taylor, *Current Affairs: An Endangered Species?,* Bournemouth University, 2003

Jeremy Potter, *Institute of Contemporary British History,* 1999

Leslie Woodhead, *DocHouse,* 2004

INDEX

MY BOOK
BOYFRIEND

KATHY STROBOS

Cover Design: Cover Ever After

ISBN: 9781958894002 (EBook)

ISBN: 9781958894019 (Paperback)

www.kathystrobos.com

Published by Strawbundle Publishing

New York, New York

To my readers.

Also By Kathy Strobos

New York Friendship Series
A Scavenger Hunt for Hearts
Partner Pursuit
Is This for Real?
Caper Crush

New York Spark Series
My Book Boyfriend
Love Is an Art

For giveaways, updates on new releases, behind-the-scene news and what's going on in my life, please subscribe to my mailing list at https://kathystrobos.com/sign-up-for-monthly-letter/

Chapter One

Lily

MY PHONE RINGS. THE library is relatively empty today, just a few patrons. Bella, my best friend, is practicing her stand-up comedy routine for our resident septuagenarian, Mr. Devi. I step away from the front desk to the back to take this call.

"We received a cease and desist letter from Strive Developers. It says Oasis Garden does *not* have the right to its land. Strive Developers wants its lot back now," Mrs. Potter says, her voice rising.

"What?" I sink into a chair.

Twenty-five years ago, this lot was an abandoned eyesore full of rats and weeds and broken glass. Mrs. Potter crawled through the opening in the rusted, wire fence and slowly turned it into a space full of green trees and yellow flowers. It's been five years since Mrs. Potter asked me to be her co-director, and I've spent all my extra time working with her to create the community it is now.

My body is shaking.

"They can't do that," I say. My stomach feels queasy.

Mrs. Potter reads me the letter. "We have to stop our activities in the garden."

"We're not going to do that," I say. "It's our land now. We own it via adverse possession." I try to sound reassuring. But I can't stop shaking.

"I'll call my friends," I say. "Tessa is a lawyer. She'll know what our legal rights are. Don't worry. I'll see if they can all meet tonight. They can't take the garden away."

I hang up the phone and stare at the poster on the bulletin board across from me, which invites families to come to the Oasis Garden to plant vegetables.

Bella comes around the bend. "I just realized I lost my earring. What's wrong? You look ill."

"Strive Developers sent us a cease and desist letter. They want Oasis Garden back."

"Well, they can't have it." Bella hugs me, and I hold on to her.

I pull away and text the rest of my friends that we need to hold a Save the Garden meeting after work at our local bookshop café, Banter & Books. My hands are still quivering.

"You sit here," Bella says. "I'll man the desk."

Get it together, Lily. You pride yourself on being a master at compartmentalizing. Here's your chance to prove it.

SOMEHOW, THE NORMAL ACTIVITIES of my job as a librarian—suggesting books to patrons, helping teens find the information they need, shelving—were just what I needed. My body has finally stopped shaking. Thankfully, my story time with the toddlers was right after Mrs. Potter called. Their rapt attention and warm hugs took my mind off the letter and its threat to demolish the Oasis

Garden. And Bella has stayed here the whole day to help me when she should be home practicing for her stand-up gig tonight.

I peer under the counter, searching for Bella's lost, gold hoop earring on the library floor, the wood floor hard on my knees. Enormous dust bunnies abound. Maybe we haven't had any water bugs or mice lately because the clumps scare them off.

At the sound of the smooth *r-r-r* of the wheels on the shelving cart, I look up to see my best friend steering into my space behind the library counter.

"No luck?" Bella asks. "I didn't see my earring anywhere on the floor either. But I did pick up the last of the books left on tables." She pushes her red glasses up on her nose and gets down on the floor on the other side of the book return bin. "Maybe it fell off when I reached in here earlier."

"Thanks again for staying to help me out." I swallow the lump in my throat.

"What are roommates for?" Bella's voice is muffled. "Are you feeling better now?"

"I'm over the initial shock." I am.

I swipe my hand gingerly over the floor under a shelf to see if Bella's earring slid into this hidden cavity.

"You're not really going to ask Aiden to the Lions Gala, are you?" Bella asks from the other side of the book bin.

My facade of normalcy must be working if Bella feels free to harangue me about my crush on Aiden.

"I asked him this morning, and he said yes." I crawl over to peer under the bookshelf where we store the books transferred from other branches around New York City in case the gold hoop slid under there.

"I know you guys can talk books for hours, but do you actually feel any electricity with him? Like you can't breathe because he's the one? Spine-tingling kisses?"

"As in the pages of your novels? You should talk. It's not like you're dating anyone."

"Found it!" Bella shrieks. "It was under the book bin." She holds up the earring and looks at me. "But I may meet him tonight, which is why I need my lucky earrings."

"He bought us cat grass. Look. He sent me a text." I sit up on my knees and show it to Bella.

Bella, sitting cross-legged, puts her earring in and peers at my phone. "All right. He gets some credit for that."

"Ahem." A very pointed throat-clearing comes from above, on the other side of the checkout desk. And then a deep, male voice says, "Excuse me, do you have *He Had No Idea*? It's a mystery that just came out today. It was sold out already at the bookstore nearby."

I stand, dusting off my jeans, and blink. Tall, dark, tousled hair, chiseled cheekbones, green, hazel eyes. It's like a book boyfriend just stepped out of the romance novels I read and into the library. His fitted suit does little to hide his muscular physique. He cocks one eyebrow. His lips are compressed into a thin line. He stares back at me. His hair is longish, a sharp contrast to the corporate vibe he gives off. Maybe he's been too busy raiding corporations to get a haircut lately.

And behind him stands Mr. Devi, back again, as he is most nights, with a book in his hand, ready to check out right before closing time.

Lovely. I'm so thrilled they both heard that conversation. I can feel my cheeks heating up.

Bella gets up to stand next to me.

"You've got some fluff on your hair." She pulls something off my ponytail.

The corners of the guy's mouth twitch.

My blush deepens. It must match the color of Bella's red-framed glasses.

"I'll straighten your hair for the gala so it will look all sleek and sophisticated, like Grace Kelly," she says.

This is *not* helping. Is she not aware of the attractive guy standing *right there*?

"So, the book ... do you have it?" he asks. "If not, I'll buy the e-book so I can read it tonight. I just prefer paperback."

"Did you check the shelves?" I ask, looking up its status on the computer, relieved to be able to focus on the screen.

"Yes. No copies, I gather? That's too bad." He pauses a minute, staring at me.

Do I still have dust bunnies in my hair? I resist the urge to check.

And then he walks away. His footsteps punctuate the silence as he turns and strides swiftly around the counter, past the rows of blue-screened computer terminals with the lion graphic, toward the glass doors.

I should let him go. He can clearly afford to buy the e-book. And I had just grabbed a copy for myself, since it was almost closing time. But it's not like I don't have a million other books on my #TBR that I could read instead. And here's a chance to promote the library.

"We do have *one* copy left," I say, but I don't yell it. If he's too impatient to wait, so be it.

He stops. Good hearing.

"You do?" His voice holds a hint of hope. He strides back. Mr. Devi gestures for him to take his prior place ahead of him in line. He hesitates and motions for Mr. Devi to precede him. Mr. Devi insists that he go first. Thanking Mr. Devi, he comes back to the front of the line.

"I do." I turn around and pull the book out of my backpack, which is slouching on the back counter, ready to go.

"I can't take your copy." He leans over the counter—too close now. His eyes are like a forest, green with flecks of hazel, giving a feeling of light breaking through the canopy of leaves to illuminate a mossy grove. My heart races.

Clearly, I've been reading way too many romance books lately.

I plunk the mystery book down in front of him. *Between us.* Maybe my friends are right. I need to stop living in the pages of books and get out more if this is my reaction to a handsome library patron.

"You can take her copy." Bella plops *A Devilish Dare* down on the counter next to *He Had No Idea* and turns to me. "Lily, read this one tonight instead and tell me if you still want to go with Aiden to the gala."

Tall, Dark, and Handsome stares at the racy cover of the barely dressed couple locked in an embrace.

I will not be embarrassed.

His slender fingers pick up *A Devilish Dare*. "Maybe I should take this one."

"I'm sure it would be an education," I say.

"Do you think so?" he asks, a teasing note in his voice, those forest eyes studying mine, an eyebrow raised.

I swallow. "Maybe not."

The corner of his mouth slants up.

I push *He Had No Idea* toward him. "Do you have a library card?"

"No. But I can just apply with an ID, right? Do I have to give my home address? Or can I use my business address?"

"We need your home address," I say. "Proof of residence is required."

He takes out his ID but then pauses, as if reluctant to hand it over.

Probably because I've just been crawling around on the floor, discussing spine-tingling kisses—not exactly the most professional behavior.

He hands me his ID with his address, and I type it into the system. Rupert Evans. He looks like a Rupert. Penthouse. *Of course.* I hand him his new library card and *He Had No Idea*, with the due date slip tucked in.

Mr. Devi seems to be inspecting our newest patron, his head craned around to look at Mr. Evans's hands.

"You married?" Mr. Devi asks him.

The guy glances at him, his brow wrinkling. "No."

Ah. Mr. Devi must be trying to match up his granddaughter. His daughter lives in California. His family has also moved away. Is his granddaughter getting a job in New York? That would be good. Then he wouldn't be so lonely.

"You're not married?" Mr. Devi confirms.

"Not married," the guy says.

"This one here is a good catch." Mr. Devi points at me. "Reminds me of my late wife. If I were forty years younger, like your age, I'd ask her out."

I blush *again*. And I can feel it. A deep, dark red. *Great.* Mr. Devi is trying to set *me* up. I really do need to get a life if my library patrons are resorting to matchmaking.

The guy looks startled, his eyes widening. I busy myself, gathering all the scattered pens and placing them in the pencil mug.

"I'm sure she can do better and that she's taken."

"No. She's definitely not taken," Mr. Devi says.

Thanks for that, Mr. Devi.

Mr. Devi continues, almost to himself. "I can't understand it, personally. Young men nowadays. And I agree with Bella. You went with Aiden last year to the gala, didn't you? And he still hasn't stepped up. Don't give him a second chance."

My neck feels hot. It must be as red as a tomato.

"Thank you—" Rupert pauses. "What's your name?" I look up, and our glances meet. His head is tilted.

"Lily."

"Thank you, Lily." The way he says my name is like a caress. Way, way out of my league.

I'm a professional. *Get it together.*

Rupert leaves the counter. Mr. Devi watches him go. Frankly, I'd like to watch him go too, but I don't dare turn around.

"Mr. Devi, do you have a book to check out, or are you just here to meddle with my love life?" I ask.

"I do have a book to check out, but as you said, a little matchmaking never hurt anyone. It's just a date."

I did say that when I set up Mr. Devi with Mrs. Potter. That was *not* a successful match. But they are my two favorite septuagenarians, so it was worth a try. And I think Mr. Devi is lonely because he spends so many afternoons and evenings here. But he says that his Prasanthi was the only one for him. True love is real—and not just between the pages of books.

"But since we don't know him, you should only meet him in a public place."

Great. Mr. Rupert Evans is *never* going to return to the public library again.

The heavy, wooden door clangs shut, and Rupert's footsteps recede. I shake myself. *Whatever.* I'll never see him again. I scan Mr. Devi's book and hand it back to him with the due date slip. My phone beeps.

Tessa: *Running late.*

I sweep underneath the counter and in the area behind the checkout counter. Turning off the computers and the lights in the back is my good night ritual for a slumbering library. Bella and Mr. Devi wait by the doors.

I do one quick walk-around through the stacks to make sure all the books have been put away. No books lay scattered on the circular, birch tables with their matching chairs in the reading section at the front. I straighten the bright covers of the books we're highlighting this month that stand on top of the short bookcases next to the red-and-white signs announcing that we have books in Chinese, Japanese, and Spanish. It's ready for another day of neighborhood learning tomorrow.

I lock the doors as I let myself out with Bella and Mr. Devi. We walk down the short set of steps and say our goodbyes. The St. Agnes library is a beautiful limestone building with arched windows built in 1920. The rest of the block is buzzing with small stores and restaurants. Mr. Devi walks south.

And then I turn around, and there is Rupert. His coat is buttoned up to his neck, and he's giving undercover spy vibes—or maybe bookish, literary genius. Either works for me. I should've done something with my hair. And my oversize red parka, while great for the winter, is definitely not the most flattering for my figure.

He walks up to us. "I feel bad for taking your copy."

"It's fine," I say. "Honestly. My #TBR pile is huge. I can always read something else."

He nods. "Okay, then." Then he glances south. Mr. Devi is slowly making his way down the street. A truck rattles and roars its way up Amsterdam Avenue.

Bella hits me hard with her elbow, and I look at her. She raises her eyebrows and then gestures at Rupert with her chin. I shake my head and raise my eyebrows back at her. I have no idea what she's trying to tell me.

Rupert turns back to face us, the book in his hand, looking unsure. I feel bad that *he* feels bad about taking the last copy.

"But here's a quiz to see if you're worthy," I say. "Why did Ms. Wilhelmina Chrissy start writing?"

"She watched a mystery on TV and thought she could do better."

"What are the main themes of her mysteries?" I ask.

"Found family and the cracks in relationships."

I nod, impressed. The streetlight is blinking to life, as if it's going to whisper a better question. "And what attracts you to her writing?"

"The characters, the themes, and I usually can't figure out who did it. Did I pass?" He steps closer.

I step back. "Yes. Enjoy the book." There. That should get rid of any guilt.

"Lily will be leading a book club on *He Had No Idea* at Banter & Books on Friday," Bella says.

"Then you need the book," Rupert says.

"It's okay. Banter & Books said they'll have additional stock tomorrow." I turn to head north, and Bella hooks her arm in mine. The dusk makes the green traffic lights pop out. A bus sighs across the street and pulls away from the curb. Bella's arm is warm against mine, and I butt shoulders with her affectionately.

As we near the corner, Bella says, "You should have asked him out. He just stood there, waiting for you."

I snort. "Then he can ask me out. I don't need another Aiden, where I do all the pursuing."

Not that I've given up on Aiden. He seemed enthusiastic about going to the gala again. He said yes immediately. And he just bought me cat grass. That's sort of romantic—in its own way.

But this guy looks like he can ask a woman out if he wants to.

As does Aiden.

But Aiden hasn't asked me out, even though he'll text me funny memes or thoughts on what he's reading. I should give up. Bella always psycho-analyzes me, saying that I only find men who are not interested romantically because I'm afraid to fall in love and get hurt after my mom's death.

That's not important now.

Tonight is about saving the garden. And if my date with Aiden doesn't go well, I'll regroup and consider going back into the dating pool again.

At the corner, the red light holds steady as cars turn into the side street. Next to us is a flower store. Pots with tulips and roses abound in all the colors of the rainbow. I look back.

Rupert has caught up with Mr. Devi. *That's kind of sweet.*

"If that guy asked you out, would you say yes?" Bella asks as we cross with the green light.

"What guy?" Probably too late to play innocent.

"The one who just made you all flustered inside the library and who waited outside for you. And the one you just turned around to check out."

"*You* made me all flustered inside the library," I say.

"I wanted to make sure he knows we have high standards for our men," Bella says.

Neighbors bustle home, their coats zipped up against the cold. We pass restaurant after restaurant, and the whiffs of coconut curry, pizza, and fried food are making me hungry. There's not much space to walk here, between the tables set out for dining in the wooden sheds and the delivery bikes tangled together, all locked to a single pole.

"And you haven't answered the question," Bella says.

"Yes. I'm not a complete idiot. I know that Aiden probably isn't romantically interested, and that guy seems like a good guy."

"And he reads."

"And he reads."

"Where does he live? You should take some walks near his block."

"That's confidential information. And he was dressed in a very sharp suit, so he probably works very late."

"Still, it's always good to take a walk and clear your head. Next time I take a plot-walk for one of my books, if you want to come and lead the way, I will happily follow."

We reach 86th Street.

Bella drops my arm and faces me. "Shouldn't you just ask Aiden what the deal is? Tell him you like him and ask him if he likes you? It's just that last year, you had high hopes for the gala and then you were disappointed."

"I have to see him every day if he says he doesn't like me," I say.

"He travels enough that you probably wouldn't run into him that much in the hallway between our apartments."

"I don't want to put him on the spot," I say. "If nothing happens at the gala, I promise you I'll give up on Aiden."

Bella harrumphs and pulls the strap of her bag higher on her shoulder. "You asking him to the gala again should have been a pretty clear sign, but he probably thinks this is an extension of your brunch-buddy relationship."

"Brunch-buddy relationships have their place." But granted, do not give much hope of a passionate romance.

"Did you at least yell at him for standing you up for brunch this past Sunday?"

"No," I say. "What would be the point?"

"The point is that he takes advantage of your good nature, and you let him."

"In the end, it was more food for us."

"Oh, this got delivered to our neighbor by accident." Bella hands me a postcard. "She gave it to me in the hallway."

The postcard has a photo of some stone elephants on a gate in New Delhi. I flip it over to read the back. "Found some friends for Patience and Fortitude—Dad." Patience and Fortitude are the names of the lions that guard the New York Public Library Fifth Avenue branch. I sigh. That's it. Nothing personal from my dad.

"Have you talked to him lately?"

"No," I say.

"You should call him. Anyway, I'm off to my stand-up gig," Bella says. "I'm sorry I can't make the meeting tonight."

"Thank you for coming by the library to help me out. Break a leg. I'm sorry I won't be there to cheer you on."

"No worries." Bella turns left to head to the subway downtown. "Saving the garden is more important. See you at home."

Banter & Books is a few more blocks up on Amsterdam Avenue. I zip my large overcoat and trudge up the street past empty sheds, closed up for the winter. The glowing holiday star hanging from the lamppost provides festive cheer amid the deepening dusk. *Will we be able to fight Strive Developers?* I bite my lip. The only other community garden in the neighborhood was demolished a few years ago to make way for luxury housing.

I open the door to Banter & Books, immediately enveloped by warmth. Hanging plants and shelves filled with books line the whitewashed walls. Bright book covers and green plants give such a cheerful, welcoming vibe. It feels like a cross between a café in Provence and a greenhouse. French-blue settees and armchairs scattered around form little nooks for private conversations or reading. Around each cluster of chairs is a mass cane, an Areca palm, or a peace lily, providing some additional seclusion. At the back, half of the yard has been converted into a conservatory. The books at the front are for sale, but they also have a small, free library in the back where people can exchange books.

I order a peppermint tea at the counter from Miranda, who appears to be the only one working today—and busy. She hands me a stand with a number on it, and I move to the end of the counter.

I check the book club discussion binder. A good number of people signed up for the book club discussion for *He Had No Idea*, and quite a few men listed Chrissy as one of their favorite authors. Banter & Books runs a very laid-back matchmaking service where they will match you up based on reading interests. And if you're too shy for that, you can just join a book club to discuss a particular novel.

I scan the names. No Rupert Evans. Not a surprise. I shouldn't even be looking for his name. He definitely doesn't need a dating service, and he exudes a "time is money" motto. And I don't do blind dates anymore—not since the last few dates when the men seemed disappointed to meet a librarian for a drink rather than some svelte model. Not to mention the last guy who seemed to be seeking some mythical, prim-and-proper librarian who was a wildcat underneath.

Miranda passes by me with a tray to deliver some very full mugs. On her way back with an empty tray, she gives me a warm pat on the back.

"Do you have any copies of *He Had No Idea* left?" I ask. He had to have checked either this bookstore or the Strand a few blocks down.

"No. We sold out, but we're getting more stock in tomorrow. I sent the last guy to the library. Now, he was *hot*. Did he stop by?"

"Because it would definitely be the same guy?"

"This guy was steaming. Are you getting a plethora of hot guys at the library?" Miranda raises an eyebrow as she puts down the tray. She re-ties her Banter & Books apron around her waist. The dark-blue apron highlights her red hair and bright-blue eyes.

"He came by. I gave him the last paperback copy. All the e-books were borrowed almost immediately." The door opens with a whoosh of cold air, and Iris enters, unzipping her heavy parka. She's wearing an enormous, knitted neck warmer that practically covers her entire face. She pulls it off as she joins me at the counter and shakes out her dark-brown hair. It seems like the neck warmer does double duty as a hand muff.

"He was hot, right?" Miranda asks.

"Yes," I say. "Mr. Devi tried to set me up with him."

Miranda snort-laughs. "Go, Mr. Devi."

"Who was hot?" Iris shoves the hand muff into her ever-present backpack.

"This guy who came in here looking for *He Had No Idea* but they're out, so Miranda sent him to the library," I say.

"Did you get his number?" Iris asks.

"I got his address—but only so I could give him a library card," I say.

"He didn't have a library card?" Iris asks. "That's insane. He's not a good match for you, then."

"He looked like the type who buys all his books," Miranda says. "What can I get you?"

"Cappuccino," Iris says. "Someone clicked on a phishing link in an email and installed malware, so I've still got some work ahead of me tonight." Iris works in cybersecurity for an up-and-coming entertainment company.

"You didn't have to come out, then," I say.

"It's fine. This morning was relatively quiet, so I spent some time researching Strive Developers then."

"I can design posters for you to publicize what they're doing and protest it." Miranda pulls out her pad and sketches a few lines. She just had a hugely successful art show. "And I can create a painting we can auction off to raise money."

"That would be amazing," I say.

Another whoosh of cold air, and Mrs. Potter enters with Maddie.

"This place really needs one of those curtains around the entrances," Miranda says.

"But then you can't see who's entering," Iris says. She's definitely the one focused on security. She made us all take jujitsu self-defense.

Mrs. Potter's curly, gray hair is held back by a black kerchief, and she seems to walk a bit slower than usual. I only hope I age as well as Mrs. Potter has. She could easily pass for sixty, with her barely wrinkled, brown skin. Mrs. Potter and I have worked so hard to build this garden and the community around it, staying up late for nights on end, applying for grants and organizing activities.

We take our beverages and join Mrs. Potter and Maddie at a grouping of armchairs in the front. Miranda waves goodbye as she moves to help another customer.

I sit next to Mrs. Potter, who turns to me with a reassuring smile. I probably didn't hide very well how shaken I was this morning when she called me.

Maddie presses her palms to her face, trying to warm it, her flushed cheeks bright against her white skin. She opens up her always-overflowing bag. We tease her that it's like Mary Poppins's bag, but she insists that she can find everything in it. And because she's a reporter for *The Intelligencer*, she never knows when she's going to be sent out on an assignment, so she always carries everything with her. She digs out her notepad.

The door opens one more time, and Tessa enters. Her heels click on the wooden floor as she walks over to drop off her briefcase.

"Why are you wearing a suit?" Maddie asks in her typical leave-no-question-unasked fashion.

"I had an appearance in court today," Tessa says. "Has everyone ordered? Can I get something for anyone?" She takes orders from Maddie and Mrs. Potter and then walks over to say hello to her roommate, Miranda.

"I still can't believe they're kicking you out," Iris says.

"And I thought I'd finally gotten rid of all the rats threatening the garden." Mrs. Potter hands around copies of the notice for the Oasis Community Garden to "cease and discontinue its unauthorized use of the property."

My stomach plunges. Seeing the text in black and white is even worse than hearing Mrs. Potter's reading it on our phone call this morning. The notice looks so official and final.

How can we win? We're just a ragtag bunch of volunteers up against a Goliath real estate developer.

My hands feel clammy at the thought of confronting them, and I rub them against my jeans under the table. "What can we do to stop them? We can protest outside their office building. The demonstrations for more library funding at City Hall always have some impact." I usually create a book costume. I guess this time, I can create a garden costume.

Tessa sits down in her seat, crossing her legs. The gang—Tessa, Maddie, and Iris—is all here except for Bella. Tessa's blonde hair is up in a bun, and she looks like the professional lawyer she is. Plus, we've got a reporter and a cybersecurity expert. And Mrs. Potter, with her network of community activists. We're not a completely ragtag bunch. Tessa pulls out a legal pad.

"I pitched my editor, and I can write an article about the garden for *The Intelligencer*," Maddie says. "I'll need to interview you two. I thought I could also interview some of the families who have vegetable plots, and the fifth graders from the nearby public school who plant in the garden as part of their science class. And I put a call into Strive Developers to get their side. Maybe we'll get some useful intel."

"I also did some legal research, and I asked my law firm if I can represent you pro bono. We have a strong adverse possession argument." Tessa flips over to the next page of her legal pad.

Mrs. Potter says sadly, "I talked to some of my friends, but they weren't that reassuring. Several community gardens have lost lately. Some are still fighting. I'm going to meet with them tomorrow to get advice. They suggested we try to get it designated as a critical environmental area. That could save it. But it might be difficult now. The Upper West Side has both Riverside Park and Central Park, so it's not actually short on park space compared to other neighborhoods."

"That critical environmental area designation seems key," I say.

Maybe we do have a chance.

Iris pulls out her laptop from her backpack. "I did a little digging on Strive Developers. What you can find on the web nowadays is scary. First, it's family-run. There's a grandfather at the top with two sons who don't get along after a bitter battle for who would be CEO. The first son is CEO, and the second son works in advertising for a different firm. Each one has a child, and there's another fight for control between the two kids." Iris takes a sip of her coffee. "The granddaughter started in business school but then switched to architecture, and the grandson has been working his way up through Strive Developers. Unfortunately for us, this garden lot is part of the project that seems to be at the heart of the power struggle. They've bought the adjoining three smaller buildings on the block and are planning to tear those down and build a larger, twenty-story building."

Miranda walks over with a tray and sets down each of the coffees and teas we have ordered. Wisps of steam drift out of each mug. It smells of hazelnut coffee with a slight whiff of Earl Grey tea.

"Anyway, the grandfather's name is Robert. Here's a photo of the CEO, Tom Evans, and here are photos of the two grandchildren—Rowena Evans and Rupert Evans." Iris turns the laptop to face us.

"Did you say Rupert Evans?" I ask.

But his photo is right there, staring me in the face. I just gave the library's last copy of *He Had No Idea* to Rupert Evans, the man about to destroy my garden.

Chapter Two

Rupert

I OPEN THE DOOR to my office and see the red, suede boots on my coffee table first. It's hard to miss that splash of bright color in my otherwise two-toned room of maple wood with white chairs and white walls. Rowena has made herself comfortable, as usual. But then, her office is also my second home at Strive Developers.

"You're late." A voice comes from the interior of my very comfortable reading chair.

"I was up late finishing *He Had No Idea*."

And thinking about a certain blushing blonde.

That older gentleman, who introduced himself as Mr. Devi, was quite persuasive as I walked him home. The librarian was pretty, especially when she blushed. And good taste in books.

But she seems to be in love with some other guy. Aiden or something. It's fine.

I'm off the market.

Rowena swings her—my—chair around. "Was it good?"

"Very."

"You found a book buddy?" Rowena waves her phone in the air. I sent her a text yesterday after meeting Lily telling Rowena she might be off the hook for being my book buddy.

"I did."

"Where did you meet her?"

"At the library."

"Good place for you. And you clearly found her attractive."

"Yes. Why?"

"Because you're not usually texting me about meeting random strangers. Did you ask her out?"

"She's running a book discussion on *He Had No Idea* on Friday, so I can wade in slowly and see how it goes."

"Always a good idea to do some covert due diligence on potential dates and how they act in public before you meet up and *The Intelligencer*'s *Page Six* blows it all out of proportion for click-bait gossip," Rowena says.

"Exactly," I say. "But at least they refer to you by name and not as 'New York's most eligible bachelor.' One of many, I might add." I hate that designation. Because if I go out, there's always that whisper: "You know, he's Rupert Evans, the heir to Strive Developers." I never know if I am wanted for myself.

As I sit down at my maple desk, Rowena plops her boots back on the floor and walks over. She picks up the photo of Grandpa with the two of us and smiles. She has pigtails in the photo and barely resembles the very stylish woman who stands before me now. Granted, I've got chocolate ice cream smeared on my nose in the picture, so I look quite different as well. Grandpa had taken us to Coney Island for the day.

"This is my favorite picture of us," she says.

I lean my head on my laced fingers, my elbows on the tabletop. "We're still agreed, right? We're not going to compete against each other when we want to be co-CEOs." She just got back from a family trip to Florida, strategically timed by her dad, my uncle Tom, to convince her to go for CEO alone, I'm sure.

Rowena nods. "Agreed. Even though I have my doubts about the likelihood of our success. Did you see the Oasis Development project? It requires tearing down the four small buildings that we own, razing that community garden, and coming up with the design for the new, twenty-story building. And Dad and Grandpa want us *each* to pitch for it, proposing how we're going to get it done, and then Grandpa will select the winner."

"A total nightmare. I already got a call from PR that a journalist called about it. And I like that community garden. It's a great spot to read. And to buy organic vegetables. Anastasia used to shop there sometimes."

The development for this project is not complicated. Other than the community garden, it's similar to several projects we've done in the past three years. *The community garden aspect has to be the test.*

"Anastasia. That's a name I haven't heard in a while. That was messy. I remember how surprised I was when I came over and her stuff was everywhere."

"Not as surprised as me."

"It was pretty ballsy on her part to move in. Most get scared away by your brusqueness. You must have shown your softer side."

I snort. "I don't think so. I was just working all the time on that project by the East River, and she took advantage of my absence. But when I came home late one night and she had five friends over and I felt like a guest in my own apartment, that was it. She also complained that I worked all the time."

"You do work all the time."

"She liked the *idea* of me more than the *real* me."

Rowena pinches my cheeks. "How could she not like the real you?"

"Ouch," I say, without any heat.

"I thought *Page Six* had you dating some *YouTube* star."

"Grandpa set that up. He met her grandfather at a college reunion."

"And so of course you went," Rowena says.

"And so of course I did."

"Grandpa's little yes man."

"Within reason." I shrug and study Rowena. She and I both know that Grandpa calls the shots in our family. Rowena is less biddable, but her dad is CEO. He's in her corner, politicking for her to take his place when he retires.

And I'm not prepared to scare off my dates like she did with the last one Grandpa set up. She gave him the supercilious silent treatment. I reserve that for our business competitors.

"Did you even watch her *YouTube* videos before you went on the date?" Rowena leans forward.

"I watched one of them. She had a sense of humor."

"What was the problem then?"

"She wasn't into reading." I lean back in my chair. Lily definitely reads.

"That shouldn't completely rule Ms. YouTuber out."

"No. But I'm pretty busy right now anyway, especially if we're actually going to do this project. And she seemed very social, so she'd be disappointed, like Anastasia, when I completely disappear for work."

"The project is not a total nightmare. It's a great location, and although it's a PR problem with the Oasis Garden nonprofit, it's not like they have a lease to the land," Rowena says. "We own that land. We can always counter it by giving some money to support the farmer's market near the Museum of Natural History. I can't imagine that anything grown in New York City is that safe anyway. The layer of dust I have on my windowsill if I leave it open belies that, and I live in Brooklyn."

"It's a good idea to donate money to the farmer's market," I say. "But I still hate these kinds of PR problems. And that garden has been there for twenty years. They have programs with the library, the local school, and some retirement centers. That's a lot of different constituents that I don't particularly want to mess with. Particularly Upper West Side moms and retirees."

"There's my idealistic Rupert. You like to be the knight in shining armor, coming in and creating affordable housing."

"What I don't like to be is the Grinch." Not again, anyway. And not when bad press could hinder my bid for co-CEO.

"But you weren't the Grinch, exactly. You paid for that family's two-month hotel stay out of your own pocket until we could get them settled in open, affordable housing units."

"That's still not the same as having a home at Christmas." At least that first project had prepared me for a negative tsunami of press coverage. "Grandpa was so nonchalant about kicking them out. Business is business. No room for emotions." At least Grandpa had been impressed by my actions. "It's good you're not a softie," he'd said. He hadn't known about my footing the hotel bill.

Rowena folds her arms. "As if Dad and Grandpa aren't emotional about the business. They're just fooling themselves if they think they're not. But whatever. I'm going to play this game until he gives us the CEO title."

"Even with the CEO title, I'm not sure it will stop," I say. "He's always holding that carrot, and it's like every time, we have to prove ourselves again and again." There's no escape. Even my father, who refused to work for the family business, felt the pressure to prove himself to Grandpa.

"He'll have less power if we're CEO. The business world has changed."

My glance meets Rowena's. That's the reward. We both adore Grandpa as our grandfather but much less as our boss. Independence is the prize. For Rowena and I to have the final say in the locations, the designs, the funding—to make the CEO decisions. It's been thirteen years of working around the clock for my family business, conforming to the wishes of my uncle and my grandfather, while Rowena and I bide our time for the chance to do more daring, creative projects and expand internationally.

The business world is different nowadays.

"But isn't there a way to build so we can keep most of the garden?" I ask. "We were planning on having some garden space. Can't we just incorporate this already-existing community garden instead?" I turn on my computer and click on the file that shows the space.

Rowena narrows her eyes. "Possibly. Architecturally, it would be cool, but Grandpa ..."

"Grandpa should realize that this will get us community goodwill and the same twenty-story building."

"It would probably give up some profit."

"We can afford to give up some profit," I say. "We also have to meet the requirement, anyway, to have a green roof. We could add solar panels and install one of those 'intensive' green roofs. That will even give us tax breaks."

"But shouldn't we play this by the book since we're already challenging him enough with our insistence that we be co-CEOs?"

"You're right. I'd feel a lot more confident suggesting we keep most of the community garden if Grandpa wasn't framing this as 'the' project to show we're CEO material."

"He'll say you're soft. And I have to be realistic here. If I save the garden by architecturally incorporating it into the plans for the building, he may cut me out as CEO."

"I know I'm asking a lot," I say. "I wouldn't accept CEO without you as my co-CEO."

Rowena, her face so similar to mine, stares back at me. I trust Rowena absolutely. Her father is another story. There's so much bad blood between my father and his brother. And my dad's constant warnings not to trust my uncle have taken their toll.

"Okay," Rowena says. "I'll look into it to see if it's feasible. It's a cool challenge. And it would save us landscaping costs. Anyway, you're hardly soft. Grandpa should have seen you last week when you had to fire that subcontractor who used shoddy materials. How's Ernesto?"

"He's better."

"I guess the sub thought he could get away with it once he'd heard our foreman was sick and the corporate guy was coming in to supervise."

"Probably."

"It's not every child who's grown up on a construction site."

My phone buzzes, and I glance at the caller ID. "PR."

"Good luck." Rowena stands. "I'm glad this is in your purview and not mine."

I talk to PR, and she emails me the packet they've compiled about the Oasis Community Garden. I click on the folder and open it up. A lawyer is definitely advising them. They've achieved 501(c)(3) status and even have a board. And there's the lawyer: Tessa Jackowski, Esq. My matchmaker friend, Mr. Devi, is the treasurer. He worked as an accountant for fifty years.

A romantic accountant. Not a bad source for a recommendation.

I glance at the list of names and then look closer. Lily Burton.

The librarian last night was named Lily. *Couldn't be the same one.* And then a Mrs. Potter and an Iris Murphy round out the board.

I unpack my bag and take out my hardback of *He Had No Idea*. I still want my own copy. I call up Banter & Books. "Hi, yesterday, the saleswoman mentioned that you might get more copies of *He Had No Idea* in stock today. Did you happen to receive any?"

The woman at the other end replies that they did. I ask her to hold one copy for me and ask if they can deliver another copy to Lily at the New York Public Library branch nearby.

"We don't usually do that, but since I know Lily, I'm happy to do it. Do you want to include a note?"

She knows Lily. My face flushes. I don't want to seem like some weird stalker guy. I give a short note to include.

"Don't forget that we have a book talk on *He Had No Idea* on Friday at 7 p.m. They're lots of fun. Lily is leading it."

I note it on my calendar. I am free, and it would be good for me to get out more. And find people who also like Wilhelmina Chrissy—an entire crew of book buddies.

I should have gotten her last name. I google Lily at St. Agnes, but there are no photos of the librarians. I pull up the website of the Oasis Community Garden. No pictures of their board members either.

But she is in a photo on the site, reading to a group of pre-K kids out in the sun, with a caption explaining the garden's partnership with the library.

This is ridiculous. I need to focus on making sure Rowena and I become the next CEOs, and instead I'm googling some woman I met last night. Who wasn't even interested.

I turn back to my computer monitor. PR has sent another email with additional material. And there it is. I frown.

They've created information dossiers with photos of the entire board. And Lily Burton is the librarian I met last night.

A coldness fills my gut.

I stare at her face, a mischievous smile lighting up her eyes just like last night when she quizzed me.

That's too bad.

That's not good.

I close the dossier, my teeth clenched.

We just sent them a cease and desist letter.

I can't afford to be a "softie." It's business.

Our legal team is next on my list to call to find out our options. We're playing hardball. Because this company is my dream and my life.

Chapter Three

Lily

I PULL ONE OF Miranda's posters protesting Strive Developers' threat to our community garden out of the portfolio stashed behind the library checkout counter. I spent the morning posting them in store windows and on school and day care bulletin boards around the neighborhood. The places were all very supportive.

Jade, a high school student, thanks me as I hand her one. She saw the posters and decided to do her second semester paper on the importance of community gardens.

"A package for you." The security guard holds up a bag. "Just delivered from Banter & Books."

I take it and look inside. It's a copy of *He Had No Idea* with a handwritten note.

Dear Lily,

Thanks for giving me your copy.

I hope you'll accept this gift of *He Had No Idea*
in return.

– Rupert

That's kind of thoughtful.

I shake my head. *Don't think you can butter me up, Mr. Rupert Evans, Evil Developer. If you'd just returned the copy you borrowed yesterday, I'd be fine.*

Did he know I am involved with the community garden? Maybe he came in to check out what he was up against. And was vastly reassured to find some distracted, casually dressed librarian, so pathetic that even elderly patrons are trying to set her up. Somebody who is holding on to the hope of some guy, even when it seems pretty unlikely. Somebody who has crushed on a guy for a year instead of confronting him and telling him she likes him.

I sigh. I do hate confrontation.

Mr. Devi comes up to the counter. "That was a very nice, young man yesterday, that Rupert Evans. He walked me home to make sure I was safe." He shakes his finger at me. "I did my best to sing your praises. And I told him the days you work here."

My skin flushes again.

"I just found out he's also the developer who sent us the cease and desist letter about the garden," I say.

"Oh." Mr. Devi's face falls, but he recovers quickly. "Plenty more fish in the sea."

"Plenty of piranhas too," I say.

Mr. Devi laughs.

At five, I am off to the garden—my oasis.

I breathe a sigh of relief as a clean, wire fence comes into view. No new threatening letters. This morning, I had ripped off a copy of the cease and desist letter from where it was taped to the metal bars and opened the gate. We were definitely *not* going to cease and desist using our garden.

Four elderly people, all bundled up in blankets, are playing bridge at the stone table near the wall of still-green bamboo. They're here every day, unless it's raining or snowing. The bamboo hides the street, muffling the noise, and creates the illusion that we're far from the city. But it was a lot of work to put in the preventive plastic around its roots to keep the bamboo from overtaking the whole garden.

Our cherry tree is still bare, its brown branches twisting and stretching up toward the sky, each bough a fair distance from another, giving space to grow. The brick wall of the building that abuts our garden forms a soft, hazy, pink patchwork background. A blue jay alights on one branch followed by its partner.

"Hey, Miss Lily," Jade says from the gazebo, where she's hanging out with a bunch of other teenagers. They wave. I say hello back.

I walk over to my favorite little enclave in the middle of the common juniper, next to a tall, white pine and sit on the iron bench. There's the smell of wet dirt, pine needles, and possibility. A crow caws. Some birds chirp. A shout and a burst of laughter from the gazebo make me smile. Across the way are the elevated, wooden boxes we've built for planting vegetables and fruit covered by tight, iron wiring. Next to them is a milkweed patch for bees and caterpillars. I hope we can do that project again. The children love taking home their caterpillars and then releasing them into the garden when they turn into butterflies.

A sense of peace comes over me.

It will work out.

A mom comes in holding her daughter's hand. She passes by me. "Hi, Lily. She just wants to see if any of her pansies have come up yet. She's not very patient."

On her way back, the mom says, "I saw your poster, and we both wrote letters to Strive Developers asking them to save the garden." She shows me a picture on her phone of her daughter's letter, the childish scrawl in black crayon accompanied by pictures of butterflies and daffodils and carrots.

Tears come to my eyes. I get down to her daughter's height. "It's beautiful. Thank you."

Some things are worth fighting for. *I'm just getting started, Strive Developers.*

I walk over to Jade and her friends. "Jade, you have a pretty active *TalkTack* account. Do you think you can create some videos supporting the garden?"

"Sure. That will be fun," Jade says.

We brainstorm some ideas, and Jade is very enthusiastic.

At six, I lock the entrance to the community garden and walk home. The temperature is dropping again, and people stride by, desperate to return to their warm apartments and families.

I unlock the front door of our building and check my mailbox in the foyer. Another postcard from my dad, this time with a picture of the Taj Mahal.

"Having a great time" is scrawled on the back.

He's not one for a lot of words. My mom always said he was the strong, silent type. Still. He could write something more or call via WhatsApp, except he refuses to believe me when I tell him it's free.

I take the elevator up and unlock the door to our apartment just as Aiden comes out of his. He looks like he's dressed to go out. He's wearing a white, button-down shirt and a blue jacket with jeans, carrying a small, navy backpack.

"Hi," he says, smiling. He runs his hand through his blond hair.

"Hi."

"I've missed seeing you these past few mornings," he says.

We usually leave for work at the same time and bump into each other in the hallway, when he's not traveling.

"I thought you were away," I say.

"No. I had to get to the office brutally early for work," he says. "Trust me. I was not a sight to be seen."

He comes over to where I stand, my door barely open. Tiger sticks his head in the crack, trying to escape into the hallway.

"Do they like the cat grass?" he asks, standing close, just a little bit closer than necessary, as if he wants to be near me.

"Tiger and Darcy like it. Bennet is a little suspicious."

"I found you these great reader socks at the airport bookstore. I'm on my way out now, but I'll drop them off later."

Socks? That's not remotely romantic.

But they are *reader* socks.

"Did you get a chance to read that Pam Houston short story I sent you?" I ask. In the story, the man always talks about the future but never makes it clear if the woman is included. It seems apt.

"No. Work has been brutal. But I will. And we can discuss it when we next have brunch, okay?" He tucks my hair behind my ear. "I've got to go." He dashes down the stairs.

I pick up Tiger so he doesn't escape into the hallway, nuzzle his furry face, and then put him down in our apartment. Darcy greets me, rubbing against my legs.

Should I tell him I like him as more than just a friend? It's been a year. *Why am I putting up with the Sunday brunch spot when I want to be so much more? Don't I want to be something more?*

Bella comes out from her room and says, "I bought snacks for our meeting tonight."

"Excellent." I shrug off my coat, make my way to the kitchenette, and pour some water into our electric kettle to make tea. I pick up Tiger and hug him, petting his fur. Bennet and Darcy appear in the kitchen, meowing. Bella and I are both softies for cat rescues. Bennet and Darcy were up for adoption outside GreenGrocer this past summer, all curled up together, and we didn't have the heart to separate them. They're Bella's, while I adopted Tiger when my mom died.

I add a tea bag and pour the boiling water into my mug and then sit down at our small, square, dining room table and pull out my laptop.

We've made our one-bedroom apartment into a two bedroom by using the living room as another bedroom. Our dining table is smack in the center of the foyer. And that tiny space also serves as our library, so bookshelves cover every wall. Our narrow bedrooms are lovely, though, because both rooms have a bowed window. And we have high ceilings.

"Rupert Evans sent me a copy of *He Had No Idea*."

"He did?"

"Yes. I think I should send it back and say I can't accept this, as a library employee."

"But you're allowed to accept gifts under fifty dollars."

"Okay, how about, 'I can't accept this because we're about to sue your ass in court'?"

Bella laughs. "You should accept it and then offer him a home-cooked meal as a thank you. While we're suing his ass in court, you should butter him up. Flies are caught with honey, not vinegar."

"There is no way any buttering up is going to work," I say. "I did some research, and he seems to be dating some famous YouTuber." And if Mr. Devi really wants to get into the matchmaking business, he needs to up his game and ask the guy if he's single—not just married.

The downstairs buzzer rings.

I feed the cats as Bella says, "It's Tessa and Iris." She buzzes them in.

A few minutes later, there's a knock on the door, and I let them in. I hug Iris hello and then give Tessa an awkward hug because she's carrying a pizza box. I take their jackets and Iris's scarf muffler and put them in the closet. The crocheted scarf probably deserves its own hanger. No suit today for Tessa.

"I cleared off my desk so we can eat in my room," Bella says. "Let's put it all in the kitchen, serve it there, and take our plates into the bedroom."

"I can't represent you guys." Tessa frowns as she places the pizza box on our kitchen counter. The melted cheese smells delicious. "The firm found it a conflict of interest. They definitely don't want to piss off Strive Developers—or any other developers, for that matter. I'm so sorry. Even though I can do a lot of pro bono at White & Gilman, it's not a blank ticket, unfortunately. They don't want to set any precedents that could hurt their clients. But I found another lawyer for you guys." She unwraps her scarf from around her head and shakes out her blonde hair. "And Miranda was sorry she couldn't come, but she started a painting to auction as a fundraiser." Tessa shows us a photo on her phone.

"It looks mesmerizing."

Iris hands over a bag of Chop't salads, and I take it into our kitchenette to unpack. Bella already set up plates and wineglasses and opened a bottle of white wine. Maddie arrives next, and we all crowd into the kitchen, filling our plates with pizza and salad. It's tight but cozy.

"I did some research on him during lunch," Maddie says. "In his very first project, he was labeled the Grinch because he threw the tenants out of the building they were tearing down right before Christmastime. This is nothing compared to that."

That's not good. But he doesn't come across as a Grinch.

"Mrs. Potter will be late," I say. "She said not to wait for her. She'll eat at her friend's house and then come over."

Everyone takes their plates, and we adjourn to Bella's bedroom. Large, framed versions of her first paperback covers dot the walls. Tessa and I climb over the bed to reach the far side of the converted Ikea table that is Bella's desk. She's pulled it away from the wall, piled her writing stuff on her bed, and put all our chairs around it. Bella lights some tea candles as Iris pours the wine into our glasses. Everyone sits down at the table, leaving one open seat for Mrs. Potter.

Iris raises her glass. "To defeating Strive Developers and saving the Oasis!"

"Hear! Hear!" I say. We clink glasses and sip our wine. Even without the wine, I feel such a warmth spreading through me. I have the best group of friends. Bella and I have been best friends since college, but I met Miranda through the garden when she came to paint there. I convinced her to hold a class for teenagers. Miranda introduced me to Tessa, who is her roommate, and Iris.

"We should hold a protest at their headquarters next Friday," I say. "The moms suggested that's the best day because a lot of them work part-time and have Fridays off."

"That sounds good," Maddie says. "I'll update the press release I wrote. I also drafted these sound bites for when the press interviews you. I'm not sure I can cover it because we're friends." She hands over a press release and a list of sound bites.

"These are amazing," I say. "Where'd you get all these statistics?"

"New Yorkers for Parks did research and compiled them. Overall, the Upper West Side does not do that badly because it has both Riverside Garden and Central Park. The city parks per seniors, however, is half the New York City average. There are only 4.5 acres of parks for seniors on the Upper West Side, and the citywide average is thirteen acres. There are also only four community gardens versus a New York City average of nine community gardens."

The doorbell rings.

"I'll get it." Iris picks up her empty plate.

"We should research requirements on whether we can protest outside their building. Do we need a permit or something?" Bella asks as she wipes her hands on a napkin after finishing her first slice.

"Mrs. Potter may know," I say. "But I'll research that if not."

"Do we know any architects?" Maddie asks. "We should ask one if it's possible to save the garden but still construct a twenty-story building with the lots that we have. That would be a better angle for a story—that they have the choice *not* to destroy the garden. I'll ask some of the other reporters."

"I only know lawyers," Tessa says. "Other than Miranda and you guys. Lawyers tend to hang out with lawyers." She takes another bite of her salad.

"I must know some assistants or caterers who work at Strive Developers," Bella says. "I feel like, at this point, I've worked so many part-time jobs that I know everybody."

"Your network is insane," I say.

"Your network is seriously the best when I'm trying to write a story," Maddie says.

"It definitely helps to know the people nobody pays attention to," Bella says. "I'll check. One of them might have an inside scoop."

We may be small, but we are mighty. Rupert Evans has no idea who he is messing with and what's he in for.

Mrs. Potter bustles in, waving a cluster of papers. "Strive Developers sued us for back rent. That's all our money. We can't afford a lawyer."

And just like that, my hope floats away like a balloon let go by a child, buffeted by winds, a red circle outlined against tall, overpowering, Manhattan skyscrapers.

Chapter Four

Rupert

GRANDPA'S OFFICE IS DESIGNED to impress. Large, framed photos of his first buildings and his biggest developments line the walls. His desk is a mammoth antique. I take a seat in one of the leather armchairs across from him. He's added another framed photograph to his desk: a family picture, one that was taken a few years ago at a very stilted Christmas Eve dinner at his home. That's not an occasion I want to remember. My dad and my uncle had alternated between not talking to each other and slinging barbs. But at least everyone is smiling in the picture.

It's next to a photograph of Rose, my grandma, and two grinning boys—my dad and my uncle. The only other picture on the desk is one of Rowena and me with him as teenagers, wearing hardhats on a construction site. I look a little shell-shocked there. That was the day I realized how much I loved being on-site and watching two-dimensional drawings transform into physical buildings. Grandpa had spent that summer teaching us about the business. We'd shadowed him everywhere.

"What's this I hear from Rowena about you two being co-CEOs? I thought I told you no." Grandpa fixes me with his steely-blue eyes and steeples his fingers, like a craggy eagle peering down from a tree branch, deciding which small mammal scampering below it will eat.

But this is my life. It is either co-CEOs with Rowena or an outsider running the company. It's not a choice for him. Not that I should tell him that directly.

"You need a clear chain of command, or there will be politics, people playing you against each other. I saw it with Fell Developers," Grandpa says.

"We're dividing it up. She has creative, and I have finance."

Grandpa waves his hand like he's swatting a troublesome fly. "And that division won't work the first time creative goes over budget. Who calls the shots then?"

"What's best for the company."

"You think it's finance." He snorts. "What you're saying is that you're the top dog. How's Rowena going to feel about that?"

"First, Rowena doesn't usually go over budget. And if she does, she has a valid reason. You know we won the bid for that development in Queens because of her design skill. Finance is not always the determining factor. And we work well together. We've been working well together for ten years."

Grandpa doesn't look entirely convinced. "You're just being soft."

Soft. That's what he called me right before the Grinch debacle. I'm not soft, but I'm not going to be an a**hole again. At least not like that.

Time for some tough love. If we're fighting for the chance to be co-CEOs, then at least let's be honest about why.

"It's better than one of us leaving the company." Leaving has to be on the table.

There's silence.

"And it's better than losing our relationship. We've all seen the consequences of that." I gesture toward the family photo on his desk.

Grandpa growls and looks off to the side.

Yes. That was a low blow, but my father and my uncle barely talk to each other, ever since my uncle betrayed his brother to become CEO.

"This job is all-consuming. That's why Uncle Tom has decided to retire," I say. Uncle Tom's recent health scare convinced him it was time to step down. "And if we ever get married and have kids, we'd like to see them." Another harsh truth.

"Maybe I should hire an outsider," Grandpa says. "Then you both can have plenty of time to find a partner and don't need to risk your health to run this company."

Shit. I'm being too confrontational.

Our playbook has always been to agree with Grandpa.

Telling him Rowena and I want to be co-CEOs is the first time we've openly disagreed with his wishes.

"I'm sure we can both find a partner *and* do this job. You and Uncle Tom managed," I say.

"Apparently, Tom has not managed so well. As if I have meeting your partner to look forward to. You're not even dating anyone."

I look away, and Lily's face pops into my mind. I'm excited to see Lily tonight at the book club. Even if a relationship between us is impossible.

"You're seeing someone?" Grandpa's gravelly voice snaps me back into the room. "You're looking besotted."

I shake my head. "I can't exactly date right now when I'm in the middle of trying to convince you that Rowena and I can be co-CEOs—and come up with an idea for this development that will prove to you we both merit the position."

"Excuses," Grandpa says. "I'd like great-grandchildren while I'm still capable of seeing them and playing with them."

I soften. Grandpa really did make up for lost opportunities with his sons by spending so much time with me and Rowena. Why can't he understand that's one of the reasons Rowena and I are close and don't want to compete against each other?

"And you should find someone like your grandmother—someone feisty, someone who is a risk-taker."

I can feel my eyebrows raise. As if Grandpa wants someone to stand up to him. He wants his own way—and only his own way.

Grandpa stares at me. "I don't think I ever told you and Rowena this, but your grandmother is the one who persuaded me to start my own business."

"You never told us that," I say.

Grandpa gazes at the photo on his desk. "She was the one who insisted we buy that first piece of land. It was crazy. Even now, I can still feel that cold fear in my stomach when I bought that lot that I could lose everything. You guys have it easy." And then he shakes his head and glares at me. "I also haven't seen any articles published yet countering the garden-biased crap *The Intelligencer* printed."

I rub my brow. "I talked to *The Intelligencer*, *The Gazette*, *The Squirrel*, and a bunch of other papers. I explained that we are providing affordable housing units ... plus, there will still be green space, so the development will actually be better for the community."

"Harrumph. It's clearly better."

A tap sounds at the door.

"Come in," my grandfather bellows.

It's our press person, Alison.

"I heard you were both here. Unfortunately, there's a *TalkTack* video and Instagram reel trending that takes a dim view of the proposed development," Alison says.

"What's *TalkTack*?" Grandpa asks.

"It's a social media platform where people post videos," Alison says. "This looks like it's made by some of the teenagers who hang out at the garden." She turns on her iPad.

The video shows the garden and all the various communities using it, and then a big hammer smashes a dollhouse-size garden into bits with the words "Save the Oasis."

Grandpa's eyes bulge.

"I already showed it to Tom," Alison says. "And we're looking for some *TalkTack* influencers to counter with stories from our families whose lives have been changed by moving into our affordable housing units."

"That sounds good," I say. "Let's get on that as quickly as possible."

She looks at her phone. "Oh."

"What?" Grandpa asks.

"There's another one. Aww. That's pretty compelling." She chuckles and then composes her face to look more serious.

She turns the video to face us.

An older couple show two teenagers a swing dance, and then the two teenagers show the older couple a trending *TalkTack* dance routine. And the older people try to follow it—try being the operative verb there. I almost laugh but catch myself in time. But the effort is valiant, and the teenagers are doing their best. They also seem super concerned that the older gentleman doesn't hurt himself. It's definitely well done. Did Lily come up with the concept?

"I'll get some videos up as soon as possible." She clicks off her phone and strides out.

Grandpa looks miffed. I should have gone with her to figure out what we can do to counter these.

This doesn't look good for me. I didn't expect viral *TalkTack* videos. I stand and head toward the door.

"Don't think I won't search for an outsider," Grandpa says. "I have to do what's best for the company. I hired a consultant to come up with options."

I don't flinch. It's not like I didn't expect Grandpa to play hardball. I turn around, my back straight, my eyes hard. "I look forward to the competition. No one knows this company or our market better than Rowena and me."

"You think it's my fault that your dad and your uncle fell out." Grandpa leans across the desk. "Yes. I said only one could be CEO. But your dad didn't take that seriously enough. He thought this was still family and there'd be allowances. But this is business. You can't let your emotions get involved. You'd do well to remember that."

I walk out the door.

Dad *didn't* think there'd be allowances. He didn't think his brother would lie to him and say he supported their being co-CEOs.

Don't people lie for deals?

Never trust what your opponent says. Another one of Grandpa's business dogmas.

Grandpa can't *really* be looking for an outsider to take over the company. *No way.* He always told us he built this company for his family—to make sure we'd be protected.

But if he truly believes that co-CEOs won't work? If he's worried now that stress has caused Uncle Tom's recent health scare?

The Fell family is completely different from Rowena and me. Those three brothers barely got along and didn't want to work, so each was milking the company for what he could get.

That's not me and Rowena.

I walk down the hallway to my office, shut the door, and sink into my reading chair. Is Rowena right? Should we do whatever it takes to win—even if that means bulldozing the garden?

My empty, minimalist office, my books hidden behind the white panels, provides no answers. *If I lose the company, I lose everything I've worked for over the past fifteen years—and all our dreams of seeing Strive evolve into the next generation.*

I've worked so hard at this company to prove myself that I've barely kept in touch with friends. Only my best friend, Sebastian. And that's because we play squash together every week, and we live in the same apartment building.

Not that my college friends don't understand. They're all working their asses off too. I certainly haven't made any new friends, except for the women I've dated—and I can't say any now qualify as friends.

By the time I get home, I just want to relax, read a book, and take my mind off work.

Dad walked away. But he also admits that he enjoys marketing far more than he enjoyed real estate development. That's not me.

Was Dad also at fault? Should he have suspected his brother would lie to him?

Can I *not* trust Rowena?

When I see the picture of my dad and my uncle smiling together as teenagers, it looks like they used to have a similar relationship to Rowena and me.

I'm boxed in. Grandpa's way doesn't work anymore, but to win, I need to play his way. And yet, if we keep the Oasis Garden, we could immediately defuse these protests.

Time to call PR and up our game.

But playing his way would also mean not trusting Rowena.

Chapter Five

Lily

I WAVE TO MIRANDA at the counter and head to the back where the book club meets. Banter & Books is busy today. Almost every table is taken, and Miranda has a line of patrons in front of her.

The book club is held in the rear conservatory, so called because of the slanted, glass-paned roof and the huge windows. A white-washed, maple table, long enough for ten chairs to fit around, holds center stage. A row of bird of paradise plants shields the book club from the view of the rest of the patrons. Hanging plants break the expanse of windows. French doors lead out onto the small backyard, closed now for the winter. A vase with fresh hydrangeas decorates the table.

And there is Rupert. I stop short. The enemy. He glances up and lifts an eyebrow.

I lift an eyebrow back and take my seat across from him, placing my tabbed copy of *He Had No Idea* on the table. And then I take out the copy he gifted me. I'd brought it to donate to the free library in the back.

"I can't accept this." I slide it across the table to him.

"Because I'm from Strive Developers?" he asks.

"Yes. So you know who I am?" I ask.

"I do now."

"Did you know who I was then?"

"No. I wouldn't have taken your last copy if I had known. And not when I bought that book for you either." He slides the book back across the table to me.

I pick it up and shelve it in the free library. I take my seat back at the table. He frowns.

What is he doing here? Is he trying to curry favor with the locals? I didn't expect him to be mixing with the plebians.

Maybe he's doing some on-the-ground research.

I'm sure he didn't expect us to find a lawyer so quickly (thank you, Tessa) and file counterclaims. Another community garden was recently victorious in court, and the judge ruled that an environmental impact statement was required. And as Maddie noted when creating her press talking points, community gardens are lacking in our neighborhood. Clearly, this proposed development would remove yet another one. We have a fighting chance at winning.

Our lawyer is working pro bono so we don't have to worry about the legal expenses. We've also raised some funds from families in the neighborhood, and Miranda's painting will raise some more money, giving us a cushion.

Our *TalkTack* video has gone viral, and Jade has gotten even more friends to create shorts. I came up with another idea for a new dancing one today after school—with the bridge players and the toddlers. The teenagers did cartwheels off the handles of the walkers and the baby strollers. I convinced a nearby gym that offers parkour classes to use the garden as their playground, and they agreed to be filmed. Wait until that video hits *TalkTack*. I chuckle. Maddie's colleague is writing an article about the garden and all the community support for it.

Really, Mr. Rupert Evans should be at the office worrying about this bad media coverage.

Unless it doesn't matter.

It's a large group today, with two women I don't know and two other men. Bella and Jing are already seated. Iris is there, her laptop open on the table, that huge scarf warmer next to it. I forgot to tease her about it last time. She closes the lid as I move the vase of hydrangeas to the windowsill behind me. I sit across from her. Maddie joins us a few minutes later, grabbing the last seat next to me.

I take out my list of questions. Bella's handwriting is scrawled across the top with her first question. She always wants to know what attracts people to a book. I ask everyone to introduce themselves.

"Why did you pick up the book?" I ask.

Rupert says, "She's one of my favorite authors, but also because it was about a bunch of old friends who'd fallen out but who were trying to reignite that old spark. And that last sentence in the blurb." He picks up the book and reads it aloud: "'When one of them is murdered, it reveals all the fissures underlying their relationships.'"

Yes.

"Same," says the woman next to Rupert, leaning toward him and smiling.

I probably looked like that at the library.

Like a moth drawn to a flame.

But I'm not going to get burned.

Others give different reasons for why they picked up the book, like the New York City setting. Most chose it because they will read anything by Wilhelmina Chrissy.

"What did you like or dislike about the book? No spoilers yet." I might as well start with the basics.

"I couldn't figure it out, and yet, once it was revealed, the clues had been there all along," Jing says.

"I really liked the way she captured old friendships—that easy familiarity and how when you get back together after a long time apart, it's like the intervening time disappears, and you just pick up right where you left off," Maddie says.

This group of ten people seated around the table, books or e-readers in front of them, all engaged, with the soft lighting and the green leaves as background, reminds me of a scene in the book. Wilhelmina Chrissy describes how when these friends all lived together, they would gather around the kitchen table and swap stories, catching up on the day. It sounded so idyllic.

"Except that I found it disheartening that they'd fallen out," I say. "The author described it so realistically that I found it believable, but it made me sad." But I didn't want to. I didn't want to believe that just like that, a group of friends could fall apart.

"Well, it was partially because Ashley and Herbert broke up," Maddie says. "It seemed like they were the center of it all."

Like how my parents and my family home had been my anchor. Now gone. But I've found my new family among my friends and the community I've built with the Oasis Garden. Bella smiles at me warmly from across the table.

"I did *not* expect Herbert to be murdered," one woman says.

"Didn't you read the back of the book?" Bella asks.

"No. I usually don't. I like to go in blind," she responds.

"Interesting. I always read the blurb, but that's also an occupational hazard of being a writer," Bella says. "I want to know how they hooked a reader into buying the book."

"I also liked how Herbert went back to the neighborhood where they'd all first become friends and bought that apartment where they'd lived before," Rupert says. "Wilhelmina Chrissy is really good about weaving in the importance of place. I loved when Ashley had that flashback to Herbert asleep in the living room, the sun lighting his long legs, and his feet sticking off the edge of the chaise lounge, and her cozying up to him. I really felt that uncertainty of young love and how much she loved him by the vividness of her memory of him in that room."

I stare at Rupert. That was one of my favorite paragraphs of the book. It reminded me of my memories of my mom in our kitchen. So, he does understand the importance of a place. Maybe that's a prerequisite for becoming a real estate developer.

I can still see my mom baking in the kitchen, but I worry that memory is fading, and it's not like I can refresh it because the kitchen is gone—renovated by the new owners when my dad sold the apartment, according to our old neighbors.

"What did you think of the main character?" I ask.

"I liked her." Rupert looks straight at me. "She was intelligent and resourceful."

Strike two for my expectations that Rupert was just here because of the garden. He is enthusiastically participating in this discussion.

"Too intelligent and resourceful and calculating," another guy says. "I thought she killed her ex-boyfriend." And we're already into the mystery portion of the book.

"She clearly still loved her ex, so I didn't think she'd killed him," the woman says.

We talk about our perceptions of the characters and how well the author defined each one.

"All right, let's discuss who we thought killed Herbert," I say.

"I thought it was the new boyfriend," Rupert says. "I didn't like him at all."

"Oh, no," another woman says. "He was so romantic."

"I didn't trust him. He wasn't straight with her from the beginning." I stare at Rupert. "I didn't believe him when he said he was in love with her already. He barely knew her."

"Same," Maddie says.

"Did you think he killed Herbert?" another guy asks.

"I thought it would be too easy if he was the one who killed Herbert," I said. "And jealousy over an ex didn't seem like enough of a motive."

"I thought it was the neighbor who wanted Herbert's apartment to expand his own. Real estate in New York City makes people do crazy things," Rupert says. "It becomes personal when it's just a business decision."

Rupert smiles benignly at me.

I grimace. Two can play at this. "What could be a more personal decision than where you live and the community you create there?"

"Touché," Rupert says.

I feel like Rupert's eyes have an appreciative glint, and it warms me up inside.

"I thought it was the older woman down the hall who hated his dog and was into gardening. She had the means since she knew about all those plants that killed people without any trace," the other guy says. He was at my last book club.

"I did wonder about her and her plant expertise." Rupert stares at me.

"You learn so much from gardening. Such a handy thing to know," I say. Not that I've learned about any poisonous plants yet, but my repertoire can always expand. We should add some poison ivy in the garden if they're going to tear it down. I meet Rupert's glance and try to make a face like, *Who, little innocent me?*

Rupert's eyes widen. Looks like I succeeded. I chuckle.

Bella coughs across from me.

"Was there any point when you knew for sure who killed Herbert?" I ask.

"No," the guy who suspected the older gardener says.

"I was reading it too fast to try to figure it out." Rupert smiles at me. "But that is one of the reasons I return to this author—she always surprises me, and I never know what she's going to do next."

"I'm always happy to discuss this author's books," says the woman sitting next to Rupert. She smiles at him, leaning closer.

Be careful you don't fall into his lap.

He seems oblivious to her overture and faces me. I turn back to my list of questions. He's fair game for her.

"What did you think of how the mystery was solved?" I ask.

Everyone chimes in with their thoughts. This is one of the best book discussions I've led in a while.

"Why do you think it was titled *He Had No Idea*?" asks one woman.

I stare at Rupert. "Because he had *no idea* what he was up against."

Rupert blinks and clears his throat.

"The new boyfriend, right?" says the woman. "He didn't realize he was going to star as a prime suspect in a murder mystery."

"And he didn't realize how much Ashley was still in love with Herbert," Iris says. "To be fair, Ashley didn't realize it either until she saw Herbert again that first night when they had dinner at the apartment—before he was murdered. She'd built up so many protective defenses."

There's silence at the table as we all seem to take a moment to digest these last points.

"All right, any other things anyone wants to discuss? Any burning questions or points?" I ask.

One guy talks about his favorite things about Wilhelmina Chrissy, and then we call it a night.

The guy who was at my last book club turns to me. "I'm Matt. What are you reading next?" He slides his chair closer to mine.

He's kind of cute. Bella had said he seemed interested after the last meeting, but I'd waved that off. But maybe she's right and not just tired of watching me futilely pursue Aiden.

"I'm not sure." I finished *A Devilish Dare*—and yes, Bella was right that that book set really high standards. I look over at the bookshelves to see if any of the new releases pop out.

Matt moves his chair back, the legs scraping on the floor.

"Well, hopefully, I'll see you around." He shoves his book into his bag and stands.

That was abrupt.

I look to see what happened ... right at Rupert, who's walking toward me.

I raise my eyebrow at Rupert. What the hell? First, he wants to destroy my garden, and now he's actively foiling my romantic life? I frown at him. But he just smiles—a cocky grin that makes me see red.

I raise my eyebrow at Rupert and turn to Matt, putting my hand on his arm. "What are you reading next?"

Matt looks like a deer caught in headlights. *Buck up, dude.* I'm not impressed that he's conceding so quickly to some guy who just glared at him. *Hold your ground.*

"I'm not sure yet," he says.

"Lily." Rupert is right there. I don't even need the panic in Matt's eyes to tell me. It's like a fire heater ignited next to me.

Matt skedaddles out of there. I turn to Rupert. I put my hands on my hips and step closer to him. I *will not* be intimidated.

That was a mistake.

He smells like fresh pine, and he's got a very broad, muscular chest, which is currently way, way too close.

I refuse to step back.

I look up at him. "What was that?"

"What?"

He tries to look all innocent, but it's like a wolf in sheep's clothing trying to hide that he doesn't have a fuzzy, white snout with pink nostrils.

"Can I take you out to dinner and Bumper Cars on Ice at Bryant Park some night?" he asks. "It seems like a fun winter date activity."

"You're asking *me* out?" I ask.

Stupid idiot. Because doubting some guy wants to ask you out is a surefire way to make him doubt he should ask you out. *Rephrase that.*

"*You're* asking me out?"

That does not sound better. He probably already thinks he's some god, and I just reinforced that.

I close my eyes and wave my hand no. "Are you trying to butter me up so we won't oppose your taking over our garden?"

The thing is, I'm attractive, but I'm not the type of woman hot mega-developers are lining up to take on dates. I've been pursuing Aiden for a year, and I'm still in the Sunday brunch time slot. This is not just suspicious. He's totally playing with me.

He blinks. "Would that work?"

Depends on the buttering up. "No."

"I didn't think so," he says. "But still, this proposed development is just business. I don't think it means we have to be enemies. I bid against Rob of Pear Developers all the time, but he's still one of my closest friends."

Just business.

No.

"No. This is not just business to me. The garden is not a business. It's a refuge and a community. There's no other open-air space like it on the Upper West Side. It's a space for teenagers to hang out safely. It's a place for older people to find their friends and—" Tears well in my eyes, and my voice cracks. I'm sounding weak and emotional. I stop short. He's tilted his head, listening. That's the last thing I need to do, *cry* in front of him. I take a deep breath and stare off at the bright covers of the books in the nearby bookcase.

It's the self-help section. Of course.

He's so sure of himself. He probably thinks I'm just another lap dog, about to roll over and expose my belly so I can date him.

He reaches out his hand and pats my shoulder awkwardly, then pulls his hand back as if burned.

Maybe I should go, just to see if I can get any further intelligence.

"I see. It's not just business. I thought maybe we had a connection." He clears his throat. "I'm sorry. I like the garden too. But this is critical for my career."

A connection.

He feels it too.

Or says he does.

Crap. There's no way I can date him. I'm too attracted to him. And I'd be forever parsing his words, hoping he meant what he was saying. And not just saying it to get me to drop the lawsuit.

Just draw the line, Lily. Rupert is the enemy. That's his compartment.

But I don't want to. That book club banter was fun. Our connection is like a magnetic, fizzy electricity that's pulling me forward.

"Can I walk you home, at least?" he asks. "I didn't mean to upset you."

Chapter Six

Rupert

THIS IS A TERRIBLE idea. We're enemies. And it's not going to get better if wrecking balls destroy the garden. *If.* Rowena and I might be able to save the garden. Not that I can reveal that.

But that book club was fun, and I want to get to know Lily.

"I just thought bumper cars seemed appropriate. You can bump into me and get all your anger and frustration out about our dispute." I am rambling.

She glares at me. If this were a cartoon, steam would be pouring out of her ears.

But then she smiles, and her whole face lights up. I've just been sucker punched. My breath catches. I stare at her.

"Okay," she says. "But first, we're walking Maddie, Iris, and Jing to the train station, and then Bella and I are walking home. We could also escort you to your apartment building since we're two and you're only one."

"And we've all taken self-defense training," Iris says as she joins us, wrapping a huge scarf around her neck.

"I feel safer already," I say.

Lily laughs. It's this lovely, no-holds-barred laugh—not some polite rejoinder.

Bella and Jing join us, waving goodbye to the red-haired woman at the counter. It feels festive, like a warm family. I can tell a lot about a person from the friends they have, and this group speaks well for Lily.

"Can you guys make our Lunar New Year celebration at my apartment on Sunday?" Jing asks. "I just sent out the email invite this afternoon. My parents really enjoyed meeting you all last year."

"What can I bring?" Bella asks.

"Your mom's dumplings are so good," Maddie says. "I can't wait."

"She'll be happy to hear that," Jing says.

"Did someone crochet your neck warmer, Iris?" Lily asks.

Iris's laughing, hazel eyes just barely peer out from above the rim. "Why? You don't think it's too small?"

"It could serve as an anklet for an elephant," Lily says.

I chuckle.

"I know." Iris sighs. "Patrick took up crocheting, briefly, and made this for me. He likes to stick it on me before I leave the apartment."

"Patrick usually dresses pretty sharply," Maddie says.

"Are you sure he's not just marking you as his and scaring off anyone else who might be interested?" Bella asks. "That looks like it's swallowing your whole head."

"At least it does keep me warm." Iris shrugs. "And he looked cute when he was crocheting it."

Should I take up crochet? Would Lily wear something I made?

At first, we walk six in a row, but as soon as we have to pass someone, Bella, Jing, Maddie and Iris move up and leave me and Lily together. Not bad.

I didn't think they'd be on my side.

Lily doesn't look as happy as I am about it. Her turquoise-blue hat brings out the color of her eyes.

But now I'm not sure what to say.

There was real pain about losing the garden.

We need to meet on some neutral territory. We walk side by side, a foot between us. A foot of distance that I feel. I shorten my steps to match hers.

"That was a great discussion you led," I say. "Is there a particular Wilhelmina Chrissy you recommend to patrons at the library?"

"The first," she says. "Start at the beginning and read them all."

"I agree. I noticed you didn't put yourself on the matchmaking list at Banter & Books," I say.

She tilts her head and looks at me. "Were you checking that out?"

"I got there early."

"Did you add yourself?" she asks.

"No." I smile at her. "I seem to have a very reliable matchmaker in Mr. Devi."

She laughs. "I'll tell him that."

"Who are your other favorite authors?" I ask.

"For a librarian, that's like asking who your favorite children are. I feel I have to be kind of open and can't pick favorites," she says. "It also depends on my mood. What books have you read recently and liked?"

"That's a much better phrasing," I say. "Although my favorite modern author is probably Fredrik Backman. And other favorites are Nick Hornby, Richard Osman and, of course, Wilhelmina Chrissy. And the classics like Hemingway and Fitzgerald."

"Lot of male authors there."

"Yes," I say. "I'm happy to take suggestions." I pull out my phone, ready to note them down.

She laughs softly.

Bella drops back. "I'm sure you can think of some suggestions, Lily. How about *A Tree Grows in Brooklyn*?"

"That poor tree—giving everything," Maddie says.

They were listening in.

"There's *Our Life in Gardens*," Lily says.

"I liked *Green Thoughts: A Writer in the Garden*," Jing says. "We read that last year as part of the Oasis Book Club."

"We read all the books recommended by Vivian Swift on a list she compiled for *The Guardian*. Just search books about gardens, Vivian Swift, and *The Guardian*," Lily says.

"I'm sorry I missed that book club," I say.

"So are we," Lily says wryly.

"We would have had a lot more time to sway you," Maddie says, popping up next to me. "Isn't there a way to save the garden?"

I falter. Maddie is very direct.

And normally, I like direct people.

But now I feel like I'm just giving them hope. When there isn't any.

Or not much.

If it were my company, yes. I'd save the garden.

But it's not going to be my company if I save the garden.

And my first priority is to save Rowena and me.

"I'm sorry," I say again. "I should go home. It seems like you're quite able to defend yourselves."

And I turn around and swiftly walk in the other direction toward my apartment.

I'm a fool. First, I'm afraid a woman is going to date me just because I'm the grandson of the founder of Strive Developers. And now I've gone in the total opposite direction and am attracted to some woman who won't date me precisely because of my role in Strive Developers. Good going. *Congratulations on perfecting the art of bad dating choices.*

But I like that she isn't falling over herself trying to pick me up. When she threatened to poison me ... I snort-laugh.

A delivery guy on an e-bike whizzes by me.

And she'd highlighted the same section in the book as me—about families and friends.

That passage about friends was key. Because it's hard to make new friends nowadays, now that I'm the presumed heir to Strive Developers. Most of my friends are from high school and college. I could never make friends at Strive Developers as the boss's nephew. That's also why Rowena and I are so close.

For that reason alone, sometimes I think I should've worked somewhere else first. My college friends made close friends in their law firms or in their residencies. But I never wanted to work anywhere else.

All I ever wanted was to build on the Strive legacy established by Grandpa—to be the co-CEO with Rowena, to build affordable housing, and to establish our name and our company as synonymous with good development. As Mom always says, "With power comes responsibility."

These *TalkTack* videos are smearing the Strive Developers' name. For that reason alone, I should hate her. And if Grandpa knew I had asked her out on a date, "softie" would look like a compliment.

I text Sebastian.

Me: *Free for a squash game?*

Sebastian: *Sure. Half hour. Just finishing up at the office.*

Chapter Seven

Lily

"YOU SCARED HIM OFF." Jing pulls her hat down to cover her ears. The bright flags of the various small restaurants that line Amsterdam Avenue wave in the wind. Nobody is eating in the outdoor sheds tonight.

"Let's not pretend we're all friends," Maddie says.

"He is really attractive, though," Bella says. "He's got such long legs, and the way he walks ..."

"Bella," I say.

"I'm sorry. I am a romance writer. I wish I could describe how he walks and put that in a book."

We all stare after him. He does have really long legs and a magnetic way of walking. But he also looks a little lonely. And he seemed so happy discussing the book with all the club participants.

I pivot and walk in the opposite direction. My friends follow.

We turn down one of the side streets to cross over to Central Park West. Warm light spills into the street from the illuminated windows. A striking, red-and-white painting with *love* in script hangs on a wall, visible through one window. Tall, bare trees line the block. We skirt around the piles of black garbage bags set out for tomorrow's pickup.

"And he definitely likes you," Bella says. "He didn't pay any attention to that other woman, and she tried so many times to get his attention. He was fully focused on you."

He *did* completely ignore that other woman.

"And I don't think it's because of the garden," Maddie says. "Or not solely. I'm sorry if I scared him off."

"It's okay. You're right," I say. "We can't really pretend we're all friends." *Much as I want to.*

No. *Don't go down that route.* I can't like another guy who's not for me.

"Maybe you can see how you feel after the building is finished," Maddie says. "He does seem like a good guy."

"Yes. He's not telling you that he can save the garden and lying to you," Jing says. "And he was definitely there for you. Before you got there, he kept checking the door every time it opened, and once you arrived, he stopped."

"I like him much better than Aiden," Bella says.

"You like anyone better than Aiden," I say.

"That's true. Aiden is not worthy of you," Bella says. "Aiden has never once come to a book club or any of the events you've hosted at the garden or the library. And this guy already joined a book club you were leading. He did some research."

"Even if he destroys the garden?" I ask.

"It's business," Bella says. "He's in some succession fight. He probably doesn't have much of a choice."

"He's the grandson of the founder. He should have some power," I say. "Otherwise, what's the point?"

"That's true," Jing says.

We nod hello to a person walking a poodle. The moon is visible as we turn to walk south on Central Park West. A nearly empty bus passes us. Trees cluster behind the stone walls marking the border of Central Park. The wind whistles through the branches.

"I did some more searching on that point you mentioned about how he kicked out that family right before Christmas. It turns out that although the family was evicted, he paid for a hotel room for them and eventually settled them in an affordable housing unit," I say. "The mom said that that building should have been torn down—everything was falling apart, and it was best fit for its rodent occupants—and staying at the hotel was like a two-month spa vacation. And the new apartment was so much better than the first. The follow-up was buried because it didn't have a catchy headline like the Grinch."

"Really?" Maddie asks. "I'm relieved to hear that."

"It made me feel much better," I say.

"Because you like him?" Bella asks.

"Because he's not a totally evil person, and maybe he'll have a heart when it comes to the garden," I say.

Ahead of us, a doorman rushes out to open the door to a taxi stopping right at the awning.

Maddie yawns. "Sorry."

"Maddie, why do you look so tired?" I ask. "You didn't have to come if you have a lot of work to do."

"My annoying 'rock star' neighbor was up all night again practicing a song."

"I thought you were using ear plugs now," Bella says.

"Those were brilliant at first," Maddie says. "But then I woke up with my ears hurting. I'll have to try another brand."

"If you can stand to hear more rock music, don't forget to put Patrick's next gig on your calendar," Iris says. "It's at my family's bar."

"I asked around the press room for architects we call when we need a consult for an article, and so I talked to a few of them," Maddie says. "One was reluctant to say anything, but one said you could feasibly keep at least half of the garden because with a development this size, extra green space is a selling point. He did note that maybe a community garden wouldn't be the right kind of green space, but something more landscaped."

"Still, spatially, you could keep it?"

"Yes," Maddie says.

We reach the 86th Street subway station and say goodbye. Maddie, Jing, and Iris jog down the steps.

"Still, despite the garden, if he truly likes you, I think you should give him a chance," Bella says.

"Well, that is the question, isn't it? If he truly likes me ..." I say.

"Not really." Bella puts her arm around my shoulders. "The question is whether you can date him even if he destroys the garden."

Chapter Eight

Rupert

I HIT THE BALL hard against the front wall of the squash court. It rebounds, and I swing forcefully. *Whack.* What a mess. I wipe away the sweat on my brow.

Sebastian steps through the little, red door. He's tall like me, but with blond hair.

I hit the ball to him, spinning it slightly.

"Frustrating day at the office?" Sebastian asks.

"You could say." I hit the ball hard. "It turns out it's very difficult to counter compelling videos of small children planting carrots while teenagers and grandparents teach each other dance moves. We put out a video with a mom talking about how life-changing this apartment opportunity was, but it's not like we gave it to them for free."

Sebastian grunts as he hits the ball back to me. It's a drop shot in the corner. Sneaky bastard. I race to get it. I miss.

"The coverage has been very positive for them," Sebastian says. "Have you thought about dancing in a video and praising Strive Developers? You definitely could be a thirst trap."

"What?" I stare at him.

"My sister told my mom that if she really wanted to marry me off, she could just post a picture of me on social media because, as much as she hated to admit it, I'd definitely qualify as a thirst trap."

"I don't even want to know what you're talking about."

"It's an attractive picture of an individual posted online. She showed me some hilarious videos around Christmastime of some guy wearing flannels who said his car had just broken down near a small town, and he was waiting for his 'one and only' to find him."

I look blankly at him.

"It's a riff on *Hallmark* movies."

"You watch *Hallmark* movies?"

"You can avoid them over the holidays? Both my mom and my sister watch them." He serves. It's another shot with topspin. I miss.

"It is true that I cannot see Rowena or your mom watching *Hallmark* movies." Sebastian serves again. I manage to get it this time. He returns my ball easily.

I hit it off the corner. *Focus. Get your mind in the game and off work ... and Lily.*

"I'm just saying, I'd even be willing to dance with you if it would take that frown off your face." Sebastian chuckles.

I'm so glad he's amusing himself.

"How about we do a video of you alone?" I ask. "Rowena can script it."

"Not even for you, mate." Sebastian grimaces. And hits another drop shot. I run for it and slice it back to him.

"So, Grandpa's not happy about that bad press," I say. "And ..."

"There's more?"

Should I even bring up Lily? What's the point? It's not something that is ever going to happen.

It's my serve. I focus on the red line on the front wall.

"There's a woman," Sebastian says, a note of surprise in his voice.

For a guy who doesn't date anymore, he's remarkably perceptive.

"Yes, there's a woman."

He tilts his head. "Shouldn't that be good? Consoling hugs at the end of a hard day at the office? Why are you here playing with me?"

"She's the co-director of the garden we're considering destroying."

"That does make it difficult."

He doesn't say anything more, but I feel better.

I raise my arm to serve. My head is back in the game. The squeak of our shoes on the wooden floor, the sound of the ball hitting the wall, the exertion, the twist of my body to get a shot ... there's nothing like squash.

We play five games. Sebastian wins.

Sebastian takes a swig from his water bottle as he wipes the sweat off his brow. "How'd you meet?"

"She's a librarian at St. Agnes. I met her at the library when I checked out a book. I didn't know who she was." My lips curve up, recalling the quiz outside. "But she was cute and smart. This other patron tried to set me up. Elderly guy. I walked him home, and he couldn't stop singing her praises for two blocks. How she's a good person. Described all the programs she's set up at the library. 'A catch,' as he said."

"I didn't realize you were in the market for dating advice."

"Obviously, that alone wouldn't have swayed me. If I hadn't already met her." I towel the back of my neck.

"Let me get this straight. You met her once at the library while checking out a book, and you're still thinking about her?"

"I saw her again at a book club discussion she hosted at Banter & Books."

"You've been busy."

"I should be busy focusing on how to become co-CEO with Rowena," I say grumpily.

"You definitely should," Sebastian says. "Maybe that's why you think you like her. You need something to take your mind off the stress of this decision, and she's perfect. Because ultimately, she's unattainable. Thus, you can think you like her, but once the deal goes through, you can forget about her."

"That's some great psycho-babble bullshit right there."

"I thought it was pretty good myself," Sebastian says.

"I'd be a lot less stressed if she wasn't posting videos about how horrible Strive Developers is."

"You'd still be stressed. You've only been working for this for ten years, fifteen years if you count summers during college." He tips his water bottle toward me. "Your uncle is brilliant too."

"Thanks. This is helping so much." I can feel my shoulders and neck tensing. I roll my head and stretch my arms again. So much for this being a good idea.

"But he does have a weak spot," Sebastian says.

"Rowena," we say together.

"Which is to your favor if Rowena does want to be co-CEO with you."

I nod. "Enough about me. What's happening with your job? Any chance of promotion?" Sebastian worked at a law firm for three years and then moved in-house at Capital Management, where he's been for the past two years. He still doesn't seem satisfied.

"I'm exploring an offer from an entertainment company."

"That would be different."

"The work at Capital Management is great, and I especially like my boss, Brooke. You've met my friends there. But again, I don't see great promotional opportunities. Brooke is young, and she's not leaving anytime soon. She's a great boss, and she completely looks out for me, so I think I'll be promoted this next round. But this company is offering me an Associate General Counsel position. The General Counsel is older and said he might be looking to retire soon. He wanted the start-up experience first."

"Are you sure he's not telling you that to entice you?"

"He could be. I have to do more due diligence and find some associates who worked for him at his last firm."

"And then you could date Brooke."

Sebastian snorts. He pushes the little, red door open. I bend my body and follow him out. The squash court is located on the upper floor of our apartment building.

"I have no desire to date Brooke. She's my boss. She's like ..." He shudders. "Believe me. Stop trying to set me up. I'm very happily single."

I slip out of my squash shoes and back into my sneakers. Sebastian puts on his slippers. We walk over to the elevator, and I push the button.

"Classy," I say. "Where's your robe?"

"Don't tell me you're going to take the elevator with the rest of us plebians when you're one flight up."

The elevator door opens.

"I was just seeing you off like the gentleman I am," I say.

Sebastian puts both hands on my shoulder and looks at me. "Forget this woman. And concentrate on becoming co-CEO. This is the opportunity of your lifetime. No pressure." He smiles and slips into the elevator. The elevator doors close in my face.

He's right. *Forget about Lily. Focus on the end game: co-CEO with Rowena. Do what I need to do. Don't try to save the garden.*

Chapter Nine

Rupert

I STEP INTO THE elevator at GreenGrocer, holding my plastic basket with groceries, and press the button for the second floor with organics.

Just as the doors start to close, a cart noses in. The doors retract, and in comes Lily, bringing with her the smell of fresh air.

I blink. It's like my thoughts conjured Lily up. But it's definitely her.

"Hello," I say.

She glances up, sees me, and I seriously think she checks if she can back out, but the doors have shut.

"Hi," she says. She faces forward, ignoring me.

I do the same. Focus on the end game: co-CEO. She's just a distraction.

A very enticing distraction.

Suddenly, the elevator growls and stops short. Lily falls slightly back against the metal wall.

"Are you okay?" I put down my basket and step toward her.

She waves her hand. "I'm fine."

I press the red call button. "Hello, hello, the elevator has stopped."

"It has to go to a central company, right?" she asks. "Or do you think it goes to the fire department? Bella is going to be so envious."

I turn and stare at her. So much for my thinking that most women would be thrilled to be stuck in an elevator with the heir to Strive Developers. Instead, she's elated that the fire department is coming to rescue us.

"Is the love interest in *A Devilish Dare* a fireman?" I ask wryly.

"No. But the hero of one of her favorite romances is." Lily smiles. "Don't worry. Maybe there will be a firewoman for you."

I harrumph. "That's exactly what I need. I'm here late because I've spent all afternoon combatting the fires from your *TalkTack* videos."

She grins at me. "That's excellent news."

At least I've made her happy.

A gruff voice from the intercom says, "We are working on it."

"So, the *TalkTack* videos have been successful? I'll have to tell Jade. She'll be thrilled. She's thinking that maybe she can write her college essay on this next year. Could she interview you?"

"You seem to think you'll prevail. But yes, sure."

"I certainly hope we'll be successful. I also thought you'd agree to an interview."

"Why'd you think I would agree?" I'm the Grinch. The cold, cruel real estate developer.

"You walked Mr. Devi home."

"Oh." I can feel a red flush crawling up my neck. I shrug. "I spent a lot of time with my grandfather growing up."

She takes that in.

Why did I say that? I should be playing up my Grinch demeanor so they give up.

There's silence, and we both stare at the very quiet intercom. Her stomach growls. Or my stomach. I'm not even sure. I'm starving.

But I just don't think being the Grinch is the way to play this project. My heart isn't in it.

"Mr. Devi was very flattering about you," I say. "He did fail to mention your take-no-prisoners approach to saving your garden."

She blushes. She looks adorable. "I'm normally very peace-loving."

"I find that hard to believe. I'm beginning to think you're descended from the Amazon warrior women."

She laughs. "Bella would say that's a good thing."

My heart beats faster as our glances meet, and there's a zip of electricity.

Her eyes widen as if she's been shocked.

She licks her lips, and I can't help focusing on them. They're very full and plump. Pink. Kissable.

She's still staring at me, her hands gripping the metal bar of the shopping cart. I want to kiss her and definitely make her forget about any firemen.

The intercom buzzes. "Sorry. We can't figure out the problem yet." The gruff voice fills the space again.

I've figured out the problem, and I need to put a stop to these feelings. *Shit.*

She looks away at the back wall and stares at it, as if she finds the poster on the wall announcing a sale on pasta fascinating.

The one day I don't have a book in my backpack.

She faces me. There is only so much text on that poster.

Those huge, blue eyes look up at me.

"What food do you have?" I ask.

She leans forward over her cart. "Bread, milk, fruit. We can eat the bananas. Did you have dinner yet?"

"No. Did you?"

"No," she says.

"I've got prosciutto and sushi for our main course, with fresh baby carrots, and Leibniz chocolate-topped biscuits for dessert."

She smiles. "Not bad."

The elevator shudders but then stops, heaving a big sigh.

"We're calling the Fire Department," the raspy voice says.

"Would you like some sushi?" I open my plastic container.

"If you're willing to share."

I slide the chopsticks out of the paper wrapper, separate them, and pick up a piece of salmon. I should just hand her the chopsticks and let her pick up her own. But that would be no fun.

She looks up at me as I bring the sushi close to her mouth. She narrows her eyes but opens her mouth.

Oh, God.

She holds my glance as she savors the salmon sushi.

I swallow, and my pants feel tight. I turn slightly. I pick up my own piece and eat it, the fresh salmon taste and the soft, white rice melting in my mouth, with a nice wasabi kick at the end.

There must be more to eat in my shopping basket. Paper peeks out from under my plastic deli package. Another pair of chopsticks. That's a relief.

I hand them to her along with the open container. "Help your-self." I take another salmon roll, facing forward. Out of the corner of my eye, I watch her take another bite.

"I didn't realize the sushi here was so good."

I nod. "It's especially good when you're pressed for time." We finish up the carton, and I put it back in my basket.

I open the package of prosciutto. "Would you like some?"

"Sure." She pulls out her loaf of bread, rips off a chunk, and hands it to me. We both sit down on the floor and eat the prosciutto on bread. I open the bag of pre-washed carrots and put it between us.

"Where did you grow up?" I ask.

"Here."

"I did think you seemed very comfortable in this elevator."

She snorts. "On the Upper West Side. Where'd you grow up?"

"In the village. My parents still live there."

"You're lucky. My dad sold our apartment after my mom died."

"I'm sorry about your mom."

"It's okay. It was several years ago, and she was in pain for a while, so at least now I know she's not suffering anymore. My work with the garden has been helpful. My mom liked gardening."

Of course. *Just twist that sword in my chest.*

"I'm sure she'd be proud of what you've accomplished with it." And I wish I could tell Lily we can save it.

"That's what my dad always says when he comes to visit."

"He moved away from New York?"

"Yes. He's retired and spends his time traveling."

"Do you join him sometimes?"

"Maybe someday. It's complicated."

"I know all about complicated family dynamics," I say.

"It sounds like it—from what I've read in the paper."

"You've read about me? I'll take that as a hint of encouragement."

"Please. Didn't Sun Tzu say 'Know your enemies'?"

"Is that why you've followed me into the elevator?" I ask.

"I didn't—" She stops short. "You're teasing me."

"I am. You were so cute when you were blushing that night at the library."

She blushes, and I lean closer. "Like now."

She covers her face with her hands but then peeks through her fingers. "So if our *TalkTack* videos are causing trouble, do you think you'll give up the garden?"

"Giving up is not a word in the Strive Developers' vocabulary," I say.

Voices sound from above. *Screech.* A crowbar appears between the doors as they're wrenched open to reveal a brick wall and elevator cables, boots on the floor above. Now, knees appear in the space at the top. An older guy with a fireman's helmet peers in at us.

That's too bad they arrived so quickly.

"Everyone okay?"

"We're fine," Lily says. "We just had dinner."

"I can lift you up," I say. "Do you want to put your groceries in my basket?"

"Okay." She piles her groceries on top of mine in my basket and then hands up her backpack. I pass up my backpack and the overflowing basket of our food to the outstretched hands in the opening at the top.

"Are you ready?" I ask.

"How will you get up?" she asks.

"Hopefully, I can pull myself up with some help," I say. "All that gym work has to be good for something."

She glances at my chest. "Definitely good." She blushes and turns around to face the opening. I grip her around the waist and lift her up as she reaches for the floor of the opening. Two firemen grab her arms and assist her to safety.

Now me. The opening is higher up than I expected. I turn the shopping cart upside down and step on it, then get pulled to safety by the same two guys.

Two young firemen are assiduously asking Lily if she's okay. And she's exchanging names. They agree to be interviewed by Bella. I huff.

I pick up our basket of combined groceries to interrupt this cozy conversation. "Do you want to use the basket, and I'll take my groceries out?" I ask.

A store manager then apologizes to us, giving us our groceries for free as compensation. We thank the firemen. A cashier bags up our food, and we walk out.

Outside, the lights of Broadway are bright. The air tonight is warmer, at least in contrast to the recent arctic breezes. We're in the New York spring-of-deception phase, when a few days of warmer weather make New Yorkers believe winter is over. But this balmy breeze does give me hope.

"Do you want to go out for dinner?" I ask. "Or dessert? We didn't get to eat the cookies."

Lily stops and turns to face me. "We *cannot* be friends."

"I don't know. I like you."

She stares at me. "Probably just because I'm not falling all over myself to charm you."

"That does make it more interesting," I say.

She shakes her head.

"But I think you should take me up on dinner for the goal of getting to know me better," I say.

"I think I'm getting to know you pretty well."

"Nobody's ever called me an open book before. Are you sure?" But then, I'm being so honest with her. I should hold back.

She shakes her head. "Yes, I'm sure. Goodbye!" She practically dashes away.

I'm going to take that as a good sign. She'd want to eat dinner if she didn't feel anything for me. She wouldn't run away if she wasn't feeling confused.

I watch her. She's right that we can't be friends. And I don't want to be friends.

Chapter Ten

Lily

THE NEW YORK PUBLIC Library is all dressed up for the gala, the three arched, stone entrances bathed in a warm, golden light, with red-and-white flags streaming in the night air. The lions, Patience and Fortitude, are even wearing crimson bows. I lift up my green, velvet skirt like a princess in a fairy tale and climb up the stone steps with Aiden. His eyes had widened in appreciation when I'd opened the door in my strapless gown.

I grin, feeling all bubbly, even though I've yet to have a glass of champagne. Maybe tonight is the night I'll finally move from friend to girlfriend. A gift of red tulips had to mean something—especially when Aiden was usually so careful *not* to cross that line.

Forget those pesky, traitorous thoughts about Mr. Rupert Evans. He is not for me.

I don't know. I like you.

That's been playing like a soundtrack in my head ever since our GreenGrocer escapade. The meal in the elevator felt like both a first date and a rendezvous with an old friend. A year of pursuing Aiden and no clarity, and this guy straight up says he likes me. Right after I've told him we can't be friends.

We're not friends.

You don't want to be friends.

Stop.

Rupert and I are enemies.

This is my chance to date Aiden.

A shrill sound cuts through the buzzing chatter. Aiden's phone. He takes the call, excusing himself. Aiden, phone to his ear, forges forward, fully immersed in conversation with whoever is on the other end. I trail behind. The couple ahead of us holds hands, their heads close together as they walk through the door on the right.

I enter Astor Hall as Aiden waits by the entrance, still on the phone. I hand over our ticket for two guests to the woman at the reception table. She checks off our names, and I turn to Aiden. His brow furrows—that adorable look he gets when he's concentrating—as he waves at me to precede him. *Is it a work call? Is he going to have to cancel?*

The coat check is behind the reception tables, under the stone staircases that flank the spectacular Beaux-Arts hall. Aiden stops.

"Hold on for a minute," he says to whoever called him. "I'll take your coat, Lily."

I remove my coat and hand it to him, but no appreciative glint in his eyes warms me this time.

"I'll join you shortly. Don't go too far," he says and leaves to get in the coat check line.

I move off to the side under the arches next to the band stage.

The sound of a saxophone serenading the night fills the cavernous, stone hall, and then a jazz singer croons the lyrics to "I Got It Bad (And That Ain't Good)" melding with the saxophone and trumpets. *Longing.* For the wrong man. My chest tightens. Ella Fitzgerald knew how to make you feel that pain.

Astor Hall is dimly lit, with black-tie couples standing around in groups of two or four. It smells of orchids.

"Here's your coat check." Aiden hands me a plastic, numbered ring. His gaze sweeps the room. It's like he's searching for someone. Not me.

"There you are," a high-pitched voice squeals off to my left. A woman in a bright-red dress bounces up and hugs Aiden. She has the blonde, Grace Kelly hair Bella tried to give me.

"You're finally here," she exclaims. She locks her arms around his neck and leans back to stare at him. His arms go around her, his hands splayed against her skin. A backless dress.

Who is this?

A cold heaviness fills my stomach.

I step back, shocked. And because she's kind of pushed me out of the way. Accidentally.

Aiden *finally* releases her. But she doesn't let go of him. She promptly holds on to his arm with both her hands.

Definitely not accidentally.

"This is Lily." Aiden gestures to me. "And this is Everly." He beams down at her.

Beams.

Looking at her like I want him to look at me.

My stomach knots.

"I've heard so much about you." She shakes my hand enthusiastically but is most definitely checking me out.

I haven't heard about her at all.

"Aiden and I met two weeks ago on a flight back from Texas. I asked his neighbor to switch seats." She giggles. "And when he mentioned last night that you guys were going to this, I told him I was too."

I smile. Weakly.

"I was so impressed with Aiden's green thumb, but then he explained that you gave him that plant when he moved in," she says. "And that you don't mind watering it when he's traveling for work. And that you have a ton of cats."

I sound like I'm ninety years old. Like I'm his neighborly, pushover cat lady.

That's how Aiden sees me.

"We have three cats," I say. *Say something witty. Not about the cats.* Aiden pats Everly's hand on his arm. I don't know what to say. Those interlocked arms. My stomach roils and churns like I'm on a boat that just hit a swell.

A server offers us crab cakes, and we all take one. Everly has to release Aiden's arm, but she still stands very close to him.

"We should get drinks," Aiden says. "What can I get you ladies?"

Oh no. This is not a hi-and-bye situation.

Does he like Everly? She clearly likes him. And he's not telling her goodbye. But then, he does like to avoid conflict.

"I'll come with you," Everly says.

"I'd like a white wine," I say. The bar is off in the stone hallway, and the line snakes down the corridor. That is a long time for the three of us to make conversation. She could be a friend who wants to catch up. *Then Aiden will return to me.* "I should say hello to my boss and some of my other colleagues, so I'll catch up with you after that."

Everly puts her arm back through Aiden's as they walk toward the bar. I stare after them. He has to return, right? Is my date being hijacked? I shake my head. It's just a momentary blip. Maybe she just wants to hang out with him until her other friends arrive.

I'm the one who didn't volunteer to get the drinks with him. I could have.

But the way he looked at Everly ...

He doesn't look at me like that.

We are just friends, after all.

But still, I asked him to be my date for this gala, and he agreed. That means he should hang out with the girl he arrived with.

I turn to look for my boss. My first instinct was right. I should get my work obligations out of the way while those two catch up, and then Aiden and I can spend the rest of the night dancing, like last year.

The place is packed, but from experience, my boss usually hangs out in the Polonsky Exhibition of Treasures. As I make my way over there, stopping to say hello to some colleagues and their dates, I see Rupert. He's standing with a short, dark-haired woman, very attractive.

My stomach dips. Again. *Fricking roller coaster.* He looks very dashing in a tux.

Of course, he has a date.

And I'm not interested in him. *Garden destroyer.*

Keep telling yourself that, and maybe you'll believe it.

He was just trying to confuse me.

Men.

I knew it.

I continue on my way and find my boss, wearing a red sari, holding court, standing by Charles Dickens's desk. She looks amazing. She compliments me on my green dress. She introduces me to her husband, who excuses himself to get them drinks. Without another woman hanging on him. As it should be.

"Thanks for alerting me to that issue with the community garden," she says. "We'll have to stop officially meeting and holding book talks there if it's going to rile Strive Developers."

I nod. I figured as much. I'd seen them on the list of donors to the library, as evidenced by Mr. Strive Developers' presence.

She frowns. Uh-oh.

"But what you do in your free time is your business."

Phew.

Not that it would have stopped me. But I love my job, and I definitely don't want to lose it.

"I was able to book some local romance authors to come speak on a panel for May, and I have a great panel lined up for Juneteenth," I say.

She thanks me, and we discuss a few more things going on with the library. We walk out of the room as she leaves to join her husband. No drinks are allowed in the exhibit. I excuse myself to find Aiden. The glow from the chandeliers warms up the white, marble walls. Groups of chatting friends cluster together.

There's Rupert again, this time hanging out with another guy. Blond but also tall and fit and attractive. Maybe their dates went to the bathroom.

They look like they're good friends. Rupert shakes his head at something his friend says and then laughs.

His face is much more relaxed when he laughs.

I wander through the dressed-up crowd back to the bar area, but Aiden is not there. I finally look out on the dance floor, and he's there with Everly. Dancing.

It's fine.

I get in the line for the bar.

"We meet again," that deep voice that seems to resonate in my stomach whispers in my ear.

I turn around. "We do seem to be meeting a lot lately." Someone jostles me in the crowd, and he puts out his hand to steady me. His touch is warm and sure. I stand straight, and he drops his hand. Thankfully.

"I thought you were coming with some guy named Aiden. Or did you read *A Devilish Dare* and change your mind?"

"I didn't change my mind. I'm the faithful type," I say. "Where's your date?"

"I didn't come with a date. I'm single, as I told Mr. Devi."

No date.

A little bubble of hope expands inside of me. I squelch it down.

"I'm impressed you remember the title of *A Devilish Dare*," I say. "Maybe you want to join our next book club discussing it at Banter & Books?"

"I could hardly forget it, with your colleague's ringing endorsement."

I'm totally sending him a copy.

"And would I be welcome at that book club?" He raises an eyebrow.

"We have quite a few male romance readers," I say. "And it might give you a few insights and help your dating life."

He narrows his eyes. "I've never had any complaints in that department." One corner of his mouth kicks up, and he leans in closer. "But I'm open to tutelage, if you're willing to teach me."

My breath catches. My heart races.

His hand reaches out like he wants to touch my hair, but then he stops. I stare at his hand, but then look up to meet his dark-forest eyes. *Danger.*

His glance is solely focused on me. "Is it helping your dating life?"

Off limits. *The enemy.* The man who is going to destroy the community garden.

"My dating life is fine." Just as soon as Everly finds her friends. "Thank you for your concern. Anyway, the only meeting you wouldn't be welcome at is our next book club, when we will discuss how to stop your proposed plans to destroy our garden."

"That sounds like the one I *should* attend."

We've finally made it to the front of the line.

"One white wine," I say, ignoring Rupert. He orders a red wine. As the server hands me my drink, I turn to Rupert. "See you in the trenches."

He raises his wine glass to me. "I look forward to it."

Is this a game to him?

I leave hastily to search for Aiden. If he didn't want to go with me, he should have just said so. This can't be some weird, passive-aggressive way to tell me that he's not interested. I stand at the edge of the dance floor, drinking my wine, and Aiden finally sees me. He leans down to say something to Everly, and they both come over.

"Where'd you go for so long?" he asks. "I'm sorry. I drank your white wine. But come, let's dance now." He pulls my hand and smiles at me. *Take that, Rupert Evans.* I have a date. I put my empty wineglass down on the table and join Aiden on the dance floor. Everly disappears. I smile at Aiden. *See?* Just a momentary blip because he didn't want to hurt his friend's feelings.

The bass pounds, and we both move to the beat. But that previous feeling of potential is not there.

Rupert's heated gaze. *That* matched the electricity described in *A Devilish Dare.*

And then Everly is back, twirling around Aiden.

Aiden smiles at her, and my chest constricts.

She smiles at me, but mostly at Aiden. The song changes, but it's still the three of us dancing.

With me on the outside. The sad friend hanging on this couple.

She dances up against Aiden's back, putting her arms around him but holding them out so she's not actually touching him.

I don't want to be the third wheel on my date. *Good job, Aiden. This is definitely killing my feelings for you. If that was your intention, A+ for effort and effect.*

I excuse myself to go to the bathroom. I can find some other friends to hang out with. Someone else must have come without a date. If only Bella had come. She didn't want to pay for the ticket, and she's making good progress on her next novel. I order another drink and meander around the side of the dance floor, looking for a familiar face, weaving through the few, small cocktail tables set up.

No one so far. I don't recognize anyone. It's a slow song now, and couples are dancing cheek to cheek. Definitely not something I want to see. I order another drink and stand in the corner. *Why?* Why did I pin my hopes on him? Everybody told me Aiden wasn't interested after last year's gala.

I thought he was worried that we were neighbors. He just needed to see that we would last. Yup, me doing a great job of rationalizing.

I'm such an idiot.

Should I go home?

Such a waste. I smooth down my velvet dress, the softness soothing me.

I saved up for this party—this one night that was supposed to be magical. One for the books.

It was definitely one for the books, but not the happy ending sort. I stand. *Enough.*

At least now I know Aiden isn't interested in me romantically. Even if I should have known before. It has been over a year of my making clear my interest with only friend vibes back from Aiden. Even Mr. Devi knew. I straighten my shoulders.

There must be someone I know here. I should at least get some of my money's worth by having a glass of champagne.

As I wait in the line for a drink, I order *A Devilish Dare* from Banter & Books to be delivered to Rupert at Strive Developers. I chuckle. It will be even better if his assistant opens his mail at Strive Developers. I turn off my phone.

"You look like you're plotting mischief." Rupert appears by my side again.

Why does he have to be so attractive?

"So that's the infamous Aiden you were with earlier," he says. "I have to agree with Mr. Devi. He's a fool."

"You have a remarkably good memory for names and titles."

"I have to," he says.

We both order drinks and then make our way to one of the small cocktail tables in the back. The tea light flickers.

I don't look at Rupert. "I'm the fool here."

"You're not the fool. You asked him as your date, and he agreed to be your date. Dancing with another woman the whole night is not being your date."

I turn to Rupert. His face looks concerned, caring. It's hard to square this consideration with the cold, heartless developer who is going to tear down our community garden.

"Thanks," I say. "But it is remarkably effective for killing my crush. And I don't want to waste my night pining over him. Do you want to dance?"

"I thought we couldn't be friends."

"As long as you can accept defeat, I think we'll be fine."

He snorts. "Are you trying to butter me up so I won't destroy the community garden?"

"Is it working?" I grin at him.

His jaw clenches. "I can't save the community garden."

"I'm not going to withdraw the lawsuit," I say.

The music switches to a slow song.

He holds out his hand for mine. "Well, as long as we're both clear …"

I put my hand in his, and my heart buzzes. "All clear. For tonight, anyway."

We walk to the dance floor, and he pulls me into his arms. We're so close. He smells of warm pine spice. He sweeps me around the room as I grasp his shoulder. He feels comforting. And he manages to stay on the side of the room where Aiden is not.

"I had fun at the book club." He holds my glance.

I smile. "I'm not sure the others have recovered yet from our sparring."

"I'm not sure I've recovered yet," he says. "I'm still wounded you thought I was so nefarious."

"You accused me of knowing which plants I could use to poison you," I say.

He chuckles and tightens his grip, pulling me closer. He rests his cheek against mine. I stop breathing for a moment. "Can we have our own book club? What book should I read next?" His breath whispers against my ear, sending shivers down my body.

"*A Devilish Dare*. I bought it for you."

He laughs, and that sound reverberates throughout my whole body. I'm melting. He's holding me so tightly and he smells so good, like pines and male and red wine and chocolate.

"I look forward to discussing *A Devilish Dare* with you," he says.

For one night. I can pretend for one night this is real and has a future.

Wouldn't that be something?

I might as well salvage my pride so that if Aiden does come looking for me, I look like I'm having a good time.

Bella said I should try to make Aiden jealous and see if that inspires any reaction.

But I hate playing games.

Even if this is an even bigger game.

Rupert trying to beguile me to drop the lawsuit.

Wait until we start picketing his business.

The music switches to a pop song. He releases me, but it feels reluctant. "Shall we go check out the Treasures exhibit?"

"Yes," I say.

We enter the exhibit, where glass cases filled with books, clothes, and other key markers of literature and art reside. Strains of music from the hall murmur in the background, mixed with the hum of conversation. There's a line in front of the case with Winnie-the-Pooh and his friends.

"What made you want to become a librarian?" he asks as we stand in front of Thomas Jefferson's Declaration of Independence.

"I get paid to read and talk about books all day. What job could be better? I thought about going into publishing, but I like all the library programming. It's one of my favorite parts of the job. I feel like I'm having an impact and making a contribution to society."

He nods. "That's what I like about my job too."

"I wanted to be a librarian, even when I was a little kid. I organized my books into my own library, and for my tenth birthday, my mom gave me one of those date stampers." I peer closely at the case in front of us. It has a copy of Nelle Larson's book *Passing*. I read the text on the card underneath. "I didn't realize she was a librarian too. Wow. Have you read *Passing*?"

"No."

"It's set in Harlem in the 1920s. It's about two friends who meet up. Both are Black, and one is passing as white. Her white husband doesn't know she's Black. It's very good."

"I will have to read it," Rupert says.

Rupert points out how bright the colors still are of the manuscript copy of Ptolemy's map. It's amazing what they have here: the 1789 Bill of Rights, a Gutenberg Bible, a home video of Malcolm X visiting Egypt, a decorated Jewish marriage contract from the thirteenth century, among so many other items.

"Did you want to work for your family company?" I ask. "Or did you have dreams of doing something else?"

"I've always wanted to work for my family company. My father was the rebel. I was the one fixing it all."

Before us is the New York section. Rupert peers closely at the architectural drawing of the plans for Grand Central.

"So cool," he says. "Imagine being the architect designing this."

"Rumor has it that you're competing against your cousin," I say.

He tilts his head. "Rumors are not always correct. *Page Six* will have us married by tomorrow."

"There are still twelve hours left in this night," I say.

He laughs. "Are you proposing?"

"Not on the first date," I say. "I usually save that for the third date." I do tend to be way too up front about my feelings. I sent Aiden a fricking valentine cupcake last year. But he did give Bella and me flowers the next day. Maddie pointed out that was conveniently the day flowers go on sale. She's such a cynic.

"Are we on a date?" he asks.

Our glances meet, and the air between us becomes zippy. And I freeze.

Yes. No. I don't know. I can't date him when he's trying to tear down the community garden. Not just because he's the enemy but because it's clear he doesn't share my values. But I pride myself on not judging a book by its cover—much as I do like some elements of this cover.

I take a deep breath. "Yes. Sort of. For tonight."

"Then I'd better make it count."

It's too much pressure for one night.

He takes my hand and pulls me along. "We have to say hello to Winnie-the-Pooh."

"One of my favorite bears," I say. "I still remember my mom reading me that story and both of us crying at the end."

"But the message was happy ... that memories of a little boy and his bear playing in these hills would always remain," Rupert says.

I stare at him. "That's true."

I had forgotten that was the message of Winnie-the-Pooh and only remembered that the boy had to leave the bear behind when he grew up.

But the memories remain, just as I will always have my memories of my mom.

"Are you okay?" Rupert asks.

"Yes, I am," I say. "What made you want to work for the family company?"

We join the line in front of the glass case of Winnie-the-Pooh and Tigger and his friends.

He looks away, as if considering what to tell me. "This is all off the record. Off the record for our dispute and any press, right?" He gives me a tight-lipped smile, but it's really more of a grimace.

I stare at him, sad for him that he has to clarify that.

"This whole night is off the record for our dispute and any press," I say solemnly. "I know from my friend Miranda Langbroek how terrible the press can be. Her stepfather was the Manhattan Borough President, and one reporter in particular seems to love following her and creating drama."

"You know Miranda?" There's a slight lift to his shoulders, as if I've said some magic word that strengthens my credibility. "I don't know her well, but the press was pretty terrible to her when they published that photo of her crying on the front page, her mascara smeared."

I put out my hand to shake his. "Deal?"

"Deal."

We finally take our turn in front of the stuffed animals. Audio of an excerpt from a Winnie-the-Pooh book plays. The bear and his friends were with A.A. Milne's American publisher, who then donated them to the New York Public Library.

We walk out the exit, and I gesture to a bench in the hallway. "Can we sit down for a moment? It's been a while since I've worn heels."

We sit, and he stretches out his long legs. I lean back, relieved to be off my feet.

I'm not missing Aiden.

I don't feel anything for Aiden. Maybe I'm in shock, and I'll feel something tomorrow.

I should feel something. I wanted to date him.

I narrow my eyes.

I feel mad.

Mad at Aiden for being such a jerk. For stringing me along. For saying yes to my invite. Mad at myself for building this fantasy about him.

I sigh.

Rupert coughs. "You just sighed. It seems like I may have to read *A Devilish Dare* if I'm making you sigh. I really must be losing my touch."

I glance at him. "Sorry. I'm pissed at myself for thinking Aiden liked me."

"I'm sure he gave you some good reasons." Is there a thread of bitterness in his voice?

"Just enough to keep the flame of hope alive," I say wryly.

"He might realize the error of his ways once he dates her for a while."

"No thanks," I say. "I'm not a complete idiot."

"Did you really order a copy of *A Devilish Dare* for me? I thought you hated me."

I glance at him. "It would be easier if I hated you. But you were very sweet to walk Mr. Devi home. And Mrs. Potter recognized you as someone who reads periodically in the garden. And obviously"—I wave at his face and body—"you're not unattractive." How am I even sitting here with him?

He's Rupert Evans, someone who periodically features on *Page Six* and in pictures of events from charity functions.

Remember. It's not me. It's the garden.

Still, as another woman strolls through the hallway and her gaze sweeps over us, then stops and returns to Rupert, my poor, battered ego feels just a slight boost. She walks past but then turns around again to look at him.

"Do you want to make him jealous? We could dance near him."

I shake my head. "I'd rather not spend any more time thinking about him." And I wish I wasn't going to run into him again in the hallway. Ugh. "You never answered my question. Why did you want to work for the family business?"

"A few reasons. My father wanted to prove that he could make it without the family name, but in a sense, he has still been stuck proving himself to my grandfather his whole career. And he just worked. I actually didn't spend a lot of time with him growing up. Instead, I spent time with my grandfather. And my grandfather loves this company. I guess he gave that to Rowena and me."

He looks away as if he suddenly regrets sharing so much. I stay silent, to encourage him to continue.

"My grandfather admits he didn't have much time for his sons because he was so busy building the company, so he wanted a second chance with me and Rowena. And he wanted to spend time with my grandmother. She got sick."

He stops. I wait.

He looks off into the distance. "He made me want to continue what he started. Plus, there's nothing like that excitement when you first review the architectural plans, and then when you watch the building emerge. Or meet the families who are getting the affordable housing units. When the skyline changes because of a building you developed. When I see people living in what I envisioned."

I look down. Do they already have the architectural plans that destroy our garden? I want to enjoy this time together, but his history only reminds me of why the garden is so important to me.

"We will also include affordable housing in this project, so there's that."

It's true. I've been impressed by what I read about many of their projects.

The strains of "New York, New York" filter out from the dance floor.

"That's probably the last song," he says. "Shall we head home?" He stands and takes my hand to pull me up.

As we walk down the hallway to the front entrance where the coat check is located, he also looks like he's searching for someone. My time is already done.

He stops, and when I glance at him, he looks pale.

"Did you check your coat? I'll get it for you if you want to meet me by the exit," he says. "There's a bench there where you can rest your feet."

"Okay. I should tell Aiden I'm leaving." I hand my plastic chip to Rupert, but he seems to be dismissing me. My stomach sinks a little. The spell is over. This is probably the end for us. He will probably disappear into his waiting limo, and I will go my separate way by subway. Because even if he offers me a ride, the clock has struck midnight, and I need to return to my reality.

I sit on the bench by the door and check my phone. Not even a text from Aiden.

I was so stupid. I can't believe I crushed on him for a year. He was the one who first left a book in a bag on my doorknob with a note: *Thought you might enjoy this.*

And then I gave him that plant and invited him for dinner to thank him.

Then we took turns inviting each other over for Sunday brunch. He clearly liked me as a person, but not as a partner.

Did he plan this? Couldn't he have just said no when I asked him? Or at least paid for his own ticket.

I text Aiden that I'm leaving.

Couples leave holding hands, some tottering as if they've had too much to drink, some giddy with joy from the evening. The grandeur of Astor Hall is imposing. The walls are filled with written inscriptions giving thanks to farseeing, wealthy benefactors who established the library. To paraphrase our former library president, a library serves democracy, as all it asks of its patrons is curiosity. It makes me feel proud to be a librarian. I'm part of this world of education, providing access—and chances—to everyone.

And then I see Aiden and Everly, kissing by the archway.

I stare at them for a moment but then turn away and look for Rupert, who is still standing in line. I got the better end of the deal. I'm lucky Rupert was here. He turned this date disaster into a fun night. Rupert's glance meets mine, and he grins at me from his place in line.

Yes. Everly can have Aiden.

Chapter Eleven

Rupert

THE COAT CHECK LINE winds down the corridor behind Astor Hall.

I like Lily. *More than like.* I need a moment alone to process that.

I knew I liked her, but not enough that I couldn't say goodbye.

I'm still here. I'm not going to run away. Even if for a second there … I take a deep breath.

I cross my arms. *This is not good.*

Or it's very good. I run my hands through my hair.

I loosen the bow tie of my tux.

I stand in line across from carved, solid, double, wooden doors that look like they'd hide a bank vault, hinting at the treasures that lie beyond. The line moves up several spaces, and now I'm under an arch. Janus was the god of arches, also known for new beginnings. This may signify a new beginning with Lily—except for the truckload of obstacles between us. The line moves again, and another heavy, imposing, wooden door is to my left.

Mr. Devi was right. I'm surprised she doesn't have a boyfriend.

I am screwed.

Charity benefits are usually tolerable as a necessary evil for networking, but let's face it. I looked forward to this one because I knew Lily was going to be here. The line moves quicker now.

"New York's most eligible bachelor does not appear to be by himself tonight. I was wrong." Jenna, Ms. *Page Six* reporter, dressed in a very bright, purple gown, has snuck up on me. I am off my game.

"I'm hardly New York's most eligible bachelor," I say. "And I'm still single. Even if you did portray my last meeting with a woman as an engagement announcement."

"Your self-deprecating humor is one of the things I like most about you," she says. "But you did spend a significant portion of tonight with one woman."

"It's business," I say reflexively. The last thing I want is for Lily to be hounded by the press. Especially if she knows Miranda. She's not going to have a positive impression of me if socializing with me crowns her with a nickname as bad as Miranda's "Weeping Willow" moniker.

"Nobody seems to know who she is."

"She's a private citizen."

"Very protective of you." Jenna smiles.

The line finally reaches the corner, where I can turn and disappear into the coat check area hidden by a green, velvet curtain, softening the edges of the sharp, stone walls. I'm happy to end this conversation and disappear behind those drapes.

I pick up our coats. Lily is by the bench, but I don't want the *Page Six* reporter to catch us leaving together. I pause, making sure there is no Jenna in sight. There must be some more interesting news to follow. Some other unexpected couples.

I quickly cancel the car waiting for me outside. No need to remind Lily I'm some wealthy developer. She'd probably say no if I offered her a ride. And a subway trip together will give me more time with her.

I reach Lily and hold out her coat so she can put her arms into it. She zips it up and pulls on her gloves.

And then Aiden and Everly appear.

"What happened to you?" Aiden asks. "You disappeared."

Is he serious?

Lily's eyes widen and she steps back, but then her eyes narrow. "I'm surprised you noticed. You seemed to have arranged a date with Everly here, and I didn't feel like being a third wheel at my one black-tie event of the year."

Good for you, Lily.

"I told him he should tell you—that you might consider him more than a friend," Everly says and then turns to Aiden. "But now, at least you don't need to drop her off at her apartment, and we can go straight back to mine." She smiles at Lily. "He's spent the whole week sleeping over at my place."

Lily looks shocked.

Because she likes him so much?

I peer down at Aiden, giving him my best superior sneer, and lace my fingers through Lily's. "Let's go."

Aiden stares at our clasped hands.

We turn away from Aiden and Everly and walk quickly out the door. A gust of cold air greets us. I glance at Lily, and she's frowning.

"He had the perfect opportunity to tell me," Lily says. "He said he hadn't been around the last few mornings because he'd been going to work early. He could have said he'd started dating someone."

"Are you okay?" I drop her hand, in case Jenna is around, and zip up my parka to my chin.

"I'm fine," she says. "The telling him off part was quite satisfying. And I'd already figured out they're dating. Obviously. But I can't believe he flat-out lied to me."

"He didn't look too happy about our holding hands. I think he wasn't quite ready to give you up, even if he is dating someone else," I say.

"Maybe." She smiles up at me. "Thanks for trying to boost my ego. That's enough about Aiden. I've clearly spent way too much time thinking about him already."

"Shall we take the subway?"

"Sure," she says.

I follow her down the stone steps, past the lions guarding the entrance, both decked out with red bows for the evening festivities.

Black sedans, cars, and taxis are lined up outside the entrance as people call out their goodbyes, making plans to meet up again soon, and pile into the waiting vehicles.

We stroll to the corner in silence and turn left to walk west along the wide boulevard of 42nd Street, past the New York Public Library facade, reaching the row of bare trees that mark Bryant Park. I want to hold her hand, but I can't be sure *Page Six* is not following us.

Off in the distance, an ambulance siren wails. The flags of the tall office buildings on the north side flutter in the night breeze.

"What kind of community activities do you plan?" I ask.

"I see the library as a free community center. We plan various afternoon programs, including coding classes for teens, a book club for kids, and, of course, daily story time for our pre-school children.

Homework help has been outsourced, but we can always help with research for reports."

Her whole face lights up when she talks about the library and its programs. It makes me want to bask in that warmth.

"And then, as you may know, in the Oasis Community Garden, I'm running a children's gardening book club. We're growing tomatoes and peas, and the children participating are writing books about it. Peas are especially great for New York because they're vertically growing plants."

My stomach sinks.

"I hope we grow enough so that every child can take home a tomato and some peas."

Maybe we can move the planted seeds somewhere safe before construction begins.

"What about the squirrels and rats?" I ask.

"We do our best to make it as unattractive for rats as possible. Mrs. Potter does a fair amount of offense to keep them out and prevent them from gaining a foothold." She glances at me. "She's very good at dealing with rats."

I smile. "And here I thought your opinion of me had improved."

She chuckles. It's this joyful sound that warms me up inside.

Bryant Park is closed, all the small stalls of the Winter Park shuttered, including the hot chocolate stand.

I point at it. "Hot chocolate would be perfect right about now."

"With marshmallows or whipped cream?"

"Either."

We reach the green, metal entrance of the B and D subway lines on Sixth Avenue and jog down the subway steps as a bunch of people emerge. We must have just missed a train.

Someone says to us, "Uptown is not working. There's a signal problem."

We turn around on the staircase as Lily says, "We can take the 1, 2, or 3."

"They're out too," another passerby says. "Water main break."

We trudge up the stairs.

"Citi Bike?" I ask, but even as I suggest it, I realize it's impossible with her dress. And across the street, no bikes are left at that station.

We both pull out our phones and check the various ride apps, as does everyone around us. But nobody is available for another thirty minutes. Taxis race up Sixth Avenue, but they're all full of passengers.

"Let's walk," Lily says. "We can probably walk it in thirty minutes."

"Sounds like a plan." I take her gloved hand and stick it in my coat pocket with mine. I'm worried about Lily's feet in heels, but I'm happy to walk uptown with her.

She shakes her head at me but smiles. She doesn't let go of my hand.

"What are some of your favorite book scenes? The ones that you still remember long after you've finished the book?" I like holding her hand in mine. For once, I give thanks to the subway Loki for a breakdown that allows me more time with her.

"That's a good question."

We wait for the light at the corner of 48th Street and Sixth Avenue. Although a wide avenue, the buildings are so tall here that it feels like we're walking up New York City's equivalent of a ravine, with cliffs on either side.

"Bella has a scene in her romcom debut when everything around the couple is going wrong, but it only makes it obvious that these two people are so right for each other. And the scenes in *The Undomestic Goddess* by Sophie Kinsella when she has no idea how to cook or iron."

"I'd identify with those."

"You can't cook?"

"Not well. I work pretty much all the time. I eat pre-prepared meals most nights." Left by my personal chef. "Rowena asks me why I even have a kitchen. Can you cook?"

"Yes," Lily says.

I don't want her to think we're too different. "I can make scrambled eggs."

She raises an eyebrow. "That's handy."

I need to get off cooking. "I just read *The Hired Man*, and I was struck by the scene when the British woman stubs out her cigarette, not looking, and kills some ants, sending the rest of them panicking around their dead comrades. It happens right at the beginning, and up until that moment, she's described positively—or so I thought. But that description was not. It really stood out for me."

"And that foreshadowed what she did to that town." Lily glances at me.

"Exactly." I grip her hand tightly. "You read that book too?"

"Yes. And that scene totally struck me too, for the same reason. Because usually someone killing a lot of bugs or animals signals someone is psycho."

"Here, she was oblivious."

"And indifferent," Lily says.

Don't say anything. It's confidential.

"I'm not indifferent to the plight of the garden." I turn to her. "I'm searching for solutions to save it."

"You are?" She gazes up at me, her face shining, her lips parted.

I want to be the man who deserves that look.

"But I can't promise anything. My first priority has to be making co-CEO with Rowena."

"I understand." She squeezes my hand. "I appreciate that you're considering options to save it."

"I don't want to get your hopes up." Shit. Now I've set some impossible goal.

"I don't have very high hopes."

What? I'm Rupert Evans. She should think I can get this done.

But right now, I'm not the CEO.

I rub her hand. "Are you sure you're okay with walking?"

"Yes," she says. "What's the funniest book you've ever read?"

"*A Confederacy of Dunces.*"

"I was reading that on a train in Holland, and I remember someone said to me in Dutch that the book must be really funny because I kept laughing."

"Best book about New York City?" I ask. "I'd pick *Bright Lights, Big City.*"

"I have to pick Bella's. She captures the New York I know," she says. "Did you ever want to be a writer?"

"No," I say. "I enjoy reading too much. I definitely don't want to turn my respite into my job."

"That's a good point."

The streets of New York at this hour are empty, the stores closed, but it doesn't feel lonely because there's still so much life, even if sleeping. The blinking neon lights of store signs, the lit-up window displays, the zoom of the cars passing us, the spray of water from the fountains diagonally across from Radio City Music Hall, Lily's hand in my pocket—all of it works together to make the night feel alive.

We discuss some more of our favorite books.

"What lines from a book made you pause and think, 'That's brilliant'?" I ask.

"I love the line in *Cowboys Are My Weakness* by Pamela Houston when the protagonist says her lover pretends he's not good with words, and yet, when he talks about next fall or summer, it's impossible to tell if she is included in those plans. That's one of my favorite lines ever."

I glance at her. "That's not a very nice reflection on men."

"No," she says, "perhaps not. Dating in New York, though, is tough. You saw what happened with my date for the evening. I basically got dumped in some public, passive-aggressive maneuver. It wasn't even quick and painful. And maybe we were just friends, but I still wouldn't treat my friend that way. As you said, if I've agreed to be someone's date, I've made a commitment." She appears to be hobbling slightly.

"Are your shoes bothering you?"

"I didn't really plan for a long walk in them—after dancing too. But I'll be fine."

"You know what I thought when we passed Bryant Park? That I'd like to go there in the summer with you when they're having a movie night."

"It is easy to say that, but there's a good chance that we can't actually be a couple—because we'll be on opposite sides in a lawsuit."

I don't know what to respond to that.

We reach 59th and Central Park. The entrance to the park, usually crowded with bicycle cabs for hire, is empty. The bare tree branches sway in the light wind.

"Can we sit for a moment?" she asks. We take a seat on a bench. The iron is cold under my legs. It must be even colder under her dress.

"You can sit on one of the Citi Bikes, and I can wheel you," I say.

"It looks like there are three bikes. I'll bike," she says. "I can hike up my dress."

We walk over to the Citi Bikes. We each pull up the app on our phones, but it turns out only one is available. The others are out of service.

"Let's take that one," I say. "Hop on, my lady."

She laughs and sits on the seat sideways. "Are you sure it's okay? It's probably going to be a pain."

It's great. She's so close to me. She smells of lilies and laundry. I wheel the bicycle forward as she kind of leans on me. It's definitely not smooth.

"Maybe you need to grab on to me," I say.

"If you insist." She hooks one arm around my waist. "It's like we're doing a three-legged sack race but with a bicycle. I'm not sure this works."

I glance at her. "It's working for me."

She blushes.

Like that evening at the library.

It makes her blue eyes sparkle.

I push us along. "At least the body heat is keeping me warmer."

"Do you want to come over for hot chocolate?" she asks. "We'll have to be really quiet because Bella is sleeping, probably, but you did seem sad that the hot chocolate stall near Bryant Park was closed."

"I'm always up for hot chocolate."

As we reach Columbus Circle, a homeless man shouts out, "Baby, you need a man who can afford a limo. Don't settle for less."

Lily laughs and yells back, "I don't know. I think a man willing to push me along on a bicycle is worth keeping." She snuggles her head into my neck and whispers to me, "You get points for creativity and effort."

Snuggles. I stand still. For a minute. I could climb a mountain, wheeling her along. I glance down at her, and she looks up at me. Questioning, asking. But also acknowledging that there's some definite chemistry here.

I think I could kiss her. I lean my head down, and she seems to move her head closer.

No.

This will not end well.

I kiss the top of her head.

Like an idiot.

"Let's get that hot chocolate," I say gruffly.

"Look. They've restocked those Citi Bikes," she says. "We can get a bike for me here."

I like pushing her. But it makes sense. I hold the bike still, and she hops off. "Maybe you should return this one so you start the clock running again."

I return my Citi Bike and take out another one as she also pulls one out of the slot. She gently slides her dress up. I should look away, but I don't. Long, muscular legs in black tights.

I avert my glance and clear my throat. "Do you want my jacket? You could wrap it around."

"It's okay. It's so dark anyway. Let's go. I live on 88th Street," she says.

We zip up the path marked for bicycles on Central Park West. It's empty enough at this hour that we can go side by side. I look over at her, and she smiles at me.

"Shush," Lily says as she slowly closes the door behind us. A table for two is right there. She puts our coats on a chair. To my left is a door, and there's another door to my right that must be a closet. Bookcases cover almost every wall.

I take off my shoes, following her lead. A cat comes over to sniff me. That explains Aiden's cat grass gift.

"Should I hang up the coats?" I open the closet door, and various posters fall out.

"Save Our Community Garden!" "People Before Profit." "Community Over Corporations!"

I stare at them in silence.

"Oh." She rushes over, picks them up, and shoves them back in the closet. "It's not like it should be a surprise," she whispers.

"No." I pick some up from the floor. "I particularly like 'Healthy Vegetables Over Profit!'"

"One of my five-year-olds made that. The marching carrots really add that extra emphasis."

"You do know that we are including affordable housing units."

"Like, five?" She shakes her head. "Versus the whole community that this garden creates. A place for the older people in our neighborhood to find friends, for families to grow their own vegetables, for teenagers to hang out in a safe environment? And it's a false division. You can build affordable housing somewhere else. There are other lots in the city."

"Should I go?" I want to stay, but I should go.

"I promised you hot chocolate. It's not like the posters were a surprise to me. Were they really a surprise to you?"

"More of a painful reminder," I say.

She stares at me, her eyebrows raised, and then pulls me by the hand into their kitchenette. This is a small apartment. The oven and dishwasher have been slimmed down. A hose seems to run from the dishwasher to the kitchen faucet. She clicks on the under-the-counter lighting, pulls a saucepan off a wall hook, grabs milk from the small refrigerator, checks the dishwasher, turns off the tap, and unscrews the hose—all completely efficient, like this is something she does often.

The white, metal cabinets stand out against the royal-blue kitchen wall. Red potholders hang off a hook, and an orange, clay pitcher holds a wooden spoon and other cooking utensils. It gives off a very cozy, cheerful vibe.

I can *never* invite her to my empty, cavernous apartment. I'll look like a total, spoiled millionaire.

"We don't have a living room," she says. "We used it to create another bedroom, so maybe we should take the hot chocolates to my bedroom? That way, we won't wake up Bella."

She takes out two packets of milk chocolate mix. "Marshmallows or not?"

This kitchenette is so small that we're right next to each other.

"Definitely marshmallows."

"Good choice." Her arm brushes mine as she pours the milk.

"Can I do anything?" I ask.

"There's really nothing to do." She stirs the milk.

Nothing can happen. This is merely a friendly overture. If the signs that fell out of the closet are any indication, soon we'll be on opposite sides of a picket line.

I shouldn't have come over here. In the dim lighting, next to her, whispering, surrounded by the smell of chocolate, the temptation to kiss her is too great.

She glances at me, tilting her head. I want to run my fingers along her slim, pale neck, down to where her green, velvet dress meets her shoulder, slipping that down, trailing kisses. Spine-tingling kisses.

Chapter Twelve

Lily

I GLANCE AT RUPERT. His eyes have gone all black, and the air is suddenly very heavy.

I feel myself leaning toward him.

No.

I grab a mug of hot chocolate and shove it into his hand.

Fooling around is not a good idea. No matter how attractive he is. No matter if I was tempted to kiss his neck when pressed against his hard body as he wheeled me uptown.

No matter that he makes me laugh.

No matter that I think he has a heart.

I can't lose *my* heart.

I turn abruptly and lead the way into my bedroom.

Bad idea.

The bed looms. My bedroom is small; my queen bed, up against the brick wall, takes up most of the space. I motion to my tiny nightstand so he doesn't trip over it. A bookshelf hangs above the bed. A small desk for my computer sits between the foot of my bed and the large window seat. And in front of that, trying to capture as much sunlight as possible during the day, struts my bird of paradise plant, like a peacock spreading out all its feathers.

The dark night outside the glass windows doesn't reveal any answers.

But I plop down in the reading nook I've created in my bow window and pat the seat next to me. It's a little cramped, but there's still space. And it's definitely safer than the bed.

Or he could sit in my chair by my small desk.

But I want him next to me.

For one cup of hot chocolate.

He sits down beside me, and my heartbeat races. He drinks his hot chocolate as I sip mine, the marshmallow melting perfectly to add sweetness. He puts his cup down on my handy, little table placed near the window for precisely that purpose and swings my legs over his thighs. And he massages my stockinged feet. Gently.

The shivering sensations cascading up my body are not gentle, though. I close my eyes and lean back. Yum.

"Are they okay?" he asks, his voice deep and quiet.

"They're a lot better now."

Bella's voice: *Can you date him even if he destroys the garden?*
I don't know.

His fingers knead the soles of my feet. I let the sensations relax me.

And Bella's voice whispers in my head, again, from when she told me to ask Aiden how he feels. I should have done that.

The only way forward is to be totally honest and up front.

I swing my feet off his lap and open my eyes to face him. "You seem like a great guy. Like an amazing guy. The kind that doesn't exist in real life. But the garden saved me."

I look down and bite my lip. He is silent. Outside, the noise from the wheels of one lone car cruising down the street pierce the quiet.

"The thing is, after my mother died, my father sold our apartment to travel. Somewhere where there were no memories of my mother. He couldn't stay here for me." I wasn't enough. I swallow the lump in my throat.

"And it was the right decision for him. He sounds really happy now and a lot less destroyed. But the thing is that Mrs. Potter and the rest of the Oasis gardeners, as well as all my library patrons and my friends ... I found them and built a new community. A new family. And yes, affordable housing is crucial for those families—the ones who get it. I recognize that. It's fine. I realize you can't save the community garden. I can't ask you to do that, just like you can't ask me to drop the lawsuit. But I think we may need to table this until there's a decision either way and then see if we can have a relationship. It's too conflicted now."

"I'm not asking you to drop the lawsuit," he says. "Do your worst. I want to save the garden, and whatever pressure you can put on, that helps."

I stare at him. The light from the streetlamp outside illuminates his square jaw.

"It would be a lot easier, obviously, if we could just demolish the garden and move forward with the building." He shrugs. "But I'm up for this challenge. I can't promise I will succeed. I don't want to make any false promises."

He leans in close to me and smiles crookedly. "So do your worst, Lily. Don't hold back."

Our glances meet. My heart races.

Don't hold back.

I reach out to run my hand through his tousled hair. His eyes go dark, and he watches me, still. I lean in closer, keeping eye contact. He reaches out his hand—to stop me?

No.

He pulls me closer. "I'm going to kiss you. Okay?"

"Yes. Do your best." I grin wickedly at him. "Don't hold back." I brush his hair off his face as he cups my head and leans in to kiss me firmly.

Mmm. He tastes of chocolate and red wine as I kiss him back, running my hands through his soft hair. He growls and pulls me onto his lap. I hug him tightly. He's got one hand in my hair and one hand holding me against him. I arch forward as his fingers tease a hot trail of desire across the bare skin of my back. His hands come back up to caress my face as our tongues explore and tease, like this may be our only chance to taste each other and show each other that we fit together. All my frustration and desire pour out.

I want to forget about the garden. I want it to be just us—two people who are attracted to each other.

He trails kisses down my neck to the swell of my chest. And then pauses. Torturing me. He kisses my neck as I strain toward him. His five-o'clock shadow scrapes my shoulder. I'm holding on to him, tightly grasping his shoulders.

His hands reach back into my hair to angle my head for another kiss. *Yes.* I reach up to hold his head. His mouth is so sure.

I can't believe this is happening. And it is so good.

Then he picks me up, cradling me, carries me to the bed, and lightly lays me there. "I want you all to myself. You're so beautiful."

He goes back to close the curtain and takes off his bow tie.

"Although I am wondering if I should read *A Devilish Dare* first. I feel like I might not live up to its expectations."

"Your last kiss definitely lived up to my expectations." I sit up and put my hands behind my back to undo my dress. I don't want him to leave.

He stops, his gaze fixed on my chest, and then smiles. "Can I help?"

I tilt my head. "Yes."

He gets on his knees in front of me and enfolds me, his hands undoing my dress zipper as he kisses me on the lips quickly and then presses kisses on my bare skin above my decolletage, teasing. Soft, then firmer touches against my flushed skin, fluttering feelings.

I surrender, swaying into him. I want more.

I quickly undo his shirt and slip it down his shoulders and arms.

My dress falls down to reveal a strapless, black bra and tights.

He shrugs off his shirt. Released, I stand to slip out of my dress. He takes off his pants. I take off my tights.

Both in our underwear, we jump back into the bed. He chuckles. He's hard against me as he folds me into his arms. I run my hands up and down his muscular back. He cradles my face again, kissing me, almost reverentially, softly, small, sweet kisses.

But as I open my mouth slightly, he deepens the kiss. I can't get close enough. I want him, his hard body pressing against mine into the softness of the mattress. The fresh laundry scent of my sheets, the firm touch of his lips, his hands caressing my body. We roll together so that I'm on top, astride him, my hair forming a halo around our faces, our own private world. Everything else fades away.

"How are you still single?" he asks. As he kisses me again, my hair gets in the way.

He lifts up my hair into a ponytail.

"Do you want me to put it in a ponytail?" I reach for one of my ever-present ponytail holders on the nightstand.

"No. I like it down." He takes the ponytail holder from my hands. He scrunches his hair up into a tiny ponytail on top of his head. "Ancient warrior style."

"Hmm. That's not the vibe it's giving me."

"It's not?" He pinches his face up into a stern expression and growls. And flips me so I'm underneath him once again. He kisses my neck, and I moan. "You like that."

"I do," I say. "You still look adorable."

"My grandpa is always telling me to get my hair cut." He looks over at the nightstand and picks up another hair tie. "I'll give you a matching one."

He shifts back, and I sit up.

He gently sweeps some of my hair into a ponytail on top of my head. "Now we match."

Kissing me, he presses me back against the bed.

"Are you okay?" He holds his upper chest on his elbows.

I pull him closer. "I like your weight."

"I like you." He nuzzles my neck. "What I really want is a date. A proper date. Can I get my bumper car date now?"

Chapter Thirteen

Lily

My phone buzzes with a text.

Rupert: *Miss you already.*

Me: *Miss you too.*

Last night definitely lived up to the books. Is Bella right … that I always find men I can't actually have because I'm afraid to fall in love and get hurt? Rupert is the best evidence yet. Except that I'm *not* falling for him.

Nope.

I've already fallen for him.

I'm definitely going to get hurt.

I eat my oatmeal breakfast and then pull out all of our picket posters.

My phone rings. It's Maddie.

"That's you on *Page Six*, right? Did you end up on a *date* with Rupert Evans at the library gala?"

"What? Sort of." I google *Page Six*. And there I am. The back of me in my bright-red parka, hand tucked into Rupert's coat pocket.

I stare at it in shock. My stomach sinks.

He wasn't kidding about *Page Six*.

The caption underneath reads: *Is the elusive, always-single, Strive Developers CEO-to-be off the market? It certainly appears that way. It looks like the type of developing feelings we should all be striving for.* *#relationshipgoals*

Maddie reads the caption out loud. "That last line is so cheesy. But I want the scoop. Off the record, of course."

At least they didn't print a picture of me biking with my dress around my butt.

Bella emerges from her bedroom, still sleepy, and ducks into the bathroom. I stack our picket posters by the door.

"Another woman showed up on my date with Aiden. She danced with us the whole time until I decided I didn't want to be the third wheel on my date, and I left." The toilet flushes, and the sink faucet runs. Thankfully, Rupert didn't get to hear the poor acoustics of our bathroom door.

I continue, "I ran into Rupert and we chatted, and danced, and walked home together. And he came over for hot chocolate."

I put Maddie on speakerphone. "Bella is up."

Bella emerges from the bathroom. "Can I use Aiden's behavior in my next novel for the shitty ex-boyfriend part?"

"Why do I always feel like we're research fodder for Bella's writing?" Maddie's voice asks from my phone speaker.

"It's like compensation when you realize your date is going totally awry. At least Bella can use this," I say.

"This photo is great," Maddie says.

Bella looks at me, questioning, and I show it to her.

"It's like a romance book cover," she says. "I'd totally buy that novel."

"Except you wouldn't. Because I'm not sure it has a happily ever after."

"Oh," both my friends say at the same time.

Last night was amazing, and when Rupert was here, everything seemed possible. But waking up alone this morning, Rupert having kissed me goodbye earlier, I'm not so sure. I grab my empty bowl and mug and walk into the kitchen, still holding my phone, while Bella follows. She pours water into the electric kettle.

"I'm off to meet Mrs. Potter and a whole group of senior citizens and moms to picket Strive Developers." I rinse my bowl and put it in the drying rack. It sits alone, upside down—kind of the way I feel right now. I'm conflicted. I don't want to picket Rupert.

But I will. Because saving the garden means everything to me.

And I don't know what I'll feel if I see a wrecking ball demolish the garden.

Although he is sweet and smart—and crazy good in bed.

And all that is not something to dismiss.

I'm so fricking conflicted.

Was that his plan?

No. Couldn't be.

He doesn't seem that devious.

That picture. The chemistry is so palpable that it's evident in a photo. You can't fake that. But movie stars fake it.

"Good luck," Maddie says. "I'll see you there."

I hang up the phone. I try calling my dad via WhatsApp. No answer.

Bella puts her hand on my arm. "But it was more than hot chocolate. I ran into Rupert in the middle of the night on my way to the bathroom. And I was half-asleep and not wearing my glasses, but he looked pretty rumpled to me."

I blush. "We did fool around. It was spine-tingling and every other adjective in *A Devilish Dare*. But we stopped. We're both trying to limit the depth of possible heartbreak." I pick up the stack of posters. I decide not to go as a carrot in case I talk to reporters. "Now, let's go protest his company."

Strive Developers is located on Sixth Avenue in one of the glass-fronted office buildings that command midtown.

As soon as I see Mrs. Potter waiting there, I rush up to her. I kiss her cheek, and she hugs me. I breathe in her comforting smell of shea butter moisturizer.

I can't help but feel I've betrayed the cause by falling for the enemy.

And so I blurt it all out: "I actually ended up kissing Rupert Evans last night—the potential CEO heir. We met at the library, and then he came to the book club, and then we met again last night when Aiden dumped me, and things turned pretty serious."

Mrs. Potter's wise, brown eyes study me. "Do you think his intentions are good ... that he likes you?"

I nod. "I thought so at the time. He didn't say he could save the garden. He said he would try, but he couldn't promise anything. And he said that I should fight as hard as I can for the garden. He saw the picket posters."

Mrs. Potter pats me on the back. "I hope he doesn't hurt you."

I nod. *That's not reassuring.*

Mrs. Potter takes out her bullhorn and leads our group of volunteers in a chant. About thirty of us mill around with huge signs and hand out flyers protesting Strive Developers and their proposed destruction of the community garden. It's a better turnout than I expected for a cold, wintry day. And then an access bus pulls up and lowers the ramp. Three of our most loyal patrons roll out in their wheelchairs, all bundled up.

I rush over. "Oh. You shouldn't have come. It's too cold."

They wave their protest posters vigorously as they form a line.

"These capitalist scoundrels. How dare they take our park after all our efforts to make it what it is today?" one says. "Nobody wanted it when it was an abandoned, rat-infested lot."

"A little protesting warms the blood and keeps us young," Mrs. Smith says, hobbling over to greet her friend.

"Can you wheel me over next to Mr. Devi? He always makes me laugh," another says.

Maddie is the first reporter to arrive on the scene. But she's followed by a few others. Our senior citizens are huge hits with the press, garnering interviews with reporters from multiple outlets.

"It's very hard for me to walk to either Central Park or Riverside Park. The Oasis Garden is right in the middle and serves the senior citizen population who need that green space." Mrs. Smith leans heavily on her cane. As the photographer snaps a picture, she asks, "Did you get the cane? And make sure you add that it's freezing today, but we're all committed and we're still out here."

Another reporter interviews a mom and her five-year-old, holding the marching carrots poster.

"Did you make that yourself?"

"Yes," says the five-year-old. "Last year I grew four carrots." She holds up her hand with all five fingers sticking up.

"Wow," the reporter says.

"But my mom says that if the garden is destroyed, I won't be able to grow carrots there." Her eyes well up with tears. The reporter gestures vigorously to his cameraman to make sure he's got the shot. "Please save the garden."

Chapter Fourteen

Rupert

"Mr. Evans Sr. wants to see you in his office immediately," Gertrude says as she knocks on my door. "And this came for you. I didn't realize it was personal, so I opened it."

She hands me a copy of *A Devilish Dare*. The bare-chested guy is hugging a very voluptuous woman and doesn't seem to want to let go. Understandably.

Well played, Lily.

"Expanding your reading tastes?" Gertrude asks.

"Apparently." I put the book in my desk drawer.

"Can you send down some coffee and tea and hot chocolate to the protestors and the press?" I say to Gertrude. "It's cold out there. Oh, and tell them they can use the restrooms in the lobby. Alert security."

My executive assistant raises her eyebrows but nods.

As I pass by Gertrude's desk, the newspaper is open to the picture of Lily and me. No secrets here. At least my warning worked, and the photo doesn't show Lily's face.

I stride down the hallway to Grandpa's office. I have no plan for dealing with the protestors outside. Or rather, my plan involves saving most of the garden, but that's not what Grandpa will want to hear.

I walk into Grandpa's office, and he stands up from behind his desk.

It's not like we haven't had protestors before. We usually let them do their thing and come to an agreement behind the scenes, if we can.

"Are you dating someone?" Grandpa waves around *The Intelligencer*.

"Potentially," I say cautiously. My dating life is not what I want to discuss with Grandpa. Not when I'm trying to persuade him that I'm completely committed to being co-CEO of Strive Developers.

"*Potentially?* What does that mean? You've got her hand in your pocket. That looks like dating to me. I know it's different nowadays, but I wasn't holding hands or putting anyone's hand in my coat pocket if I didn't have intentions." Grandpa sits back down.

I sit in the chair in front of him. "I do have intentions." Why do I feel like I'm back in the eighteenth century and Grandpa's the irate father of the girl?

Grandpa looks at the picture. "It's a good picture. But I wish I could see her face."

"I told *Page Six* she was a private person, so they probably didn't dare risk printing an image of her face. I walked her home last night."

"What kind of intentions?" Grandpa asks.

"I intend to date her."

"Don't you have a picture of her face? You young people take selfies all the time."

"I'm not that young," I say. "Did you have anything else you wanted to see me about?"

"So, you're not *actually* dating her? You're *intending* to date her? Why are you still in the intentions phase? What's wrong with you?"

"I have a date." *What the hell, Grandpa. This is my dating life. Don't judge me on that too.* "It's complicated."

"She's playing hard to get? That's good. You should have to work to date someone. Too many women throw themselves at you."

"She's definitely not throwing herself at me," I say wryly.

"What's her name?" Grandpa picks up a pen and pulls his pad toward him.

"Lily," I say.

"No last name?"

"I don't want you running some Google search on her."

I turn around and race back to my office, only to find Rowena sitting on my desk, waving *The Intelligencer*, a portfolio under her arm. I should send the editor and Jenna a thank you. Grandpa didn't even mention the protestors. He's now fixated on trying to figure out who I'm dating.

"Make yourself at home," I say.

"She's very attractive." She places her portfolio on the side of my desk.

"You can't even see her face, thankfully. At least they heeded my warning that she's a private person."

"I saw her outside—same red coat." She smirks. "No need for a face. That picture is enough. I didn't think you were the kind of guy who shared pockets. Will wonders never cease."

"Why wouldn't I be that type of guy?" I ask.

"I thought you told me you don't like to hold hands. You find it awkward."

I pause. I think I did say that. "I'm still worried she's only dating me to change my mind about the garden."

Because yes, that thought is still there, at the back of my mind.

But even more present is the feeling that I can't wait to see her again.

"I always worry that guys are dating me just because I'm wealthy," Rowena says. "But then there are the guys who find out who I am and run as fast as they can in the opposite direction because their ego can't handle it. It's not easy." Rowena gets up from my desk and wanders over to my bookshelf, her back to me.

"I like her."

"What happened last night?" Rowena turns around. I walk over to sit in one of my reading chairs. Rowena sits in the other one.

I explain about Lily's date—Rowena growls in disgust—and how I then approached her.

"You approached her?" Rowena asks.

"Yes."

"It doesn't sound like she was thinking about seducing you for any nefarious means."

It's true. I approached her. And I initiated the kiss. And she was the one who stopped me when I was about to kiss her ... when she shoved the steaming hot chocolate into my hands.

"So anyway, then we walked home together, which is when they must have snapped that picture."

"Why didn't you call CarFast? It's not like they wouldn't have figured something out."

"I didn't want to make a point of my wealth. And I kind of enjoyed that extra time with her."

Rowena nods slowly. "Tricky. I always test my dates if I think they want to date me solely for my money."

"How?"

"I suggest something totally extravagant, and if they're too into it, that could be a red flag. And I almost always do the camping test."

"What's the camping test?"

"I suggest a sleepover at whatever site we're working on or, if no sites are available, the Henry House."

"The haunted Henry House?"

"If it was actually haunted, that might be romantic. But yes. I mean, I usually do a sleepover at our sites—to get a feel for them and what the night noise is like. It's like that old adage that you should live in a house for a while before you renovate it because you'll have a better idea of what it needs."

"I don't think suggesting a sleepover at the Oasis Garden is going to go over well. Or it may go over *too* well because she'll think it will convince me to save it."

"You already want to save it." Rowena grins at me and stands, walking over to open her portfolio. "And I'm super excited. Look at what I've designed. We lose some ground space, unfortunately, so I made the entrance hallway a little less grand inside. I took out the two-level entrance we had in the original plans. But honestly, I think if I were a buyer, I'd prefer the garden over a two-level entrance space."

I follow her to my desk. She lays out the plans on my desk, holding the edges down. It's a cantilevered structure. Most of the garden is still there.

"It's amazing," I say.

"We do lose six small apartments."

"It's still amazing."

"I also prepared a backup plan that doesn't save the garden. In case we can't convince Grandpa. Because ultimately, Rupert, we need to win as co-CEOs first."

I know. I know. But I don't want to lose Lily.

There's a knock on my door, and my assistant sticks her head in. "Security just emailed the visitor logs you requested."

I thank her, and as the door closes, I open my email.

"Why did you request the visitor logs?" Rowena asks.

"Because Grandpa said he might hire an outsider, so I wanted to see if he was bluffing or if he met with anyone."

"He's definitely bluffing," Rowena says.

I stare at the logs. My stomach sinks.

"Nope," I say. "He's not bluffing. Look. Grandpa met with Percy Anderson last night." Percy Anderson is the CEO of a company very similar to Strive Developers in Chicago.

"What?"

I can hear it in Rowena's voice, the same shock I feel.

I show her the logs. She underlines his name with her finger.

"He's brilliant," she says, worry tinging her voice.

My speaker buzzes. It's Grandpa again.

"What are you doing about these protestors?" His voice bellows in my open office. "My inside source at *The Squirrel* called and said that those protesters are compelling."

I look at Rowena. I open my mouth. I close it. I can't suggest yet to Grandpa that we keep the garden.

Chapter Fifteen

Lily

I STOMP MY FEET to warm them up. The wind whips my hair around. I pull down my hat to cover my ears.

"Strive to Save Oasis!" we shout.

"Strive to Do Better!"

"Save Our Community Garden!"

A few more moms arrive. They've dressed their children as vegetables. The potato costume works particularly well over the winter coat. The carrot is definitely a chunky one because of the puffer jacket underneath. Next to the carrot is a pea and another potato. The children march around with signs: "Save Our Carrots!" "Save Our Peas!"

The reporters love it, and one mentions that it might get on the six o'clock news. I take a video. We're under strict instructions from Jade to film as much as possible, and she'll see what she can use for *TalkTack* videos.

A man in a black-and-white catering outfit wheels out a cart with three carafes on it, plus cups and milk.

"Strive Developers was worried you might be cold, so we brought you some hot beverages," he says.

"Don't drink it," one of our elderly protesters says. "They want us to have to go to the bathroom and give up."

"And you're free to use our bathrooms in the lobby. Ask for the key from the receptionist," the catering staff person says.

My phone beeps.

Rupert: *Are you okay down there? It's cold out. Should I send sandwiches or some hot food?*

Me: *Keeping toasty warm by marching.*

Rupert: *I'd rather be keeping you toasty warm.*

I blush.

Mrs. Potter joins me at the cart and stirs sugar into her paper cup of coffee.

Mrs. Potter sips her coffee. "You know, Lily, if it's love, keeping the garden may not be more important that finding a life partner. Don't let us hold you back. I don't want you feeling all conflicted and torn about this. It's hard enough to find love in New York City without adding this into the mix. We will still do all we can to save the garden."

That is so Mrs. Potter.

"I won't let you down," I say. "My priority is the garden."

A reporter comes over. "Are you two the co-chairs of the Oasis Garden? I'm with *The Squirrel*."

"We are," Mrs. Potter says.

"We understand your desire to save this community garden. But surely, affordable housing and giving homes to families is more important than preserving a small community garden?" the reporter asks.

Not a friend of Maddie's.

"It's a false dichotomy," I say. "They can build a development that has affordable housing *and* keep the community garden. The community garden draws about fifty thousand annual visitors, offers diverse programming, provides organic vegetables for low-income families, and serves as a community center. Not to mention that this is one of the few community gardens on the Upper West Side and is accessible for seniors." I cite the statistics that we found earlier.

"How do you know they can do both?" the reporter asks.

"We did research. Ask them. Ask them if they can do both." *I'm not holding back.*

The reporter backs off. "Okay. Thanks for your time."

Another man in a black suit wheels over a cart of drinks to the reporters who have shown up. Buttering up both sides.

Next follows a man with a cart full of sandwiches. Rupert is definitely taking the honey approach. We decide to take shifts eating. Half of us will keep up the chant while the other half eat. Mrs. Potter rallies us to eat as much as we want. "Might as well take what we can."

"Oh, I know that guy," Bella says, pointing to one of the catering staff members. "I worked with him on a catering gig at this fancy Upper East Side party. We had such a fun time. Nobody ate anything. There was so much food left over, and the hostess said we could take it. Remember that grilled chicken that fed us for several days?"

"Yes, and those strawberry dessert tarts."

"I'll be back. I want to say hi."

Bella runs over to where he's serving the reporters. The guy looks cold, dressed as he is in his black-and-white catering outfit with no coat. Bella puts her hat on him. He pats her on the head.

I don't remember her saying she thought he was a possibility, although she did say he was great to work with.

Mrs. Potter gives an interview to another reporter. As do I.

Once those reporters disperse, Mrs. Potter says to me, "We've done what we could for the morning. Especially since it's so cold. After school, we'll come back with the teenagers and hit them when they're leaving the office." She turns to face our crowd of supporters. One of the moms steps out from the crowd to film it. "Thank you so much for coming out to support Oasis. It means the world to us to know that you gave up your time and energy on this cold and windy day to support the Oasis Garden and to show Strive Developers that this garden means something to such a diverse community of people. It's not just a plot of land. It's sunshine, sunlight, organic food, laughter, and love. It's a community, and we're not going down without a fight!"

The crowd vigorously cheers, waving their placards wildly in the air.

AT 4 P.M. OUR teenagers arrive, and I hand out the placards again. There are about twenty of them, a small melting pot of New York

City. Two of the moms return with their potato- and carrot-cos-
tumed children.

The two children exclaim excitedly, "You're wearing a potato
costume!"

I bend down to their height and say, "I wanted to join in the fun."
And the video.

Jade leads us in some choreographed dance moves, asking the
potato and carrot children to wave their hands in the air, me behind
them, while her friend films the whole performance.

After a dip here and some fancy footwork in sync, the teenagers
freeze and yell, "Strive to Save the Oasis."

I wipe away a tear as Rupert exits the building, a baseball cap
pulled down low over his brow.

Our glances meet. He holds mine for a moment, then ducks his
head as if to say he's sorry. He turns and walks south. And just like
that, I feel like I've swallowed a handful of lead nails.

This relationship can't work, can it?

Maybe he never meant to save the garden.

I couldn't even attract Aiden, and I believed that Rupert Evans
was interested. When I'd told myself not to be a fool about love
again.

Chapter Sixteen

Rupert

GRANDPA WAS NOT THE only family member intrigued by the *Page Six* photo. Mom and Dad invited me over for dinner. And frankly, I need to talk to them. I'm in over my head. Will Grandpa really hire Percy Anderson over his grandchildren? I still want to save the garden, but how to get Grandpa on board?

I let myself in with my key to my parents' townhouse in the Village. The smell of fresh bread baking means my dad is already home. He bakes bread when he's stressed. As the door clangs closed, he comes out, apron on.

I hang up my coat in the closet in the back of our entrance room. A huge bed for the dog has been added to the décor, right next to the comfy couch across from a TV hidden behind wall paneling. Upstairs on the parlor floor is the more formal living room.

"What's happening with this project?" my dad asks. "Your mom is out walking Freckles."

No preliminaries. We stand facing each other, the staircase leading up to the second floor off to the side.

"Rowena and I are working together, and we've both told Grandpa we come as a package."

"Did you hear Rowena tell him?"

"No."

"Your grandfather doesn't believe in co-CEOs," my dad says.

"So he said."

"What did you say?"

"I told him that he basically destroyed your relationship with Uncle Tom."

Dad flinches.

"And the Fell family situation was completely different."

"Tom is never going to let you win. He's worked too hard to allow the company not go to Rowena. His whole life has been devoted to it."

"Exactly. And neither Rowena nor I want that."

"You can't trust him. I trusted Tom. He told me we were going to be co-CEOs, and he totally backstabbed me, stealing the company from right under me. I'm telling you—you cannot be paranoid enough."

Is Dad also to blame? How was Tom going to finagle co-CEOs when Grandpa has always been dead set against that? All this time, he's been blaming Tom.

I shake my head, frustrated.

"Why don't you become CEO and then you can appoint Rowena as co-CEO if that's what you really want?" Dad asks. "Although, that gets Tom back in the mix. He'll scheme to push you out."

"I don't trust Tom a bit, but I do trust Rowena," I say. "I'm sure she's having the same conversation with Tom that I'm having with you." *Or not.* Rowena is not as close with her dad as I am with my parents, primarily because her dad worked all the time when she was growing up. She's close to her mom.

The door opens again, and a white furball races to greet me. I sit on the bottom step of the staircase to let Freckles, my parents' white terrier mix, greet me.

"Okay, okay," I say as I pet him.

"He misses you." Mom hangs up her coat next to mine. She kisses me on the cheek and my dad on the lips. "Rough day at work?"

"Yes," I say in unison with Dad.

"What happened at your work?" she asks.

"Client hated the marketing campaign," my dad says. "But I think I figured out how to fix it while kneading."

"And you?" my mom asks. "I saw some of the coverage of the protest outside headquarters. Cute kids. And pretty feisty retirees. Can't you save that garden?"

"I'd like to save the garden." I follow my mom into our dining room, behind which is the kitchen.

"You want to save the garden?" my dad asks. The timer beeps, and my dad hastens into the kitchen to pull out his tray of bread.

My mom and I follow.

"But I know Grandpa is opposed," I say. "He met with Percy Anderson yesterday."

"He met with Percy Anderson?" my dad asks. "Way to bury the lede. So, he's considering letting an outsider run the company?"

"There's no way your grandfather would let an outsider run the company," my mom says. "Nor would your uncle. No way."

"If Dad gets to keep control, he would," my dad says. "And this way, the company still provides for his family, and he doesn't risk what happened in the Fell family company."

Dad's right. Maybe talking to him wasn't the best idea. He's getting me more stressed.

"Does Rowena support keeping the garden?" my mom asks. She hands me the glasses to set the table as she puts the plates on the kitchen counter.

"She is supportive," I say, "but not at the cost of our not being co-CEOs. She came up with a kick-ass design, though."

My dad turns to my mom. "What if Rowena is playing him the way Tom played me with this whole co-CEO crap?"

"Rowena is not Tom," my mom says. The doorbell rings. "I ordered Thai. I'll get it."

Rowena isn't playing me because she's told me becoming co-CEOs comes first. She's not telling me she can make us co-CEOs.

As my mom leaves, my dad removes his apron and leans against the sink. "A kick-ass design, huh? Still, Tom sacrificed so much for the company."

"You also never thought Tom would retire, and now he is. He's mellowed since his health scare. I think Tom might realize that co-CEOs would be best for us. It's mostly Grandpa and this Fell family history that has created a total block in Grandpa's mind on even considering co-CEOs."

"Tom wants you to *think* he's mellowed," my dad says. "He wants you to lower your guard."

But Tom has mellowed. Dad doesn't know.

It's best for Dad if Tom is an ogre. Then Dad doesn't have to admit that he made mistakes too.

Shit. This is making me question my dad.

I grab the water and finish setting the table. Dad feeds Freckles. We're both silent.

Mom comes back in with two plastic bags and sets them on the kitchen counter. She proceeds to take out the various containers. "Help yourself."

"If Rowena is on board with the co-CEO idea and came up with a kick-ass design, I think you're in the clear." My mom finishes filling her plate and sits at the table. "Tell your grandfather what you want to do. If he's going to make either of you CEO, he's giving you the decision-making power anyway."

"That's very rational of you," my dad says, following her with his plate.

"I'm allowing for irrational decision-making as well. I do teach game theory," my mom says. My parents met at business school, and my mom is a tenured professor at Columbia Business School. "But Rupert's relationship with Rowena is different than yours with Tom."

I sit down at the table with my overflowing plate and pick up a piece of chicken with my chopsticks.

"You only met me after we had the fallout," my dad says.

My mom shrugs and turns to me. "Isn't that what you want to do?"

"Yes." I stare at my mom. I don't have any doubts about what I want to do. "I need to convince Grandpa that this is the right way."

Lily wiping away that tear. And me powerless to go comfort her because I was the cause.

But I was also sure Grandpa was bluffing until I saw Percy Anderson's name on the visitor logs.

"He can't save that garden," Dad says. "Dad will choose Percy Anderson to run the company. Percy Anderson is brilliant, and it's not like Rowena or Rupert will leave. Dad can dangle that CEO carrot for a little longer while he gets the benefit of Percy's expertise."

"Ultimately, as CEO, these are the decisions you and Rowena have to make," my mom says.

"You're right," I say. It's up to us.

"But you can also leave," Dad says. "I know you think this is your dream, but leaving was the best thing for me."

I can't leave. I want to grow my family's company. I certainly don't want to compete against it.

"Who was the woman in the *Page Six* photo?" my mom asks. "I know that's not as important as the CEO decision, but I am quite curious."

"What? Did you also not think I was the hand-holding type?" I ask.

"Are you not? I quite like hand-holding," my mom says.

"I like holding your hand," my dad says.

I eat my food. I hope to find a relationship like theirs, but I could do without this when my hopes of something similar are in the hands of a "don't be emotional" businessman.

"No comment?" my mom asks.

"Her name is Lily," I say. "She's a librarian. I met her at the library."

"And you invited her to the New York Public Library Gala? That's quite on brand," my dad says. He takes a bite of his shrimp dish. "Unless she'd have work colleagues there."

"I'm not quite that clever," I say. "I met her there again, and we ended up talking and walking home together. But ..."

"But?" my mom asks.

"But she's the co-director of the Oasis Garden. She was out protesting in front of the office today."

"The co-director?" my dad asks.

Freckles barks as if to emphasize the point.

"Oh, then there should be a picture of her among the protestors." My mom opens her phone.

"Does she know you're Rupert Evans?" my dad asks.

"Yes."

"Can you trust that she's for real?" my dad asks, frowning, as my mom holds up her phone.

"Same red coat, right? I see her." My mom grins as if she's solved a puzzle. "If you guys are holding hands despite being on opposite sides of this conflict, it seems like a pretty strong start to me."

"But do you have any advice about how to convince Grandpa? I thought I'd write a memo detailing how Rowena and I being co-CEOs will be different from the Fell family fiasco. And now I'll have to research how our leadership would differ from Percy Anderson's."

My dad nods. "Confronting that head-on would be good."

If I can. I've always admired Percy Anderson's work.

THE TALK WITH MY parents helped. I stand at the stainless-steel island in my open-concept kitchen and drink a glass of water. The cursor at the end of my memo on my open laptop in front of me blinks. There were a fair number of articles detailing why the Fell family real estate dynasty imploded, including some details I hadn't been aware of, and I was able to distinguish most factors.

But Grandpa seems emotionally affected by the Fell story. Rowena is right that it's ironic how he says it's all business, and yet rationally, there is no way the Fell brothers are comparable to Rowena and me.

Percy Anderson is a brilliant businessman. He's a formidable foe. I don't have any answers on that front.

Choices. Do I play it safe and not save the garden? We're already going against Grandpa by proposing we become co-CEOs. Do I risk even more and pitch the design that preserves most of the garden?

I need to call Lily and make sure today's protests didn't change her feelings for me. She picks up. My shoulders loosen. That wasn't guaranteed.

"I'm sorry about walking by you earlier," I say. "What I wanted to do was hug you."

"Oh." She sounds surprised.

What if she wants to cancel the date now?

"And the *Page Six* article. I presume nobody realized it was you."

"Maddie recognized me. She's seen me in the coat and the dress before, and she knows we're acquainted."

"She's a good reporter." Her first article about the garden was quite compelling—not overtly in favor of the garden, but with enough subtle, heart-wrenching details to leave a reader rooting for it.

My hand grips the phone as I stare out at the black stillness beyond my living room windows. "I reserved 6 p.m. for bumper cars tomorrow night for our date." I don't ask. But I know it is a question.

There is silence, and my breath catches. *Please.* One more chance to persuade her that we suit even if I can't save the garden.

"Yes," she says softly. "I don't break my promises."

I haven't said I will save the garden. I can't promise that.

Chapter Seventeen

Rupert

THE ORANGE, BLUE, YELLOW, and green bumper cars slide around the ice as I wait by a short, vinyl, banner barrier. The bumper cars resemble large donut rafts on wheels with a plastic seat in the middle. I offered to pick Lily up, but she had some event at the New York Public Library on 42nd Street. Bryant Park is busy, though. Disco music plays as ice skaters glide around the pop-up ice skating rink next to the bumper car arena.

Over a loudspeaker, I hear the time check for the ice skaters: "Ten minutes until Group B is over."

I check my watch. Our timed slot starts in four minutes. I pull down my beanie hat around my ears. It's crispy out right now. But then I spot her. Same bright-red coat.

And she grins and waves as she sees me.

I smile back, relieved that she is happy to see me.

She joins me. "I love bumper cars. I hope they don't hit really hard, though. I once did bumper cars in Amsterdam, and I think they have different safety rules there. Those hits hurt. But I'm glad you suggested this."

"It looked fun."

We're ignoring the garden issue. That works for me.

I show our tickets to the guy at the gate, and he lets us into the waiting area.

They announce that the ten minutes are up and call for the current participants to exit the ice. They smile as they depart. Then the guy demonstrates how the cars work and explains the safety measures. And then we're allowed in. It's a little slippery on the ice, but Lily and I each climb into a car and buckle up.

"Watch out," she says. "I'm not going to go easy on you."

"Watch yourself." The cars start, and I pull my lever back and reverse into the arena. But Lily comes right for me, and I grimace as I wait for the hit. But it's a side bump—not front-on. More playful than painful.

"Argh. I was aiming straight for you, and then it veered," she yells. "No killer instinct."

But she's definitely hitting hard with the negative press coverage of the planned demolition of the garden.

I aim for her, but I also end up going slightly sideways when I hit her donut tube.

No killer instinct either.

Isn't that what Uncle Tom says?

Isn't that why Percy Anderson will be a better CEO?

Another guy hits me hard on my back bumper.

Lily is aiming straight for me again, her face tightened with a look of determination. She is adorable. All I want to do is kiss her.

She's pushed the lever all the way forward. She hits me front-on, but still, the impact is a small jolt. I careen off to the side, bumping into another driver.

She shouts happily, "Got you that time."

I push the lever forward, chasing after her. She tries to escape to the other side of the ice, laughing, as she darts a glance over her shoulder at me. Bumped by another car, she is pushed even farther away.

Argh. Another car hits me, and my tube streaks straight for the side bumpers, spinning around. I look behind me. She's escaped. Three other cars are in the way. I turn myself around and head back toward her.

"And your ride has come to an end. Please park your cars by the west side wall. We hope you enjoyed your ride!"

She raises both hands above her head with her fingers forming a V. She's certainly not shy about rubbing it in.

She carefully steps on the ice over to me as I wait for her.

"That was fun." There's that huge smile that got me last time. The second time around is no less gut-punching.

"How was your day?" she asks.

"I wished I'd woken up next to you, but other than that, it was fine. I played squash and did some work. Yours?"

"Good." She smiles at me. "I missed you too, but I caught up on sleep after Thursday night. And then spent the day helping out at the library."

"I made a reservation at Le Ciel on 42nd Street. It's a French restaurant." No half-assed date attempt here. "Or we can eat sushi at Hatsuhana?"

She bit her lip. "That sounds expensive."

"It's my treat." I may not always have the magic touch, but Le Ciel does romance in all capitals.

"I'd feel weird accepting that."

"I can cancel." *She doesn't want to eat at Le Ciel.* But the mouth-watering French cuisine ...

"Will you have to pay a fee?"

"No. We do enough business there." I call them to cancel, and they accept it graciously. "Where do you want to go?"

"Iris's boyfriend's band is playing downtown at this bar. They serve food before the show starts. Do you want to go there?"

"Yes." I'm all for a more casual night out. That's not usually what women who date me expect—or want.

We walk to the subway, and this time it's running. She glances at me as if in silent acknowledgment of that night.

The memory of her face, all flushed in desire, her lips all swollen, flashes before my eyes. And my body heats up. I nearly groan.

Get a grip.

A year of abstinence was *not* a good idea.

And dating your opponent right before the CEO decision is an even worse idea.

We jog down the metal steps, tap our cards, and enter the subway.

She bites her lip. "I hope you like it. The food isn't fancy, but it's delicious. And his rock band is good."

I take her hand. "I'm just happy to be with you." It's true. It has to be a good sign that I'm being invited into her life.

The subway arrives, and we get in. It's crowded with rush-hour traffic, so I'm pressed tightly against Lily, my arm curving around hers to grab on to the pole. Her hair smells of lilies again. The top of her head reaches up to my chin. I've never enjoyed a crowded subway so much before. Let's hope the subway stays full all the way down. Also not a thought I've ever had before.

It's not ideal for talking, though.

She tilts her head and looks back at me. "Are you okay?"

"Very much so." I hug her with my free arm. She leans against me. It feels so right. Is it only because she thinks I will save the garden?

The subway races, rattling and squeaking through the stations, down to Broadway-Lafayette Station, where we get off. We follow an elderly, Asian woman with a bag on wheels to the stairs.

"Can I help you carry that?" I ask.

She nods. I bring it up the stairs as she follows more slowly, Lily behind her.

"Were you a Boy Scout when you were younger?" Lily asks me.

"No. Do they even have Boy Scouts in New York City?"

"They do. Troops come to the library every once in a while."

"How do you get to be a librarian at St. Agnes?" I ask.

"I got my master's in Library and Information Science at Queens College. I applied to the New York Public Library upon graduation, and I was accepted. St. Agnes was my local library growing up, so that helped a bit."

The one-way streets down here are closer together and the buildings shorter. Cafés populate nearly every corner in this area.

"Are you working on a lot of building projects at the moment?" she asks.

"A few, but my main one is this Upper West Side development. That's the one Grandpa set as the test for CEO. Not to be a downer."

"I appreciate you being honest about it."

Up ahead, an electric sign with the words LIVE BANDS glows.

"Is that it?"

"Yes."

The front of the bar has floor-to-ceiling doors that look like they are open when it's warm. Today, the entrance is at the side door. I open the door and gesture for Lily to walk on in. ABBA is playing in the background, under the happy hum of conversation punctuated by the clink of glasses. This bar is narrow and opens up toward the back into a dance floor in front of the stage.

A long bar with barstools lines one side. On the other side are worn, dark, wooden tables with chairs. A beer bottle with a melted candle and a plastic placard with various ale choices are on each table. Signed band posters line the walls. The one nearest me says "Thanks for taking a chance on me."

"Hey, Lily." A hostess comes up to greet us. "Table for two?"

"Thanks, Jen," Lily says and takes my hand as we follow the hostess to a table in the back by the stage. We sit down and study the menu.

"I recommend the fish and chips," Lily says.

The waitress comes to our table and pours us each a glass of water. "Can I take your order, or do you need some more time to think about it?"

I order fish and chips, as does Lily. We each order a beer.

"You know everyone at Banter & Books, and you know everyone here too?" I ask.

"That's because I frequent these places the most. My friend Miranda is in a band and she plays here. And then Iris's boyfriend's band also plays here. That's how they met."

"It seems like you form a community wherever you go."

She tilts her head. "Maybe."

The waitress brings us our beers.

"I have my favorite coffee place, but I'm not on a first-name basis with anyone there."

"Different worlds," she says. "I'm not usually appearing on *Page Six* after a night out."

I'd forgotten about that. "Oh, shit. I'm still sorry about that."

"At least they didn't get a photo of my face."

Anastasia was upset when *Page Six* only had her in profile instead of showing her full face. And she thought that the picture was too small. She wanted our relationship blared from the rooftops. And the YouTuber approached the *Page Six* reporter to suggest we pose for a photo for her.

"I told the reporter you were a private person."

"The reporter asked about me?" Her eyes widen.

I wince. "She was teasing me about not being single anymore."

She shakes her head. "Wow."

"I don't think I'll be of much interest if I'm in a serious relationship," I say. "It's only because I've been single for a while."

"When was your last relationship?"

"A year ago. When was yours?"

"I've dated a fair amount, but I haven't had a relationship since college. I was working, my mom died, and I was not in a place to be dating. And the community garden is like a second job, with all the programming we arrange and seeking grants. And then, as you know, I met Aiden a year ago when he moved in across the hallway, and I thought we had something." Her eyes dim. "I really read that wrong."

"I'm sure he must have given you some signals." He must have been attracted to Lily. She's far more beautiful than the woman he was dancing with. But also a very different type. Not showy. More elegant. More hidden depths. At least for me. Thankfully, not for him.

"Brunch almost every Sunday. But Bella did warn me that the brunch was the friend spot."

Enough with Aiden. "You're not reading me wrong," I say. "I like you."

"Or you're even more ruthless and you're weakening my resolve to fight you." Her glance meets me in the candlelight.

She likes me back.

But those blue eyes, so unsure.

She's the one weakening my resolve.

I reach out to hold her hand.

"It's mutual. And I didn't see any weakened resolve when you were out picketing our building."

She grins and leans forward. "Well, you know, I had to put up a strong front in front of all our constituents. But really, I would've preferred to spend the day kissing you into submission."

I can feel my eyes widen. "We'll see who folds first." I stroke her hand.

The waitress sets down the two plates of fish and chips. Perfect timing to cut the tension.

I take a bite of my fish. It's crisp on the outside and flaky inside. "This is delicious."

"Iris's family actually owns this place. Her dad is from England originally, and his father owned a pub there. Family recipe."

I'm impressed. But what I like most about the place is the relaxed and friendly vibe.

We talk about growing up in New York and Wilhelmina Chrissy's previous book. I don't want this to end. I want to stay at this table in our own bubble.

"Why do you always include affordable housing?" she asks.

"I think it's important. I don't want a New York full of pieds-à-terre for millionaires. This is my city too, and I want to live here, and I want the people who work here to be able to live here. Many of the guys on our construction crews travel over an hour to get to a worksite in Manhattan." I sip my beer. "But it's not completely altruistic. The company gets some tax breaks, and it helps smooth the process."

"Is the competition for CEO between you and your cousin?"

"No," I say. "Rowena and I want to be co-CEOs."

"Isn't it a sure thing, then, that you will be CEO?" she asks.

"Not anymore. This is confidential, but my grandfather has found a very qualified outsider to potentially be CEO." I can feel my jaw tense. Today, Grandpa and Percy Anderson toured our various projects under construction—without Rowena and me.

"Are you worried?" she asks.

"Yes," I say.

"I'm sorry."

"It's part of the process," I say.

As we finish dinner, she says, "They're going to move these tables to the side so they can open up the dance floor. Should we grab a table by the bar in the front, or do you want to dance?"

"I want to dance with you," I say.

Her phone beeps. "Iris can't make it. She has to work late again. Patrick is not going to be happy." She frowns.

"He must understand."

"He takes it so personally when she can't make his performances because of work. He doesn't seem to understand it's work. She doesn't have a choice."

"My last girlfriend hated that I worked all the time," I say.

"Who doesn't work all the time in New York?"

I feel for Iris, but I'm relieved that Lily is so understanding about being a workaholic.

I look away, to the band posters that line the walls. "My last girlfriend, Anastasia, didn't work all the time. She was getting a cooking degree at the Institute of Culinary Education in New York, but she wanted to be an actress."

"She must have been a good cook."

"She was," I say.

"I'm not a particularly good cook," Lily says. "Tessa, my friend who is the lawyer, is ironically the best cook out of all of us. But she says it helps her to de-stress."

"My dad bakes bread to de-stress," I say.

"Is his bread good?"

"Delicious. We can have some tonight with Nutella."

I pay the check, and we get up.

The emcee announces the first band, and they enter.

"The lead singer is Patrick, Iris's boyfriend," Lily says.

A woman next to us says, "Isn't he magnetic? Those eyes. And that body."

Her friend says, "And that British accent."

Lily glances at them and then murmurs, "I want to tell them he's taken."

"I'm sure she doesn't need to worry." I lean close to her ear so she can hear me.

Lily nods as she sways to the music. She whispers in my ear, "He did pursue Iris. She actually resisted him, saying he seemed to be a player."

They sing a ballad, and I pull Lily into my arms. She rests her head against my chest. She feels so good. *More ballads, please.* Can she hear my heartbeat?

As the opening chorus of the next number fills the space, the crowd roars. The place is packed. I release Lily. This is a fast-paced rock song with lots of fans jumping up and down. Mostly women crowd the front near the stage.

I hold Lily's glance as we dance, our moves mirroring each other's. She puts her hand on my chest as she sways back and forth. I clasp her hand and then take it and twirl her around.

The music pauses as the lead singer introduces the band members. Lily checks her phone and types something.

"My friend Maddie is coming."

The set is over, and the conversation swells again as we go grab a drink. Iris's boyfriend comes down from the stage, and a cluster of women surround him.

He breaks free and comes over to Lily and hugs her. Very tightly. He's my height. I cough.

"Lily, so good to see you. Who's this?"

"Patrick, meet Rupert, my date."

"About time someone snatched you up." Patrick tousles her hair.

I put my arm around Lily. Yes, I'm acting like a possessive caveman. And yes, I'm a bit embarrassed I'm staking my claim. But not enough to stop.

He grins like he's amused I'm acting all territorial. "Hope you're worthy of our Lily here. Iris is definitely not someone to mess with." He smiles fondly. "I can't believe she has to work late again. Well, I'll leave you to your date. Need to go and help pack up." He merges back into the crowd but stops to talk to quite a few female fans along the way.

We head back to the bar. As we order our drinks, an attractive, dark-haired woman joins us. She was at the book club.

Lily introduces us. Maddie is a reporter. My eyebrows raise. Reporters are generally not my best friends.

And indeed, her demeanor is frosty.

Without looking at me, Maddie loops her arm through Lily's. "I need to talk to you. In private?"

And I watch as she practically drags my date away.

Chapter Eighteen

Lily

"HE'S ATTRACTIVE, RIGHT?" I ask Maddie as she pulls me outside. A few smokers stand off to the side, huddled in their oversize coats. A group of young guys pass by us, arguing over which bar to go to next.

"He also told the *Page Six* reporter he was dating you for business," Maddie says.

I step back. "No." My stomach clenches.

No soft preliminaries, my Maddie. Right for the jugular.

No. It's all fake. He *is* just trying to woo me so I give up.

But when he kissed me ... How can you fake that kind of passion? That way he looks at me.

The way he got all possessive when Patrick hugged me ...

That's all fake?

I bite my lip.

"Oh, shit. You really like him," Maddie says. "I'm sorry. But I wanted you to know."

"How did you find out?"

"I was in the newsroom, and one of the other women said, 'I can't believe Rupert Evans is off the market.' And Jenna, the *Page Six* reporter, said, 'I'm not sure he's off the market. He said it was for business.'"

"I'm such an idiot," I say.

It's not just business.

"No. You're not," Maddie says. "He is very attractive, and it would be a challenge for anybody to resist a full-court press from him. And he looks at you as if he likes you. If I hadn't overheard this, I would have thought he really liked you too." She hugs me. "But I have even worse news. Or what I thought was worse. The reporter who covered the protests said he was staking out the Strive Developers' building to see if he could catch the CEO and get a quote."

I stare at Maddie. "I should stake out the building to catch the CEO so I can make my pitch to save the garden directly to him."

Maddie shakes her head. "It didn't work. My friend thinks the CEO leaves via a car service that picks him up from a restricted, mid-block driveway. But he said he saw Percy Anderson leaving the building."

"Who's Percy Anderson?" I ask.

"He's the CEO of a very successful similar company in Chicago. Very well-respected. It seems Rupert has a competitor for CEO."

"He told me he had a competitor, but he didn't tell me the name or any details."

"I researched him, and he's very much a by-the-numbers guy. He's even quoted as saying that business is all about the numbers and doesn't leave any room for emotion. He doesn't seem like the type to save the garden."

"So if Rupert wants to be CEO, he can't save the garden either." I stare at Maddie. "I don't know what to do."

Is Rupert just dating me for business?

I can't believe that. But is he not going to even try to save the garden? How can I continue to date him?

I should be able to do that—to compartmentalize. There's the garden, and there's Rupert. But I can't. My feelings are all intertwined and are not going to stay contained in separate boxes. My eyes tear.

"I can't ask him to save the garden if he might lose the CEO position. But I can't kiss him and fool around while knowing he will probably destroy the garden." I put my face in my hands. "And if I was just business to him?"

Maddie hugs me.

My stomach feels like I'm a passenger on some upside-down, spinning ride at a carnival.

I should've known.

I take a deep breath. *Men.* I'm not your Sunday brunch option in case nothing better happens on Friday and Saturday night. And I'm not playing second fiddle to some development that could be built while still saving the garden.

I'm worth more than that. All those trees and flowers I planted in the Oasis Garden, the dirt cool between my fingers, watering them, nurturing them, giving them the space to feel the warmth of the sunlight.

I hug Maddie back and then pull away.

Across the street is a graffitied, brick wall next to a corner deli. The red "OPEN" light blinks on and off. Hot and cold. Truth and lies. Next to it, the graffiti asks, in big, black, scrawling script: *Where is the real New York?*

Where is real love? Who is the real Rupert? The one who kissed me or the Grinch developer?

I shiver.

You don't want me to hold back, Mr. Rupert Evans?

Good.

Because I'm not going to hold back.

My blood feels like it is boiling now. Like I'm one large tea kettle about to blow.

"Are you okay?" Maddie asks. "Because you look scary right now."

"Good," I say. "I'm done being played."

"You should probably get his side of the story, though," Maddie says. "Maybe I was too hasty. I was wrong with the Grinch article."

"Wait here. I think I'll do that." I march back into the bar and right up to Rupert. Rupert's eyes widen as he sees my face.

"Is everything okay?" he asks.

All innocent.

"No. Maddie just told me that you told the *Page Six* reporter you were dating me for business reasons. I'm done here. I liked you, despite the fact that you're about to destroy my garden and the community I've worked so hard to build for the past five years. But it turns out you're playing me. That's horrible."

Rupert pales, looking shell-shocked.

I turn around and race out the door. I don't want to hear his excuses. Or worse, listen to him admit it.

"Wait," Rupert says. I turn briefly, but he's been blocked by the crowd, and he can't reach me. I keep going.

Maddie stands outside, her hands jammed into her pockets, her face creased in concern. I grab her arm and say, "Let's get a cab."

"Wait." Rupert is next to me. "Wait. I did say that to the reporter, but that was to give you some privacy so she wouldn't be all over you, trying to figure out who you were and running an exposé on the woman I'm seeing. I'm not dating you for business reasons. Dating you is the absolute last possible thing I should be doing for my career."

"I'm going to go inside," Maddie says. "Say hello to Patrick." She slips through the door to the bar.

"The absolute last possible thing?" I turn to him.

"That didn't come out right," he says. "I mean, if I didn't want to date you, I wouldn't be trying to save this garden. And pissing off my grandfather and looking like some soft touch. And worrying that I'm risking the CEO position."

"Then why did you tell me not to hold back?"

"Because you shouldn't hold back on my account. And because then I can argue to my grandfather that saving the garden under-cuts the strong community opposition and works in our favor. The stronger your opposition, the more it helps me to save the garden."

That makes sense.

I narrow my eyes.

"I'm being totally honest here," he says. "I really like you. And I've tried to be as up front as possible—that I may not be able to save the garden." His green eyes are huge in his face, pleading with me to believe him.

I look away. Shit. I still believe him.

"I believe you." I take a big breath. "I believe you." I clutch my stomach. "This isn't good. This is going so fast, and I'm afraid I'm going to get hurt."

He hugs me. "I'm sorry I said that. It was an idiotic thing to say. I wasn't thinking. It's what I usually say because usually, it is business. I tried to course-correct by saying you were a private person, but I should have clarified that dating you was not business. I can text her right now."

"You have *Page Six* on speed dial?" I laugh. Not that it's funny, but I'm so relieved that I wasn't being totally played. And his world is so different from mine.

"No. I have my PR person on speed dial, and I would call her and she would tell *Page Six*." He looks down at me. "Thank you for believing me."

"I still can't help but think we should take a break," I say. "Because I don't want you to regret anything. You should fight as hard as you can to make CEO, and I'll fight as hard as I can for the garden. We shouldn't be conflicted. And then when the decision is made, we can date in earnest."

"What if you don't want to date me?"

"Then that's better too. I need to know how I feel once the garden decision is made. I don't want to get my heart broken. I want to be all in on this relationship. No doubts."

He's shaking his head no.

"When are you making the decision?" I ask.

"This week."

"All right. We can hold off on dating for a week. That's practically nothing."

"I wanted more of a chance to persuade you that we suit," he says ruefully. He grips my hand. "I get a second date, though, even if I don't save the garden? I'm going to try to save it."

"I'm telling you. You don't need to. Do what you have to do to be CEO." I pull my hand away.

"But I don't want to lose you." He shoves his hands into his pockets, his coat still cradled in his arm. He ran out after me without putting it on. "Can I take you home?"

"I think I prefer to go home alone. I need to check in on Maddie."

"Okay." He turns away, his back resolute.

"Okay," I say. *I'm not okay.* I walk into the bar and don't look back. Oasis Garden has to be my first priority for this week.

Another band is now on stage playing pop music. Couples dance all around me. Laughter breaks out behind me. Maddie seems to have disappeared. And wading through the crowd of swaying, happy people is not an appealing option. I stand there, on the edge of the dance floor, alone. Maybe I made the wrong decision. Maybe I should have enjoyed this time, come what may.

That's not me.

Because he can date me even if the garden is destroyed. It's just business to him.

I thought he'd protest more. Maybe he isn't that interested in me. He's Rupert Evans, and I'm just a lowly librarian.

My own father didn't stay. Shouldn't we have held each other to get through our grief over my mom's passing? Instead, he disappeared, and I had to do it on my own. Not quite on my own. My friends helped.

I take a deep breath. Someone bumps me as they pass by. I retreat into the corner and close my eyes.

Now that Rupert has real competition for the CEO position, won't he abandon me and the garden? We've just met, and he's been working toward being CEO for ten years. What if he tries to save the garden, fails, and his grandfather chooses this Percy Anderson?

I made the right decision. I want him to focus on trying to make CEO. If he doesn't make CEO because of me, how could we date?

I could lose *both* him and the garden. I slump against the wall.

I open my eyes and stare at the signed band posters on the wall. All these photos of people looking cool and like they couldn't care at all.

I care too much.

Chapter Nineteen

Rupert

SHE'S RIGHT. SHE'S ABSOLUTELY right. We should wait until the Oasis Garden issue is resolved.

But this doesn't feel right.

I hail a taxi, and one swerves over to stop in front of me. I sink into the back seat. The cab driver has Frank Sinatra on the radio.

I do think Lily likes me—and not because she wants to persuade me to save the garden. But I don't know if she likes me *enough*.

Not enough to keep holding hands this week while we go through this together.

I take a deep breath.

That bodes ill for our relationship continuing if Grandpa vetoes saving the garden. And if he does, how can I ever prove to Lily that I tried to save it? The board minutes are confidential.

What happens with the garden shouldn't determine whether we date.

Outside the window, New York City flashes by as we drive uptown. As we cross west on 14th Street, we pass one of the first buildings I ever worked on. During college, I spent my junior summer at the office. It was awkward to work with my uncle. As if I was betraying my dad. But Uncle Tom was fair then, willing to teach me with Rowena.

I want a relationship like my parents, and the last thing I need is one forged in conflict and opposition. My family has had enough of that.

What if Sebastian is right that I'm using her as a distraction? Her laughing face flashes before mine. My heart hurts. I hit my chest.

The taxi turns up Sixth Avenue.

Sinatra's smooth tenor croons the lyrics to "My Way" on the radio. Grandpa loves that song. *Why does Grandpa have the photo on his desk of that horrible dinner?*

He doesn't care about appearances. It can only serve as a grim reminder of his failure in the last succession fight. And yet, he set up a competition again as if he wants to repeat history. My eyes narrow. What if this is a test to see if we succumb and compete against each other?

It couldn't be. What happens in this succession fight has serious family consequences, in addition to its impact on my love life. But if we don't turn on each other here—when the CEO position is the ultimate reward—doesn't that also show that we are not going to repeat either our family history or the Tell debacle?

I have to do it my way. The only way to show Grandpa we're CEO material is to stand up for what we believe in. I need to save my family. If Rowena and I were no longer friends ... I shudder.

Percy Anderson can't just come in and take what Rowena and I have worked for.

Now the taxi races up Sixth Avenue, where Lily and I walked after the New York Public Library Gala. I take another deep breath and swallow the lump in my throat.

Chapter Twenty

Lily

OUR APARTMENT DOOR SLAMS behind Bella. I emerge from the kitchen, Tiger in my arms. He's been consoling me with his constant purring. But I still haven't figured out what more I can do to save Oasis Garden.

"I feel so bad," Bella says. "Remember the friend I saw at our protest, the one who freelances at Strive Developers? He has the main conference room on his schedule for Thursday with breakfast, lunch, and possibly dinner. And the menu is high quality, so it seems like top executives will be there."

"That makes sense. Rupert said it was going to be decided this week." That's good. It's better to know and get it over with rather than drag this out and hope Rupert's feelings survive. I definitely held on too long to Aiden. I put Tiger down.

"But this is the kicker. My friend has a call-back audition that day, so he's looking for someone to replace him. He's desperate. He called me, but I'm volunteering at a local high school on Thursday. I can't do it but—"

"I could do it," I say.

Bella says, "You should take his place. This is your chance to find out whether Rupert is advocating to accommodate the garden or if he's been stringing you along."

"Won't I find out when Strive Developers files the plans?" I shake my head. "I can't do it."

"And what if there is no garden and he says he tried really hard, but he couldn't get it approved by his grandfather? You won't know for sure that he did try. But here, you can see if he does."

"There is that," I say slowly. "But maybe I want the pretense that he tried so I can still date him."

"No. You don't. That's not a solid foundation. And if he lies to you about that, he could lie to you about something else." She hangs up her coat in our closet.

I can't believe that Aiden lied to me.

Rupert could be lying to me. *If I couldn't tell that Aiden was lying to me, how can I possibly know if Rupert is lying to me?* And how could I date him then?

"Rupert hasn't lied to me so far. He's been honest that he probably can't save the garden. Although he did omit that he'd also told the reporter he was with me for business reasons when he told me he'd warned the reporter I was a private person."

"But last time, he said he was trying."

I stare at Bella. "He did say that." Tiger meows and rubs against my leg. "I can't take his place. Rupert will recognize me." If only I could cater in my book or potato costume.

"Miranda can disguise you. You can wear one of her wigs. Like that silver one. He'll never suspect that an older woman on the catering staff is you. And would he even notice the catering staff?"

"When Miranda dressed up as an older woman, William still recognized her."

"But William had context. Miranda was at an art gallery, where her painting was being shown. William knew that Miranda's uncle was a costume designer. William probably also knew that Miranda periodically disguised herself to avoid the press. There is no way Rupert will think you dressed up as an older woman to masquerade as a member of the catering staff. It's worth a shot."

That's true.

"My friend said it's a really easy job. You just have to wheel in the food, set it all up, and roll the cart out. And you'd be doing my friend a huge favor because he needs to make this audition," Bella says.

"But what if I get caught? Won't he lose his job?"

"He's planning to quit anyway. He's only an outside contractor, and he was just offered a full-time position elsewhere."

"But I'm the enemy," I say. "I can't do it. If Rupert finds out, he'll realize I didn't trust him."

The bell buzzes, and I let Iris in. She and Bella are going to a workout class in Central Park together.

I wait out on the landing for Iris to arrive. It's not worth the risk. I have to trust Rupert.

Iris emerges from the elevator, we hug hello, and return to our apartment.

"I'm sorry I missed you at Patrick's concert," Iris says. "And Maddie told me you and Rupert are taking a break. I'm so sorry."

I slump down in a dining room chair. "It's for the best. I was getting too emotionally involved, and I'm not sure how I'm going to take losing the garden. Although now, Bella thinks I should work as the catering staff for the board meeting and see if I can overhear what Rupert advocates. Then at least I'll know if he tried to keep the garden. But maybe it will be worse if I get discovered and he realizes I didn't trust him?"

"We have a saying in information security: Trust but verify. But I don't think it applies to personal relationships," Iris says. "Then again, with Patrick, I sometimes feel like it should."

"My friend said they often discuss business while he's there, though he can't guarantee they will. He doesn't usually pay attention because it's not like he cares," Bella says. "But he's definitely seen building plans up on the screens and blueprints out on the table."

To see the building plans. A shiver runs through me. *I would know.*

"My friend is desperate to do this audition, and he said he'd still have to run your name through security, leaving it to them to bounce you," Bella says.

"Run my name through security?" I ask. "Then Rupert will definitely find out."

"That's usually just a check to make sure you don't have a criminal background," Iris says. "And it's not like the results are reported to senior executives. But they're idiots if they're leaving confidential information around in front of vendors. We constantly run training to remind employees to wipe whiteboards clean and not to leave documents lying around conference rooms to ensure only authorized personnel see what is discussed."

"See? You'd be doing the company a favor. Pointing out their vulnerabilities. It's not like Rupert is holding back. He's using every means possible, and then some. They've sued you and even gone after your funding." Bella holds her hand up. "And are you allowed to hold library events at the garden now?"

"No. But I'm not sure that Strive Developers explicitly banned those events."

"Exactly," Bella says. "They're using their soft power of influence. And you'll have to sign a confidentiality agreement, so it's not like you can tell anyone else. It's just for your own knowledge of what they did. Provided you pass the security test."

"That's fine. I only want to know for myself," I say. "At this point, we've done what we can." We've tried to sway public opinion against Strive Developers and, for the most part, succeeded, with all the positive press coverage of the Oasis Garden. And the lawsuit is proceeding. Strive Developers has to be feeling some heat. But is it enough? That is the question.

I feel helpless that I have to wait and find out what will be decided at some board meeting where I can't even counter any naysayers—can't even make my case directly to the CEO and Rupert's grandfather. *But I could if I went to the board meeting.*

"And what if he *isn't* presenting anything to the board in favor of the garden? Then I have to speak up. They should have held a public hearing and let the community be heard. They think we'll give up by the time the city government hearings roll around in a year. This could be my chance to make my case to the board," I say. "But I don't want to hurt his bid for CEO."

"He's not CEO yet. If there's a security breach, that's on the current CEO and the head of security," Iris says. "And if he really is supporting the garden, it should help demonstrate the passion of the opposition."

"He should be able to handle public dissension if he wants to be a CEO. He said you shouldn't hold back," Bella says. "If you didn't care about him, wouldn't you take this opportunity to present your case directly to the board?"

"I would." Like a bear that is normally shy and passive but becomes aggressive once their critical space is attacked, I'm prepared to do whatever it takes to save the community garden. "And it's not like he's even said, 'Trust me, I'll save the garden.' He's said he is looking at options, but his first priority is becoming co-CEO. Okay. I have tomorrow off. Tell your friend I'll take his place."

"I'll text Miranda and see if she can do your makeup first before I commit you." Bella types quickly on her phone.

Commit me—like I'm being committed to an insane asylum. This idea is so insane that it might work. But Bella sometimes has some crazy *bad* ideas, and this might be one of them.

I pace back and forth. I'm just not sure.

Bella's phone beeps. "Miranda says she can do your makeup. We're on." Bella grabs her workout bag. "And we need to go."

"Good luck," Iris says as they disappear out the front door.

I'm tempted to call Bella back and say I can't do this.

> Bella: *Thank you! My friend is so happy he can make the callback. And he said he'll tell the chef that you'll be dressed as an older person because you're practicing for a role.*

No turning back now. I need to work on my speech. But first, I should try calling my dad again. He had just texted me that he was back in the UK. I sit on my bed and call him.

He picks up. "Is everything okay?"

"Yes, I just miss you," I say.

"I'm glad to hear your voice," my dad says. "Your mother would have loved that trip to India. We always intended to go there. The ten-day tour in Rajasthan was magical. Your mother would have gotten such a kick out of it."

He does miss mom.

"You should meet me on your next vacation. Let's pick a country. Your mom always wanted to go to South Korea," he says. "We could go there. Visit some of the spots from the Korean dramas she watched."

My eyes tear. "I thought you didn't miss Mom."

"I miss your mom every day. But I thought the best way to honor her memory was to visit all the places we meant to see before life got in the way. We thought we'd both live longer than she did." My father's voice catches. "And sitting in that apartment missing her ... I thought I wouldn't be able to get up every day. I'd want to give up. And she wouldn't want that. And then, what good would I be to you? Instead of enjoying your late twenties and thirties, you'd be worried about me."

It wasn't really about me. It was more about my dad attempting to cope. He was trying to protect me. But I wish he'd told me that directly.

I sniffle.

"Are you okay?" My dad's voice is concerned.

"I miss you," I say.

"I miss you too," my dad says. "I'm sorry. I'm sorry I didn't say all this when I left."

"Why didn't you?"

"I was barely holding it together. I went to England and sat in my hotel room the first few weeks. I didn't leave."

"But you sent me happy postcards."

"I didn't want you to worry," my father says. "Are you sure this call doesn't cost anything?"

"I'm sure. Let's visit South Korea together. I will figure it out," I say. "And now you can call me more regularly. Now that you see how easy this is."

"Is the garden okay? I saw some articles in *The Upper West Side Rag* that its existence was being threatened by some developer."

"We'll see. We're fighting it."

"Good luck. If anyone can defeat them, it's you and Mrs. Potter. I should go. But I'll call you more often. I love you."

"I love you." I hang up. A sense of completeness fills me. I also feel bad that he was hiding his pain from me. But then, I was also hiding my despair from him. I pretended to be okay when he said he was going to travel.

I did tell him once that I didn't want him to sell the apartment.

And he said, "But it's too big for me, and it has too many memories."

How could a place have too many memories?

And when I'd wandered through the empty apartment the day before it transferred to the new owner, taking pictures and trying to commit it to memory, he'd said, "You don't need a place to remind you of your mom. She's in you and me."

Maybe I don't need the garden. I've created this community, and it will go on even without the garden.

I need to prepare for that mentally. Mrs. Potter and I have discussed contingency plans. We could raise funds to organize a monthly get-together for the seniors at Banter & Books. Maybe we could have planting sessions with the kids at the library and grow seeds in small pots in our windows.

I stare at the photo of my mom on my desk. It's the two of us at an environmental protest. I'm about ten and dressed as a polar bear. She looks so healthy and vibrant there—no sign of the illness to come.

My mom was a fighter to the very end.

Ultimately, it's up to me to save the garden. It's not Rupert's responsibility. It's mine. I can't wait on the sidelines for him to resolve this.

Chapter Twenty-One

Lily

I WAIT FOR THE elevator in our hallway, Miranda's words echoing in my head: "Remember to move like an older person. Be a little stiff. I think that's where I went wrong."

I pat my black pants pocket, which has my index card with notes for my speech, if necessary.

Everly's high-pitched voice pierces through the door to Aiden's apartment. It's been impressive how little I've seen Aiden since they started dating. Bella said I should take it as a compliment—that we weren't entirely just friends because then he wouldn't have ghosted me once he started dating someone. But apparently, we weren't friends at all.

Everly comes out and does a double take to find me—an older woman—in the hallway.

I look like the seventy-year-old neighbor Aiden described.

I ignore her. That's one benefit of this disguise. I don't have to act friendly or nonchalant, like she didn't crash my date and all my expectations of dating Aiden. Though, I should probably thank her for saving me from him.

"Are you visiting someone?" she asks.

"Yes," I say. Short and sweet. The joys of being older and not giving a hoot about what anyone thinks.

This elevator is so slow. It's stopped on the fourth floor. Normally, I'd walk. But I need to practice this persona.

"You must be Lily's grandmother. You look a bit like her."

"Yes," I say. "And you must be her neighbor." I press the button again.

"I don't actually live here; I'm dating her neighbor."

"In my day, we didn't advertise that we'd slept over. And if we did, we certainly expected him to see us to a taxi at the end of the date."

Everly huffs, and I smile sweetly at her.

I WHEEL THE BEVERAGE cart into the large conference room. Floor-to-ceiling, glass windows form one wall, giving an expansive view of midtown Manhattan. A huge, cherry conference table sits in the middle of the room, surrounded by about twenty Herman Miller chairs.

My heart is pounding so loudly, the whole room must be able hear it. I suck at subterfuge.

I place the hot carafe of coffee on the side console. Thankfully, Bella's friend even drew diagrams of where everything should be placed.

Rupert enters, and I stare at him like a lost traveler in a desert staring at a mirage of water. Because I'm hoping against hope that he does actually suggest saving the garden and that I haven't completely misjudged his character.

He's cut his hair. It's shorter, more corporate. That doesn't seem like a good sign. Is he conforming to his grandfather's wishes?

A woman who looks similar to him comes in next. I turn back to the coffee setup. I stack the mugs, add the three different containers of milk, and remove the Saran wrap from the first tray of breakfast muffins.

"You're sure about this?" the woman asks.

"Yes. I'll present the concept, and I'll say it was my idea," Rupert says. "Don't worry. I won't leave you hanging out there."

This could mean anything. Don't get your hopes up.

She shakes her head. "We're in this together. That's our winning card."

"Let's hope."

An older woman bustles in, carrying a pile of presentations. She places one at each seat and then leaves.

I remove the Saran wrap from the fruit tray and place it next to the muffins. Now to add the tray of utensils. Everything is set. There's no reason for me to hang out here anymore. I bend down slowly by the cart to pretend to be looking for something on the bottom shelf. If they leave, I can sneak a peek at the printouts.

But no. Rupert takes a seat at the head near the front of the table, by the screen. The woman sits next to him. He drums his fingers.

"Don't tell me you're nervous?" she asks.

"You're not?" he counters.

"I am, but I didn't expect you to be."

"Impatient. I want to get this done with."

Not nervous? That's not a good sign. If he was proposing to keep the garden, he'd be nervous—or she'd expect him to be nervous. I stand, falter a bit. I'm stiff from crouching, even if I'm not seventy. I wheel my cart out the door, my heart heavy.

I head back to the kitchenette on the twentieth floor. As I walk in, the head chef greets me.

"All good?"

"Yes." Not at all.

I look at the sheet to see where I deliver the next set of beverages. It's a small conference room on twenty-two. But at ten thirty, I'm back in the main conference room to remove the breakfast food and refresh the drinks. At least Rupert didn't recognize me.

My stomach feels queasy. That could be the moment of truth.

Chapter Twenty-Two

Rupert

FINALLY, THE ROUTINE BUSINESS matters are finished. Grandpa, Uncle Tom, our chief financial officer, and our general counsel flip to the next page. Agenda Item 4: The Oasis Development, West 84th Street. We should have code-named it Pandora.

Grandpa steeples his fingers. He never responded to my memo detailing the differences between the Evans and Fell families. But his assistant assured me he definitely read it.

I click on my next slide.

"We plan to build a twenty-story unit with a cantilevered design so we leave two-thirds of the garden untouched." Right up front. No hiding that we are keeping the garden. "We see the garden as a selling point for residents, especially with all the programs they offer. I've run the analysis, and outdoor amenities, like this garden and the green rooftop, will add significant value to the development." I list the numbers we've calculated.

Grandpa frowns.

That smirk on my uncle's face is also not a good sign. But then his eyes narrow as he looks at his daughter. Is he hoping she hasn't agreed to this?

My stomach tightens. Because there is a possibility she will support the plan with no garden. And she'll be the CEO.

I've given it all up for a garden. And a woman. A woman who broke up with me.

Repeating my dad's mistakes by trusting my cousin and thinking I can persuade Grandpa that this is the right approach.

"Are you crazy? You're giving up all that land?" Grandpa asks. "And residents aren't going to want to mingle with the public in some ramshackle, rat-infested garden."

"Have you visited the garden?" I click on the next slides, which show the garden oasis. It really is a marvel—the way they've planted trees and bushes that grow in shade. All the nooks for reading. The spots for gathering, especially the picnic table where the senior citizens socialize and play bridge. The teenage hangout gazebo. The family gardens.

I'm still a businessman, and this garden has value.

With or without Lily.

"You're too soft," Uncle Tom says. "Just because they're picketing. I heard you sent down food. What was that?"

"Keeping the garden will cost us very little because of this cantilevered design," I say. "In fact, we would save some money by asking the nonprofit to help design the rooftop garden and to run similar family gardening programs. Rowena will walk us through the design. It was my idea to keep the garden, and I asked her if she could create a design with that in mind. It shows us as responsive to the community, and frankly, when you see Rowena's design, I think you'll be blown away by its brilliance."

"Do you agree with keeping the garden?" Grandpa asks Rowena.

I hold my breath.

It's the million-dollar question.

"Yes," Rowena says.

I release my breath, and she shoots me a dirty look.

"No faith," she says under her breath.

"To be honest, this was a stimulating challenge—to design a building while keeping most of the garden," Rowena says. "And the garden really does have a very special feel. I'm proud of my cantilevered design. We could even enter this design in various competitions, giving Strive Developers more international exposure and possibly more cachet when we pitch for projects."

Rowena takes the remote from me and clicks on the slide showing the architectural plan. "Because the building grows as it ascends, the upper floors have more generous layouts and additional exposures. With the air rights we bought, we cantilevered it over the adjacent supermarket so as not to create too much shadow over the garden. We're offering fifty-six units. If we took out the garden, we could make a double-story lobby and four one-bedroom apartments, or we could add six more one-bedroom apartments and leave the lobby as it is."

"Is the Upper West Side really going to support that kind of design?" Grandpa asks. "Won't they argue it's too modern and not in keeping with the neighborhood?"

"We'll use clad limestone to be contextual at the street level," Rowena says. "We think the design's accommodation of the garden will lessen any critiques. It's really the perfect opportunity to build something more modern while benefiting the community." She stares at her father.

Rowena has her own reasons for supporting this.

"Six apartments at two million each ... so that's a twelve-million difference in profit," I say. "But if the lawsuit delays our start date—and that's likely as it takes its time winding through the court system—or if they win the lawsuit, our losses will be even greater." I run through the numbers we've crunched.

Grandpa snorts. "We can't lose."

I glance at our general counsel. "You wrote a memo that the adverse possession and the critical environmental area designation claims were strong arguments in their favor." I pull out the memo. "And it was addressed to you." I slide the memo across the table to my grandfather.

The general counsel says, "We can't be sure we will prevail, and this lawsuit could take several years. Two years might even be optimistic. I would advise settling."

"A delay of several years would be a far greater loss than twelve million," I say.

Grandpa harrumphs.

I gesture to Rowena to click on the next slide, showing the mock-up of the structure.

As the design comes up, Grandpa whistles. "It's not bad."

Not bad. That's high praise from Grandpa. He's warming up.

The conference room door opens as the catering staff pushes in a cart with refreshments for the coffee and tea. It's already ten thirty. We all quiet to let her clear the dishes and replace the coffee. It's the same silver-haired woman from earlier. Someone new. I haven't seen her around before.

"But giving up six apartments to save a garden—I'm not convinced. Although it is a smart move to get rid of that lawsuit and the bad press," Grandpa says.

The caterer gasps. Loudly. We all look at her.

And Lily's eyes stare right back at me.

My mouth drops open. Lily's eyes in a seventy-year-old face with silver hair. *Is her grandmother spying on us?*

What the hell?

"Is something wrong?" Grandpa asks.

"I spilled some coffee on my hand." A low, gravelly voice emerges from Lily's grandmother.

"Rupert, call for some ice," Grandpa says.

She waves her hand. "No. No. It's fine. I'll finish setting this up and then get some ice in the kitchen." She turns around and quickly switches the carafes and empty trays.

Very quickly. Very fluidly.

I walk over. "Let me see. We don't want a lawsuit."

She glances up at me, startled.

It is Lily.

"We should get this checked," I say. "The nurse's office is down the hall. Please come with me." I pull her out of the room and into a small conference room next door.

"What are you doing here?" I ask.

"I'm so sorry." Lily stares up at me, and her face crumples. "I know this looks really bad, but I wanted to know that you tried to save the garden. And you did. Thank you. Thank you so much." She hugs me.

But I don't know what to say.

She didn't trust me.

She was spying on us.

I wouldn't have trusted that I would save the garden either.

She's hugging me, and I want to hug her back.

"You didn't trust me," I say.

"No." She leans back to look up at me but doesn't stop hugging me. "I didn't trust you."

"My grandfather hasn't approved it yet."

"Is that okay?" She still doesn't let go of me.

"I'm not sure I would have trusted me either," I say.

Lily's face breaks out in a huge grin. "You tried to save the garden." She does a little hop of joy.

I run my hand through my hair, frustrated that I haven't yet saved the garden, as Lily looks at me.

"It's kind of jarring seeing you as a seventy-year-old."

"How did you know?"

"Your eyes. And your movements. And just you."

She shakes her head. "I was afraid you'd recognize me. I'm really sorry. I wanted to trust you. I wanted to date you, and I didn't want the garden to divide us. I decided that it wasn't your responsibility to save the garden. It was mine. So when I was given a chance to be here today—long story—I had to come to make my speech to the board in case you were not trying to save the garden."

"You're willing to date me now?"

"Yes."

I smile and kiss her lightly on the lips. "Okay. Then let's go back in there, and you can persuade Grandpa. But you can't dump me tomorrow."

"I'm not going to dump you tomorrow. Even if we don't succeed. You were right that even if the garden goes, I can probably save the community I created. And I have my family and my friends. I'll be okay. So do what you have to do to be the CEO."

"I hope we're still together when you're actually seventy. You're still beautiful to me," I say. "But how'd you get this job?"

"Bella has a friend who works here. He had an audition, so he was looking for someone to fill in for him, and I volunteered. I signed the confidentiality waiver. I won't reveal anything. Please don't punish him."

"I'm not going to punish him," I say and grab her hand just as the door opens. And there's my grandfather.

He stares at our clasped hands.

"Your concern seemed very suspicious," Grandpa says.

"This is Lily, the woman I'm dating, and the co-director of the Oasis Garden Board," I say.

Grandpa coughs and bends over slightly, grabbing the wall. "She's a bit old for you. Of course, she turned you down. What are you thinking?"

"Actually, I disguised myself as an older woman so Rupert wouldn't recognize me, and I could sneak into the board meeting to make my pitch for the garden," she says.

"Your Lily is spying on us?" Grandpa asks.

"Apparently," I say.

"And is she the reason you want to save the garden?" he asks.

"Not the whole reason," I say. "I wanted to save the garden because it makes good business sense. But I was more willing to take the risk of saying this is the right solution because I don't want to lose Lily."

"This is the right solution," Lily says. "The Oasis Garden is so much more than just plants and flowers in a lot. It's a community that brings together people from all ages and walks of life to be there for one another. We have families with young kids who get advice from grandparents, older people who can't make it all the way to the parks, teenagers who hang out there because there are few other free places to hang out. They interact with the older people who mentor them, while the teenagers teach them about how to use their phones. Oasis Garden gets about fifty-thousand visitors. It's worth saving, and it's a legacy worth sharing."

Grandpa nods and turns to Lily. "You remind me of my Rose."

Yes.

"We could even call it the Rose Evans Oasis Garden," Lily says.

We enter the conference room. The immediate silence is deafening. Five heads turn to us. Including Percy Anderson.

Percy Anderson is already here?

Grandpa says, "We've invited Percy Anderson in to give a presentation on what he'd bring to the table as CEO."

I school my face to appear calm.

Grandpa glances at Rowena and me and seems to be surprised that we're not shocked by his announcement.

Lily looks up at me, and I can see the worry in her eyes. I squeeze her hand.

I introduce everyone to Lily and explain that she dressed as a seventy-year-old to infiltrate our meeting. "And I think she'd like to share why she wants to save the garden."

Percy Anderson smiles a very derisive, self-satisfied smile.

Lily explains again how important the garden is for the community and ends with: "It's the first week of March, and the daffodils have just popped up. Daffodils symbolize new beginnings, so I hope we can start our relationship again."

I want to clap.

"Anyway, I'll finish clearing the dishes, and then I'll be out of here," she says.

Up on the screen is the 3D rendering of our other design—the one with no garden.

Shit. Did I get ambushed? I glance at Rowena, but she's watching Lily.

No. Rowena wouldn't do that.

No way she'd betray me.

I walk over to where Lily is changing the coffeepots and help her by placing the last of the cups on the cart.

"You didn't trust Rupert?" Grandpa asks.

Lily turns around to face the table. "I trusted Rupert, or I wouldn't be dating him. But Rupert didn't actually say he would save the garden. It's my responsibility to save the garden, so I can't rely on him. That's not fair to him or our relationship."

Grandpa chuckles. "I do like spunky women. She'll keep you on your toes, Rupert. I'll expect you both at dinner tomorrow. If you're still dating after this."

That doesn't sound good. Lily glances at me, but I shrug.

"Thank you for the invitation." Lily wheels the cart out of the room. The door clicks shut behind her.

I take my seat back next to Rowena.

Rowena says, "As you can see, this design is more in line with our other projects, less visually and architecturally engaging than the cantilevered option. I much prefer the first design."

"Will the Oasis Community Garden withdraw the lawsuit if we go with the first option?" my uncle asks.

"I didn't ask," I say. "I didn't want to make any false promises. I can ask her if that's how we want to proceed."

"I have to note that we can't build any design until the litigation finishes," our general counsel says. "We're under an injunction that the garden must remain as is, as of ten this morning when the judge released this decision, until the matter is decided."

"I move to table this until we finish Agenda Item 5: CEO," my grandfather says. "Percy. We're honored you've chosen to join us today."

Percy Anderson's presentation is good. Not earth-shattering. Not innovative. But maybe that's what Grandpa wants. When I ask Percy which design he would pick, he chooses the one without the garden because it garners more profit, presuming we can settle the lawsuit with less money.

Rowena and I then give our presentation of our vision for the company—all of it, not just what we think Grandpa would like.

"Give me and the rest of the board some time to confer. Let's convene back here in half an hour," Grandpa says.

Rowena and I stand and leave.

Rowena smiles when we're out the door. "Percy's presentation was good, but I expected it to be better. There's no way Dad is going to vote against me. I think he'll be able to convince Grandpa." She punches my arm fondly. "And Grandpa likes Lily. She's a formidable enemy." Rowena laughs. "I think it may have helped her cause—and ours."

"I thought we might have a chance when I saw the photo of our horrible family dinner on Grandpa's desk," I say.

"I gave Grandpa that photo," Rowena says.

"You did?" I never suspected.

"When I told him that we wanted to be co-CEOs. As a reminder that his approach last time had serious familial consequences."

"I think it worked."

Rowena smiles. "I'm off to my office."

"I'll check on Lily." Lily is actually *in* my building.

I take the elevator to the kitchen and peek in. Lily is there, rolling out dough as she asks the chef some question about consistency. Her face is scrubbed clean of makeup, her hair up in a ponytail, the wig sitting on top of an upside-down vase.

My heart beats faster. We are back together.

She smiles at me.

"They're conferring." I walk into the kitchen.

She looks up at me. "I hope we win. And I think your dad is right, that playing with dough is a good way to relieve stress."

Our chef smiles. "We've finished this batch, or I'd offer you a chance too."

Lily washes her hands and says, "I've got to deliver lunch to one of the small conference rooms. I'll go get the cart from the back."

I follow her through the connecting doors to the storage room behind the kitchen. As the kitchen door swings closed behind us, I lean against the second door archway, backing her up against the frame. "I didn't get a chance to really kiss you earlier."

She tilts her head up.

Mmm. She tastes of cookie dough and tea. I pull her tight against me. It feels like it's been much longer than a week.

My phone alarm goes off.

"Time to get back." I reluctantly release her. "Would you withdraw the lawsuit and agree to maintain the garden and plan the roof garden if we approve Option A, where we keep two-thirds of the garden?"

"Are you trying to kiss me into submission?" she asks.

"I'm willing to throw the kissing in for free," I say.

"Mrs. Potter has to approve it, and we have to run it by our board, but I think yes. We'd be thrilled."

I walk back into the conference room. Rowena is already seated, but she looks the most relaxed I've seen her in weeks. She's very good at reading her dad. And Percy Anderson is not there.

Grandfather clears his throat. "We've decided to appoint you both as co-CEOs. The decision about the building is yours." The general counsel hands him a resolution to sign.

As Uncle Tom co-signs it, he says, "I look forward to your stewardship. And my own retirement."

I turn to Rowena. Her huge smile must mirror mine. We did it.

I gesture to Rowena to take the floor.

"I motion to approve Option A as our proposed architectural design for West 84th Street," she says.

"I second," I say. "I'll negotiate terms with the Oasis Community Garden board, but they seem amenable."

"This meeting is adjourned," says our general counsel.

Everyone stands, and there's a round of handshaking.

"I was afraid you and Rowena were not brave enough to take risks, but I was wrong," Grandpa says. "You need to take risks in business. And maybe you need some emotion too. I want you to feel passionately about your career and this company. And I definitely don't want to stand in the way of you dating Lily. She's a keeper. Between the lawsuit, the protests, the press coverage, and now her infiltrating our company, I'm glad she's going to be on our side in the future."

Grandpa winks at me as he slaps me on the back. "Good luck with her."

I text Lily.

Me: *We approved Option A, pending negotiations with Oasis.*

Lily: *And you're co-CEO?*

Me: *Yes.*

Lily: *Hurray! Congratulations! Thank you!*

I turn to Rowena as the room empties out. "Shall we go celebrate?"

"I've got a date." Her half-smile teases me. "And I'm sure you want to go celebrate with Lily."

"You've got a date? Who?"

"You're practically as bad as Grandpa. I need to find my own partner before he decides to try setting me up again, now that you're in a relationship." Rowena gathers up her files. "You'll be the first to meet my date if all goes well. But for now, I'd rather not jinx it. Go have fun with Lily." She leaves the room.

The room is empty. I walk over to the windows. A feeling of awe inspired by the midtown Manhattan skyline against the bright-blue sky—the glinting, glass skyscrapers, the cream sentinels of the old, distinguished guard, the shorter, red brick buildings—sweeps over me. The desires and ambitions of plucky New Yorkers crowded together, each building striving for individuality yet also contributing and co-existing, all summed up in that view.

I'm co-CEO of Strive Developers. A shiver runs through me. We really did it. Rowena and I will contribute our own vision to this city. The sun warms certain facades, leaving others in shadow. Like Fell Co. That was Grandpa's main competitor when he started, but the company went into debt when the three brothers squabbled. And disappeared. I take a deep breath. With great power comes great responsibility. The sky suddenly darkens as a cloud covers the sun. So much authority and obligation.

I can do it. The sky brightens again as the cloud edges away.

Time to negotiate terms with Lily.

Chapter Twenty-Three

Lily

WE ADJOURN OUR EMERGENCY zoom meeting of the Oasis board, having approved the parameters for my negotiation with Rupert. He'll be here in a half hour. Tiger sprawls across the empty space of my desk next to the computer, his paw on my mouse pad.

We did it.

I swing around and stare out the window at my familiar street below.

A man runs in shorts toward Central Park. The weather is getting warmer. A taxi meanders down the street as if searching for the right address. It stops at the apartment building awning a few houses down. A mom walks by the cab, holding the hand of her toddler. She leans down as if to listen to what the child is saying. We, the little people, made Goliath listen. Two pigeons alight on my windowsill and make loud, trilling sounds. Tiger gets up on his haunches, still, watching them, his tail switching, ears back.

I pet him. "We're celebrating."

Bella: *Date with guy from stand-up. Lucky earring worked! Will be home late.*

The bell rings. It's Rupert. I buzz him in. Our tiny dining room table is clear except for two glasses of water. All set for the negotiation.

I open the door as Rupert exits the elevator. I run and hug him.

He laughs and picks me up, swinging me around. "We did it!"

I hook my legs around his waist and kiss him. Then I slide down his body, still holding tight.

"C'mon." I scoop up Tiger, who's exploring the hallway, and pull Rupert into my apartment.

Bennet winds herself around Rupert's legs, meowing. Darcy is on a shelf on the bookcase, looking aloof. I put Tiger down, and he scampers into Bella's room.

I gesture to the table. "Choose your seat."

Rupert sets up his laptop and takes a seat. I grab my pad with notes and sit across from him.

We stare at each other with serious expressions. Rupert breaks first, grinning. He slides his hand across to caress mine. "I'm looking forward to this partnership."

"Are you buttering me up?" I ask.

"Yes." He runs his foot up my leg. "I'm definitely planning to use all the weapons at my disposal."

I shake my head. "You might be sorry. You may be more susceptible than me."

He raises an eyebrow but then reaches back into his messenger bag and pulls out a piece of paper from a folder. "Here's our proposal."

Shit. It's good. It's basically exactly what we wanted. It's twice the amount of money that we have now to maintain the community garden.

And on top of that, there's another pot of money for creating and maintaining the roof garden.

I school my face. He's probably already seen that I'm fricking delighted.

"This is your opening offer?" I ask as if it's not enough.

He narrows his eyes. "It seems pretty fair to me."

"Hmm." I whistle through my teeth and get up. He pushes his chair back from the table and leans back, his feet sprawled out.

"You're looking for a better offer, Burton?"

"I am, Evans, I am." I stride over to him and put my hands on his shoulders. His laughing eyes look up at me. "We were thinking 10 percent more in funding."

"You'll have to do some persuading."

I sit on his lap and kiss him, running my hands through his hair. He kisses me back, holding me tight. I lean back and loosen his tie.

"Five percent more," he says.

"Done," I say.

"Done." He pulls out a version with a 5 percent increase. I think I just gave in too easily. But it's a fair deal.

He signs it and hands me the pen. I turn to face the table and sign it, his arms embracing me. He unbuttons the top button of my shirt, pulling it slightly off my shoulder. He softly traces my collarbone. I shiver. His gaze is intense, reverential. I unbutton his shirt so I can wrap my arms around his bare skin. He smooths the hair from my neck and trails kisses down to my shoulder.

"Shall we go celebrate now?" he asks, his voice gravelly, his glance heated on mine.

I sink into him and rest against his warmth. We did it. And he's here. He still wants me.

"I have a gift for you," he says, his voice muffled against my hair.

"You do?"

"Yes." He reaches down to his bag with one arm and pulls out a copy of *A Devilish Dare* with colorful tabs sticking out of it. "There are some things I definitely think we should try."

I laugh. "We'll need to compare notes. I tabbed some sections too."

Rupert kisses me firmly on the lips. "I think this book club is going to be very fun."

"Mmm," I say. "I was impressed at the book club when you were struck by the same paragraph as me—the one where she describes Herbert in the living room."

"That's when I impressed you?" he asks, a slight pout to his lips. "Not when I passed your book quiz?"

"You definitely impressed me when I first saw you. But then I disliked you because you were the Rupert Evans who was about to tear down my garden."

"The book club banter must have redeemed me somewhat?"

"Somewhat," I say. "But I was really grateful to you for turning around my night at the gala. And I think I ended up with the right guy. I am lucky Aiden wasn't interested."

"I still agree with Mr. Devi—I have no idea how he wasn't." He pulls me close against him again. "You didn't even vent or moan about what a shit he was. You decided to turn your night around, and you did. Rowena has a test for seeing what stuff guys are made of, but I could see right there your resilience and strength." His eyebrows rise. "Although, those qualities were also very obvious from the fight you put up to keep the garden. Those dancing vegetables and the high school kids. And the interviews with the retirees. They were moving. You were so determined and persistent, so effective with those incredibly creative ideas."

"Thank you for saving the garden."

He runs his hands though my hair and then holds my face gently. "You, Mrs. Potter, and your whole team saved the garden."

"Thank you for telling me not to hold back," I say. "I didn't know I could enjoy causing so much trouble." I was proud of myself for fighting so hard for the garden.

His glance holds mine and he says, "I think you might be the one for me."

"I feel the same way about you." I caress his face, already so dear to me. "Should we compare notes now on what we tabbed in *A Devilish Dare?*"

"I'm all yours. Starting with this." And with that, he picks me up and carries me to the bedroom. I loop my arms around his neck, laughing, as he gently closes the door with his foot.

Chapter Twenty-Four

Epilogue – Rupert – 4 Weeks Later

THE GARDEN LOOKS FANTASTIC, especially the cherry blossom tree, its pink petals brightening up the sky, dropping pale polka dots on the ground. The daffodils have also opened. Lily stands on a ladder, hanging the last of the fairy lights in the gazebo. I honestly can't keep my hands off her and have fully converted to hand-holding at all times. But similar to my dad, I think it's Lily's hand that I like holding.

The birds are chirping as if they've all just returned from Florida and are sharing their adventures.

My private chef, along with the catering crew from the office, including Bella's friend, are manning the tables of food prepared for a picnic, with little burners underneath the steel pans.

Lily turns around as I walk over. "What do you think? Does it look pretty?"

I stare at her. "Beautiful." I reach up and lift her from the ladder, letting her slide down my body, torturous as that is.

Her eyes heat up for a minute, and then she shakes her head. I chuckle.

"Is your tall, male friend from the gala coming?" she asks.

"You saw my friend?"

"Yes."

"You noticed me before I came over? You never told me." I squeeze her hand.

"You were the enemy. Of course I was keeping my eye on you." She looks away as if trying to appear innocent.

"If you want to believe that," I say. "But no. He can't make it. He has to work late again on some litigation."

She pouts. "That's too bad. I was hoping to set him up with one of my friends. Who do you think would be a good match for him?"

"Sebastian is a tricky one. I have no idea."

"Does he have a girlfriend?"

"He does not. And he's rather committed to remaining single right now."

The next one to arrive is Miranda, with her band. They set up in one corner. Then Mrs. Potter carries in a bowl of her famous dip, her tall, twenty-six-year-old son following, a few bags of tortilla chips in his arms. After they set down their gifts, Mrs. Potter introduces us. He's getting a PhD in math at CUNY.

And suddenly, everyone shows up at once. Jade arrives with her band of teenagers, along with the moms who let go of the hands of their children so they can play tag among the bushes, and the retirees who grab the nearest chairs. Mr. Devi is next, proudly announcing that he set us up. He's immediately swarmed by several of the older ladies.

Bella arrives. Lily hugs Bella as if she hasn't seen her in weeks. To be fair, she has been staying over a lot at my place.

Bella hands me another book. "For your reading pleasure." She smirks.

"You have to sign your books for me." I walk over to my backpack and pull out a stack. I've bought every book on her backlist. "I'm three in. They're excellent." Bella blushes.

Lily beams at me like I've done the most wonderful thing ever. For a smile like that, I'll stock Bella's books in all of our buildings' free libraries.

Miranda walks over at that moment. "I told you he looked like the type who bought all his books." She shakes my hand. "You probably don't remember me, but I'm the one who sent you over to the library. I'm taking some credit for getting you two together."

"You and I actually met when we were teenagers," I say. "I didn't recognize you that night at Banter & Books, although I should have. Out of context, I guess."

Lily hugs Miranda. "Good job. Is William coming?"

"Yes. It's tax season, so he'll be a bit late." Miranda turns to me. "My boyfriend is an accountant."

"Miranda is the one who made the posters," Lily says.

"Those posters were works of art." I point at the one we framed that currently hangs from the garden fence. "We're going to keep one for the foyer of the building. They have a very Milton Avery feel."

"Let me know if you want any more." Miranda grins.

Next to arrive are Maddie and Jing. Maddie assures me she's off-duty, but she might write a positive article about Strive Developers now.

"I Got It Bad (And That Ain't Good)" is the first song sung by Miranda as the band plays. I requested that one. The composition is different without the saxophone and trumpets, but it still packs a potent punch.

"My dance." I pull Lily into my arms. She melts into my embrace—like she fits there perfectly, which she does.

"I love you," she says.

"I love you more," I say.

Around us, the teenagers are swing dancing. Those lessons filmed on the social media videos worked. Mr. Devi is swaying slowly with Mrs. Potter.

I whisper to Lily, "Could they be a couple?"

"No. I tried, but they're good friends."

"It's a good foundation." Lily and I didn't start out as friends, but she's becoming my best friend. Not that I want Rowena to feel displaced. I keep inviting her over, but she says she's busy. And she's not revealing if it's the phantom date or if she doesn't want to feel like a third wheel, hard as Lily and I try to make it like we're all good friends hanging out. Mom and Dad say hello to both of us and then circulate around, meeting others.

The next song is faster, and we go over to grab some food and mingle with more of the guests.

At the buffet table, we join Maddie, who has piled her plate high with miso-glazed salmon and salad.

"Look." Maddie shows Lily a note and opens her phone to *YouTube*. "My rock star neighbor wrote me a song. See? It's dedicated to 'my neighbor who always complains.'"

"You're someone's muse," Jing says.

"That's so sweet," Bella says.

"Not really. At the end of the note, he said that instead of getting soundproofing, he used his saved funds to hire another music editor. But he hopes I'll forgive him because he dedicated a song to me." Maddie snorts. "He's such a prima donna."

"But the song is good," Jing says. "The lyrics are funny. And he clearly thinks about you."

"Oh, yes, the line about how he looks forward to incorporating my banging on the wall telling him to shut up into the rhythm of the song. Touching," Maddie says.

Grandpa comes with Rowena and her family. Unfortunately, both Uncle Tom and Dad still ignore each other, but not even that can dim the festive spirit.

I introduce Mr. Devi to my grandfather. "You both have a shared interest in matchmaking."

Mr. Devi smiles. "I'm responsible for this match."

"I played a part. I agreed he could be co-CEO and keep the garden," my grandfather says.

"That was critical. That was very smart of you," Mr. Devi says.

"Why did you think they would make a good match?" my grandfather asks as he and Mr. Devi walk away. "My granddaughter is still single."

Rowena doesn't stand a chance. Unless her mystery date is still in play.

I glance at Lily as she smiles at me. A warmth steels through me.

Tessa shows up. A wrench sticks out of her bag.

"Now, that's something I don't have in my carryall," Maddie says.

"I had to fix a tenant's bathroom," Tessa says. "It's part of my latest pro bono case. I've been calling the landlord for three weeks with no action, and I finally decided I needed to learn how to fix it myself, courtesy of *YouTube*."

"And did you?" Lily asks.

"I think so," Tessa says.

"You're the lawyer," I say. "Our general counsel was impressed with your arguments."

"I wasn't actually the lawyer. I found the lawyer," Tessa says.

And I found the woman I want to spend the rest of my life with. Dusk falls, and Lily and I sit at a very full table with our friends and family, laughing and making plans for the future.

THE END

I hope *My Book Boyfriend* left you with a warm, fuzzy feeling. The New York Spark world continues with *Love Is an Art*, which is Tessa's story, a fake-identity romantic comedy: *He hates lawyers. So I'm a lawyer pretending to be an artist. Forgetting one tiny detail: I can't paint.*

And for Miranda's story, an opposites-attract romantic comedy, read *Caper Crush*.
She's an emotional artist. He's a reserved accountant. When they team up to solve who stole her painting, will they find love?

FREE NEWSLETTER EXCLUSIVE BONUS EXCERPT!
Find out what Rupert thought during Chapter 10 at the New York Public Library Gala!
For a bonus Chapter 10 from Rupert's POV, sign up for my newsletter at https://books.kathystrobos.com/MBBmore and receive that exclusive newsletter subscriber benefit!
For more information about the books of Kathy Strobos, please find them at https://kathystrobos.com/books/

Chapter Twenty-Five

Love Is an Art Blurb

He hates lawyers. So I'm a lawyer pretending to be an artist. Forgetting one tiny detail: I can't paint.

Tessa: There's something about the way the blond guy laughs and leans in to listen. My gaze keeps returning to him.

The only problem is, we're at an art gallery after work, and I've swapped my lawyer suit for a paint-splattered shirt. I'm pretending to be a struggling artist, acting as bait to entice a scammer who conned my friend out of thousands of dollars.

I look pathetic. But still, I approach Hot Guy. Our glances meet, and an awareness shimmers across.

He offers to buy me a drink, we're definitely flirting, and then he asks me what I do.

Just when Scammer Guy is in earshot.

I have no choice but to say I'm an artist. I can tell Hot Guy later I'm not.

But then he says he *hates* lawyers.

Now what?

Zeke: She's the worst artist I've ever seen.

And I hate that that makes me suspect that she's lying to me. After my ex-girlfriend cheated on me, trust is in short supply.

She makes me laugh, and it's one adventure after another with her.

Definitely different from my workaholic lawyer ex.

Maybe it's time to give love a second chance.

All is fair in love and litigation, but when truth and deception clash, can you trust your heart?

The romcom books in this series are interconnected standalones set in the same world. Each can be read as a pure standalone with a guaranteed happily ever after.

Chapter Twenty-Six

About the Author

Kathy Strobos is a writer living in New York City with her husband and two children, amid a growing collection of books, toys, and dollhouses. She previously worked as a lawyer before switching careers to write romantic comedies and get in shape. Born and raised in Manhattan, she loves writing about New York City and the accomplished heroines who live and fall in love there, amidst its vibrant energy and the aroma of homemade chocolate chip cookies. She is still working on getting in shape.

Also by Kathy Strobos
A SCAVENGER HUNT FOR HEARTS
PARTNER PURSUIT
IS THIS FOR REAL?
CAPER CRUSH
My BOOK BOYFRIEND
LOVE IS AN ART

Acknowledgements

Thank you to all my readers.

It makes me so happy when readers tell me that they enjoyed my books. I can float for days after reading a positive review.

Thank you also to my ARC team, my newsletters subscribers, the librarians, book bloggers, bookstagrammers, and booktokkers who recommend my books and help me find my audience. You make it possible for me to follow my dream of being an author.

Thank you, as always, to my critique partners: Giulia Skye, Ellen Gilman, and Vicky Tiseros. I am always in awe at how they pinpoint exactly how to improve my story. I'm also very grateful for their friendship. We can talk for hours about crafting romance novels and the ups and downs of publishing, and still, there is more to say. Giulia and I email weekly, and I feel like we are colleagues in a small publishing venture.

Linnea Sinclair's class and Jessica Redland's class were also inspiring and invaluable.

Thank you, as always, to Emily Poole of *Midnight Owl Editing* (my developmental editor and line editor), Sharon Coleman of *Twisted Metaphor* (my story editor), and Joyce Mochrie of *One Last Look* (my copy editor and proofreader) for making my story the best it can be.

Thanks also to my cover designer, Lucy Murphy, of *Cover Ever After*. I love my covers.

Thank you to Parinyarat Cutone for hosting book talks and for my author photograph.

I researched community gardens in New York City; in particular, the website of the Elizabeth Street Garden in SoHo was very helpful. It is an absolutely lovely oasis and under threat of demolishment. See the pictures on my blog, and you can read more about their journey at https://www.elizabethstreetgarden.com/. Thank you also to the St. Agnes Library librarian who answered my questions. Any errors are my own.

The New York Public Library Lions Gala is actually in November. I took an author's liberty and moved it to February. I've also never attended it, so my event is entirely fictional. I did visit the Treasures room, which is well worth it. And I can attest that Bumper Cars on Ice in Bryant Park, another "tough author research" project, is a lot of fun.

The Oasis Community Garden is fictional, but for photos of various community gardens in New York City and the St. Agnes library, please check out my website at https://www.kathystrobos.com for various behind-the-scenes blog posts.

Thank you to all my friends who cheer me on. I am so touched by your support.

And thank you to my family, who encourage me and put up with me disappearing to write at my computer.

Milton Keynes UK
Ingram Content Group UK Ltd.
UKHW011833041023
429950UK00004B/256